PRAISE FOR *THE MVP MACHINE*

"Travis Sawchik and Ben Lindbergh brilliantly capture the next frontier of major-league teams' 'evolve or die' mindset: the league-wide movement of using data, technology, and science to revolutionize the way players are developed. Baseball has seen a rapid influx of high-curiosity, growth-mindset players and coaches, creating the perfect environment for innovation and rethinking convention. *The MVP Machine* provides tremendous insight into baseball's latest transformation."

—Billy Eppler, General Manager, Los Angeles Angels

"*The MVP Machine* isn't just the purest distillation yet of baseball's information era and how it came to be. It's a seminal road map for the game today and treasure map to find—and understand—the gems baseball soon will offer."

—Jeff Passan, MLB insider, ESPN

"As the game of baseball, and more specifically the teaching methods within, continue to evolve, *The MVP Machine* paints a real-time portrait of player development. Players and coaches are in a constant search for advantages that will push their personal limits on the field in order to maximize their abilities. Ben and Travis provide fascinating details of how individual players pushed the boundaries of innovative coaching, self-reflection, and a willingness to make even the smallest of adjustments in order to reach new heights as players. This book is a very accurate portrayal of modern-day player development and the ongoing pursuit of individual greatness."

—Mike Hazen, Executive Vice President and
General Manager, Arizona Diamondbacks

"A lot of books have claimed to be Moneyball 2.0, but this book actually delivers. It chronicles the changes that are transforming the game of baseball at a fundamental level and shifting power back into the hands of players and coaches."

—Mike Fast, Special Assistant to the General Manager, Atlanta Braves
and former Director of Research and Development, Houston Astros

"High-speed cameras and radar-tracking devices have revolutionized training and are now giving baseball players accurate, detailed, and actionable feedback during practice. This captivating book details step-by-step how merely good major-league players have recently been able to transform themselves into great ones and reach previously unattainable levels of mastery by purposeful and deliberate practice."

—K. Anders Ericsson, Conradi Eminent Scholar of Psychology, Florida State University, and author of *Peak: Secrets from the New Science of Expertise*

"Travis Sawchik and Ben Lindbergh are always at the forefront of the analytics revolution. *The MVP Machine* brings us the newly emerging competitive advantage whereby players are joining the intellectual advancement of the game and utilizing the new tools available to build a better major-league player. Make no mistake, this is how games, divisions, and World Series titles are now being won."

—Brian Kenny, MLB Network

THE MVP
MACHINE

THE MVP MACHINE

HOW BASEBALL'S NEW NONCONFORMISTS ARE USING DATA TO BUILD BETTER PLAYERS

BEN LINDBERGH & TRAVIS SAWCHIK

BASIC BOOKS

New York

Basic Books
Hachette Book Group
1290 Avenue of the Americas, New York, NY 10104
www.basicbooks.com

Printed in the United States of America

First Edition: June 2019

Published by Basic Books, an imprint of Perseus Books, LLC, a subsidiary of Hachette Book Group, Inc. The Basic Books name and logo is a trademark of the Hachette Book Group.

The Hachette Speakers Bureau provides a wide range of authors for speaking events. To find out more, go to www.hachettespeakersbureau.com or call (866) 376-6591.

The publisher is not responsible for websites (or their content) that are not owned by the publisher.

Editorial production by Christine Marra, Marrathon Production Services.
www.marrathoneditorial.org
Book design by Jane Raese
Set in 9.5-point Caecilia

Library of Congress Control Number: 2019934700

ISBN 978-1-5416-9894-9 (hardcover), ISBN 978-1-5416-9895-6 (ebook)

LSC-C

10 9 8 7 6 5 4 3 2

TO MY PARENTS, FOR MAKING ME A PROSPECT

—BEN LINDBERGH

FOR ALL THOSE WHO DIDN'T MAKE THE CUT

—TRAVIS SAWCHIK

CONTENTS

PROLOGUE

POWERING UP

> The only way of discovering the limits of the possible is to venture a little way past them into the impossible. . . . Any sufficiently advanced technology is indistinguishable from magic.
> —ARTHUR C. CLARKE, "HAZARDS OF PROPHECY"

Trevor Bauer steps onto a makeshift pitching mound at Driveline Baseball in Kent, Washington, a suburb south of Seattle. The throwing platform consists of a pair of black, rubberized weight-room mats covering a sloped plywood structure that mimics the shape and height of an actual mound. It's January 3, 2018, three months before Opening Day.

The Driveline campus, where inquisitive and often desperate ballplayer pilgrims gather to get better, consists of three buildings strewn about a drab industrial park that also serves as the site of a sewage disposal service, a glassblowing business, and a hydraulics company. Driveline's R&D building, where Bauer spends much of his offseason, is a warehouse of a place, carpeted wall-to-wall with Kelly-green artificial turf. The main entrance is a roll-up garage door, usually left open to a vista of neighboring business units' beige, vertically corrugated metal facades and an asphalt parking lot where a collection of modest cars rests. Opposite the door and along the far wall of the facility, occupying nearly the entire length of it, is the bullpen-like pitching area where Bauer is to begin throwing. The home plate he's aiming for has a backdrop of black nylon netting to protect the nearby employees and desktop computers from ricochets.

At the front of the mound is a wooden board, to which cling three small tracking devices used for biomechanical evaluations. Sawdust from the recently assembled, jury-rigged contraption has spilled onto the front of the mound. So much at Driveline is improvised because what was needed was either nonexistent or cost prohibitive. But this unpolished place has become Bauer's lab. Every off-season he tries to get better at something, focusing his efforts on gaining a new skill. His goal this winter is to create a much-needed additional pitch.

In his first three full seasons with the Cleveland Indians, 2014–2016, the right-hander was a roughly league-average starter, a useful player but far from the star he thought he could be. Then, at the end of May 2017, Bauer regressed. Hitters started crushing his fastball, giving him the worst earned run average in the majors (6.00) among qualified starters. There were calls for him to be sent to the Cleveland bullpen. His postgame press conferences grew testier and shorter; after one mid-May start, he ripped off and slammed down the television mic attached to his undershirt. Thanks to an increased reliance on his best pitch, a curveball, and greater use of his slider-like cutter, he was able to turn his season around and posted a strong second half. But he knew he could not be successful long term with the curve as his lone elite pitch, and the cutter variant he was throwing was uncomfortable and hard to command.

Bauer believed the lack of a lateral breaking ball—a pitch that moved more east–west than north–south—was holding him back. He'd turn twenty-seven later that month, an age at which most players, particularly pitchers, have already reached their prime. But coupled with his fastball and his 12 o'clock-to-6 o'clock, vertically diving curveball, a dependable pitch that moved side to side could flummox hitters and elevate him from inconsistent to elite. He prescribed himself a new pitch: a slider.

In a navy-blue, Indians-issued compression T-shirt and red shorts, Bauer moves to a table behind the indoor mound, where he's positioned two cameras. One is his personal iPhone, which he employs to log and label each of his pitches. The other is an unusual-looking camera, a Carolina-blue colored cube with a protruding circular lens. That high-tech gadget, an Edgertronic SC1 manufactured by the San Jose company Sanstreak, is focused only on his grip of the ball and the initial flight of the pitch. Under tightly grouped pairs of fluorescent lights, Bauer goes to work on his great project of 2018.

Clean-shaven, with his hair closely cropped, Bauer looks into the iPhone lens and speaks.

"Normal slider arm slot, full spike," he says.

He looks down at his right hand, which is gripping a ball. The familiar horseshoe of red stitching makes contact with his skin in an unfamiliar way, running along his right thumb and middle finger. He digs his index finger into the white leather cover just inside his middle finger. He steps on the pitching rubber and then launches into his throwing motion and releases the pitch. As the ball travels, it seems to fall off an invisible table, moving more north–south than east–west. It bounces well before the plate. A speed of 71.7 mph registers on the electronic radar-reading board, which sits on the carpet just behind the left-handed batter's box.

During the season, television cameras and pitch-tracking systems capture the movement of all of Bauer's pitches from major-league mounds. But those technologies can't tell him what the little blue box behind the mound at Driveline can: exactly how the ball is coming out of his hand. At hundreds of high-def frames per second, the Edgertronic shows with perfect clarity how his right arm moves and his fingers impart spin to the ball as it's released. Examining the video between sets of pitches, Bauer sees the ball first lose contact with his thumb and then separate from his middle finger. His spiked index finger, its fingertip and nail raised vertically and jabbed into the surface, touch the ball last before it flies, subtly altering the axis of its spin. If he times this sequence just right, he'll create the perfect spin axis and produce the pitch movement he wants.

Bauer checks his grip and his wrist position, looks toward the cameras, and speaks again. "Normal slider arm slot, half spike, pitch number two."

Again, the pitch dives too vertically, but less vertically than with the full-spike slider grip. Bauer subtly adjusts his fingers. Working in concert with the Edgertronic video at Driveline is a Rapsodo radar and optical tracking unit, a portable system that measures velocity, spin, and spin axis. Under an array of electronic eyes, Bauer extends his right arm to the camera once again: "Normal arm slot, no spike."

He sets into a ready position and makes his move down the mound. This time the pitch moves more laterally, breaking in toward an imaginary left-handed batter. The offering is closer to what he's seeking: a pitch whose shape and movement would fit between his fastball and curveball.

Bauer throws his second no-spike slider, releasing it with a grunt. This one is his best pitch of the morning. It moves sharply and laterally at 73 mph and, with a thud, smacks into the rubber pad attached to the L-screen, roughly where a catcher would squat. Next, he tries a half spike with a drop-down angle. The pitch has more vertical break and looks closer to his curveball: an adjustment in the wrong direction.

The cluster of expended baseballs widens around the home-plate area. After about fifty throws, Bauer collects the balls in a bucket. Then he begins again.

1

SAVIORMETRICS

Welcome to the machine
Where have you been?
It's all right, we know where you've been
You've been in the pipeline, filling in time
Provided with toys and Scouting for Boys
    —**PINK FLOYD, "Welcome to the Machine"**

In the early and late hours of October 27, 2018, the baseball world (or at least the part that was awake) focused its attention on a group of high-performing players that no one had thought much of a few years before.

Shortly after midnight in Los Angeles—seven hours and twenty minutes after the first pitch of World Series Game 3 and four innings after the fourteenth-inning stretch—the Dodgers' Max Muncy drove a fly ball over the fence in left-center in the bottom of the eighteenth to beat the Boston Red Sox in the longest postseason game ever played. In one way, Muncy was an obvious candidate to end the ordeal with one swing: during the regular season, he hit a home run every 11.3 at-bats, the best rate of any hitter who played at least fifty games. Considering his history before that, though, Muncy's hero status was astonishing.

In limited playing time with the Oakland Athletics in 2016, Muncy was one of the worst hitters in baseball. The A's released him the following spring, and he sat on the sidelines for almost a month until the Dodgers handed him a minor-league contract. While he was waiting (and pondering a future outside sports), he returned to his high-school batting cage and revamped his approach at the plate, lowering his stance, shifting his hands on the bat handle, and learning to take more aggressive swings. He hit well in 2017 at Triple-A, but the back of his uniform still said "Muncy," so he stayed in the minors in 2018 until the injury-depleted Dodgers, desperate for a healthy hitter, called him up in mid-April. He homered in his first start and raked for the rest of the year, slashing .263/.391/.582 to finish the season as the second-best batter in the National League. Muncy, a marginal player in no demand, entered 2018 with a career record in the red and, at age twenty-eight, became the most valuable full-season player on a pennant-winning team.

The pitcher who gave up the walk-off winner after unexpectedly being pressed into service for six-plus innings in that extra-long game was Red Sox swingman Nathan Eovaldi, another twenty-eight-year-old who was released after the 2016 season, setting up his own dramatic turnaround. Eovaldi sat out 2017 after tearing his ulnar collateral ligament, but even before the injury, the righty had been a below-average run preventer for three consecutive seasons, despite possessing one of the game's fastest fastballs. When he resurfaced after Tommy John surgery, Eovaldi boasted not only a new ligament but also a new look, featuring fewer (and higher) four-seam fastballs, more cutters, and less indication of which one was coming. The modifications made all the difference: in 2018, he posted the highest strikeout rate and lowest walk rate of his career, which prompted Boston to acquire him at the trade deadline. After the series, he qualified for free agency, and the Red Sox re-signed him to a four-year $68 million deal, banking on the altered Eovaldi being better than the original.

With the Dodgers' bullpen depleted after a parade of nine pitchers got them through Game 3, the team turned to an unlikely left-handed savior in Game 4, which began less than seventeen hours later. A few months away from his thirty-ninth birthday, with pouches under his eyes and a goatee graying at the edges, Rich Hill was the oldest player on either roster and a product of perhaps the most improbable path to the series. From 2008 to 2015, Hill was released three times and changed teams ten times, pitching a total of 182 below-average big-league innings, mostly in relief, amid injuries and minor-league exiles. At the end of that span, the Red Sox signed him out of independent ball, and one conversation with Boston's Brian Bannister—a former fringy major leaguer turned analytical coach—convinced him to trust his underutilized curveball, a special, high-spin pitch that immediately made him one of baseball's best inning-per-inning arms. Of the 190 pitchers who amassed at least seventy-five innings in 2018, only 11 threw slower fastballs, on average, than Hill, but Bannister's former protégé allowed only one hit over 6 1/3 innings against his old team, baffling Boston to such a degree that his removal from the game, and the Dodgers' subsequent defeat, prompted the President to send a second-guessing tweet.

Playing behind Hill were third baseman Justin Turner and left fielder Chris Taylor, co-MVPs of the 2017 National League Championship Series. Turner was an itinerant twenty-eight-year-old utility type with a below-average bat in the winter of 2013–2014, when he changed his stroke and his future with the help of a nearly unknown swing whisperer named Doug Latta, who transformed a nondescript industrial-park unit in suburban Los Angeles into a factory for line drives. Latta helped Turner tap into power no one knew he had, and over his following five seasons for the Dodgers, this reject of the Mets and Orioles organizations was one of the fifteen best hitters in baseball at an age when players typically decline. Before his own breakout, Taylor's slap-hitting, low-leverage stroke had produced only one homer in almost three hundred at-bats in the big leagues. Then a *second* suburban Los Angeles swing instructor took a sad swing and made it better. In 2017, Taylor hit twenty-one homers.

Boston's cleanup hitter in Game 4, J.D. Martinez, was another face of the fly-ball revolution who rejected a swing designed for singles the same winter Turner did. Martinez's team at the time, the Houston Astros, released the twenty-six-year-old the next spring, not knowing what they had. He went on to top Turner, rating as one of the *five* best hitters in baseball over the following five years. After signing a five-year free-agent contract with the Red Sox in 2018, Martinez became the first player to win *two* Silver Slugger Awards (outfield and designated hitter) in the same season, doubling up on an honor bestowed annually on the best offensive player at each position.

Some standout players took less circuitous paths to the series. Red Sox right fielder Mookie Betts, for one, made the majors at twenty-one and excelled immediately. But even elite players have room for improvement. In 2018, Betts secretly tweaked his swing and learned from his teammate Martinez. He then vaulted toward the top of virtually every offensive leaderboard, outpacing all other players in both batting average and slugging percentage and winning a well-deserved MVP award. In Game 5, both Betts and Martinez hit home runs off Clayton Kershaw as Boston beat LA to take the Series 4–1.

If there was one theme to October—other than really long games— it was the presence of players like these, who embodied a movement that's transforming (and transcending) the sport. It wasn't just the last two teams standing whose rosters were studded with stories of deliberate, dramatic development. The full playoff field featured many more. Inside a rented retail space in Harlem that he turned into a high-tech pitching lab, Colorado Rockies reliever Adam Ottavino built a new pitch from scratch and gained command of an old one. Atlanta Braves catcher Tyler Flowers studied data to make himself baseball's best pitch-framer, capable of stealing extra strikes by receiving borderline pitches smoothly. The team Boston toppled in the American League Championship Series, the defending-champion Astros, bounced back from their big whiff with Martinez by becoming the kings of acquiring underperforming pitchers—including Collin McHugh, Charlie Morton, Justin Verlander, Gerrit Cole, and Ryan Pressly—and implementing a few fixes to help them reach greater heights.

No individual player has pushed the movement forward more than the innovative and controversy-prone Trevor Bauer, who has proclaimed himself "the foremost expert on pitch design" and "one of the most scientific players in MLB." Those aren't empty boasts. Bauer has attacked tradition, unafraid of the friction it created, and embraced every idea and piece of technology he thought might make him better. In the winter of 2017–2018, he designed a new and nasty pitch in a nondescript Seattle facility that's become a hub for bleeding-edge ballplayers, Driveline Baseball. The addition to his arsenal made him an AL Cy Young Award contender.

In each of these cases, and many more, a player made the choice to use new methods and technologies to systematically address his deficiencies. Sometimes it was a mechanical adjustment that unlocked the latent power in a swing. Sometimes it was a more strongly instilled sense of the strike zone. Sometimes it was training to add velocity a pitcher didn't know his body was capable of producing. Sometimes it was a pitch designed from scratch or promoted from secondary status to a more prominent role. And sometimes it was a modified mindset or meal plan or gym regimen. These overhauls are happening in hundreds of places across the sport, from professional clubhouses, bullpens, and batting cages, to colleges, high schools, and international leagues, to the independent petri dishes where this drive to reconceptualize talent began: boundary-breaking facilities outside of the professional game. Curious, scuffling players linked up with little-known coaching iconoclasts to spark a revolution. Now some savvy MLB teams are taking their insights to scale and lapping the rest of the league.

Veterans who've looked lost are reclaiming careers, while an emerging generation of information-friendly players is seeking out stats from the get-go, fueling a youth movement in the majors and contributing to a constantly increasing level of play. "During the '80s and '90s it was steroids," says Seattle Mariners director of player development Andy McKay. "And now it can be new information."

Mainstream baseball commentators haven't quite figured out how to talk about this new era in baseball development. On almost every broadcast during the 2018 playoffs, national commentators fretted about jargon like "launch angle" and "spin rate," lamenting the game's new scientific focus. But though the language is new, these terms don't describe new phenomena: Babe Ruth's batted balls had a launch angle, and Bob Feller's fastball had a spin rate. In earlier eras, there was just no way to track them. Today's technology tracks everything, allowing progressive players to dissect their performance with unprecedented depth. The better they understand their current technique, the easier to analyze how it could be better.

Not every player wanders from team to team until he's bitten by a radioactive hitting coach and triples his home-run total or meets a sabermetrician on the road to retirement and suddenly sees the light. Enough of them have, though, that it's swaying player performance on a league-wide level—changing the composition of coaching staffs, scouting departments, and front offices; altering the way general managers construct rosters; popularizing formerly frowned-upon training techniques; and determining who wins the World Series and individual awards. Even in its early stages, though, this movement is also raising privacy concerns, exacerbating baseball's anti-spectator trends, and possibly leading to labor strife.

On a more fundamental, broadly applicable level, it's overturning old beliefs about the immutability of talent. In baseball's old-school scouting parlance, "guy" is a versatile label, employed, one scout says, "like how Smurfs use the word 'smurf.'" A non-prospect is *not* a guy, or (said dismissively) *just* a guy; a prospect is a guy; and a top prospect is a "GUY," or a *guy*-guy. Players aspire to "guy" status. As former Red Sox prospect Michael Kopech said after Boston traded him to Chicago for ace starter Chris Sale (who recorded the first and last outs of the 2018 World Series): "All I wanted to do is show them I could be a guy for them." Players also hope to hit their "ceilings," a scouting term for an athlete's alleged best-case outcome.

Mike Fast, a special assistant to the GM of the Braves and a former Astros research and development director, says that whereas traditionally teams subscribed to labels like these, the franchises at the forefront of the latest, greatest revolution are realizing that "everything" is subject to change. We've entered an era in which the right type of practice produces more perfect players, and the earliest adopters of data-driven development are leaving the laggards behind. "I think the idea that analytics is leveling the field is completely backwards," Fast says. "Analytics is tilting the field far beyond how it has ever been tilted before." Fast's colleague Ronit Shah, an Astros scout turned Braves R&D analyst, echoes that sentiment, saying, "The possibilities and the upside are pretty much limitless."

Talking in terms of "guys" and "ceilings" suggests that there *are* identifiable limits. Yet more and more players are figuring out how to go from non-guys to guys or from regular guys to *guy*-guys, which raises a radical possibility: Maybe there's no such thing as an absolute ceiling, or the ceiling is high enough that no one knows where it is. And maybe more *guy*-guys are out there than we ever believed before.

These new peaks in performance aren't just the product of better technology. They're a manifestation of a new philosophy of human potential. Increasingly, teams and players are adopting a growth mindset that rejects long-held beliefs about innate physical talent. One of the only innate qualities may be how hard players are willing to work. Scouts have historically graded players based on five physical tools, but in an era of optimization, a player's approach to practice is a once-unsung sixth tool that affects the other five.

"This decade of baseball," Bannister says, "is all about an inefficiency on the player-development side." To elaborate, Bannister borrows an analogy from *Forrest Gump*. "For a long time, baseball players were almost viewed as a box of chocolates," he says. "They came in endless varieties, and you were just trying to find the best ones. As we started to be able to collect information on players and learn at a rapidly growing pace, we started to realize that the reason the best players are the best players is that they got closer to perfection with the way their bodies moved, as far as executing a certain pitch or taking a certain swing." For information-friendly teams, Bannister continues, the pursuit of perfection has shifted from "finding bodies that are already doing things well or close to perfect" to asking, "How can we leverage the data and what we've learned from the data to get closer to that perfect pitch or perfect swing?" That, Bannister says, is "where the rabbit hole begins."

It's also where the outlying lives of big leaguers begin to apply to our own. Only a small subset of people needs to get great at baseball. But if experienced players in a centuries-old sport can be better than they thought, it suggests something exciting. Maybe we all have hidden talent. And maybe *everyone* can be better at whatever work they do.

The index of Michael Lewis's *Moneyball*, the 2003 book about the Oakland Athletics that became a bestseller and the source of such severe front-office FOMO that copycat teams across the sport soon molded themselves in Oakland's analytical image, contains nine subheadings for the listing "players, professional." There's "tools of" (the first page of the book), "scouting and recruitment of" (all of chapter two), "sight-based evaluation of" (three entries), and "trading of" (all of chapter nine). There's "use of statistics in evaluating" (somewhat misleadingly, only one reference). There's even an entry for what happens when "players, professional" fail to produce: "designating for assignment."[1]

But *Moneyball*'s index omitted an important potential tenth entry: "development of." The oversight stemmed from a blind spot of the book—and until recently, of baseball at large. Perhaps in part because of his own history, then A's general manager Billy Beane—a former first-round pick with raw talent to spare who never learned to translate his tools into on-field success—didn't devote much time or attention to developing players, at least as Lewis told the tale.

Much of the drama in *Moneyball*'s narrative arises from transactions: picking players in the amateur draft, trading for undervalued relievers, and signing the unsung Scott Hatteberg, whose patience at the plate went underappreciated at a time when runs batted in and batting average still reigned as the game's most prized offensive indicators. As *Moneyball* portrayed it, Oakland's ability to compete despite noncompetitive payrolls was about being better at acquiring players. "You can identify value or you can create value," says former San Diego Padres senior quantitative analyst Chris Long, one of a wave of stathead hires who flocked to front offices in *Moneyball*'s immediate aftermath. Ideally, you'd do both, but Oakland's cutting-edge efforts, initiated by Beane's nonplayer predecessor Sandy Alderson, were focused on the former. *Moneyball*'s subtitle promised to reveal "The Art of Winning an Unfair Game." Apparently, developing players wasn't part of that art.

That's not to say the A's weren't promoting players from within; though one would hardly know it from *Moneyball*, they did have homegrown heroes. Some of them, though, had been top draft picks, always slated for stardom. In Lewis's book, Beane adopted a deterministic view of player performance, downplaying the idea that players could be capable of changing their ways. Oakland's draft strategy was akin to clever actuarial work: the A's determined that picking certain types of players had panned out in the past, so they made more of those picks (college pitchers) and fewer of the riskier kind (high-school pitchers). They also noticed that walks were worth more than the market realized, so they targeted hitters who took them. As a consequence, the homegrown half of Oakland's early-aughts lineup was less patient than the half acquired through trades, leading Lewis to note that "the guys who aren't behaving properly at the plate are precisely those who have had the [proper] approach drilled into them by A's hitting coaches from the moment they became pro players."

Because his own prospects had proved unable or unwilling to master traits that the players he imported already possessed, Beane concluded that if plate discipline could be taught, "we'd have to take guys in diapers to do it." In 1984, another A's firebrand, Oakland manager Billy Martin, had expressed the same sentiment in even more absolute terms: "You got your mules and you got your racehorses, and you can kick a mule in the ass all you want, and he's still not gonna be a racehorse."[2]

In fairness to Beane, no one else in the early 2000s was thinking too much about making mules into racehorses. The year *Moneyball* debuted, Mark Armour and Daniel Levitt, coauthors of *Paths to Glory: How Great Baseball Teams Got That Way*, wrote: "Other than some analysis of the influence of pitch counts on young pitchers, there has been little research outside of the professional baseball community on such things as methods for developing a young hitter's power or how to teach a young pitcher to gain better command of his breaking ball."[3] Matters weren't much more advanced *inside* that community. Current A's general manager David Forst, Beane's longtime top lieutenant, remembers the team dictating that its minor-league pitchers throw a certain percentage of changeups per game and talking about bumping every minor-league hitter up to a 10 percent walk rate, partly by forcing them to take pitches until the opposing pitcher threw a strike. Those methods, Forst says, "seem pretty rudimentary now compared to what we're capable of doing," but more advanced development was difficult because "we didn't have the tools to implement it or measure it."

Granted, there wasn't much need for a forward thinker like Beane to focus on remaking mules when there were so many discount horses around. The A's could construct a winning team on the cheap by pairing the players their draft approach produced with other clubs' low-hanging Hattebergs. Hatteberg himself signed with the A's in 2002 and went on to be their third-best hitter for a single-season salary of $900,000, only three times more than the MLB minimum. "Evaluating was way ahead of developing," Forst says.

But Beane's edge at adding players gradually dwindled, partly because *Moneyball*'s success inspired imitators and partly because sabermetrics—a movement formative figure Bill James described as "the search for objective knowledge about baseball"—was starting to sweep the sport even before the book became a flashpoint. As Beane said just two months after *Moneyball* made it to stores: "The old days of getting something for nothing are over. There are too many good [GMs] out there now."[4]

Suddenly, other teams were holding on to their Hattebergs, and in Oakland, economic realities reasserted themselves. The A's missed the playoffs in 2004 and '05, failed to finish with a winning record from 2007 to 2011 and, after a brief renaissance, finished in last place from 2015 to 2017. Ironically, the young prospect whom Beane had traded in 2002 to clear room for Hatteberg, Carlos Peña, later blossomed into a far better hitter—and a more prolific walker—than Hatteberg had been. It took time, but the first baseman broke out, even though there was little in his recent performance profile to suggest he would.

By 2015, when Peña retired and the A's finished in the cellar for the first time since Beane's rookie year as a GM, almost every front office was heavily invested in identifying value via stats and analysis, and the most sophisticated clubs were way ahead of where the A's had been at the turn of the century. That spring, MLB introduced Statcast, a network of cameras and radar that records the speed of every pitch, the velocity and trajectory of every batted ball, and the paths of every player in the field and on the bases in every big-league ballpark. That system supplanted the PITCHf/x and HITf/x systems, which had recorded the speed, movement, and inferred spin of every pitch and the speed and angle of every batted ball for several seasons prior. Below the big leagues, TrackMan (a component of Statcast) soon monitored all thirty teams' minor leaguers from the highest level to the lowest.

Although teams differed in how deeply they delved into tracking data, the info was widely available and far more revealing than the best low-tech alternatives from a decade before. Not until 1988—the same year that the influential James published the twelfth and last of his annual *Baseball Abstracts*—had baseball's data collectors even noted the outcome of every MLB pitch. Less than thirty years later, a system that once would have seemed like a sci-fi figment was capturing the process that produced every outcome on the field at forty thousand frames per second.

Bigger data required bigger databases and bigger departments devoted to analyzing their contents. In April 2016, a study Ben coauthored for FiveThirtyEight, a website that specializes in statistical analysis, charted the rapid increase in analysts employed by teams over time. By then, more than five full-time front-office members per franchise, on average, were working in research and technological development (a figure that's still swelling, topping 7.5 per team by spring 2018). Every team in the majors employed at least one analyst, and every team but the parsimonious Miami Marlins employed more than one. Although the study found that the early adopting data-centric teams had reaped rewards worth as many as several wins (and tens of millions of dollars) per season from mining baseball's big data before their competitors could, those benefits have shrunk as the front-office brain race has intensified. As baseball analyst Phil Birnbaum once observed, "You gain more by not being stupid than you do by being smart."[5] Teams have long since stopped being stupid about recognizing the good players right in front of their faces.

Although the term "Moneyball" has come to be associated with specific strategies the A's deemed most advantageous, it was never actually tied to any one method of team building or in-game management. It was more of a philosophy, one aimed at finding inefficiencies wherever they lay. "When people think of sabermetrics and Moneyball, a lot of it is what they see on the field, the way the game is played," says Long, who has consulted for multiple teams since departing the Padres. "And most of [the value] is really off the field." On-the-field changes are easy to see: in recent years, counterproductive tactics that statheads have decried for decades (and that the Moneyball A's eschewed), like sacrifice bunting and inefficient base stealing, have fallen out of favor. But eradicating bad bunt and steal attempts offers only modest edges. Championships and playoff appearances depend on procuring—or creating—quality players. In the 1920s, teams called the experts who combed the country searching for fresh talent "ivory hunters." In the 2010s, they call them "quants," short for quantitative analysts. The goal is the same, but the methods are always evolving.

In the summer of 2014, hundreds of stat-obsessed seamheads, including quants from fourteen teams, gathered in Boston for an annual analytics conference known as Saber Seminar. Most of the speakers at Saber Seminar present research about running regressions or writing complex queries to expose some unsuspected sliver of value. But that year's keynote speaker, then Red Sox GM Ben Cherington—whose team was fresh off a 2013 title—announced that the days of detecting hidden value that players were already providing were quickly coming to an end. "It sure felt like in '02, '03, '04, we could more easily create a talent gap between the best teams and the worst teams, and you could more easily count on a bunch of wins before the season ever started," he said. "That feels harder to do now. . . . Finding ways to optimize player performance and get guys into the higher range of possibilities is more and more important."

The higher range of possibilities: it may not sound sexy, but that's where the wins are in a world where teams aren't being bullheaded about on-base percentage and other once-overlooked contributions. Cherington was speaking a language in which his audience was well versed. A few months before *Moneyball* made it to the shelves, a young analyst named Nate Silver, who would go on to project political races, unveiled a new framework at the sabermetric-minded website Baseball Prospectus for projecting player performance. His creation, PECOTA—which ostensibly stood for player empirical comparison and optimization test algorithm but was really a "backronym" tribute to former infielder Bill Pecota, who represented a roughly typical player—became the standard for public projection systems. PECOTA presented its estimate of each player's stat line as a single likeliest projection, accompanied by a range of less likely (but still conceivable) outcomes: a 10th-percentile projection sketched out a season where nearly everything went wrong, whereas a 90th-percentile projection presented one where the player far exceeded what the system expected.

PECOTA and its successors, both public and private, brought a new level of accuracy and rigor to baseball prognostication by counteracting the cognitive biases that steer humans wrong. A projection system doesn't fall for a player because it saw him have a hot home stand or smack a game-winning hit. Nor does it write him off because it happened to catch him on a day when he went 0-for-4 with four strikeouts or hit into hard luck. Although projection systems are smart, they've traditionally lacked imagination. Public projections are based largely on a player's past performance, weighted by recency and adjusted for his competition, ballpark, age, and other factors. PECOTA assigns greater odds of a breakout to particular players, based on their builds, ages, skill sets, or comparable players from the past, but only up to a point; it will never predict great things for a player who's only been bad before.

On the whole, that reluctance to expect unprecedented performance serves such systems well, insulating them from fans' willingness to persuade themselves that every hot streak reflects a permanent improvement flowing from a new stance, a new swing, a new grip on a pitch, or some other magical mechanical tweak. Sometimes those tweaks are irrelevant; sometimes they're real but tough to sustain. At other times, though, a player who appears to be a changed man actually is one. And the first team to find him—or to make more like him—will leap closer to first place. Every team now knows which players are projected to be good. But the best teams are discovering ways for players to accomplish what they aren't projected to do.

"There are real stories out there of guys who in another era would have just flamed out as minor leaguers and were able to change their profile to turn themselves into big leaguers," Forst says. As Andy McKay puts it, "All bets are off."

Player development has inspired fewer titles in the boundless baseball library than any other vital aspect of the game. It's an arduous, opaque process that unfolds far from view, on back fields, in bullpens and batting cages, and in seemingly low-stakes games that until recently most fans had no way to watch. As far as many fans are concerned, players disappear after draft day, encased in cocoons from which some emerge as beautiful baseball butterflies, while most wither away, forever forgotten or, if they're particularly talented, lamented for failing to molt.

But there's magic in the moments that propel polished players to major-league mounds and batter's boxes, even if they often occur off camera. Scouting stories supply the thrill of love at first swing, and books in the *Moneyball* mold chronicle the moments when the wins come fast and furious and the champagne pops. Development sits somewhere in between, but without it, many of the scouting discoveries would be wasted, and many of the wins wouldn't come. "For all of the unceasing talk of money in baseball, of salaries, of taxes, of revenues shared and unshared, the only path to success is through player development," wrote Baseball Prospectus cofounder Joe Sheehan in October 2018.

In November 2015, Russell Carleton published a piece on the BP website that was part plea and part clarion call, titled "I Want to Write about Player Development." He acknowledged that it wouldn't be easy: below the majors, there's less publicly available data, less knowledge of what players are working on, and less importance attached to wins and losses. But prying open baseball's last black box and settling its final frontier would be worth the work. "Everyone's always looking around for the #NewMoneyball and, frankly, it's staring right at them," Carleton wrote. "Young, cost-controlled players return value—on average—at a dollar-per-win rate that's about half what a team would pay on the free-agent market. And that's just the average. If a team is any good at player development, it can assemble a roster of young, cost-controlled players and ride that wave for a long time. If a team could nail down player development, they'd have a bit of an edge, wouldn't you say?"

We would, and we will.

"I don't think people realize that if you're a Moneyball team right now, you're getting your ass handed to you," says one quant for an MLB club. "When you hear the smart teams saying they use analytics now,

they're not saying they're doing Moneyball. They're saying they're doing the thing that comes after." This new phase is dedicated to making players better. It's Betterball. And it's taking over. As Mariners GM
Jerry Dipoto remarks, "We're moving at a hyperpace compared to the
prehistoric crawl of the saber revolution."

Minnesota Twins chief baseball officer Derek Falvey is another of
the architects trying to build a team that embodies this movement.
"We talk about what's the next frontier," he says. "Analytics. OK.
[Player] selection? We have models. Don't get me wrong, we need to
improve those selection models. But I think development, if we can
find ways to do that better than the other twenty-nine clubs, that's
where we have a chance to make an impact."

In ballparks and seemingly modest independent facilities across
the country, we're witnessing the fruits of an incipient revolution
in player development—one with the potential to upend the sport's
competitive landscape. Teams have a stronger grasp than ever on
what makes players valuable. Now they're zeroing in on how to turn
nonprospects into prospects, middling major leaguers into MVP candidates and, less dramatically but on an even more widespread scale,
good big leaguers into *better* big leaguers. And it's not just teams: curious and data-savvy players are now empowered to improve *themselves*, sometimes acting in concert with the outside instructors who
started the movement. Moneyball began above the field level, in executives' offices and number-crunchers' cubicles. Its successor and
supplanter started far from MLB's bright lights.

2

A NATURAL MANIAC,
AN UNNATURAL ATHLETE

No bird soars in a calm.
—**WILBUR WRIGHT**

John Boyd worked as a tactical instructor at Nellis Air Force Base in the Nevada Desert, like a proto-Viper from *Top Gun*. For five years in the 1950s, Boyd flew multiple times a day against fighter pilots training in F-100 Super Sabres. He observed, recorded, and analyzed the positions of his plane and opponents during mock combat engagements. He had a standing bet that in forty seconds or less, he could defeat anyone in the skies. The former fighter pilot from the Korean War reportedly never lost. During his hours in the cockpit, Boyd studied the most efficient way to gain an advantage. He knew that when turning, a plane would either slow down or lose altitude because it lost energy. "Boyd concluded that maneuvering for position was basically an energy problem," wrote aircraft designer Harry Hillaker. "Winning required the proper management of energy available at the conditions existing at any point during a combat engagement."[1]

Boyd found that a plane's top speed was not nearly as important as how quickly it could maneuver and climb. Prior to Boyd, there was little science to piloting. It was seen as an art. Then Boyd wrote the book: *Aerial Attack Study*. He applied physics to dogfighting. He changed how planes were built and how pilots fly. He played a key role in the development of the F-16, one of the most successful fighter jets in history. He was also impossible.

Author Morgan Housel, a former *Wall Street Journal* columnist and a partner at the Collaborative Fund, wrote about Boyd in a blog post on the fund's website in August 2018. He described Boyd as rude, impatient, and disobedient, writing, "He talked back to superiors to the astonishment of his peers." His behavior in meetings could be crude and unseemly. "This brilliant young officer is an original thinker," one review of Boyd read, "[but] he is an impatient man who does not respond well to close supervision. He is extremely intolerant of those who attempt to impede his program."

Housel used Boyd as an example of the personality and obsession of eccentric genius. He compared Boyd's behavior to that of Tesla founder Elon Musk. Housel described them as "natural maniacs," writing, "A problem happens when you think someone is brilliantly different but not well-behaved. When in fact they're not well-behaved because they're brilliantly different."

In the summer of 2018, Trevor Bauer retweeted the blog entry. Housel had come as close as anyone to understanding him.

The most public case in which Bauer believed he had been misunderstood occurred in October 2016. The Indians were in the playoffs, and Bauer was supposed to start Game 3 of the American League Championship Series. He took the mound in Toronto with black stitches sewed into his right pinky finger, which was caked with dried blood. He couldn't keep it bandaged because MLB rules prohibit pitchers from applying foreign substances to their pitching hands. After his first few pitches, fresh blood streamed from Bauer's finger. The stitches hadn't held. Bauer was pulled from a postseason start because of a first in baseball injury history: a drone accident.

Days earlier, when Bauer had plugged in his drone to charge its battery, the device malfunctioned. Its propellers started to whirl, slicing open his pinky. Some saw flying drones in the midst of the playoffs as an irresponsible act. But building drones wasn't just a hobby for Bauer. His construction projects were a way to give himself a break from baseball for an hour or two a day. He was obsessed with a different engineering effort: building himself into the best pitcher possible. What some didn't understand about Bauer was that few, if any, professional baseball players were as driven to become better.

The collection of curious Indians officials traveled as other hopefuls had, along Honea Egypt Road, a two-lane path of pavement in rural Montgomery, Texas (population 621), fifty-five miles north of Houston. They slowed as they approached a white, split three-rail fence, a common cattle enclosure, which marked the perimeter of the sprawling property. Then the caravan turned onto the gravel driveway. It had arrived at the Texas Baseball Ranch.

The complex, resting in the middle of grazing country, seemed an unlikely talent incubator. There were no immaculate fields or training centers. Instead, much of the work took place inside a simple, steel-arched edifice, which looked like a cheap hangar for a small plane or a giant tin can cut in half and stuck, sideways, in the ground. The facility lacked all imaginable frills, including air conditioning, even in in the oppressive heat and humidity of midsummer Texas. The office was housed in a shed-like building. There was an overgrown field at the back of the property alongside patches of AstroTurf, improvised areas for drill work. It was hard to imagine a setting further removed from the baseball establishment.

These humble surroundings suited Bauer fine; he was put off by ostentatious training facilities. As an amateur, his ball cap had been well-worn in high school and faded light blue in college at UCLA, drenched in sun and sweat. As he sat behind an elevated table for a postgame press conference at the College World Series in 2010, his hat was several shades lighter than those of the teammates to either side. He was asked about the contrast.

"I don't like hats that stick up in the corners," Bauer said. "They make you look like a conductor." The back of the room broke into laughter. Bauer smiled. "So when I find a hat that fits and the corners stay down, I stick with it."

After college, when Bauer was entertaining offers from agencies prior to the draft, he was courted by the sports division of the massive talent agency CAA. When he arrived at their fourteen-story, glass-and-steel building in Los Angeles, luxury cars lined a valet parking lane. There were reps in expensive suits. The building had its own movie theater. Those bells and whistles made Bauer uncomfortable, so he passed on CAA and chose the Wasserman agency, whose reps greeted him wearing jeans. "Good information can come from any environment, any look," Bauer says. "A lot of times I am more comfortable in lesser-looking environments. It seems to suit the idea that it's all about the information and the work and the ideas."

In the rental car arriving at the Texas Baseball Ranch in the winter of 2012–2013 were Indians president of baseball operations Chris Antonetti, manager Terry Francona, and codirector of baseball operations Derek Falvey. They were working to revamp their player-development practices, and they came in search of ideas. But the primary reason for their visit was to learn more about the subversive, iconoclastic Bauer, whom they had just traded for earlier in December, eighteen months after the Arizona Diamondbacks had drafted him third overall. Trading such a high draft pick in such a short time was highly unusual. In fact, prior to Bauer, the only top-three pick ever dealt so soon after the draft was 1973's second selection, Phillies catcher John Stearns, who was moved eight days faster than Bauer because he was blocked by big-league backstop Bob Boone.

That winter, Bauer had temporarily taken up residence at the ranch, as had become his off-season routine. He was the first major leaguer to do so.

For three days in Montgomery, Texas, the Indians officials trailed Bauer, who remembers them asking questions about his routines: "Hey, why are you doing this? Walk us through your thinking." They took Bauer to lunch. Francona and Antonetti took the rental car, and Bauer offered Falvey a ride in his sports car. As they drove to their lunch destination, they made an immediate connection. "We're pitching nerds," Falvey says. "From there, I got to see his workouts. I got to see what he was doing. Better development. At the core of it, that is what Trevor is trying to do." It was the beginning of a productive relationship and what Falvey describes today as a friendship.

Bauer says his entire career has been a triumph of development over the limits of his natural ability.

"I wasn't a natural-born athlete," Bauer told a *Sports Illustrated* reporter in August 2011. "I'm not that strong. I'm not fast. I'm not explosive. I can't jump." So how was he selected third overall in the major-league draft? "I was made."

I was made.

If that was true—if Bauer was made, and in a way that turned conventional baseball training and thinking on its head—then his career could have dramatic ramifications for beliefs about learning and skill development. Nearly six years after being traded, Bauer is an elite among the elite. Yet in the midst of his Cy Young Award chase in 2018, he insists again that he's a poor natural athlete. He believes more than ever that he's a successful baseball construction project, an engineering feat.

"My sixty-yard times are ridiculously slow. Power output? How much weight I can lift? A lot of that can be training, but the speed at which I can move [the weight]. . . . It's not powerful. I think that's a lot of what athletics is. You look at football. What makes a guy a good athlete? He's strong, powerful, he can run fast, very quickly change direction. Basketball? Can he jump? Is he quick? Does he have good hand-eye coordination?"

He pauses.

"Well," he concedes, "maybe I have good hand-eye coordination." (He was caught catching batting-practice (BP) fly balls behind his back in 2018.) "But if you look at all those sports and pool the attributes and ask, 'What makes someone a good athlete?', I am not good at them."

In college, after every home start he made at UCLA, his father, Warren Bauer, took Trevor back across the 405 Freeway to have dinner at a Denny's in Westwood Village. Trevor always ordered the Lumberjack Slam, an infusion of grease and carbs. Asked what natural gifts, if any, his son possessed, Warren doesn't hesitate. He reaches for his smartphone and pulls up a YouTube video, a TED Talk presented by Angela Lee Duckworth.

Duckworth had left a management-consulting job to teach seventh graders math in New York City schools. She soon observed that IQ alone was not a reliable indicator of the difference between her best and worst students. She became convinced every one of her students could master the material if they worked "hard and long enough." Her experience led her to believe that educators must better understand learning from motivational and psychological perspectives.

Duckworth then left teaching to study psychology. She examined the performance of children and adults in challenging settings, always exploring the same questions: Who is successful, and why? She tried to predict which West Point cadets would stick in the military. She forecasted which contestants would advance furthest in the National Spelling Bee. She administered a questionnaire to Chicago high-school students and analyzed the responses of the ones who graduated. One characteristic emerged as a significant predictor of success. It wasn't IQ. "It was grit," she told the TED Talk audience. "Grit is passion and perseverance for very long-term goals. Grit is having stamina. Grit is sticking with your future, day in and day out. Not just for the week or month, but for years. And working really hard to make that future a reality." If Trevor possessed any rare attribute, Warren thinks, he had grit.

To Duckworth, who had spent much of her professional career studying it, the most surprising thing about grit "is how little we know, how little science knows, about building it." What she did know is that natural talent did not make someone "gritty." If anything, her data showed that grit was *inversely* tied to measures of talent. "The best idea I've heard about teaching grit in kids is something called growth mindset," Duckworth said.[2]

Growth mindset is a characteristic defined by Stanford University psychologist Carol Dweck, whose research suggests that the way we think about our abilities is a key to shaping talent. Dweck defined a fixed mindset as one that assumes that a skill, ability, or attribute cannot be improved or changed in a significant way. Cultural critic Maria Popova writes that with a fixed mindset, "avoiding failure at all costs becomes a way of maintaining the sense of being smart or skilled," whereas a growth mindset regards failure not as evidence of stupidity or lack of ability but as a "heartening springboard for growth and for stretching our existing abilities."

If there is any case study in grit and growth mindset in professional baseball, it's Bauer. Back in the fall of 2012, the Indians wanted to learn how Bauer had made himself into an elite amateur pitcher and a promising professional pitcher. But they also wanted to understand why the Diamondbacks were so eager to part ways with their third overall pick. Bauer had a reputation, and Cleveland had heard the complaints: a bad teammate, a loner, stubborn, difficult, and uncoachable. Although Bauer acknowledges that he brought some of that on himself, he thinks much of the labeling was unfair. But once the labels adhered, few bothered to question their legitimacy.

Asked to recall conflict early in his amateur career, Bauer reflects.

"My high-school coach . . ." he begins, before briefly pausing to pick at the Parmesan-crusted pork chop he always orders at Yard House near his in-season accommodations in suburban Cleveland. Then he emphasizes a single word: "Jesus."

Drive north on I-5 beyond the coastal foothills in Los Angeles, where the highway brushes by the San Gabriel Mountains, and the feel of the Pacific Ocean and the California coast fades away. Eventually, the road leads to the working-class city of Santa Clarita, Bauer's hometown, an arid, desert environment about thirty-five miles from the LA city center saturated with bungalow houses and cookie-cutter subdivisions and surrounded by shrub-pocked hills.

There in the sun-baked bullpen of the Hart High School baseball complex, Bauer was told after joining the varsity team to reach a point in his pitching delivery where he would be perfectly balanced—and stationary—on his right leg. Bauer thought the exercise was absurd. It was conventional pitching advice, handed down from generation to generation. To Bauer, it was flat-out wrong. He exaggerated the motion, stopping and balancing on his right leg. Turning to the Hart High coach, he quipped, "Is this good? Can I throw now?"

It's not that he won't listen, Bauer says, it's that he rejects bad advice. He explains that he's very coachable if someone is presenting useful information and can explain its logic. He just doesn't automatically acquiesce to authority. More often, he questions it. He wants to know the logic or science behind any practice or drill he's being asked to do. This is part of the Bauer DNA.

"My dad taught me not to be blindly allegiant and to question authority and to think for myself," Bauer says. "Maybe I take it too far sometimes."

Warren's father was a World War II bomber pilot and first-generation American who had emigrated from Germany. He became an early computer programmer for New Mexico's oil and gas division, and Warren still remembers him working through sheets of code at the kitchen table. Warren was expected to be self-sufficient at eighteen and leave his parents' modest home in Santa Fe. He bought and operated his own Dunkin' Donuts, sold it, and used the money to pay for tuition and housing at the Colorado School of Mines, where he earned a degree in chemical engineering. He worked in the oil and gas industry for a few years in the oil fields of central California before returning to New Mexico, where he opened a furniture business with his brother.

Although Warren did not play sports as a kid, his son was obsessed with baseball from a young age. He first pitched at age seven in a Little League game. He was one of the few players who could keep the ball over the plate, so he kept pitching. After the season, Warren asked Trevor if he wanted to continue to pitch. He did. In that case, Warren said, he would pay for lessons so that Trevor could improve and not hurt himself—but his son had to put in the work. He had to be invested in becoming better.

They went to the local batting cages and found a pitching instructor named Silvio, who was from the Dominican Republic. He taught a practice that incorporated the first unconventional training implement adopted by the Bauers: throwing weighted balls. In the Dominican Republic, Silvio explained, pitchers threw weighted balls, or almost any heavy object they could turn into a projectile, to build strength. When they went home, Warren and Trevor filled a Tupperware container with water and soaked several baseballs. At eight years old, Bauer had his first experience with a tool that later became a well-known part of his training regimen.

"After three days the water would be all full of algae and moss and whatever. They'd smell terrible," Bauer says. "We'd be throwing soaked balls, gripping wet balls, gloves would get wet, splatter us in the face. . . . Throwing weighted balls then wasn't popularized. You couldn't go online and buy them."

Warren was commuting to New Mexico, flying into Albuquerque on Sunday and returning early Friday morning, so Bauer had to practice on his own and be fully accountable. That taught him to adhere to a strict regimen. "My work ethic started from a young age because I had to do it to get lessons," he says.

Since Warren didn't play baseball, he had no preconceived notions of what baseball training should look like. For Warren, his son's activity was a great science experiment. They began to learn about pitching together, examining and questioning everything from the ground up, like engineers. They read about how Nolan Ryan pounded nails into softballs to add weight. And after two years of working with Silvio, they felt they had absorbed all they could from him and began to question some of his methods. They needed growth.

When Trevor was ten, a family friend and former college pitcher, Jim Wagner, said he was going to begin giving pitching instruction. Bauer became one of his first clients. At first, Wagner related information gleaned from experience, pitching-instruction books, and videos. But the then pint-sized Bauer seemed to be making little, if any, progress. Wagner suggested Trevor meet with a former teammate of his, Alan Jaeger, who had become a pitching instructor and proponent of long toss—essentially, throwing a baseball as far as one possibly can—and pulldowns, which were crow-hop, max-effort, on-a-line throws from flat ground covering shorter distances. Often Jaeger would have a pitcher throw from three-hundred-plus feet and then "compress," or work back toward his throwing partner with pulldowns from increasingly shorter distances. Jaeger counted big leaguers Barry Zito and Dan Haren among his clients, but he was one of the few coaches advocating long toss, which was extreme and antithetical to conventional thought. Naturally, Bauer was interested.

One purpose of long-toss and max training is to teach intent. Throwing baseballs hundreds of feet forces a pitcher to exert maximum effort, expanding his body's capabilities and fostering gradual skill growth. From a technical standpoint, long toss is also designed to promote greater flexibility in the throwing motion by increasing external shoulder rotation, or movement away from the center of the body. To experience external rotation, extend your throwing arm straight out from your shoulder to your side, parallel to the ground, and raise your hand, bending your elbow upward to form a 90 degree angle. Then try to move your hand backward as if you were pulling a giant rubber band. Alternatively, imagine pulling a rubber band attached to the center of your chest away from your body. That external rotation of the shoulder joint also causes the elbow to rotate. Increased external rotation is closely linked to velocity gains, as it creates a "greater arc of motion over which force can be applied to the baseball," according to strength coach Ben Brewster.[3] Internal rotation is the opposite movement, motion *toward* the center of the body.

There are three basic ways to improve velocity: get stronger, adopt more efficient mechanics, or create more mobility. Pitching researchers often advise caution because so little is known about the impact of pushing the arm's limits. Yet some have quantified the benefits of pushing the body, finding that throwing from greater distances, and with greater intent, increases range of motion and arm speed. In 2017, the *Orthopedic Journal of Sports Medicine* published a study of 16 Division I college pitchers that found the pitchers' external shoulder rotation had improved from 129.4 degrees to 135.9 degrees after just three days of long-toss training.[4] A 2015 paper by Dr. Kevin E. Wilk and his colleagues, based on data gathered by following 296 professional pitchers from 2005 to 2012, showed that increasing shoulder mobility is crucial in preserving pitchers' arms, reporting that pitchers with a deficit in external shoulder rotation were 2.2 times more likely to be placed on the injured list (at that time called the disabled list) and 4 times more likely to undergo shoulder surgery compared to pitchers with sufficient external rotation.[5]

When Trevor was twelve, Jaeger put him on a routine that perhaps no other kid in the country would have recognized. Before Bauer began a throwing session, he used TheraBand rubber tubing to attach his right wrist to a static object like a fence or railing. He then performed a series of resistance exercises originally designed to rehabilitate torn rotator cuffs. The bands worked his external and internal rotation. After that warm-up, he needed space to launch throws as far as possible. He was mastering intent, and his body was learning, implicitly, to organize itself in the most efficient manner to create velocity. Long toss and pulldowns became a vital part of his routine.

It was through Wagner that Bauer first learned of the Texas Baseball Ranch. Wagner had stumbled upon an obscure, spiral-bound book

on pitching mechanics, *The Athletic Pitcher* by Ron Wolforth. The first
thing most pitching coaches taught was mechanics. Not Wolforth. He
didn't believe in cookie-cutter approaches or trying to copy or clone
the throwing motions of effective pitchers. He noted that pitchers in
the 1930, '40s, and '50s had individualized, natural deliveries, and he
argued that they threw far more innings, seemingly without suffering
more injuries (although injury data for that era is scarce, and pitchers
generally threw softer, which subjected their bodies to less stress).[6]
He studied javelin throwers to glean insights into their motions, and
he employed weighted balls and long-toss regimens. Intrigued, Wagner sent his son on a reconnaissance mission. The younger Wagner
returned from the ranch with a simple message for the Bauers: "You
have to go out there."

At the time, Wolforth was running weekend camps for $200. Any-
one who bought five camp tickets received a sixth for free. Warren
bought a six-pack for his fourteen-year-old son. What Trevor remembers about his first trip is the insufferable heat. There were fans, but
they were blowing humid, 100 degree air in from outside the training
facility. It seemed hotter *inside* the semicircular structure. The camp-
ers broke into three groups, each engaged in a different drill or activity. In one drill, a pitcher tried to throw a four-pound ball with two
hands from above his head at 40 mph, which equated, Wolforth calcu-
lated, to throwing a ball 90 mph from a mound. If a pitcher can't break
90 mph, he has little chance to be a successful major-league pitcher.
In 2008, the average major-league starting pitcher's fastball flew 91.3
mph. By 2018, that figure had climbed to a record 93.2. When he arrived at the ranch, Bauer couldn't touch 80.

When groups of pitchers at the ranch rotated from station to station, Bauer's father didn't follow his son. He was transfixed by the
facility's camera system. At home, Warren would train a camcorder
on his son and record VHS footage of him throwing. The ranch used
a more sophisticated video system, with a higher-frame-rate camera,
to analyze mechanics. For three days, Warren listened to instructor
Brent Strom—now the Astros' pitching coach—speak about analyzing
pitchers via video. He also watched video of a prep pitcher named Josh
Bohack, who went on to pitch at Northeast Texas Community College

and could throw in the low 90s. (The ranch had no famous clients.) Warren observed how Bohack's front knee completely straightened out and his torso flexed forward, creating a 90 degree angle, as he released each pitch, another sequence that correlated with velocity gain. "That image was burned into my dad's head," Trevor says. At UCLA, his delivery had similar attributes.

In his freshman season at Hart High, Bauer hit 76 mph. After visiting the Houston facility several times after his freshman year and during and after his sophomore year, he hit 94 mph in a tournament in the December before his junior season began. Coaches from UCLA and Stanford were there to see the radar readings.

"Sixteen months of being down there completely changed me," Bauer says.

The ranch is where Bauer learned how to acquire velocity. It's where he and his father were exposed to the power of high-speed video. He learned to exchange endurance training, like running the warning track, for explosive drill work that mimicked the act of throwing. He also learned concepts like pitch tunneling, a theory that the longer different types of pitches could share the same release point and path to home plate, disguising their true nature, the more effective they would be. To help him practice tunneling, Warren constructed a metal frame with a thirteen-by-ten-inch opening to target and placed it twenty feet from a practice mound. That was the distance at which a pro hitter would have to decide to swing. If two pitches both traveled through the opening, they shared a tunnel. It may have been the first tunneling instrument ever designed. This was one of the first innovations Bauer brought to baseball. It would not be the last.

Arguably, the most valuable tool Bauer had acquired was his distinctive shoulder tube or, as it's sometimes described, wiggle stick or javelin, which he continues to use. Bauer is the only pitcher who walks to and from the Cleveland clubhouse carrying a semirigid six-foot pole with weighted cylinders attached to each end. He won't throw a baseball until he's warmed up with the shoulder tube by grasping the center of the pole and shaking it at various points above his head, in front of his body, and to his side.

Bauer believes in warming up to throw, not throwing to warm up, and the tube activates muscles in the shoulder, forearm, and upper chest, increasing blood flow to those regions. He also twirls the staff like a propeller, even holding it behind his back to mix up the routine. He could fit in on the flag corps of a high-school band. Wolforth said that if he lost every piece of equipment at his facility, the first thing he would want to bring back was the tube, which he came to view not only as a warm-up aid but as a secret to the durability of pitchers' shoulders and arms. But when Bauer incorporated the shoulder tube into his routine with his high-school team as a sophomore, he was ridiculed by players and coaches. They called it Bauer's "penis pole" and "Linus's blanket."

Ridicule never seemed to bother Bauer, and it didn't stop him from continuing to carry the pole. He was so obsessed with baseball that as an elementary-school student he insisted on wearing his jersey pants to school. Bauer's mother warned him he'd probably be mocked. He wore them anyway, and her prediction came true. He kept wearing them.

Bauer's small group of friends featured fellow social misfits. "They were willing to accept his oddities, and so he was willing to accept theirs, and so they got along great," Warren says. "But the people Trevor didn't get along with are the people that felt it necessary to try to mold Trevor to their status, or their way of going about things, versus just letting him be whatever he was."

"His mom isn't a conformist, and I'm sure not," Warren continues. "So we didn't encourage him to conform, but we didn't discourage him. We just encouraged him to make his own choice."

Trevor can vividly recall approaching a crowded table in the Hart High cafeteria and seeing its occupants quickly disperse despite his status as a rising athletic star. To avoid embarrassment and loneliness, the school's best baseball player began to retreat during lunch to the classroom of his AP physics teacher, Martin Kirby. Bauer could talk to Kirby about physics and its applications to baseball, which became crucial to his career. He had little in common with most of his peers, which is still often true today. Bauer doesn't go out after games. He doesn't drink. He doesn't play cards in the clubhouse. He generally keeps to himself, and he walks to the field and training areas with purpose. He's stubborn, impatient, and fixated on training and information gathering. When he sets a goal, he's determined to reach it.

"I'm an obsessive personality type," Bauer says. "When I got a new video game, I would just play that nonstop. That's all I wanted to do. I stopped going to class my sophomore year [at UCLA] because I would play *Call of Duty: Modern Warfare 2* for eight hours a day. I would play until 4 a.m. and sleep until noon. I would get food, go to the field, do a little bit of homework, come back, and play until 4 a.m. again. I got really good at it, really quickly. Then my grades plummeted, and I was almost ineligible to play in the College World Series. At that point, I said, 'I'm not playing video games anymore because ultimately that's affecting my main job.'"

His main job was to be the best pitcher he could be.

At Hart High, he went 12–0 as a pitcher in his junior year. He continued to use the shoulder tube, and he continued to ignore his high-school coaches' advice. Tensions mounted. "My dad just told me, basically, 'You have way better information from other places, if [the coach] can't handle it, fuck him,'" Bauer says. His relationship with the program grew more and more strained.

In the evenings, after school, Bauer made a bicycle commute from his home to a park in the center of his subdivision neighborhood. An open green space there was large enough for Bauer to conduct the long-toss regimen that he still follows in the outfield before his starts, uncorking throws that routinely sail more than three hundred feet. On one late evening, Bauer continued to throw after the lights at the park's tennis facility illuminated. A tennis instructor became irritated by the constant sound of the balls rattling against the fence surrounding the courts and complained to Bauer's baseball coaching staff. The next day, Bauer says, the coaches confronted him.

Bauer was viewed as disobedient and lacking respect, but he felt he wasn't treated fairly. Unlike other players, he wasn't out partying. He was a good student who put in more practice hours than anyone else. Yet there was constant friction between Bauer and the staff and even upperclassmen on the team. They didn't care for Bauer's brashness or his training techniques. So before his senior season at Hart

High, Bauer quit the team. Rather than play out his senior year and improve his draft stock—J.J. Cooper, executive editor of *Baseball America*, says he was on the radar of professional clubs—Bauer graduated high school early and enrolled for the 2009 spring semester at UCLA, where he had committed to play college ball.

When Bauer and his father visited Bruins coach John Savage to ask him about his stance on Bauer's unorthodox training, Savage said he would allow it but that Bauer would have to participate in all team-related activities and training. Savage promised to "leave him alone" if he pitched well.

Bauer dominated, and Savage left him alone.

Savage used to show up early to the facility when UCLA played mid-week games, and he often found Bauer doing odd drills like flipping a car tire or engaged in resistance work with ropes and bands. A maintenance worker told Warren that Savage would look at Bauer, smile, and walk to his office. Bauer quickly ascended to stardom at UCLA. In 2011, he became the school's first winner of the Golden Spikes Award, given annually to the best amateur player in the country. He was determined to chase down the Pac-10 career strikeout record set by Tim Lincecum, a number—491—he had written down and pinned to his bedroom wall back in Santa Clarita.

In high school and college, Bauer was obsessed with Lincecum, the diminutive former San Francisco Giants ace, who won back-to-back Cy Young Awards in 2008 and 2009. Lincecum was one of the smallest pitchers in the National League, and likely the lightest. The idea that a pitcher with a skateboarder's hair and body—all of five foot eleven and 170 pounds—could win multiple Cy Young Awards with an unconventional delivery fascinated Bauer, who sought out MLB .com highlight reels of Lincecum striking out an outrageous number of batters. Bauer also found video from multiple angles of Lincecum in college at the University of Washington, striking out eighteen batters against UCLA.

"He was sitting 99 mph in the ninth, most electric shit ever," Bauer says. "I still have that video burned in my head. I watched it so many times. I memorized how he moved."

Lincecum moved unlike any other pitcher. The normal stride length for a pitcher is about 80 percent of his height. Lincecum's stride length was 130 percent, which allowed him to create more energy. Bauer had to create speed and energy in his throwing motion to make up for his lack of mass. He and his father saw it as a simple physics problem, $E_k = \frac{1}{2}mv^2$: kinetic energy is proportional to the mass of the object and its velocity squared. Bauer stood six feet and weighed 165 pounds as a college freshman, 170 as a sophomore, and 175 as a junior. The faster and more efficient (or direct) his path to the plate, the more he could make up for his frame. The next determinant of throwing velocity was how efficiently a pitcher could transfer energy up the kinetic chain, from his plant leg to his throwing arm.

"In order for one segment to accelerate most efficiently, the prior segment has to stop completely," Bauer says. "Any slowing of movement of the previous segment diminishes energy transfer to the second."

Lincecum was nicknamed "The Freak" due to his velocity-to-size ratio but also because of his athleticism. Bauer wasn't the athlete Lincecum was. He made himself into a star and made his way into the Pac-10 record books. Bauer fell just short of Lincecum's Pac-10 strikeout record, finishing with 460. But he did top Lincecum's single-season mark of 199, set over 125 innings in 2006. Bauer struck out 203 batters in 136 2/3 innings in 2011, when he went 13–2 with a 1.25 ERA.

Still, the team's best player didn't always mesh well in the locker room. "I can't tell you I know Bauer," former UCLA teammate Cody Decker told USA Today. "I spoke with Bauer one time, and I said, 'I'll never do that again. I'm good. I got my fill for a lifetime.'"

And despite his success, Bauer did not pitch on Fridays, the day typically reserved for the best pitcher on a college staff. Gerrit Cole pitched on Fridays. Cole was different from Bauer in almost every way. At six foot four, 230 pounds, he was the archetype of a right-handed pitcher. But while Cole was bigger and threw harder, Bauer outperformed him in almost every measurable category. They were polar opposites in personality and interests, and at UCLA they formed a rivalry that has followed them both to the big leagues.

Before the 2011 draft, *Sports Illustrated* reported that some amateur-scouting directors were put off by Bauer's attitude. They didn't like that he played Hacky Sack before games and listened to his iPod while warming up in the bullpen, and they didn't like his faded blue hat. That a six-foot, 175-pound pitcher could be viewed as a first-rounder at all was a tectonic change attributable to one pitcher: Lincecum. "I owe a lot to Lincecum," Bauer says. "He's the only reason I went as high as I did in the draft. He kind of broke that barrier down."

The 2011 draft began on Monday, June 6, at 4 p.m. Pacific time. It was a poorly held secret that Bauer's teammate, Cole, was going to be the first overall pick. The Pittsburgh Pirates preferred his size and top-end velocity to Bauer's production. The Mariners, who held the second overall pick, had long been connected to the best available college position player, Rice third baseman Anthony Rendon. But the Mariners were growing more and more leery of Rendon's lengthy injury history. Ninety minutes before the start of the draft, Bauer's agent, Joel Wolfe, received a phone call: it was the Mariners, who claimed they were going to take Bauer second overall. They wanted to know his signing demands. Wolfe called his client.

"Hey, would you rather go to the Mariners at two or the Diamond-backs at three?" Wolfe asked.

Wolfe and Bauer had wanted to meet with all of the clubs drafting in the top ten. Some teams agreed to meet with Bauer; others did not. "They thought they were interviewing us," Wolfe says. "*We* were interviewing *them.*" Bauer was willing to sacrifice dollars to land with a club that would be open to his training regimen.

The Mariners hadn't met with Bauer. Bauer preferred the Diamond-backs, whose vice president of scouting and player development, Jerry Dipoto, had gotten to know Bauer as well as any major-league executive in the predraft process.

"I felt like I developed a good relationship with him. I saw things through his eyes," Dipoto recalls. "It's almost impossible to say that he hasn't blazed a bit of a trail, because in 2011 as a draft eligible, there were so many rolling eyes and raised brows just watching his pregame routines. . . . He was the first guy that routinely got out there before a game and went through exhaustive long toss . . . and using the [shoulder tube] in the bullpen, things that you just hadn't seen before then that now, frankly, from high schools and colleges to the pro game, it's far more common."

Arizona promised Bauer he could continue his unorthodox training practices.

Wolfe called the Mariners back and gave them an absurd asking price: $20 million. (Cole, the top pick, would sign for $8 million.) The Mariners declined and hung up. Bauer would not be going second overall. A little less than two hours later, the Mariners selected University of Virginia pitcher Danny Hultzen, whose career would be sidetracked by severe shoulder injuries. The Diamondbacks took Bauer third. "This is a chance for us to really explore what pitchers are capable of doing," Dipoto said to Sports Illustrated after the draft.

Bauer signed for $7.3 million on July 25. He debuted in High-A and advanced to Double-A, striking out 40 percent of the batters he faced in his first partial pro season. But at the end of October, Dipoto was hired by the Los Angeles Angels to be their general manager. The Diamondbacks had lost their only conduit between Bauer, general manager Kevin Towers, and the coaching and development staffs. For Bauer, this is where a lack of scouting and familiarity doomed the relationship and why human intelligence gathering will always have a role. "I'm certain that to some extent my leaving affected the communication with and around Trevor," Dipoto says.

The fit with the Diamondbacks was a disaster. Teammates found Bauer aloof, conceited. It's true that he didn't speak much or try to engage, he says, but only because he often felt he didn't fit in and couldn't find common ground in the clubhouse. For instance, Bauer says, he didn't feel he could offer anything valuable to a conversation about hunting.

To make matters worse, Bauer's approach was antithetical to the team's traditional practices. Early on, things went well enough. Bauer pitched his way quickly to the majors. He debuted on June 28, 2012, a little more than a year after being drafted, allowing two runs over four innings at Turner Field in Atlanta. But after his second major-league start, this time at home in Phoenix against the Padres, a crowd of reporters gathered around Bauer, voice recorders extended and cameras

taping, as the rookie talked about the number of shake-offs and dis-
agreements about pitch calls that he'd had with veteran catcher Miguel Montero. Bauer explained that he needed to do a better job of
conveying his approach to pitching to Montero. The same pack of
journalists then flocked to Montero and relayed Bauer's comments.

"What?" Montero said to reporters. "He's going to tell me how to
do my job?"

After the season, Bauer was traded. Derrick Hall, the Diamondbacks' president, justified the trade to *USA Today* by throwing Bauer
under the bus, saying, "Trevor just had a really tough year with his
teammates." Unnamed Diamondbacks sources quoted in the story described Bauer as a "loner."

The following season, Montero remarked, "When you get a guy like
that and he thinks he's got everything figured out, it's just tough to
convince him to get on the same page with you. . . . Since day one
in spring training, I caught him, and he killed me because he threw
about one hundred pitches the first day. The next time he threw I saw
him doing the same thing. He never wanted to listen."

Falvey says, "Despite what maybe the view is of Trevor, he doesn't
think he has all the answers. He wants to dig to find more answers."

A few weeks after the initial visit, a contingent of Indians officials returned to the outskirts of Houston and invited Bauer to dinner at his
go-to spot, Saltgrass Steakhouse. They wanted to learn more about
this player the Diamondbacks couldn't handle. They wanted to learn
how to coach him.

At dinner they listened to Bauer's expectations and outlined their
own. They assured him he would be permitted to maintain his routine, but he would have to be in the clubhouse, follow team guidelines,
and be a good teammate. If he wanted to throw longer distances and
use his own brand of mechanics, the Indians would let him. This was
a clean slate.

The Indians saw a chance to acquire an undervalued pitcher, of
course. But Bauer suspected that they had other motivations.

Cleveland had begun to reconsider many of its development practices. Although the team had begun, for example, to implement a weighted-ball program, Falvey says it wasn't "robust." If Bauer was successful, he could be an agent of change. He could give the organization a firsthand look at how to build better baseball players.

"They needed a poster child," Bauer says.

After the Indians left, Bauer kept prepping for the next season. Wolforth regularly brought in speakers for his coaching clinics, and Bauer was intrigued by one of the presenters, who spoke about data collection and technology, including high-speed cameras similar to the one Bauer owned. There wasn't a lot of technology at the ranch, and there weren't many attempts to rigorously study skill improvement. After the talk, Bauer approached and said he had a problem. When he tried to record high-speed video of his delivery, frames would skip.

"Oh, you have the wrong memory card," the speaker said. "Your memory card is too slow. It should be that simple."

They exchanged cell numbers. Bauer texted a few days later to thank him and let him know that the problem was solved. The presenter's name would come to be as associated with overturning tradition in baseball as Bauer's: Kyle Boddy. Together, Bauer and Boddy would bring change just as seismic as the *first* revolution in player development almost a century earlier.

MAKING MULES INTO RACEHORSES

Can you take me high enough
to fly me over yesterday?
Can you take me high enough
It's never over
Yesterday's just a memory
    —DAMN YANKEES, "High Enough"

For several decades before Bauer arrived at the Texas Baseball Ranch, most major-league teams were set in their ways when it came to development, either hostile or indifferent to alternative ideas. But before *that*—for roughly the first fifty years of Major League Baseball—teams didn't develop players. It's not that they didn't develop them *well*; it's that they played almost no role at all in instructing them before they got to the game's highest level. Instead, they acquired or purchased them premade.

Well into the twentieth century, the minor leagues remained mostly unaffiliated with the majors. Each minor league and member team operated as an independent entity without a "parent club" to pay its expenses and reap the rewards by promoting the most appealing players. Before major-league teams could call up promising players from Triple-A, as they do today, they acquired talent by trading for or purchasing players from other big-league teams or minor-league teams, drafting players from the highest minor leagues who hadn't already been auctioned off, or scouring the country for big-league-ready amateurs who had somehow eluded the network of other minor- and major-league teams that were trying to find them.

Because players might pass through the payrolls of any number of autonomous organizations as they climbed the minor-league ladder, player development was—as Armour and Levitt put it in their 2015 book *In Pursuit of Pennants*—a "much more haphazard and less efficiently regulated" process than it is today.[1] That system was, in today's tech parlance, ripe for disruption, and the primary disruptor would be Branch Rickey, the baseball executive now best known (and deservedly celebrated) for signing and promoting Jackie Robinson, the first black player in the big leagues since the nineteenth century. Rickey, who'd briefly been a big leaguer before he made his name in management, was Bill James, Billy Beane, and Billy Graham rolled into one cigar-smoking, bushy-browed, bowtie-wearing athlete-intellectual. Decades before he and Robinson broke the color barrier—in Rickey's case, both to right a glaring wrong and to tap a rich source of intentionally overlooked talent—Rickey, then a St. Louis Cardinals executive, revolutionized baseball by pioneering a method for stockpiling players and standardizing their development: the farm system.

Rickey, who realized that trying to go dollar-for-dollar with wealthier clubs was a losing proposition, wired prized scout Charley Barrett, "Pack up and come home—we'll develop our own players." Starting in late 1919, Rickey and Cardinals president Sam Breadon began building a Cardinals-owned and -operated network of minor-league teams. In a pattern that repeats itself across centuries, baseball's old guard belittled a boundary-breaking concept. "It's the stupidest idea in baseball," legendary Giants manager John McGraw said. "What Rickey is trying to do can't be done."[2] It could. Frequent tryouts, Barrett's scouting, and Rickey's relationships with college coaches—along with his creative, quasi-legal approaches to retaining the rights to minor leaguers—fostered the first player-development machine, a factory for big leaguers.

When roster rules relaxed in response to the Great Depression, the Cardinals upped their total from 3 farm teams in 1931 to 11 in 1932. They expanded further from there, inspiring copycat clubs (including the Yankees) that belatedly realized Rickey had stolen a march on the rest of the sport. As a writer for the *Sporting News* noted in 1937, the industry was rapidly "Rickeyized". In 1920 there had been 3 affiliated farm teams, but by 1939 there were 168.[3] The Cardinals' count peaked at 32 in 1940, not counting a number of "working agreements" with teams the club didn't own directly, which reportedly brought the total number of players at its beck and call to almost 800. As Armour and Levitt noted, in the first ten years of the relaxed roster rules, some teams averaged fewer than 3 farm teams per year, while the Cardinals averaged more than 20.

Rickey later opined, "The farm system is the only vehicle that a poor club has available to it to use to mount into respectability competitively."[4] The Cardinals, whose strategy was predicated on Rickey's player-development principle that "out of quantity comes quality," quickly managed much more than respectability. From 1922, when Rickey's first farm-system product debuted, through 1942, when Rickey decamped for the Dodgers, the Cardinals won more games than any team but the Yankees, claiming six pennants. After his departure, the club Rickey had constructed won three more pennants and two titles in four years and wouldn't suffer a losing season until 1954. By then, the Rickey-built Dodgers were a perennial powerhouse, and Rickey himself had moved on to the Pirates, where he was collecting the core of a club that would win the World Series in 1960.

At that point, nearly every minor-league team was beholden to a big-league organization, completing what Armour and Levitt labeled "the most significant changes to the nature of team-building and talent acquisition during the first half of the twentieth century."[5] Rickey had been both the driver and the biggest beneficiary of those changes, but his contributions to development didn't end there. Although he believed in buying players in bulk to stock his "chain store" system, Rickey recognized that the recipe for developing players wasn't as simple as "sign and let simmer for several seasons." A well-seasoned player requires some stirring.

Rickey's rivals believed players could improve only by playing in games, but he subscribed to the importance of practicing specific skills. During his four years as head baseball coach at the University of Michigan, Rickey, who years later invented the batting helmet, had designed the batting cage, which he conceived to help catchers like him, who had less time to hit because they were busy keeping balls from sailing away whenever their teammates swung through practice pitches. He also invented the sliding pit—a dirt patch where runners could perfect their approach to the base—and a system of strings that gave pitchers a primitive form of feedback as they aimed for the edges of the strike zone, helping them hone their command. Rickey brought these innovations to his inaugural big-league camp, and they were still staples of his teams' training regimes decades later, tangible by-products of his belief that "sweat remained the best solvent" for almost any player's ills.

One of Rickey's star pupils was the irascible but unbeatable second baseman Rogers Hornsby, who broke into the big leagues under Rickey in 1915. Rickey associate Rex Bowen later recounted that Rickey had helped Hornsby improve at the plate; as a young hitter, Hornsby had a tendency to pull balls foul down the third-base line, which Rickey corrected by forcing Hornsby to hit every ball to the right side of the pitcher every morning for ten days in a row, taking so many swings that Bowen said he "almost broke his thumb on a bat, working so hard to improve."[6]

That collaborative experience, and their shared obsession with being better at baseball, didn't stop the two from frequently clashing until Hornsby was traded after the 1926 season. The year before that, Hornsby had taken over as player-manager, replacing Rickey in the latter role. One of Hornsby's first acts was to discontinue the pregame meetings Rickey had held with the team and remove the chalkboards he had used to illustrate his lessons. "It's base hits that win ballgames, not smart ideas," the best second baseman of his time asserted.

That's true on a literal level, but players must approach their potential before they can begin banging out hits, and ideas can power that process. With the Cardinals and Dodgers, Rickey implemented even more measures to cultivate what he called "the pleasing skills of the finished athlete."[7] No longer were Rickey's scouts looking for players who could be fitted for major-league uniforms immediately; now they were after the best bets long term, and those prospects would have to be handed off to trustees who would tutor the players until they were ready to, as Rickey put it, "ripen into money."[8]

Rickey's assembly line reached its fullest fruition in the late 1940s, when Dodgertown opened in Vero Beach, Florida. The massive spring training complex, constructed on the site of a former naval base, represented, in the words of Rickey biographer Lee Lowenfish, "a permanent baseball college campus where all the players could be trained by a faculty of superlative teachers." The facility's unprecedented size allowed the team to disseminate the same instruction to the hundreds of players who would soon spend their seasons under Dodgers control, from Brooklyn down to Class D. There, the players learned how Rickey preferred they play, listening to his lectures and doing drills they could take to their respective full-season assignments.

"We are in accord on what and how we teach, so that when a player leaves Dodgertown and reports to one of our managers, he can be assured that nothing contrary to what he has learned at Dodgertown will be taught," wrote Rickey acolyte and longtime Dodger-developer Fresco Thompson in his memoir *Every Diamond Doesn't Sparkle*. Surveying the array of batting cages, pitching machines, string setups, and sliding pits, Thompson joked, "Maybe next season we'll have mechanical batters and we'll be able to dispense entirely with the ballplayers."[9]

Although Rickey was baseball's bellwether, other teams that recognized and responded to the trend toward more minor-league affiliates reaped rich rewards at the major-league level. Analysis performed for us by Baseball Prospectus writer Rob Arthur reveals that between 1920 and 1960, upgrading from zero affiliates to one or more was worth about 2.25 wins per year. Going from a below-average to an above-average number of affiliates was worth an astounding 7.7 wins per year, albeit with diminishing returns after reaching twice the typical team's farm-club count. Overall, adding one farm team was worth about 11 wins, on average, to a parent club over the following five years. Establishing a minor-league system, and extracting the youth it yielded, was for years the best (and most economical) way to win.

But bargains that good never last. By 1960, only one team had fewer than seven affiliates, and only one had more than twelve. The gap between the biggest and smallest systems had shrunk, and the pace of player development's evolution slowed. Even so, the decades between

Rickey's innovations and the advent of modern player development brought four transitional, out-of-the-box experiments, three of which were prescient failures and one of which was a prescient success. The failures came first.

Chicago Cubs owner Philip K. Wrigley, who took over the team upon the death of his gum-magnate father, William, in 1932, inherited a hugely successful family business. He proved a skilled steward, leaving the company on even sounder financial footing thanks to innovative measures like factory automation, radio and TV advertising, and a partnership with the army during World War II. At times, Wrigley attempted to extend his data-driven gum-making/marketing approach to baseball, with considerably less success.

In 1938, he invited the first failure by hiring Coleman R. Griffith, a groundbreaking researcher in the fledgling field of sports psychology, to consult for the Cubs on implementing a rigorous training program. As Professor Richard J. Puerzer recounted in a 2006 essay for the Society for American Baseball Research (SABR), Griffith's work included "filming players, recommending improved training regimes, the documentation of player progress through charts and diagrams, and changes in batting and pitching practice in order to make the practice sessions more closely resemble game conditions."[10] The psychologist was speaking the language of advanced player development about eight decades ahead of his time.

"Contrary to what coaches often assume, he argued, players in the major leagues have not reached the performance limits of their bodies," wrote psychology professor Christopher D. Green in a 2003 essay about Griffith. "They have reached only the limits allowed by the regimen of practice in which they are currently engaged." In one report, Griffith complained that "the intent of the manager and most of the players was merely to regain or to recover about the same level of skill and judgment as had been attained during the previous season . . . but not . . . to acquire new skills nor to change the fundamental character of their older skills so that they would be more useful or more productive." He also asserted that "to appeal to instinct or to heredity" to explain a player's shortcomings was "a lazy, unimaginative and ignorant man's way of evading the demands of his job."[11]

The Cubs' first manager in 1938, Charlie Grimm, had succeeded Hornsby as Cubs skipper and wasn't much more open-minded than his predecessor; in his autobiography, he railed against "professors and pseudoscientists."[12] Griffith, an egghead armed with a chronoscope and slow-motion movie camera, represented a threat.

Griffith concluded that an average of only 47.8 minutes per day was being spent on practice "effective for the playing of baseball" and recommended measures such as gradually shortening the distance between the batter and fielder when playing "pepper" (a popular pregame warm-up exercise), structuring batting practice around complete at-bats, and having a hitter stand in the batter's box during pitching practice to make the simulation more realistic. But Grimm ignored or undercut him, earning Griffith's ire in increasingly caustic reports to Wrigley, one of which lamented that "widespread belief in 'baseball magic' undermined his own attempts to put the playing of the game on a more scientific footing." Griffith's association with the team ended in 1940, and as Green wrote, "the Cubs and the rest of Major League Baseball carried on much as they had before his arrival."

In 1961, toward the end of a streak of sixteen nonwinning seasons, a frustrated Wrigley decided to dispense with managers, an experiment that Puerzer called in his essay "revolutionary and radical, defying all previous baseball convention." It came to be called the "college of coaches."

Wrigley's gambit was inspired by Cubs catcher El Tappe's suggestion of hiring roving specialist coaches in the minors. Like Rickey, Wrigley sought to streamline instruction, so he extended the idea to the big-league level. The new model called for eight to fourteen coaches, equal in status and salary, who would rotate throughout the Cubs' organization, taking turns as "head coach" in the big leagues before cycling through the farm teams. The college of coaches, which Wrigley generally referred to as the "management team," would represent "business efficiency applied to baseball."

A *Los Angeles Times* writer likened Wrigley to "the scientists who are trying to put a man on the moon when they could benefit humanity a whole lot more by discovering a preventative for hangovers," and JFK, who had ordered those scientists to aim moonward, suggested that automation might not mean the end of the workforce "since it now takes 10 men to manage the Cubs instead of one."[13] The team's pitching was too thin to win with any number of managers, but even the system itself was a flop. Although the plan was designed to minimize discordant coaching styles, it ended up doing the opposite, and Wrigley conceded defeat in January 1963. "Each of the head coaches had his own individual ideas," he said, adding that as a result, "the aim of standardization of play was not achieved."[14]

Even so, Wrigley continued to rebel against orthodoxy, installing retired air force colonel Robert W. Whitlow as the team's athletic director. Whitlow, who was supposed to oversee the entire organization and report to Wrigley directly, purchased exercise equipment, formulated workout and nutrition regimens, and proposed applying psychology to the team's operations, but like Griffith before him, he was largely ignored and resigned after the 1964 season, prompting Wrigley to lament that "baseball people are slow to accept anyone with new ideas."

As the Cubs' experiment with the college and Whitlow wound down, another National League team commissioned a long-lasting but little-known study with a name as mundane as its mission was imaginative: the Research Program for Baseball. University of Delaware baseball coach Tubby Raymond approached Philadelphia Phillies owner Bob Carpenter with a bold proposal. Carpenter was a prominent patron of UD's athletic program, and he agreed to back Raymond's idea of testing the swing characteristics, eyesight, and mental makeups of hundreds of hitters, thereby establishing baselines that the Phillies could use to weed out weaker prospects or, more proactively, give them something to strive for.

Starting in 1963, Research Program personnel flocked to Florida each spring to collect information from hundreds of minor leaguers in a number of organizations. During the regular season, they tested major-league hitters in Philadelphia. To gather their data, they worked with a UD professor on psychological testing; a Bausch & Lomb representative on measuring visual acuity, depth perception, and pitch-tracking with a portable Ortho-Rater device; and physicists from DuPont on engineering a bat that could measure velocity, acceleration, force, and swing smoothness. "It was the only program of its kind at that time," says Bob Hannah, who assisted with the Research Program and succeeded Raymond as UD's baseball coach. "It was kind of a forerunner to all of the technology that you see out there today."

One of Hannah's duties was writing an annual report on the program's progress. The first sentence of his first scouting report read, "The basic assumption underlying this study is that valid and reliable measuring devices and instruments can be constructed that will be useful in the selection and training of professional baseball players."[15] That's not an assumption anyone would quibble with today, but in the '60s it was far from accepted that sophisticated technology had any part to play in player procurement or development. The program's futuristic, DuPont-designed bats had accelerometers embedded within the wood, and each hitter would wear a recording device that was wired to a strain gauge in the bat. When he swung, that sensor would convert the bat's behavior into measurable electrical impulses the Research Program reps could record.

"We were taking baby steps with all of this stuff," Hannah says. "There was no background information with which to compare the process we were using." Over time, the program developed a profile of what high-level hitters looked like. The fastest hack ever captured was switch-hitting hit king Pete Rose's from the right side, edging out other legends who consented to swing, like Hank Aaron.

Per the terms Carpenter had imposed, the Research Program's data was confined to the Phillies, and Hannah says the organization never used it in any meaningful way, although a Research Program eye exam did convince Phillies slugger Dick Allen to get glasses. "We were still in an era of Major League Baseball where the old traditional rules were the things that were applied," Hannah says. He remembers one meeting in which Raymond briefed the Phillies' scouts on the work the Research Program was doing and the ways in which it could help them more accurately identify talent. "I think there was a lot of yawning taking place in the meeting," Hannah says. "We weren't making inroads in a hurry with that kind of stuff."

The scouts persisted in trusting their own eyes, aided at most by a stopwatch. Players on the MLB bubble were even less receptive to the program's presence. Third baseman Don Hoak, who was in his midthirties and tested poorly on the eye exam, wasn't pleased that the program might give the Phillies another reason (besides his sub-par hitting) to let him go. "He actually came in and threatened that if these tests had anything to do with him losing his job that there would be some price to pay," Hannah says.

When the evaluators of outside talent proved stubborn, Hannah and his colleagues shifted their focus to applying the program to player development. The researchers realized that their readouts could give the team a method of tracking and encouraging its own prospects' progress by providing objective feedback and pinpointing potential areas of improvement. "The vision scores, when coupled with results of the bat tests, enabled the researchers to make some impressively accurate predictions each spring about the offensive production of young hitters in the Philadelphia farm system," wrote Kevin Kerrane in Dollar Sign on the Muscle, his 1984 book about scouting. [16] But predictions are pointless if no one important pays attention to them.

The Research Program continued until 1972, when Carpenter stepped down as team president. At some point after that, the products of the program's forward-looking labor disappeared—into storage, perhaps, or possibly into a shredder. "We had a room full of pages and pages of documentation over the years," Hannah says. "I have no idea what happened to it."

The annals of player development contain one more illustrative outlier along the lengthy but largely uniform path from Rickey to recent times: the short-lived but brilliant Royals Academy, which combined Rickey's centralized instruction with Wrigley's and Hannah's science.

Like Wrigley's experiments, the Royals Academy was the brainchild of a businessman who tried to broaden baseball minds. In 1968, Ewing M. Kauffman bought the American League expansion franchise that would soon be christened the Royals. Kauffman, an entrepreneur who'd started the Marion Laboratories pharmaceutical company out of his basement in 1950, was, as The Sporting News put it, "armed with

vast personal wealth, exceptional business acumen, and no knowledge of baseball." The last attribute was more of an aid than a handicap; because baseball was new to him, Kauffman wouldn't be bound
by the weight of what had happened in the past.

Legendary scout Art Stewart, now in his nineties and still a Royals adviser, remembers being at the first meeting between Kauffman
and his scouting staff at the old Continental Hotel in Kansas City.
Kauffman, who, Stewart says, was "a brilliant man . . . way ahead of
his time," was looking for answers no one in baseball had heard before. "He made a statement, 'Gentleman, how do we get talent for our
major-league club and organization?'" Stewart says. "And someone
got up and said, 'We draft, we make trades, and there's waivers and,
uh, y'know, that's the extent of it.' And [Kauffman] said there should
be more ways to develop players."

As Stewart recalls, Kauffman told the assembled scouts he'd give
the problem some thought, and at a subsequent meeting he proposed
a solution: a series of tryout camps for raw athletes, in which the Royals would look for talent in "track stars, football stars, [and] basketball
stars [and] see if it translates to baseball." Kauffman made a fortune
at Marion by avoiding development entirely; instead, he acquired, re-
formulated, and repackaged products discovered but rejected by other
pharmaceutical companies. But in baseball, his Royals would be the
ones making discoveries and trying to cultivate them in an athletic
laboratory.

To determine which skills to target in the team's nationwide drag-
net, Kauffman hired Dr. Raymond Reilly, a research psychologist who
had worked at NASA and the Office of Naval Research. Reilly tested
the vision, psychomotor responses, and psychological makeups of
roughly 150 professional players, mostly from within the Royals organization, and identified running speed (Rickey's favorite tool), sharp
eyesight, quick reflexes, and exceptional body balance as the most
desirable physical attributes. Then the Royals set out to find potential players who possessed them, advertising tryouts in which they
would consider attendees who satisfied four criteria. To meet the
minimum requirements, players had to have completed their high-
school eligibility, be neither enrolled in a four-year college nor drafted

by a big-league team, be younger than twenty, and be able to run sixty yards in no more than 6.9 seconds in baseball shoes.

Stewart was initially skeptical that the tryouts would turn up much talent, even though Rickey, whom he'd befriended early in his career, had told him how fruitful tryouts had been for his teams. He was soon swayed. Starting with a camp in Kansas City in June 1970, the Royals conducted 126 tryouts in a year across the United States and Canada, screening 7,682 candidates, from whom they selected 42 athletes from twenty-six states to make up the academy's inaugural class. To house the top tryout talents, Kauffman had commissioned a campus on a 121-acre plot of land on the outskirts of Sarasota, Florida. The campus featured five baseball diamonds—all boasting the same dimensions as the field in Kansas City's under-construction Kauffman Stadium— plus a fifty-room dormitory for players and various administrative and recreational facilities. Kauffman's chosen few would study and train at the academy for a minimum of ten months, making a monthly salary and receiving free room and board, health and life insurance, and a roundtrip ticket home for the holidays.

In the afternoons, players received intensive instruction from an eight-man faculty composed of specialists in several aspects of the sport, as well as nontraditional hires, including a track coach and a trainer who developed nutrition plans and resistance exercises tailored to particular players. "In retrospect, this cadre of professionals constituted the first concerted effort to measure, evaluate, and improve both baseball players and the way that baseball is played," wrote Puerzer in another essay for SABR.[17] Academy members spent at least twenty-five hours a week on practice fields or in games against local pro and collegiate clubs. Players attended classes three mornings a week at a neighboring junior college, and once they completed their terms at the academy, they were eligible for four-year scholarships to a college of their choice. Those expenses added up: the academy cost $1.5 million to build and $600,000 annually to operate. The Royals hoped, as Rickey had, for a crop of players that would "ripen into money" and more than make up for the outlay.

Kauffman welcomed the academy's first class in August 1970, telling the recruits that they were "the astronauts of baseball" because they were "doing something nobody in the sport has done before."[18] (By 1970, no one was mocking scientists for trying to put men on the moon.) "Baseball's power of growth is almost without bounds," said Commissioner Bowie Kuhn at the academy's dedication ceremony. "We are only beginning a new era. Obviously, if baseball is to progress, we must be prepared to grow and adapt to a world different from the world of 50 years ago."[19]

The academy's first director, Syd Thrift, was a former Yankees farmhand who had attended a postseason camp in St. Petersburg administered by Yankees manager Casey Stengel in the fall of 1950. That camp was credited with helping Mickey Mantle and others reach the big leagues sooner than they otherwise would have, but it was a short-term program that catered only to professional players. Stengel once supposedly said, "You can't teach these fellas anything they don't already know," but the academy rejected that premise. "Baseball techniques are like the weather," Thrift said. "Everybody in the business talks about them, but very little has been done about them. We have come up with some brand-new ideas."[20]

Naturally, the academy initiative was widely disparaged, both by some elements inside the organization and by rival teams. "Most clubs thought it was a waste of time, waste of money, wouldn't work," Stewart says. The Royals' experiment ruffled even more feathers when the academy sent a team to the Gulf Coast League in 1971 to compete against rookie clubs from several other organizations. Even though seven of its twenty-eight members hadn't played baseball in high school and the others had been passed over in the amateur draft, the academy team went 40–13, winning the league championship and stealing 103 bases, nearly double the next-speediest team's total.

Stewart, who evaluated academy prospects, remembers hearing an opposing manager in the White Sox system berating his players after the academy team trounced them. "He got 'em all together and ranted and screamed and yelled at those kids," Stewart says. "He said, 'Look at them across the way, those kids beat the hell out of us 10–0, and you're sitting here with your big bonuses and you can't compare with those kids.' I'll never forget that. It proved to me and made me see how important player development was, how important repetition was, how important individual instruction was."

Because players lived at the academy year-round, they put more time in than most minor leaguers: thirty minutes of batting practice a day, compared to the few minutes most players would get elsewhere. But the hallmark of the academy wasn't just more training; it was also *better* training. Instructors turned around pitching machines and used them for fielding practice, along with machines that could produce more unpredictable grounders that mimicked the appearance of batted balls. They used an orange, two-hundred-pound video machine to record and analyze swings, radar guns to clock pitchers, and stopwatches to turn taking leads into a science.

The academy was the first baseball program to feature a mandatory stretching program or to use a swimming pool for injury rehab, and it embraced diet planning and strength training at a time when such practices were still heretical. The academy also focused on the prospects' mental approach, teaching them techniques to center their concentration on specific aspects of instruction until they became instinctive. Two ophthalmologists, Bill Harrison and Bill Lee, implemented a visualization program and conducted vision testing.

The staff also welcomed guest speakers, including Ted Williams, perhaps the best hitter in history. Williams was a walking advertisement for academy-type training: burdened by an unhappy home life, he'd spent much of his childhood at a playground near his house. "That was as big a break as I got in my whole life," he later recalled. "[The] chance to play baseball twelve months a year." As a nineteen-year-old minor leaguer in 1938, he'd been tutored by a forty-one-year-old Hornsby, who helped him hit for average *and* power. In his 1970 book *The Science of Hitting*, Williams recalled that Hornsby, whom Rickey had rebuilt, taught him, "A great hitter isn't born, he's made. He's made out of practice, fault correction, and confidence."[21] Williams tried to impart the same lesson to his academy audience. "He talked about not taking one hundred swings a day, but five hundred swings a day," Stewart remembers.

The academy's first class graduated in December 1971, having played 241 games against varying levels of competition, winning 162.

One member of that class, second baseman Frank White, became the academy's first and best big leaguer, enjoying an eighteen-year career with the Royals. White later remembered the academy being a bit like a boot camp and said it sometimes made him feel like "a guinea pig in a grand baseball experiment," but he credited the experience with transforming him from an unrefined athlete into a big leaguer. Thirteen other academy products eventually made the majors. From 1973, the year White debuted, through 1982, the Royals won the sixth-most games in the majors. When they won the pennant in 1980, they did so with a keystone combination of White at second and fellow academy graduate U L Washington at short.

By then, though, the academy was long closed. The Royals ran a $1 million deficit in 1973, and with money tight, the expensive academy, with its unorthodox methods and lack of immediate major-league results, was an easy target for Royals player-development men who viewed it as a dubious, competing product. Thrift, who called his time at the academy "the most stimulating experience I have ever been a part of," resigned as director over the lack of support from anyone in management except Kauffman. Fittingly, the assistant director when the academy closed in May 1974 was Rickey's grandson, Branch III.

With the exception of the Royals Academy, much of player-development history has depended on chance occurrences. In 1988, Braves pitcher Tom Glavine led the major leagues in losses. But in the spring of '89, while standing in the outfield during batting practice, he picked up a ball that rolled toward him and happened to grip it in an unusual way, with his middle and ring fingers along the seams. He threw it into the infield, and the release felt right. He'd discovered his signature circle changeup. "If I hadn't found that pitch, picked up the ball that way . . . I don't know," Glavine told *Sports Illustrated* in 1992. In 1991, he'd led the majors in *wins*, and twenty-five years after his pitching epiphany, he entered the Hall of Fame.[22]

Some formative moments have come from teammates talking shop and sharing their craft, although not all players are open books. Twins prospect Pat Mahomes discovered as much in 1991 when he asked future Hall of Famer Jack Morris how he threw his splitter. "Get away from me, you little motherfucker," Mahomes remembered Morris saying. "You'll be trying to take my job next year."[23] More happily, Hall of Famer Harry Heilmann was a run-of-the-mill regular for several seasons before his Detroit Tigers teammate Ty Cobb, newly named to the position of player-manager in 1921, had him back up in the batter's box, move his feet closer together, hold his hands farther away from his body, and crouch while waiting for the pitch. Using the new stance, Heilmann surpassed Cobb to become the most potent hitter of the next ten years not named Ruth or Hornsby.

Cobb, by all accounts, was a hitting-instruction savant; under his tutelage, that 1921 team increased its batting average by forty-six points to .321, still a record under current scoring rules. But in many coaches' cases, tweaks were trial-and-error and hit-or-miss. Based on hunches more than sound science, and reliant on the right instructors overlapping with the right players at the right times, baseball's prevailing principles were applied in piecemeal fashion rather than as part of proven programs.

The Royals Academy pointed toward a future where relatively little would be left to chance and all players would receive personalized, scientific instruction. In the academy era, the Royals were the first franchise to assign a coach other than the manager to each minor-league team in its system, and even though the original Royals Academy closed, the academy model spread beyond the borders of the country that birthed it. "It really was a forerunner of the academies that we have in Latin America to this day," Stewart says. But for those who were there, the legacy of the Royals Academy remains one of missed opportunities for even greater gains. As a remorseful Stewart says, "Kauffman told me a year before he died . . . the worst mistake he'd ever made in baseball was letting them talk him out of having that baseball academy."

Seven years after the academy closed, Texas Rangers GM Eddie Robinson—a sixty-year-old baseball man who'd been a big leaguer and had run farm systems for a few franchises in the '60s and '70s—hired a twenty-nine-year-old non-baseball man named Craig R. Wright, a former aspiring teacher who had dabbled in baseball analysis as a hobby beginning in high school. Rickey (there's that man again) had employed a statistician as early as 1913, but Wright was the first person to work for a major-league team in the position of "sabermetrician." The term he took as his job title was then barely a year old, and for several years, the editor of the Rangers' team media guide refused to print it. Newfangled title or not, Wright soon established himself as a trusted voice in evaluating players. For the most part, he offered input on potential transactions at the major-league level and wasn't consulted on player-development decisions. But one report he produced on a potential trade led to what Wright says "might be one of the earliest examples of the sabermetric influence helping on player enhancement."

In December 1982, the Dodgers' young catcher, Mike Scioscia, was coming off a weak offensive season, and LA was looking for a brand-name backstop. The Rangers had one: thirty-one-year-old Jim Sundberg, a six-time Gold Glover. A deal was discussed that would have sent several players to Texas, including prospect Orel Hershiser.

Wright suspected Sundberg was overvalued. As Wright noted in his 1989 book *The Diamond Appraised*, catching evaluators had a tendency to "focus solely on the things that they can see: agility behind the plate, the number of passed balls, and, above all else, the catcher's throwing ability."[24] To that point in his career, Sundberg had thrown out 43.2 percent of attempted base stealers, a robust rate compared to the MLB baseline of 34.8 percent over the same span.

Yet according to Wright's analysis of Sundberg's "catcher ERA," Rangers pitchers had consistently allowed *more* runs with Sundberg behind the plate than with the backup catchers. As Wright later wrote, he was aware that "there were some players, coaches, managers, and scouts who questioned [Sundberg's] ability to call a good game," and his painstaking statistical deep dive supported their skepticism. The resulting data identified Sundberg as "a significant detriment to [the] pitching staff," which Wright says helped convince the team's decision makers that despite Sundberg's other skills, "there was a problem here. And where there's a problem, you sometimes get a chance to fix it."

When the proposed trade died, the Rangers had a dilemma. "That's when the discussion of that aspect of my report turned to what could be done to help Sundberg work more effectively with the pitchers," Wright recalls, adding, "They decided, 'We are going to address this in the next spring training.'"

Although Wright's role didn't entail much direct interaction with players, he understood that the subject of Sundberg's weakness had been broached with first-year bullpen and catching coach Glenn Ezell, a former minor-league catcher. Ezell remembers the matter being a "tough sell" because of Sundberg's status and Gold Glove Awards and his own inexperience at the major-league level. "You don't just step out of the minor leagues and say, 'Hey! Why'd you call this? Why'd you call that? And what the hell was that pitch?'" Ezell says. However, he confirms, "There was conversation."

Sundberg describes game-calling as "a learning process" and acknowledges doing things differently beginning in 1983. In a 1988 interview, he said that because of critiques of his game-calling, "I changed the way I dealt with pitchers, and it's been a change for the better." Thirty years later, he explains that the change was increased communication, which familiarized him with each pitcher's preferred approach. "I became more disciplined in talking to pitchers postgame . . . more so with pitchers who might have had a bad outing the night before," he says. "I would stand in the outfield during BP and discuss the previous night's game until I thought they felt encouraged. Once I started this, I never had another problem."

Numbers provided by Wright bear out the purported improvement. From 1977 to 1982, in a total of 1,075 matched innings—that is, equally weighting the samples of innings pitched by particular pitchers so as not to skew the results when one catcher works with more talented batterymates than another—pitchers allowed a 3.97 ERA with Sundberg behind the plate, compared to a 3.62 ERA when throwing to the Rangers' reserves. But from 1983 through Sundberg's last season, 1989—minus the portion of 1988 following a midseason trade, which Wright has found impairs a catcher's work with his pitchers—pitchers recorded a 3.80 ERA with Sundberg and a 3.94 ERA with the reserves, in a total of 2,677 2/3 matched innings with the Rangers and three

other teams. That's a turnaround of roughly half a run per nine innings, with much of the difference attributable to a nearly 20 percent
relative improvement in extra-base-hit rate.

In 1983, the year of Sundberg's game-calling conversion, the Rangers led the league in ERA for the first (and, thus far, only) time in their
history. Sundberg didn't win a Gold Glove that year or in any subsequent season, but he may have been more deserving than when he
was winning every year. In a written report after the season, Wright
concluded, "The major factor for the narrowing and seeming erasure
of the longtime gap in catcher's ERA between Sundberg and the reserve catchers has got to be Sunny's own improvement." That success
stemmed from a sabermetric observation that was relayed to a player,
crossing the longstanding barrier between baseball men and outside
input. "The evolution of the use of the science of baseball toward enhancing player development and performance depends a great deal
on that narrowing of the divide where it is most needed," Wright says.
"The success and failure of future front offices and field personnel will
largely be decided along this line."

At the time, teams hadn't invested in the infrastructure necessary to relay information from the front office to the field. "Today
there is a big difference in the amount of instruction for the MLB
players," Sundberg says, noting that he "basically learned from my
teammates throughout my career." Colorado Rockies scouting and
player-development assistant Jerry Weinstein, a progressive coaching
luminary who's taught at every level from high school to the majors
over a fifty-plus-year career, says, "In the day there was a manager
and a trainer and that was it. . . . Manager, trainer, bus driver, and a lot
of times the trainer *was* the bus driver."

Most damaging of all, dugout attitudes were often hostile (or at
least indifferent) to front-office input. Around 1998, Wright tried to
add a service to his independent business in which he would work as
a player-enhancement consultant. He sent a prospectus to a dozen
clubs he considered solid leads and got no takers. The most frequent
reason cited was that field staff and player-development personnel
would be unlikely to cooperate enough to make Wright's reports
worthwhile.

Because of all of those obstacles, Wright, like Billy Beane in *Money-ball*, didn't see player development as the greatest area of opportunity. "As I looked at it then, I probably would have said no, that the room would have been much greater in player evaluation, because you could see what the gap was, and it was considerable," he says. "But I think we're definitely getting to that point now where you would reverse that."

In 2015, the San Diego Padres commissioned a report from Wright on the best way to advance the club's long-term interests. "It was always the logical evolutionary path that the use of the science of baseball would begin at the upper level of the front office and slowly spread out from there," he wrote. "As early as 1992, I have strongly advised aspiring professional sabermetricians to keep their eye on applying the scientific perspective to player enhancement and development issues. . . . I told them that in the lifetime of *their* careers I expected the wind of circumstance to turn and make such work a large part of their future." Thanks largely to a thawing of field-level resistance and the advent of precise tracking technology, Wright argued, that future had arrived. "The explosion of information in baseball is going to push along the use of the science of baseball in player enhancement and player development," he continued, adding, "the competitive advantage is in being at the forefront, and I assure you that the way the horses are running, this is not a time to equivocate."

By the time baseball was finally ready to build, a blueprint was waiting. Much of the technology that has helped power the player-development revolution got a foothold first in another rotational, ball-based sport with an aged average viewer: golf. "The golf world is way more advanced, to a microscopic level, at tweaking elite golfers," Brian Bannister says.

That's partly attributable to TrackMan, the ball-tracking radar system installed not only in every MLB stadium but also in almost every minor-league stadium, many parks at the college level, and almost every major-league park in Japan, Korea, and Taiwan. TrackMan, which was founded in Denmark in 2003, began by tracking golf swings and ball trajectories. Cofounder and chief technology officer Fredrik Tuxen, a radar engineer who previously worked on military technology used to track projectile weapons, says the company's plan was to provide instant feedback for golfers at driving ranges, thereby making practice more entertaining but also ensuring that players were "not just hitting balls, but do[ing] it with a purpose."

Almost immediately, TrackMan corrected coaching misconceptions. Golfers were typically taught that the ball would travel in the direction they swung the club, but TrackMan showed that its path is more dependent on the orientation of the club face. "We were the ones who basically said, 'This is wrong, and by the way, here is an instrument [so] you can measure what's going on,'" Tuxen says. TrackMan also showed that the optimal launch angle and spin rate for driving distance were 12 degrees and 2,700 rpm, respectively, which meant that golfers needed to swing with a higher attack angle than had been taught traditionally. "When I first presented this, there was huge resistance . . . nobody bought into this," Tuxen says. "All the young players that come [up] now, they have that."

After getting established in golf, the company engineered a baseball product, a challenge given the need for more sensitive measurements, the lack of consistent contact and release points, and the difficulty of setting up systems directly behind batters. By early 2008, the company was making overtures to teams, and Tuxen visited spring training with TrackMan general manager John Olshan. Appropriately, the first place where TrackMan captured data on a major-league pitcher was Dodgertown. Although the speed and movement readings were intuitive, confusion reigned when Tuxen pointed out a pitcher's fastball spin rate. "Both the pitcher himself and [Dodgers pitching coach Rick Honeycutt] looked at me and said, 'Is that a good spin rate?'" Tuxen recalls. "And I [said], 'I don't know. Don't you guys know?' Nope, they never had this data."

Player development tended to be low tech, so front-office analysts were typically TrackMan's point people with teams. "Because we came in through the analyst side, a lot of the player-development people mistrusted us at first," Olshan says. Consequently, the system was a tough sell. "These meetings were surreal," Olshan continues. "I'd go into a conference room at a baseball stadium, and all these guys in baseball uniforms would come in and sit around the table, and I'm presenting a PowerPoint about a missile-tracking system, and they're looking at me like I'm completely insane."

It was clear to the statheads upstairs that spin rate was valuable, so after its official launch in 2011, TrackMan took off quickly. "It was really remarkable, the growth," Olshan says. "It's five guys in this shitty office. We felt like the Wizard of Oz, like, 'Don't look behind the curtain.'"

The history of player development, from Rickey to Wrigley, from Hannah to Kauffman, and from Wright to today, has been one of fits and starts, of miscommunications and clashes, and of isolated experiments and belated breakthroughs, all culminating in the current revolution—one in which efforts to optimize players are no longer ahead of their time but embody it. It calls to mind a line from Bill James's foreword to *The Diamond Appraised*: "It is not that we do not progress, perhaps, but that we progress like a catamaran heading into the wind, sailing at 45 degree angles to the headwind—and 90 degree angles to the course we charted just moments ago."[25] The wind has been blowing against player development since the dawn of the game. But at last the sails are starting to billow, and the boat is beginning to move.

In 2005, eight decades after Hornsby dismissed "smart ideas," perhaps history's best second baseman, committed curmudgeon Joe Morgan, would almost eerily echo Hornsby in an ESPN.com chat when he mused about *Moneyball*, "PLAYERS win games. Not theories." But as technology permeates the sport, players have finally stopped scoffing.

Chris Fetter, a former Padres minor leaguer and the current pitching coach for the University of Michigan, is only in his early thirties, but he speaks about his player pupils as if they belong to a separate species that's poised to surpass his own. "With the abundance of information that is out there now, FanGraphs is basically a homepage for everyone in baseball," he says, referring to a leading website for baseball stats and analysis. "You have these kids that every time they open up Twitter they are seeing the launch angle, they are seeing the exit velo, they are seeing all these things thrown at them. There's curiosity that is there. They want to learn." Increasingly, so do the adults. "Player development doesn't stop when you get to the big leagues," says the fifty-year-old Dipoto, who forged an eight-year major-league career during a far less information-rich era. "There is a constant churn to learn."

At long last, teams are teaching those players. But their curriculum comes from beyond the borders of professional baseball, in the unhallowed halls of the game's player-development disrupters.

4

FIRST PRINCIPLES

I know how hard it is to know something.
—AMERICAN THEORETICAL PHYSICIST RICHARD FEYNMAN

Six months before his first meeting with Trevor Bauer, Kyle Boddy boarded a bus to downtown Seattle. It was August 15, 2012, and the Tampa Bay Rays were in town. The entirety of the team's front office was on the West Coast trip. The small-budget Rays were always interested in new ideas as they tried to compete with the large-market Yankees and Red Sox in the American League East, and Rays assistant general manager Matt Arnold was intrigued by some of the research Boddy had published on his blog, Driveline Mechanics. The Rays were playing a Thursday afternoon game, and Boddy was to meet with several team officials afterward at the team hotel.

Baseball had already begun to accept one kind of outsider into its front offices: Ivy League grads with STEM degrees. But there were no outsiders in player development, and nearly every coaching position was occupied by an ex-player. Boddy was told time and again by people inside the game that his ideas were bullshit. If there was one team that would be willing to think differently, he figured, it would be the forward-thinking Rays, who had challenged conventional wisdom more than any team, most visibly by aggressively employing infield shifts.

Boddy badly wanted the meeting to go well because he hoped he had finally found his calling. The then twenty-nine-year-old had a groundbreaking goal: to turn scrubs into stars by helping pitchers throw harder and develop better breaking balls. More broadly, he argued, baseball's entire minor-league and player-development structure needed to be rethought and rebuilt from scratch. Every breakthrough starts with the right question, and Boddy was always asking questions. Why is the minor-league system set up the way it is? Why does every coaching staff and player-development staff feature the same titles, the same backgrounds, and approximately the same size? Why is there so little data and so much "feel" involved in player development?

As he traveled into town, Boddy followed the action of the game on the radio. Seattle Mariners ace Félix Hernández was in the midst of throwing the twenty-third perfect game in major-league history against the Rays. "Are you fucking kidding?" Boddy thought. Rays officials might not be in the highest of spirits as he made his pitch.

When he reached the suite, Boddy was thrilled to see that among the assembled Rays representatives was Tampa Bay general manager Andrew Friedman, regarded as one of the game's sharpest executives. Boddy made a case to Friedman for why he knew better than anyone how to develop pitchers and how he could make a difference for the Rays. Friedman listened. Then he told Boddy that he trusted his people to tell him whether Boddy was "full of shit or not." Boddy recalls that Friedman then asked a pointed question: "Why do you want to work in professional baseball?"

Friedman surprised Boddy with the question. He suggested Boddy would be better off trying to change the game from the outside and from the bottom up. If he tried to change player development from within, he'd have to contend with a massive bureaucracy. To support his point, Friedman asked Boddy what he thought about Tampa Bay's pitching development. At the time, the Rays were loaded with an excellent staff of homegrown pitchers like David Price, James Shields, and Matt Moore.

"You want me to say you have good pitching," Boddy said.

"That's right," Boddy remembers Friedman responding. "You think that I think that we do a good job of developing pitching."

"That's not knowable," Boddy said.

Friedman conceded that he actually wasn't sure whether the Rays were developing pitchers in an optimal manner. "What I can tell you," Boddy recalls Friedman saying, "is we have a lot of good pitchers at the major-league level. So what do you think our pitching coaches think?" Boddy knew the informal interview was headed south. Friedman wasn't going to disrupt his workforce based on seemingly radical concepts.

Boddy wouldn't be working for the Rays. He would have to change the game from afar. "It wasn't what I wanted to hear," Boddy says. "It was very frustrating. But he was 100 percent right."

It wouldn't be his last encounter with Friedman. But for now, he would have to remain on the outside, where he had always been.

Boddy still speaks with the revolutionary fervor that animated him on his way to what he hoped would be a momentous meeting. "There are a whole host of things that can be done that just haven't been done," he says. "That's something I'm really passionate about that will be remembered forever . . . if we make those changes. No one is going to remember weighted balls if that's all we do. No one is going to remember that it was me that really popularized them. And if they do? Who cares. But everyone remembers that the Dodgers created basically what is now the minor-league system. . . . I'd like to be that progressive. . . . I want to be talked about as the next Branch Rickey."

Becoming known as the next Branch Rickey: not the most modest aspiration for a former college dropout and Olive Garden server in search of his first job in baseball. But Boddy doesn't set small goals, and he doesn't subscribe to slow and steady progress. Even before he had a foothold in the sport, he envisioned an overhaul of existing structures and personnel.

"People argue change should be done incrementally, and I don't agree," Boddy says. "Just like with Rickey, you can't go from having no black players to having a tenth of a black player. That's not how it works. It's a step function. You go from something to something else absolutely radical. I really think that's what it's going to require on the player-development side. From, 'This is how we've done it for one hundred years' to, 'No it's not. We're not going to do that anymore.'"

Six years before his meeting with Friedman, Boddy was living at his parents' home in Parma, Ohio. A blue-collar community that became

Cleveland's largest suburb after World War II, Parma lies in the shadows of the city's steel mills, many of which have since ceased operation. His father was an electrician of Irish ancestry, and his mother, who stayed at home to raise children, was from a Japanese-American family. Boddy was a blend of both of them in appearance, with a shock of black hair, dark eyes, and thick eyebrows. Square and solid, he was a good athlete in high school who played multiple sports. But he was also intellectual and curious. He scored well on the SAT, but he and his family couldn't afford for him to attend an elite out-of-state school. His father's yearlong search for work after a layoff in a tough Northeast Ohio jobs market during Boddy's youth shaped him in ways that he can't quite articulate. Perhaps it's why he would rather lead a business than work under a decision maker. But in 2006 he was unemployed after dropping out of Baldwin Wallace University.

Boddy had opted out of his senior year of high school to accrue college credits at Cuyahoga Community College. He earned a scholarship to Baldwin Wallace, which also accepted his community college credits. He studied economics and computer science and pitched for the baseball team. But he didn't believe the coursework was preparing students to excel in the real world. He knew he wanted to be an entrepreneur; he just didn't know how to be one. College, Boddy worried, was preparing him to work as a "slave to Progressive Insurance."

Though he's always been affable and enthusiastic in his pursuits, he was also suffering from anxiety attacks and depression, a condition he'd struggled with since adolescence. He was surprised when his parents didn't admonish him for dropping out of school, but they knew he was miserable. His mother had always suggested he try working as a server. So after dropping out of school, he began working at an Olive Garden in Parma.

"It's one of the best things I could have done," Boddy says. "It was hustling, in a sense. Customer service. It was the first time where I felt my output, how much I worked, impacted how much I made."

At the Olive Garden, he brought chilled Andes mints to customers at the ends of meals. Not every server offered to grind fresh pepper on never-ending pasta bowls, but Boddy did. He was so effective that he drew the ire of his manager when, one night, four dining parties sought out the manager to compliment Boddy's service. "He was exasperated," Boddy says. "It goes to show how little you have to do to be above average."

He was still dealing with depression after college, and his friends were enabling an unhealthy lifestyle. They worked "shitty" jobs and got together to complain about them and drink. The cycle repeated itself every weekend. Boddy self-medicated. "I was abusing Ambien," he says. "I was using it to go to sleep." He suffered side effects, including blackouts and severe amnesia.

By then, Boddy had met his future wife on LiveJournal, a social networking service. She lived in Seattle, and he wanted to move to be closer to her, but no one in his family had left the Cleveland area and doing so seemed traitorous. But early one morning, he awoke in front of his laptop after an Ambien blackout to a great surprise: he had applied for several jobs online. One of them was as a game theorist in customer service for PokerStars, an online poker cardroom. He had always loved games. Boddy played poker semiprofessionally online and often traveled to the nearest casino in Windsor, Ontario; he also played in Magic: The Gathering tournaments. "I guess my drug-induced résumé and cover letter were good enough because I got an interview," he says. He also got the job and joined PokerStars' anticollusion unit, working remotely. He could leave Cleveland. So in 2006, he moved to Seattle.

To satisfy his competitive drive, Boddy coached Little League Baseball. He then coached the freshman baseball team at Roosevelt High, where Boddy's future father-in-law coached softball and had introduced him to the athletic director. He stressed the importance of on-base percentage and drawing walks, and rival coaches mocked him, calling his team's patient approach "stupid." Boddy was perplexed.

"Why wouldn't this be accepted?" Boddy says. "It's just obvious that having the most runners on base makes the most sense. That was really the start of like, 'Why the fuck don't you guys understand the game of baseball?'"

He went to coaching clinics in the area. He listened and asked questions. But the more questions he asked, the more answers he found unsatisfying. It was the root of his interest in player development.

The last year Boddy was with Roosevelt High, the varsity squad won only a single game in its conference, while the freshmen performed adequately. Yet after the season, Boddy received a call from the athletic director, who informed him that the school was going in a different direction with the *freshman* program. The varsity head coach remained in place.

Although he hadn't openly clashed with the head coach, they weren't close. "That was the problem," Boddy says. "My assistant and I were not gonna play the game. We're not baseball guys. . . . I was like, screw this."

After being relieved of his baseball duties, Boddy remained interested in training and development. He had ample time to read about it. He had left PokerStars for Microsoft, where he worked a night shift four times a week from 11 p.m. to 10 a.m., "babysitting" the Xbox Live network. "Unless shit went bad, you didn't have to do anything," Boddy says.

Boddy used that time to think about what he perceived to be a glaring lack of knowledge, data, and objective methodology when it came to training athletes. He believed that in baseball, this was especially true for pitchers. As a kid in Cleveland, Boddy had thrown all the time, often hurling balls as far as possible. He and his peers played games in the neighborhood where they threw baseballs as hard as they could at each other, crow-hopping and unleashing offerings from sixty feet that terrorized their targets.

Boddy has a radical suggestion for how we should teach children intent. "Don't ever play catch with a six-year-old," he says. "I'd put my kid by a fence, and I'd throw the shit out of the ball into the fence, like as hard as possible." That way, Boddy says, the child will learn and mimic an adult's max-intent mechanics. Kids copy the adults they're around, Boddy notes. Boddy's theory on why the children of major leaguers succeed at such a high rate is not so much genetics—which doesn't hurt—but because they've emulated more effective throwing and movement patterns. If you play catch, lightly, at low intent, kids learn the wrong motion, he says. "[Then] you yell at them at age twelve when they're not athletic," Boddy says. "But you just spent six years teaching them how to throw like an idiot, so what do you expect?" He had always intuitively believed that max-effort throwing helped pitchers throw harder, but professional baseball was moving in the opposite direction.

In 1990, Todd Van Poppel was regarded as the best pitcher in the amateur draft. He signed a three-year, $1.2 million major-league deal with the Oakland A's that included a $600,000 bonus. Van Poppel impressed scouts with a fastball that hit 94 mph in his first professional outing for the Southern Oregon Athletics in the Northwest League. As the top prospect in baseball in 1991, he was rushed to the majors at age nineteen and went on to record a negative career Wins Above Replacement (WAR) amid arm troubles. In 2001, No. 2 pick Mark Prior signed a major-league deal that guaranteed him $10.5 million. After a brilliant early stretch of pitching in the majors, injuries derailed his career. Was he overworked? Was he rushed? Wary of employing the next Van Poppel or Prior, teams became more cautious with their increasingly expensive investments and introduced strict pitch counts and innings limits.

"The Royals do this today: they play seven minutes of catch every day, and a guy yells out 60, 90, 120, and every time he yells, you move back to 60, 90, 120 feet, and that's it," Boddy says. "It's amazing that that is still a fucking organizational philosophy, but it is. Don't throw the ball over 120 feet? OK, well, you throw it from shortstop to first base over 160 feet. You do the math."

In 1998, Baseball Prospectus created a pitch-count-based metric called Pitcher Abuse Points, which the site claimed could help predict injury and which set one hundred pitches as the point at which pitchers began incurring abuse. *Sports Illustrated* published an article asserting that increasing young pitchers' workloads by twenty innings or more from one season to the next made them more susceptible to injury. Boddy says that while rules began to emerge about pitching, they were not rooted in science. And they were not working.

By the end of the 2018 season, Hardball Times analyst Jon Roegele's Tommy John surgery database contained 1,651 entries—and although the surgery was forty-four years old, half of the surgeries on professionals had occurred since April 1, 2012. No one understood precisely how to slow the epidemic of elbow injuries. "Sixty percent of what BP wrote was false," Boddy says. "Not in a malicious way, but we lacked the statistical rigor to ascertain whether these things are true or false."

During his third-shift work at Microsoft, in an open row of desks under fluorescent lighting, Boddy devoured roughly thirty books and 120 papers about athletic training over the course of a year. He was teaching himself to be an expert at training baseball players by learning the fundamental concepts on which a theory, system, or method is based.

This process is rooted in the thinking of Aristotle, who called it reasoning by first principles. It was an idea instilled in Boddy as a child by his father, who worked for a time as an electrician for British Petroleum and at NASA's Glenn Research Center when Boddy was growing up. Entrepreneur Elon Musk is also a proponent. During a TED Talk interview in 2016, Musk explained how his process of innovation begins by boiling "things down to their fundamental truths and reason[ing] up from there."[1] This method, Musk argued, is far superior to reasoning by analogy, "which essentially means copying what other people do with slight variations."

When Musk began researching how to build a rocket, he told Wired,[2] he put aside conventional methods and approached the problem with a fresh perspective. "Physics teaches you to reason from first principles. . . . What is a rocket made of? Aerospace-grade aluminum alloys, plus some titanium, copper, and carbon fiber. And then I asked, what is the value of those materials on the commodity market? It turned out that the materials cost of a rocket was around 2 percent of the typical price." SpaceX was born.

Baseball was similarly in need of fresh thinking. When Boddy began his research, coaches and teams generally had been copying what other people did with slight variations for more than a century. Little original thinking had been done on what actually mattered in talent development. Now Boddy wanted to learn about biomechanics, about the kinetic chain of the athlete, about increasing mobility and strength. About the building blocks, the first principles, of revolutionizing player development.

Mike Marshall, the 1974 NL Cy Young winner, became a significant influence. Marshall had a PhD in kinesiology and used what he learned to apply Newtonian physics to pitching, resulting in unconventional mechanics. Marshall believed that if he could run an entire professional organization, he would get "eight to ten more miles per hour from every pitcher."[3] That idea fascinated Boddy. Marshall enlisted unusual training practices (including a high volume of throwing) and unusual implements (like wrist weights and plastic javelins) to promote, as Boddy wrote on his blog, "a straight driveline towards the target," with no twisting of the pitcher's hips toward second base. The driveline was one of Marshall's favorite concepts, and Boddy borrowed it to name his blog, which he began in October of 2009 and maintained despite a small audience. Later he named his business Driveline Baseball.

In his highly technical book *Coaching Pitchers*, Marshall addressed the power of deceleration and wrist-weight training. He believed that if a pitcher's brain did not think his decelerator muscles could handle the force generated during the delivery, it would subconsciously limit throwing velocity. Marshall wrote, "If drag race cars have the ability to achieve five hundred miles per hour in a one-quarter-mile track, but the race track has a two-thousand-foot cliff only one hundred feet past the finish line, then the question is: Can the drivers stop the cars within one hundred feet? The question that their cerebellum asks baseball pitchers every time that they try to release their fastballs at higher velocities is: Can the muscles . . . safely stop their pitching arm within the distance between the release and when the pitching arm fully extends straight forward toward home plate? Baseball pitchers must have big brakes!"[4] Marshall had his pupils train with wrist weights to increase the braking abilities of muscles in the arm. They would also become a staple of Driveline training.

Marshall's critics wondered why, if he had broken the code of pitching mechanics, all of his pitchers didn't throw 90-plus mph. Glenn Fleisig of the American Sports Medical Institute (ASMI), one of the few biomechanics labs in the country that collected data on pitching mechanics, was a Marshall skeptic. Since 1990, Fleisig had studied two thousand pitchers, ranging from the youth level to major-league all-stars. Using markers attached to the pitchers' bodies that tracked the movements of their limbs, he could compare and analyze deliveries. Fleisig and ASMI believed healthy, elite major-league pitchers had developed the best mechanics and that therefore those pitchers should be studied and copied. Marshall wasn't convinced that making the majors proved that a pitcher possessed exemplary mechanics.

Marshall brought some of the pitchers he trained to ASMI to undergo biomechanical exams and have their mechanics compared to the elite group of major-league pitchers Fleisig had recorded. Though Marshall's pitchers were similar to Fleisig's group in shoulder rotation and elbow extension velocity—key kinetics in velocity creation—they threw with far less velocity.

Boddy theorized that there was a break in the kinetic chain of the Marshall pupils. Marshall believed in "powerfully pronating" pitchers' forearms to protect the ulnar collateral ligament (UCL). Boddy suspected that pronating slowed a part of the kinetic chain, which begins when a pitcher's foot hits the ground, creating a force that works its way up the body from the largest parts to the smallest.

Boddy could reason from first principles and boil down velocity creation into simple physics. For instance, velocity began from the ground up. "The legs generate force through ground reaction," he wrote. The pitcher's front leg strides and plants in the ground. His pelvis then rotates around the front leg, generating rotational momentum, and the pitching arm follows like the end of a whip.

"Anyone familiar with cracking a whip can tell you that the 'looseness' of the whip is what creates the miniature sonic boom at the end of the whip," Boddy wrote. "If you were to make a segment of the whip stiff, it would break the smoothly flowing energy of the kinetic chain down the whip, causing the final velocity of the tip to be much lower than it normally would."[5]

Boddy had other influences, including former powerlifter Eric Cressey, who worked with a number of major-league clients and who aided Boddy's understanding of how to train. Boddy studied Soviet sports science. He was forming theories, too, but by 2010, he knew he needed to test them to turn them into athletic law. Much of the information he was seeking simply did not exist.

This is a common problem for innovators. To test something completely new requires the construction of new diagnostic instruments. Consider the case of the most famous of all Ohio-born entrepreneurs, Wilbur and Orville Wright. After a failed attempt at flight in the fall of 1901 at Kitty Hawk, North Carolina, the Wrights were despondent. "It was not just that their machine had performed so poorly, or that so much still remained to be solved," wrote their biographer, David McCullough, "but that so many of the long-established, supposedly reliable calculations and tables . . . data the brothers had taken as gospel—had proven to be wrong and could no longer be trusted."[6]

Wrote Orville in his diary: "We knew that it would take considerable time and funds to obtain data of our own. . . . We had to go and discover everything ourselves." So they returned to Dayton, Ohio, and built a six-foot wind tunnel to "crack the code of aeronautics themselves."[7] Boddy wanted to crack the code of pitching. To do so, he needed the equivalent of his own wind tunnel. He needed a biomechanics lab.

Boddy wanted his lab to be capable of conducting three-dimensional analysis. There were limits to two-dimensional analysis based on video, which Boddy didn't regard as true biomechanics research. Baseball action occurs in all *three* planes of motion: frontal (front and back), sagittal (left and right), and transverse (up and down). A state-of-the-art biomechanics lab carried a six-figure price tag, but Boddy believed he could construct one for hundreds of dollars, not thousands. Like Musk with his rockets, Boddy would build on a budget.

How do you build a cutting-edge biomechanics lab from scratch? Boddy decided to go straight to the experts. He called ASMI.

ASMI researcher David Fortenbaugh, a graduate of Rocky River High School in an affluent suburb not far from Parma, listened patiently as Boddy explained what he was trying to create. It was, Fortenbaugh explained, an impossible task. That was *before* he learned that Boddy wasn't an engineer or an orthopedic surgeon or a doctor in sports medicine, but a college dropout.

Boddy wasn't deterred. First, he needed physical space, so he found an indoor facility next to a trailer park in north suburban Seattle. Boddy offered to maintain the entire facility in exchange for reduced rent on part of the space. He installed a batting cage and set up a weight room, which was just a set of dumbbells and barbells surrounded by chicken wire. He now had a space to train athletes within walking distance of his condo, and he would stay there for a year and a half. Next, he needed methods and technology to record forces like angular velocity—the speed of a point (or limb) rotating around an axis—and movements associated with the pitching motion.

Boddy read about a method called direct linear transformation (DLT), which was pioneered in the 1970s to measure an object's movement in three dimensions. To use the theory, Boddy had to be able to follow the math, whose equations looked like hieroglyphics.

So Boddy taught himself linear algebra.

After attaining a functional understanding of the math, Boddy built his markerless biomechanics lab. He first had to define the three-dimensional space in which he would observe his clients. To calibrate this 3-D space, he needed a reference object. So in October 2010, Boddy and Matthew Wagshol, a long-serving biomechanist at Driveline, went to a Seattle-area Home Depot. In a store aisle, they began building a cube-shaped skeleton of white PVC pipe to serve as a first subject. Before they left the store, they took a photo of the apparatus being built; visible in the background is a sign above a checkout counter that read "Do More, Have More."

They transported the cube back to the nascent Driveline. The plastic skeleton defined the 3-D space for the cameras and primitive software. Boddy measured its height and width and the distances to and from its joists and entered the dimensions into the DLT algorithm. Boddy and Wagshol then spent "countless hours using terrible software meant for graduate students that we twisted in so many directions to just spit out answers." For about $2,000 in cash—"I wasn't maxing out credit cards because I had done that in a previous life and ruined my credit," Boddy says—and hundreds of hours of his time, he had his biomechanics lab. He could collect data on the movements of pitchers and eventually learn how to make those movements more efficient. "Real research involves testing your own theories using as many objective measures as you can find," Boddy wrote. [8]

Pinned above Boddy's office bathroom toilet today is a sign that says, "Being rigorous is like being pregnant: You can't be a little bit pregnant."

Over time, Boddy learned that the lab had its limits, and the raw data meant little without context and regular snapshots of players' progress. There were things the lab could not record, including pronation and supination of the arm. It would quickly become outdated. But having learned how to assemble a lab from the ground up, he could do it again, bigger and better.

Boddy settled into a routine. In those early years he would take the bus home from the Microsoft office in downtown Seattle, grab dinner, and then walk to the facility to work in the evenings. He placed ads on Craigslist seeking athletes to train. Four days a week, he would give hitting and pitching lessons and, once a month, conduct biomechanics exams on each athlete.

"It was horrible," Boddy says. "The maximum number we ever had was eight athletes. For two years, we basically had an average of four kids."

No one seemed to notice his research, and he was again dealing with depression. But then he had some good fortune: a set of weighted balls was mistakenly shipped to Driveline. They sat in the corner of the gym for months. "I was cleaning out the gym, and I was like, 'These have to get out of here,'" Boddy says. His then partner Jacob Staff stopped him. "I can [still] hear [Staff] saying, 'You're an idiot. You're going to say this doesn't work? You have no idea if it works or not. You're intelligent and you're going to say this? That's embarrassing.'"

Boddy remembers thinking, "Goddammit, he's 100 percent right. . . . I am pretty sure it's going to hurt people, but I will give it a fair look." On a fundamental level, he says, "that's how Driveline started. It was me taking the scientific method to everything and asking, What else don't I know? Is lifting weights really good? Maybe it's stupid."

Boddy searched for weighted-ball research and found a paper authored by University of Hawaii professor Coop DeRenne in 1994 that reported that work with weighted balls had improved velocity in high-school and college test subjects without any adverse health effects. DeRenne studied 45 high-school and 180 college pitchers who were randomly assigned to three experimental groups, including a control. The pitchers trained for ten weeks. The two groups that were exposed to weighted-ball training, including heavier and lighter balls, enjoyed velocity gains without increased rates of injury. If that result was repeatable, the training would revolutionize development, allowing pitchers to raise ceilings that were thought to be immovable.

Boddy researched more of the science underpinning the concept, including Frans Bosch's book *Strength Training and Coordination: An Integrative Approach*, about as dense a book as one can find about how the body works and gains athletic skill. Bosch defined weighted-ball-style practices as overload training, which utilizes implements that an athlete "is not yet equipped for and that call for adaptation."[9] The overload training tool that Bauer had already begun using, the weighted ball, would become closely associated with Boddy's future company.

Throwing a heavier ball—say, seven ounces—increases *total* force. When the pitching arm is cocked back to begin the throwing motion, in maximum external rotation or lay back, the ball feels heavier. The body adapts to manage the greater total force. But overload training could also be paired with *underload* training in a complementary, two-pronged approach that could improve total force *and* peak force. The underload ball enables the arm to move much faster, creating a higher peak force that ultimately determines throwing velocity. Strengthening the body with heavier balls and greater total forces allows it to take on greater peak forces.

To many instructors, overload training seemed inherently dangerous. Still, some, like Cressey, had challenged that assumption as early as 2009, when he noted that the weight of a baseball (five ounces) was three times lighter than that of a football (fifteen ounces) but that quarterbacks suffer far fewer arm and shoulder injuries than pitchers, despite possibly throwing even more often. A typical set of weighted baseballs ranges from three to eleven ounces. "If you increase the weight of the implement [in this case, the ball], you slow down the arm action," Cressey wrote. "If you slow down the arm action a bit, the deceleration demands drop—and it appears to be more arm-friendly."[10] In 2017, Fleisig tested a hypothesis at ASMI that "ball and arm velocities would be greater with lighter balls and joint kinetics would be greater with heavier balls." He found lighter balls did produce faster throws and arm velocities, but the second part of his hypothesis was proven wrong. Overweight balls produced "decreased arm forces, torques, and velocities."[11]

But such studies, and data on player-development practices in general, were rare.

By 2011, Boddy had moved Driveline Baseball operations to a larger location, the site of a former grocery store, and had accepted a position as the strength and conditioning coach for RIPS Baseball, which trained players and ran youth select teams in Seattle. He now had access to dozens more athletes. He gathered forty-four junior-high and high-school pitcher volunteers from RIPS Baseball to test what he called his MaxVelo Program, which incorporated "advanced deceleration drills, connection balls, plyometric training, high-speed video analysis and rhythmic stabilization methods." The results were eye-opening.

The control group of fourteen pitchers practiced on their own, in most cases not very intensely. They collectively suffered a slight velocity decrease during the test, falling from an average of 70.8 mph pretest to 70.3 mph posttest. The second, basic group followed a routine throwing program. Its members averaged 68.1 mph pretest and 70.3 mph posttest, a 2.2 mph gain. The MaxVelo group of ten pitchers engaged in an assortment of training practices that Boddy had come to believe in, including deceleration training and high-speed-video analysis. That group averaged 72.0 mph pretest and 79.1 mph post test, a remarkable 7.1 mph gain.

Boddy created regimens that combined elements from his self-education, most famously the pulldown drill, which became a staple of Driveline's underload/overload velocity training program. One difference between Jaeger's long-toss and pulldown regimen and Boddy's is that winters are much less cooperative in Seattle than in Southern California, and space at Driveline grew tight. Boddy didn't have access to open fields, so instead of throwing to a partner, his pitchers threw into the nylon net of an indoor cage.

The athletes Boddy was training gained velocity. In 2016 and 2017, college pitchers who completed weighted-ball programs at Driveline increased velocity by 2.7 mph and 3.3 mph, respectively, when comparing their first bullpens to their last. (Although Driveline's first peer-reviewed velocity study of weighted-ball effects in 2018 yielded range-of-motion gains in a six-week program, it did not produce overall velocity increases. The group that did gain velocity suffered no injuries.) Still, the practice drew criticism every time Boddy posted video of another athlete exceeding 100 mph on a pulldown throw. Boddy posted some of the common doubts and criticisms, including "How hard does [the pitcher] throw from the set position on the rubber? I bet this stuff doesn't transfer." And: "Yeah, but these guys are just spraying it and don't focus on throwing strikes!"

"None of it was embraced by any coach that I knew, none," Boddy says.

Boddy responded to skepticism with the story of Casey Weathers, a former star at Vanderbilt and a first-round Rockies pick in 2007. An elbow injury and complications stemming from Tommy John surgery had derailed his velocity and career. Unemployed and adrift, he e-mailed Boddy in March 2014, explaining that he was unsure of where to go and wondered whether Boddy could help restore his velocity. Weathers's former college teammate, Caleb Cotham, a minor-league pitcher with the Yankees, had suggested Weathers contact Driveline. On his first day at Driveline, Boddy had him hurl weighted balls at max intent and also captured high-speed video and radar readings of his throws.

"The look on his face after I told him to throw weighted baseballs as hard as he possibly could was pretty funny," Boddy wrote. Weathers's first max-effort, crow-hop throw with a regulation five-ounce baseball hit 93 mph. Three days after showing up at a facility unlike any he had ever visited, his top five-ounce velocity improved to 95.1 mph. After ten days, his velocity on a crow-hop throw had improved to 96.9 mph. After two weeks? 98.7. Weathers signed a minor-league deal with the Rays later that summer. Although he never advanced beyond Double-A, he did return to pro baseball, and with improved skill.

The most common criticism associated with Driveline was a perceived increase in injury risk. Some pro teams have complained that pitchers training on their own with weighted balls have been injured, and Boddy does caution against employing weighted balls and max-intent practices without proper coaching and buildup of strength. He's aware of the correlation between throwing velocity and Tommy John surgery, but he wonders how many of the pitchers who've been injured were built and trained properly and how many would have hurt themselves even with a different type of training. And while any pitcher can become a surgical candidate, very few pitchers are capable of pitching in the majors without elite velocity, which makes some risk worthwhile.

"I'm not so arrogant to believe that we develop velocity the 'right way,'" Boddy told a Baseball Prospectus writer. "But I think we're open-minded and we do a lot of research. . . . From a macro perspective, I'm very concerned about injuries. We haven't defeated the problem, and I don't know if it is a defeatable problem."[12]

On Twitter, Boddy wrote: "The term 'risk-reward spectrum' is used disproportionately by those who are trying to only mitigate risk. If there's one thing I learned as a professional gambler, it's that far too few people maximize value and reward. . . . You can't be risk-averse all the time, because the largest risk in athletics is opportunity risk in the form of Father Time and aging kicking your ass, unrelenting and unstoppable. You have to maximize output, and often that means taking outsized risks. Period."

In other words, maybe some pitchers will get hurt trying to throw 90 mph, but if they can't throw 90, they're probably not going to pitch for a Division I college, let alone in the majors. Mocking coaches that downplayed the importance of velocity training, Boddy tweeted, "'Stop trying to throw hard! Just command it!' *cuts player three weeks later and cites poor velocity as the reason*."

Boddy has always been brash and confident, which doesn't make relationships easy. As with Bauer, the same stubbornness and self-belief that has contributed to his maverick success has also strained his relationships with the less enlightened. He has little patience for stupidity or laziness. If an employee asks him a question they could have found an answer to through a Google search, he'll scold them. He'll often engage in Twitter disputes, arguments, and challenges.

Although playing the game is often a prerequisite for acceptance within the coaching ranks, Boddy is unimpressed by pedigree or title. He views degrees from prestigious universities on the résumés of applicants to Driveline almost as *negative* qualifications. On Twitter in the summer of 2018, he lauded Google and Apple for dropping college degrees as application requirements. Boddy wants to employ outliers; after all, he was one.

In 2012, two years before Weathers arrived at Driveline and the same year Bauer was struggling through his first full professional season with the Diamondbacks, Boddy was still a relative unknown. In his day job, he was excelling: he had moved on from Microsoft to a software-development job, which earned him a $120,000 annual salary. But Boddy's passions clearly were with Driveline, and that year he quit his lucrative job to commit to running his fledgling company full-time. It was an "outsized risk," trading economic security for a paltry, poverty-level income, even though he had a wife, a child, and a mortgage. (Boddy describes his wife as "eternally understanding.") In February 2011, Boddy had begun writing for the Hardball Times, a baseball-analysis website. The platform expanded his reach and exposure within the baseball-nerd community. He researched and wrote on topics like Tim Lincecum's velocity decline and why it was wrong to bet against Blue Jays prospect Marcus Stroman despite his lack of prototypical size (he was right).

Boddy caught the attention of Ron Wolforth, who complimented him on a blog post he had written. Boddy researched Wolforth and discovered that his most famous client was Bauer, whom Boddy had watched on TV as Bauer pitched in the College World Series. The ESPN broadcast had shown Bauer using his shoulder tube, and ESPN analyst and former All-Star Nomar Garciaparra had derided the routine as "odd." Garciaparra said Bauer would not be able to continue with his exercises in professional baseball because of the injury risk. (Ironically, Garciaparra dealt with a number of injuries throughout his own career.) During the same telecast, former MLB player and future manager Robin Ventura had said Bauer was "only allowed to do all those things because he is so good." Boddy found Bauer fascinating. In his first Hardball Times post, titled "Pitching mechanics, the uncertainty of data, and fear," he cited Bauer, whom he had never met.

"We must understand that what someone did to get to the major leagues is often what will keep them there—we should not fear things like Trevor Bauer's unorthodox mechanics and training protocol," Boddy wrote. "We should be amazed by them, and we should investigate them."

He saw that Wolforth hosted periodic coaching clinics, so he sent him an e-mail, asking to present some of his research. Boddy got on the schedule for the following year. He wanted to share a piece of primitive wearable technology: an arm sleeve, constructed from neoprene and parts of a Nintendo Wii console, that measured forces and stresses associated with the throwing motion.

It was a clumsy device, as homebrew as his old PVC pipes, but it worked, measuring arm speed, rotation, pronation, and yaw, or twisting around a vertical axis. Although nothing came of the sleeve from a commercial standpoint, the project was valuable experience.

"Anything I can do to understand first-principle stuff helps me learn other parallel things that are related," Boddy says.

He spoke twice over two days at the Texas Baseball Ranch in December 2012, lecturing about data collection and technology and presenting information from the sleeve and high-speed cameras. After his second talk, he was swamped with questions, including the one from Bauer about which memory card he needed for his high-speed camera. It was a humble beginning to a relationship that would alter not only the trajectories of their own unlikely careers but also the prevailing conception of what's possible in baseball.

Bauer's and Boddy's passion for technology brought them together. But their relationship deepened over another shared passion: the biomechanics of throwing. In 2013, his first season with the Indians, Bauer had grown concerned about pain he'd developed during the previous season with Arizona. Since then he'd been dealing with groin, back, ribs, and biceps pain and discomfort that he'd never experienced before. "It was very clear I needed to make a [mechanical] change if I was going to last ten years in the big leagues," Bauer says.

He had tried to mimic Lincecum, which was logical in that Bauer was also an undersized right-handed pitcher. But Bauer was well aware that in 2012, Lincecum had started to break down; he was finished as an above-average pitcher by age twenty-eight. "The long-term effects of moving that way and not being built muscularly or structurally to be able to handle that started piling up," Bauer says. "I was on the same track [as Lincecum]."

After the 2012 season, Bauer had begun to gather information on how he could clean up his throwing motion. In addition to meeting with a Stanford University doctor to get imaging done of his hip and shoulder, which had become part of his annual after-season routine—Bauer has an archive of his elbow and shoulder images going back a number of years—he had his delivery mapped by biomechanist Bob Keyes. Keyes found that while Bauer created an elite level of speed and energy down the mound, his posture was off. He had too much spinal tilt. As he released a pitch, his spine was tilting at 45 degrees toward first base, whereas Greg Maddux and Roger Clemens—the top pitchers Keyes had tested, pillars of durability and performance—were more erect, around 70 degrees. They also produced more hip-shoulder separation. Much like twisting a rubber band, the more the shoulders can turn relative to the position of the hips, the more energy is generated. Keyes measured Bauer at 52 degrees of hip-shoulder separation, but Maddux and Clemens had achieved 72 degrees.

When Bauer was told he would not make the major-league team in the spring of 2013, he decided to rebuild his delivery. Initially, he kept the plan to himself.

As he remade his motion, Bauer was a mess. In 138 1/3 innings between Triple-A and the majors, he walked eighty-nine batters. His fastball velocity fell from averaging 93.4 mph the previous year in Arizona to regularly sitting between 89 and 91.

"All the coaches were super frustrated with me because I wouldn't listen to anything they had to say," Bauer remembers. "They would say, 'You have to throw the ball down more.' . . . What's the point? Until I fix my mechanics it does me no good to practice a skill. They didn't understand that."

The front office sent minor-league pitching coordinator Ruben Niebla to Columbus to give a homework assignment to Bauer. The Indians wanted to better understand what he was trying to achieve. On the front and back of two pages of 8½-by-11-inch paper, Bauer drew diagrams and stick figures. He returned his homework the following day to the Triple-A staff.

"They looked at me like I was from another planet," Bauer says. Indians general manager Mike Chernoff still has the drawings.

One point of contention was that some coaches wanted Bauer to extend his glove farther out in front of his body at foot plant, rather than tucking toward his torso. Those coaches were endorsing the traditional idea of equal-and-opposite balance of limbs in a delivery. "It's just wrong," Bauer says, growing animated to the point that he pounds a table and rattles a glass and silverware as he recounts the experience. "I don't deal well with someone who doesn't know as much about a subject as me trying to tell me what to do." Bauer was arguing for "positive disconnection," or folding his glove arm down and near his body as his throwing arm came through, a move designed to initiate and accelerate the twist of his torso and maximize rotational velocity, a key to increasing throwing velocity.

After the 2013 season, Bauer sent a biomechanical mapping of his delivery to Chernoff to support his argument. Bauer and his father had attached reflective tape to key joints on his body and filmed his delivery. On the first video, it looked like dots moving through space. They attached another video revealing that those dots were actually Bauer throwing a pitch. It demonstrated that the optimum upper body rotational axis wasn't around the spine, as some staff had argued, but the glove-side arm. It was likely the first such e-mail a GM had ever received from a player.

After the 2013 minor-league season ended, Bauer knew the mechanics he wanted to build. Falvey had collaborated with him on some changes, but Bauer wanted to find new ways of implementing them. Though they hadn't spoken much during the season, Bauer hoped Boddy might have answers.

In October 2013, Bauer arrived at Driveline. Boddy had relocated the operation to suburban Tacoma, to the second floor of a facility named Clubhouse 71, which had previously held low-level Ultimate Fighting events in its main gym. Bauer describes it as an attic space complete with exposed steel I-beams supporting the sloping roof of the structure.

Bauer had not intended to throw that day. But as Boddy spoke about possible solutions and drills, his words made so much sense that excitement surged within Bauer. He was wearing street clothes, including Nike Free running shoes. Nonetheless, he picked up a ball and took it to the mound.

To improve his posture and add torque, Boddy told Bauer to hold a two-pound ball, an overload implement, in his glove hand and throw a pitch. The drill was designed to keep his glove side more elevated and his upper body back with less spinal tilt while his lower body moved forward. Boddy called the practice a "linear distraction." The drill also forced his glove side to decelerate in the proper sequence because he was compelled to tuck the two-pound ball near his body as he began to throw, which increased his rotational velocity while keeping his head and body more in line with his target. He could feel the improvement immediately.

Boddy then had Bauer work on a drill called a pivot pick, a Driveline staple. The pair moved over to a plywood wall, another homemade structure erected for athletes to pelt with sand-filled PlyoCare balls. The Plyo balls are weighted and feature a malleable PVC shell, which removes the feeling of throwing a baseball and helps pitchers throw without being bound by their baseball mechanics.

Boddy instructed Bauer to begin perpendicular to the plywood board, with his right hand closer to it. His mission: to lift his right elbow to shoulder level and, without moving his feet, twist his torso until his chest was parallel with the board. From that position, he would throw the ball into the board as hard as he could. Bauer went through the drill. His hips turned. He threw at an awkward angle, his left foot pivoting as he slammed a Plyo ball into the wall with a thud. The drill created a twist in his core that Bauer could feel. It also reduced unnecessary arm motion and reinforced the concept of positive disconnection, forcing his glove arm to firmly tuck to his body to generate throwing force at the awkward angle.

Rather than *telling* Bauer how to perform an action—the foundation of coaching in baseball for one-hundred-plus years—Boddy was allowing him to learn *implicitly*, through his own organic actions, which could then form the basis of more efficient and natural movements.

"Most of the mechanical stuff I knew I wanted to do was through Bob Keyes," Bauer says. "Bob didn't have a whole lot of teachable drills or thoughts. Kyle had a way of doing it."

While most coaching advice comes via verbal cues, Boddy wrote on Driveline's website that "we don't take the time to examine their effectiveness and what we are asking our athletes to do. . . . There is little evidence to suggest that having a coach tell a player he should change a movement pattern is effective in either immediately changing the movement or creating a lasting change." He cited some commonly recycled coaching instructions and examples of accompanying confusion.

"'Use your legs more.' Produce more force? Or move faster?"

"'Don't fly open.' Upper half or lower half?"

"'Stay back.' For how long?"

Stare at the target? "Another myth," Boddy wrote. "Gaze-tracking studies don't show that locking the eyes on the target has anything to do with throwing strikes." Finish in a good fielding position? Also wrong. (It disrupts the kinetic chain.) Bauer appreciated Driveline's learning methods and that Boddy was willing to question everything. After their first sessions together, Boddy wrote that Bauer "was able to reproduce an excellent high-level pattern that should set him up for vastly improved control, velocity, and health."

In Arizona in the spring of 2014, Bauer's posture and rotational and linear separation improved. His velocity spiked. "I didn't throw a pitch below 95 [mph] in spring training," Bauer says. "Everyone freaked out and told me not to throw as hard during spring training and save it for the season."

He was recalled on May 20 for a start against the Tigers in Cleveland. His fastball *averaged* 97 mph, where it had topped out in college. On the season, his fastball averaged 94.9 mph—the ninth-highest mark among all pitchers who threw at least 150 innings and 1.5 mph harder than his average in 2012. Most important, Bauer's body felt better. Although he had an uneven season—his 4.18 ERA was slightly worse than the 3.92 AL average for starters—it was the first year in which he had thrown the majority of his innings in the majors. Driveline had delivered tangible results. It became Bauer's new off-season home.

5

A BOTTOM-UP REVOLUTION

Congratulate yourself if you have done something strange and extravagant, and broken the monotony of a decorous age. It was a high counsel that I once heard given to a young person, "Always do what you are afraid to do."

—RALPH WALDO EMERSON, "Heroism"

April 16, 2018, was an off day in Los Angeles for the Red Sox. But for Red Sox outfielder Mookie Betts, there would be no rest.

Boston hitting coach Tim Hyers suggested to Betts that he spend the day working with the silver-haired, blue-eyed Doug Latta, a self-described swing whisperer. On that Monday morning, Latta drove to the team hotel and picked up Betts, who brought with him a couple of his personalized Axe Bats, which feature handles shaped like that of a hatchet. They drove to a facility Latta occasionally used that was closer to Anaheim than his own Los Angeles headquarters: the covered batting cages at Anteater Ballpark, home of the UC Irvine college baseball team, whose coach was a friend.

The twenty-five-year-old Betts was coming off an excellent 2017 season, albeit a disappointing one for him. His .803 OPS (on-base plus slugging) was slightly above average but down significantly from his .897 mark the previous season, although his elite base-running ability and defense in right field had made him a five-win player regardless. Many athletes are afraid to change. Betts wasn't, even if that meant listening to the advice of an outside instructor like Latta, whose own playing career never advanced past junior college. Already a two-time All-Star, Betts wanted to be better.

Many of the hitters who had previously sought change were desperate, seeking to extend careers. But what if a top-shelf talent like Betts—renowned for his elite hand-eye coordination and athleticism and already experimenting with a nontraditional bat handle designed to enhance bat speed and control—adopted a better swing? What if stars started rethinking their potential and making large leaps?

Hyers joined the Red Sox after the 2017 season, following a two-year stint as the assistant hitting coach for the Dodgers. A Georgia native with a trace of a southern accent, Hyers had a brief big-league career, batting .217 with two homers in 133 career games for the Padres, Marlins, and Tigers. He had been taught to swing down on the ball. He didn't think he could be a power hitter. He thought his skill level was fixed.

Hyers sought out Latta late in the spring of 2016, after speaking with Justin Turner about the swing he learned from Latta. They met for breakfast one morning in the suburb of Silver Lake. The meeting lasted four hours.

Up to that point, few professional coaches had accepted Latta into their circles of trust. He was perceived as an unwelcome outsider who meddled with other coaches' players. But as Boston's charter arrived in Los Angeles on that early season road trip, Hyers wanted "another set of eyes"—Latta's eyes—on a swing Betts had begun to forge that spring. Latta was a master at understanding how every part of the body worked in concert.

As Latta drove Betts to the UC Irvine baseball facility, he asked him if he was sure he wanted to exert himself. Betts had been out of the lineup Sunday after injuring his left foot in a collision at home plate the day before. He said he was fine, and X-rays were negative. So they went to work as Latta does with almost every hitter. "We want the hand path to work and get length," said Latta of creating an upswing with extension, "to get the body balanced and move forward."

They worked together in private for several hours in open-air cages covered by hunter-green corrugated metal. The next day, Betts returned to the lineup against the Angels' rookie sensation Shohei Ohtani. Betts batted first, where he had taken the vast majority of his at-bats as a big leaguer. At five foot nine, 180 pounds, he had the body of a leadoff hitter in addition to elite hand-eye ability. He had shown surprising power. That threat was about to become even more significant.

In the Anaheim twilight, Ohtani threw a full-count fastball that came close to the plate, knee-high. A keen observer could have noticed that Betts's swing—already much changed that spring under Hyers's instruction—looked different. As Ohtani delivered, Betts lifted his left leg and began his stride toward the pitcher. His hands dropped lower toward his belt. As he moved forward, his hands stayed back and "under" the ball, as Latta teaches, which would enable his bat to travel on an uppercut trajectory. Pitches travel at downward angles, both because they're released from an elevated mound and because gravity acts upon them. A flat bat path is on plane with a pitch for a very short period of time. An upward path increases the odds of optimum contact.

In a blur, the barrel connected with the Ohtani pitch and drove it high into the violet sky, the silhouette of the San Gabriel Mountains still visible in the distance. Rather than wrapping around his back as it often did, Betts's follow-through traveled on a path that finished high and slightly above his shoulders. It was almost like a golfer's swing— or like Turner's.

The ball traveled 411 feet, landing beyond the left-center-field fence and ricocheting off the faux boulders and back onto the field. Betts ran around the bases, businesslike. No smile cracked his countenance.

When Betts came up in the third inning, Luke Bard had replaced Ohtani. Bard's second pitch to Betts was a hanging slider. Betts again dropped his hands lower. His bat got on plane with the pitch earlier, and he drove slightly under and through the ball with lightning-quick hands. He again finished higher in his follow-through. Betts launched the ball beyond the bullpens in left-center field, 417 feet away from home plate. He lowered his head and subtly flipped his bat.

In the eighth inning, Betts faced Cam Bedrosian. As the temperature dropped throughout the evening, Betts blew on his hands prior to grasping his Axe Bat and stepping back into the right-handed batter's box. Bedrosian's first pitch was an inside fastball. Betts swung, making contact well out in front of the plate, where most home-run contact happens. The ball soared toward center field. This time Betts watched it briefly, and a small grin appeared. The ball landed on an AstroTurf knoll beyond the playing surface, 427 feet away: his third home run of the game. And on May 2, Betts would author *another* three-homer game.

Betts was following the trail blazed before him by a select group of hitters, including one Latta had helped transform from a castoff into a star.

On September 6, 2013, Turner, then a New York Mets utility infielder, borrowed the bat of teammate Lucas Duda and walked into the on-field batting cage at Progressive Field in downtown Cleveland. It was the beginning of one of the most unthinkable transformations in modern baseball history.

Turner's former Mets teammate, Marlon Byrd, had been traded a week earlier to the Pirates. Turner and Byrd had spoken often about hitting. The public was suspicious about Byrd's 2013 breakout because Byrd had been suspended for fifty games in 2012 after testing positive for a banned substance that masks steroid use. (Byrd would retire in 2016 after testing positive for a banned substance again.) But Turner—and another light-hitting Mets infielder named Daniel Murphy—listened to Byrd in 2013 because Byrd had changed his approach to hitting in a way that had nothing to do with drugs.

Byrd was six feet tall with a 245-pound frame, and yet prior to 2013, he had been a ground-ball hitter. "I came from more of an old-school style of baseball," Byrd told Travis in 2013. "Coming up, the coaches I had played for in the 1970s and 1980s, they were taught to swing down."

Byrd's breakout 2013 season, which featured career-bests in home runs (twenty-two) and slugging percentage (.526), came at an age, thirty-six, when players are typically in decline. His preceding suspension made the stats look like a chemical mirage, but in a single off-season, Byrd had changed the nature of *how* he swung and the angle at which his bat struck the ball.

Byrd and Turner conversed during batting practice, during games, and on late-night charter flights as they crisscrossed the country to fulfill the demands of the major-league schedule. Turner was intrigued by Byrd's radical new theories of hitting. Byrd spoke about how Latta had helped him adopt a leg kick and more loft in his swing the previous winter. As a result, he was more direct in his movement to the pitch. Turner knew Byrd had decreased his ground-ball rate from 49.6 percent in 2012 (which was near his career rate) to 39.2 percent in 2013, while raising his fly-ball rate by 12.2 percentage points, the third-greatest increase in baseball. Professional batters take tens of thousands of swings between when they first pick up a bat and when they make it to pro ball, hardwiring a swing path into their muscle memory. Most coaches thought that trait couldn't be changed. Byrd challenged that notion, suggesting that hitters could evolve, and relatively quickly, even at advanced ages.

Byrd embraced a style completely different from what Mets hitting instructor Dave Hudgens advocated. (Hudgens would later adjust his beliefs when he became the Astros' hitting coach.) Early that spring, Byrd launched ball after ball out of a spring training backfield at the club's Port St. Lucie complex. The Mets' staff told him his new swing wouldn't work in games. He was sure they were wrong. Hitters were taught that home runs were blissful accidents and that they ought to try for low line drives. Byrd believed in *trying* to hit home runs in games and in practice. He was done with conventional wisdom.

Turner had not homered in his 183 plate appearances in 2013, and he started September 6 with a .639 OPS, well below the league average. He was a bench player known for his glove, shock of red hair, and amber beard. But on this midafternoon in Cleveland prior to a 7:05 p.m. game, Turner tried on a new identity.

Duda's bat was an inch longer and an ounce heavier than his own model—thirty-four inches, thirty-three ounces—which is why Turner chose it. Maybe it would help him generate more power. As he entered the on-field batting cage to begin his experiment, he thought about what Byrd had preached: "Take a large stride. Gain ground." In other words, move toward the pitcher, creating a more linear path that would transfer energy more efficiently. Byrd also harped on contact point, explaining that batters should think about catching the pitch out in front of the plate, whereas most traditional teaching held that batters should let the ball travel longer and deeper, closer to the plate. Catching the ball out front would better organize the body and allow for the ball to be pulled into the air: the most valuable batted-ball type in baseball. In 2018, MLB batters hit .565 with a 1.267 slugging mark on pull-side air balls, and 32.7 percent of such batted balls went for home runs.

All his life, Turner had been told to let the ball travel as deep as possible and to try to hit low line drives. Now, Turner, who would turn twenty-nine in November, was ready to experiment. He knew the Mets might not tender him a contract after the season. If he wanted to play more, or at all, he had to change. He had to hit.

Turner had studied kinesiology at Cal State Fullerton, where he hit seven home runs in 1,008 at-bats. While Byrd's theories made sense, Turner didn't think he could become a home-run hitter. He had hit just six home runs over parts of five major-league seasons. But unlike Betts, he had little to lose. He traded in a fixed mindset for a growth one.

"I was thinking, I'm just going to try and catch the ball as far out as I can in batting practice," Turner says.

Only a few saw the beginning. They saw Turner connect with pitches that began to fly over the nineteen-foot, left-field wall. The clank of balls against empty bleachers resonated throughout the mostly empty ballpark. It was a sound Turner was not accustomed to creating. Teammates raised eyebrows.

"I didn't even feel like I was swinging hard," Turner says. "I was like, this is amazing."

In his first two at-bats on September 6, Turner grounded out twice versus Scott Kazmir. But in the top of the seventh, he faced right-handed reliever Cody Allen. A paltry crowd of 15,962 watched as Turner caught an elevated fastball well out in front of the plate.

The feeling of hitting a home run was alien to Turner. He *ran* out of the box. His attention was fixed on Cleveland center fielder Michael Bourn, who raced backward. "Get over his head! Get over his head!" Turner exclaimed in his head, his heart hammering as he approached first base, the ball he had struck still hanging in the air. Turner was as astonished as anyone when the ball vanished into a row of trees beyond the center-field fence.

"I was like, oh my God, what just happened?" Turner says. "I didn't hit enough home runs to know what it was like when I got it."

Turner floated around the bases, trying to keep his composure, trying to be emotionless, acting as if he had been there before. Except that he *hadn't* been there before. His teammates were slack jawed. "Swaggy," as Turner was nicknamed, did that? Following the game, Turner met his then girlfriend, now wife, at the Jack Casino in downtown Cleveland. Under the lights, above the din of the casino, Turner couldn't stop talking about what he felt and what he might have found.

Two days later, the Mets and Turner faced the Indians and hard-throwing rookie Danny Salazar on a sunny Sunday afternoon. During his second at-bat, with the count three balls and one strike, Salazar challenged Turner with an elevated 96 mph fastball. Turner caught the pitch out in front of the plate. The ball soared on a majestic trajectory, landing halfway up the sun-soaked, left-center-field bleachers. It was as if Roy Hobbs had stolen Turner's jersey and hit right-handed. For the eighth time in his career—and the second time in three days—Turner circled the bases.

Turner played in ten games with the new swing that September. In that limited sample, he batted .387 and slugged .677. He knew he needed to visit Doug Latta.

Amid the urban sprawl of Northridge, California, close to a Costco, a mobile-home park, and an In-N-Out Burger, is a long, narrow business park that terminates near a set of railroad tracks. In one of the business park's long, narrow units, Latta transforms hitters.

Inside Latta's facility, the Ball Yard, are two batting cages, a couple of couches, a half bathroom, and a kitchenette. Everything one needs to hit for hours. Outside the main batting cage is a large television whose screen Latta has covered with a clear sheet of plastic so he can pause video and use marker to scribble over the image, identifying flaws—his homemade telestrator. It is a modest, white-drywalled space with a green AstroTurf floor, but as Latta tells hitters who might be expecting a more lavish facility when they first walk in, "We don't need much space to get better." The same goes for any hotbed of talent development: all that's required are ideas, information, passion, and reps. Lots and lots of reps. The Ball Yard was where, in the winter of 2013–2014, Latta helped Turner morph from a journeyman into a something more.

At the Ball Yard in 2018, Latta scrolls through his video library, finds some early footage of Turner, and plays it on the flat-screen television outside the batting cage. It's from January 27, 2014. Turner was unemployed then. He'd been nontendered by the Mets. On the video, Turner has a shorter beard and wears a T-shirt, shorts, and a hat turned backward. He takes a swing. He goes into his leg kick and takes an exaggerated stride.

"This is before he narrowed up," Latta says of Turner's stance. "Those days we were just pumping."

By "pumping," Latta means taking a lot of swings. Latta pulls up another video of Turner from April 24, 2014, after Turner had signed a minor-league deal with the Dodgers with an invite to spring training and ended up making the team as a replacement for the recently retired Michael Young. Turner was still a part-time player. In the clip, his hands are higher than they were in January. So is his leg kick. He looks off-balance several times, finishing with his feet out of the would-be batter's box as he gathers himself. As he swings, he rocks his weight on his back leg, which is a no-no for Latta.

"People forget that's how J.T. looked then," Latta says. "He's gotten narrower, the leg kicks up more. It got easier and easier and easier."

Latta and Turner weren't alone. Byrd was often there also, hitting and serving as something of a quasi-assistant coach.

"It was hard. It was tough. I had twenty-five years of habits to break," Turner says. "Marlon had talked about it all year long, so I kind of had a head start going in there, knowing what [Latta] was talking about."

Over that winter, Turner trained at the Ball Yard for three months, four days a week. He and Latta worked for three hours per session, taking seven or eight rounds of batting practice per hour, fifteen to twenty pitches per round. He estimates that he took twenty thousand swings.

Latta has documented Turner's entire evolution. Since that winter, most of their interaction has come through texting, though Turner sometimes stops by the Ball Yard for a tune-up. Latta interacts with clients he has less familiarity with through FaceTime. He watches most of Turner's at-bats live. At first, Latta sent constant reinforcements. If he saw footage of Babe Ruth's swing on MLB Network or elsewhere, he'd capture it and send it to Turner. Ruth had a narrow stance with an exaggerated stride. He contacted the ball out front. His back foot left contact with the ground. Turner laughed about the Ruth video during spring training 2018.

"'Look at Babe, he's really staying back and catching the ball deep,'" Turner said, recounting the text from Latta that accompanied the video. Ruth did the exact opposite of the conventional teaching Latta and Turner were mocking, complete with an uppercut swing.

"You look at Ruth, Mantle, all these hitters back in the day, they all leg kick or toe tap. They all gain a *ton* of ground. Their strides are huge. . . . It's the theory that whatever starts in motion, stays in motion. . . . Isaac Newton is my favorite hitting coach. The whole old-school mentality of swinging down, chopping down on the ball? It's bullshit."

Turner slammed the table with a fist in frustration. How many coaches had let down how many players?

In 2014, Turner hit .340/.404/.493. He made only 322 plate appearances, but among all hitters with at least 300 trips to the plate, his 158 weighted runs created plus (wRC+), a comprehensive rate stat, ranked ninth (100 is league average). The Dodgers were curious enough to retain the arbitration-eligible Turner on a one-year, $2.5 million deal. In 2015, he made 439 plate appearances and hit nearly as well as he had the year before, slashing .294/.370/.491 with a 141 wRC+. Between 2013 and 2015, he cut his ground-ball rate by 12.5 percentage points, the fourth-greatest decline in the game. In 2016, Turner earned a full-time role. He hit twenty-seven homers. After that season, he signed a four-year, $64 million contract with the Dodgers.

In the summer of 2018 at the Ball Yard, Latta pulls up another evolution-of-Turner video from January 2017. By now Turner is much narrower in his stance. There is no rocking back on his back leg to move forward. As his left leg lifts to initiate his swing, his hands fall to create the proper slot for an uppercut swing.

"What's J.T. trying to create? Balance and drive," Latta says.

Latta plays it again in slow motion. Turner's back leg and shoulder remain perfectly in line. There is no backward weight transfer or movement. He's balanced.

He lands with his front (left) leg well in front of his body. His hands are lowered and ready to fire. "Body is moving in concert," Latta says. "From this position he fires right underneath. He picks up his backside, and all that energy drives through the ball. He gets what we call a lot of extension." In slow motion, the swing finishes. Latta outlines the path of the upswing with marker on the plastic sheet covering the television screen. He notes that all of Turner's energy is transferred to a contact area in front of the plate.

Latta has a HitTrax radar unit to measure launch angle and exit velocity, but he rarely employs the latest technological advances. If a hitter doesn't have timing and balance and movement, he has no shot, Latta believes. He's troubled by the teaching he sees on social media, where video clips focus on creating exit velocity at the expense of balance and adaptable swings. Latta rarely uses the words *swing* or *swing plane* when talking about hitters. He tries to organize the body in such a way that the swing takes care of itself. He believes that some in the independent-player-development business are more worried about selling products than helping athletes.

Ground zero of the fly-ball revolution was arguably the Ball Yard, where other teachers and advocates of the movement met and discussed ideas. Byrd spread the knowledge to Turner and Murphy in New York. (Murphy hit sixty-two homers in more than 3,300 at-bats through age thirty, and then hit sixty more in fewer than 1,400 at-bats from ages thirty-one to thirty-three.) Turner now proselytizes in the Los Angeles clubhouse, teaching or reinforcing the beliefs of talented young hitters like Cody Bellinger and Corey Seager, and even influencing some hitting instructors like Hyers. When Bellinger was having trouble with sliders as a rookie in 2017, he wondered if his swing was too uppercut-oriented. Turner had him play a game late that summer.

They went into the team's indoor batting cage at Dodger Stadium. Turner turned on the slider machine and told Bellinger to try to swing and miss below the sliders. Bellinger couldn't do it; he couldn't miss. Bellinger produced a .418 weighted on-base average (wOBA) versus sliders in 2017 and a .341 mark in 2018, easily eclipsing the league averages of .271 and .263, respectively. His upswing worked.

The fly-ball revolution also spread thanks to Statcast, which in 2015 began to measure the launch angle and exit velocity of almost every ball hit in every MLB game. Teams started to outfit their batting cages at all levels with swing- and ball-tracking technology. The data confirmed that air balls were better than grounders: with every 10 degree increment from minus 30 degrees to 30 degrees (where zero is a level line drive), the league-wide wOBA on contact in 2018 increased, easily surpassing the all-angles average of .315. (The average home run left the bat at a vertical angle of 28.2 degrees.)

−30 to −20:	.050
−20 to −10:	.188
−10 to 0:	.245
0 to 10:	.462
10 to 20:	.712
20 to 30:	.731

Between growing awareness of that relationship and a still-unexplained change in the composition of the official MLB ball in 2015, which caused balls in the air to carry farther, hitters had more incentive to swing up. The average launch angle of a batted ball has increased in every year of Statcast: from 10.5 degrees in 2015, to 10.8 in 2016, 11.1 in 2017, and 11.7 in 2018. Over the same span, the rate of balls hit at a 10 degree angle or higher has increased by 3.3 percentage points. According to data from Baseball Prospectus, the league-wide ground-ball rate in 2018 was the lowest on record, going back to 1950.

In 2017, MLB hitters launched 6,105 home runs, breaking the previous record (set in 2000) by 412. That year, 2018, and 2016, respectively, featured the three highest rates of home runs per fair batted ball in history, surpassing the so-called steroid era.

"Elevate and celebrate" and "Ground balls suck" became batting-cage cries. In 2018, Red Sox skipper Alex Cora said, "We don't like hitting ground balls. We like hitting the ball in the air." His statement mirrored a Cubs catchphrase—"There's no slug on the ground"—as well as Pirates manager Clint Hurdle's advice to his team: "Your OPS is in the air." An outsider philosophy had spawned insider slogans.

Latta didn't set out to change baseball. He simply loved the game. He grew up in what he describes as "tough" financial circumstances and didn't play organized baseball until he reached high school. Instead he played in a sandlot down the street in his childhood Koreatown neighborhood, where he and his friends used the back of an accommodating neighbor's garage as a backstop. He went on to play at Los Angeles City College, a public community college, and later Cal Lutheran. After college he joined the Pasadena Redbirds, an adult hardball league.

"The challenge was always there to be able to build myself, to get better, and to realize that you could beat the odds," Latta says. "We were playing major-league-caliber pitchers—like Ed Farmer, Jerry Reuss, Craig Chamberlain—so we were getting challenged."

Latta turned down a chance to play in the Mexican League. He already had a better-paying job: at nineteen, Latta had begun his own business, cleaning private swimming pools. He continued to play baseball for the Redbirds until 1995. During his time with the team, he met a professional scout named Craig Wallenbrock. They developed a friendship. Latta describes Wallenbrock as "a thinking man." Wallenbrock was a devoted reader, and he applied his studies to baseball, giving private hitting lessons beginning in the late 1980s.

While his playing days were over by the late '90s, Latta thought he had information to share. He also had space to share. He owned part of a large industrial building in Los Angeles, where he stored pool chemicals for what was then a state-of-the-art chlorine-injection system. When he had an opportunity to buy the other half of the industrial structure, Latta had an idea: he would build an indoor batting cage in the other half of the building. He could give lessons and rent out the cages. He named the facility the Ball Yard.

"We didn't even have any indoor batting cages in the area," Latta says. "They just did not exist."

Latta spent four months personally doing the demolition of what had been office space. He installed AstroTurf and batting cages. Wallenbrock asked if he could hold some of his hitting sessions there. Another instructor was interested in using the space, but that instructor wanted to use "flat-bat stuff," Latta recalls. "I told myself, hell no." Wallenbrock was more aligned with Latta's philosophy, so they reached an agreement for Wallenbrock to train hitters in his space. No hitter was ever taught to chop wood, swing down on the ball, or hit grounders at the Ball Yard, Latta says. Wallenbrock brought in a great number of hitters, including some major leaguers.

The Ball Yard began to host regular meetings with other hitting coaches inside and outside professional baseball, which Latta labels a think tank. Latta kept about thirty folding chairs on hand for the sessions, which grew in size and frequency. The attendees talked about hitting philosophies, some of them out of favor or forgotten like those of the great Ted Williams, who was hitting fly balls before they were cool. "If you get the ball into the air with power, you have the gift to produce the most important hit in baseball: the home run. . . . For those purposes, I advocate a slight upswing," wrote Williams in his 1970 book *The Science of Hitting*. Former major leaguer turned instructor Don Slaught was a frequent visitor, as was Greg Walker, who had served as a hitting coach with the White Sox and Braves. The group met for years.

"I like to say that was my graduate work," Latta says, "working side by side with Craig for fourteen years seeing what [pro hitters] were going through. How do you buy that experience?"

Eventually, Wallenbrock and Latta had a falling-out, and Wallenbrock took his higher-profile clients elsewhere. Latta eventually moved into a new facility, the present-day Ball Yard. Years went by. Latta continued to teach his unusual, uppercut-swing philosophy to players, mostly local college and high-school kids. And one day in the fall of 2012, Marlon Byrd walked through Latta's door looking for a place to hit in the off-season. Byrd became his first major-league client.

On February 6, 2017, Travis published an article at FanGraphs entitled "Can More Hitters Get Off the Ground?" Fly-ball and line-drive rates had remained stable from 2012 to 2016, through the depths of baseball's offensive depression, when a pair of low-power teams in the Kansas City Royals and San Francisco Giants accounted for three World Series titles in five years. In 2014, before the altered ball took flight, teams averaged only 4.07 runs scored per game, the lowest total in a nonstrike season since 1976, and both MLB insiders and fans fretted about how offense could be boosted in a high-velocity era. A few minutes after the story, which quoted Latta, was published online, Latta received a call from Hyers.

"At 7:32 a.m. Tim called me and said, 'Andrew Friedman just called me about that article,'" Latta says. "The president of the Dodgers. Wow. Cool. I had told [Hyers] it was coming out. 'Friedman got in the office and read it,' [Hyers said]. I was like, wow, Friedman reads Fan-Graphs. He had no heads-up. For him to get in and read it in two minutes, you never actually know who is paying attention."

The article created debate within the Dodgers' hitting circles, which included both more traditionally minded voices like the club's head hitting coach, Turner Ward, and others like Wallenbrock, who had worked with the club as a consultant, and his understudy Robert Van Scoyoc, who was named as the Dodgers' hitting coach after the 2018 season. The fly-ball revolution, and the rethinking of development as a whole, had first spread from player to player via word of mouth. Now teams wanted to disseminate it throughout their entire organizations.

For decades, coaches—always ex-professional players—had enjoyed a privileged place in the vertical hierarchy of teaching and decision-making. But more and more coaches were being questioned and challenged. Many were soon to be replaced. Ideas that had begun outside the game were trickling up into the professional ranks. Latta was just one garage startup disrupting the industry.

At the end of 2017, Hyers joined the Red Sox as their head hitting coach. He and the Sox sought to revamp their hitting philosophy. Another new face, J.D. Martinez, was told by the Red Sox coaching staff to make Mookie his "project." As Martinez watched Betts hit for the first time in the spring with his 2017 stroke, he said, "I don't know that that's going to work." Betts was not offended. He wanted information.

Martinez signed a five-year $110 million deal with the Red Sox over the winter of 2017–2018, several years after reinventing his own swing and saving his career. Through 2013, Martinez had been a replacement-level big leaguer. In his first three years in the majors, he posted an 87 wRC+. He was a below-average hitter *and* a poor defender. He career was in jeopardy.

"You still talk to coaches, 'Oh, you want a line drive right up the middle. Right off the back of the L-screen,'" Martinez told Travis in 2017. "OK, well that's a fucking single."

Martinez began to question why his best swing would result in a "fucking single." The same winter as Turner, he sought a new swing. He found it in a facility in suburban Los Angeles with assistance from Wallenbrock and his protégé Van Scoyoc.

"I have this little theory," Martinez says. "When I think about the best players, I think what makes people so good is when they have that insecurity about themselves . . . because they don't want to fall off. It keeps them working. I feel like [Betts] had that little doubt. . . . Other guys have good years and they won't make the change. He was like, 'Dude, I have to figure this out. I don't have it figured out.'"

Betts' overhaul worked from the bottom up, too. Hyers and Martinez first stressed how his feet interacted with the ground. That was where the kinetic chain of the swing began. "I had to fix the ground before I fixed my hands," Martinez says. "The engine is down there." The Red Sox now travel with force plates that measure ground-interaction forces. The portable devices are set up in the tunnels of MLB stadiums so that hitters can measure their force and balance. They look something like large digital scales and, like TrackMan, were first popularized in golf. Betts had never thought about using the ground.

"He'd just been hitting away his whole life and didn't think much of it," Hyers says.

Like Turner in Los Angeles, Martinez is something of a Johnny Appleswing, a willing teacher and a clubhouse peer who reinforces Hyers's philosophy. Among the 260 MLB hitters with at least 150 batted balls in both 2017 and 2018, Betts, center fielder Jackie Bradley Jr., and shortstop Xander Bogaerts ranked fourth, eighth, and eleventh in year-to-year increase in hard-hit rate (the percentage of balls hit 95 mph or faster). Betts, Bogaerts, and Bradley also ranked first, second, and thirtieth, respectively, in year-to-year increase in barrels (a Statcast term for "balls someone hit the snot out of") per batted ball.

"I have to give a big credit to J.D. Martinez," Hyers says. "When you have a superstar and you have a guy who's already proven it, to come in and back what you're saying and have those conversations one-on-one with players. . . . J.D. was huge on saying, 'Hey Mookie, you can do this part.' And they had their own private conversations that helped a ton also."

Now Betts has become a hitting tastemaker, too, inspiring rivals to reject the round knob at a time when some bat companies, like golf-club designers, have begun to use swing sensors to determine the perfect fit for each player in length, weight, and grip. "You start seeing that [Betts] has an influence within the league," says Axe Bat's Trevor Stocking. "[George] Springer asked him for a bat, and now all of a sudden Springer's swinging Mookie's bat, so now Springer is giving the bat to another player, and [it's] kind of this wheel . . . where they're passing on the equipment."

They're also passing on the swing, and hitters are getting off the ground younger. Byrd bought into fly balls at the tail end of his career. Turner saw the light just prior to turning thirty. Martinez and Betts made the change in their primes. Now they're modeling good batter behavior for impressionable minor leaguers, including one of Boston's top prospects. Third baseman Bobby Dalbec, a twenty-three-year-old fourth-rounder from 2016 who ascended to Double-A in 2018, tied for the lead among all minor leaguers with 67 combined home runs (32) and doubles (35). For years, players talked about "selling out for power," sacrificing contact to take big swings. Dalbec turns that expression around. "I think it's a waste of an at-bat for me to sell out for contact, hit a ground ball early in the count," he says.

Dalbec wants to hit the ball hard and far, but he also wants to be smart about it. "Being on the right attack angle [and] trying to match the plane to the pitch is something I really want to get better at," he says. "It's definitely nice to be able to watch guys in my organization at the major-league level do that." Although he notes that he's nowhere near Martinez's level, he'd like to learn from hitters like him and Betts. "If they'd be willing to or if they had time, I'd pick their brains all day about it," he says. Fortunately for him, Martinez always has time to talk hitting.

6

THE 10,000-PITCH RULE

Deliberate practice takes place out of one's comfort zone and
requires a student to constantly try things that are just beyond
his or her current abilities. Thus it demands near-maximal effort,
which is generally not enjoyable.
—ANDERS ERICSSON, *Peak*[1]

In 2000, University College of London neuroscientist Eleanor Maguire
used magnetic resonance imaging (MRI) to examine the brains of sixteen taxi drivers and compare them to the brains of fifty non–taxi
drivers. London is a difficult city to navigate. The ancient metropo-
lis is a weaving, curving mess of thoroughfares further forked by the
Thames River, winding through the center of the city. According to
a *New York Times Magazine* article, to be licensed as an "All London"
taxi driver, prospective operators must know nearly every street and
structure—every hotel, park, hospital, government office, place of
worship, or other object of interest—within a six-mile radius of Char-
ing Cross, an area containing some twenty-five thousand streets and
113 square miles.

Maguire found that the posterior part of the hippocampus, a region
of the brain associated with spatial recognition and recall, was larger
in the taxi drivers than the other subjects. Five years later, she compared the brains of taxi drivers, whose jobs took them to unpredictable
destinations, to the brains of bus drivers who drove predetermined
routes. Again, the taxi drivers had the hippocampus advantage.

In 2007, Maguire recruited seventy-nine prospective taxi drivers
and thirty-one non–taxi drivers as controls. She scanned their brains
before the study, finding no difference between the two groups in

posterior hippocampus size. Four years later, she revisited the same applicants. Perhaps unsurprisingly, the MRI results showed that the remaining taxi drivers had enlarged hippocampi compared to applicants who had dropped out and the non-driver control group. Only the active taxi drivers were challenged daily to reach random destinations across London, and their brains literally grew into the job.

Maguire's study, Anders Ericsson wrote, in *Peak*, "is perhaps the most dramatic evidence we have that the human brain grows and changes in response to training." Bauer, who believes he was made into a major-league pitcher, has always understood that his skills could grow. He is obsessed with skill acquisition. If you ask him about myelin, a substance in the brain, he'll correct your pronunciation (mīələn) before explaining that myelin is a fatty tissue that forms insulating sheaths around nerve fibers in the brain that increase the speed at which impulses are conducted. Myelin is the brain's bandwidth. The more a person practices a certain act, the more myelin is created along that particular pathway, enabling the brain to send faster, more efficient signals. The power of myelin means that talent is not fixed.

"I have to go beyond 100 percent of what I can currently do," Bauer says. "I have to find a way to increase my skill set and maximize it."

In 1993, Ericsson, a psychology professor at Florida State University, published a study in which he reported the "estimated accumulated hours of practice" among various types of musicians, from novices to experts.[2] His findings suggested that people could change their performance levels more than was commonly assumed. The study, which revealed that expert musicians had logged many more hours of practice than amateurs and weren't simply more "gifted," reached only a small audience until the popular author Malcolm Gladwell stumbled across it and used it to coin what he called the 10,000-hour rule of practice, a concept he introduced in his bestselling 2008 book *Outliers*. Ericsson would later clarify that more important than the amount of time one practiced was the quality of the training. Gladwell, he wrote, "didn't distinguish between the deliberate practice that musicians in

our study did and any sort of activity that might be labeled 'practice.'"
Just practicing an instrument for ten thousand hours doesn't mean
you'll master it. The accumulation of *deliberate* practice—focused work
with intent—is the key to quicker achievement of expertise.

When it came to gaining expertise, Ericsson didn't believe in short-
cuts. Bauer, on the other hand, felt he had to find quicker routes to
acquire new skills and maximize his career. He needed to find a more
efficient way to train. Even Bauer didn't have the ability to deliberately
practice for ten thousand hours in one off-season. Moreover, he knew
that Father Time catches up with and erodes all athletes' abilities. He
was twenty-seven. By his early thirties, he'd be in decline from his
physical peak.

If Bauer wanted to achieve his lofty ambitions, he'd have to expand
his pitching repertoire. But adding a new slider in one off-season—a
pitch he could confidently throw in high-pressure situations to the
best hitters on the planet—would be no easy task.

To quickly develop his slider, he needed "more feedback in the
loop," he says, a more efficient way to acquire the kind of subconscious mastery and command (more myelin) over a pitch that is required to succeed on the mound. Pitchers call this feel. "It feels good
coming out of my hand," Bauer explains. "So when you start struggling with it, you try this and you try that. You try to get that feel back.
. . . If you're lucky, it's a monthlong process, if you happen to find it
quickly. Sometimes it's a year. Sometimes it never comes back. That
massively changes your career trajectory."

Until recently, much of the physics at work when a professional
pitcher hurls a baseball were mysterious. The hand of an MLB pitcher
has an angular velocity of thousands of degrees per second, too fast
for the human eye or even a regular high-definition digital camera
to capture clearly. Thus, the exact manner in which a pitcher's grip
imparts spin to a ball has been unknowable. Over the history of the
sport, most pitchers have pursued new pitches through a process of
trial and error. Countless pitchers have wasted countless hours in
the floundering pursuit of feel. Finding a shortcut—a more efficient
way to gain skill, to practice, to see—would be a massive competitive
advantage.

"How can I shorten the learning curve for all these new skills?" Bauer says. "That's the holy grail."

Bauer's Excalibur in this quest was the Edgertronic camera, which he calls "the most powerful tool in all of baseball."

Trevor and Warren were always looking for new ideas and technology that could help Trevor be better. They read about a high-speed camera, Sanstreak's Edgertronic SC1, whose resolution and speed represented a leap in affordability and effectiveness compared to rival devices. At $5,500, the SC1 wasn't cheap, but it was much more affordable than any similarly capable camera. In the winter of 2014–2015, Bauer and his father purchased one.

"We said, 'We are never going to know if it's useful until we have it, so let's get it and see what we see,'" Trevor says. "Then we filmed with it for the first time, and we're like, 'That's it. That's the ticket.'"

Part of what makes the Edgertronic different is its shutter. Most digital cameras, like the one in your smartphone, employ what is known as a rolling shutter, in which each row of pixels is captured at a different moment from the rows above and below. For video capture of stationary or slowly moving objects, a rolling shutter will not produce any noticeable negative effects. But when shooting fast-moving objects—like a pitcher's hand throwing a ball—a rolling shutter will produce an imperfection known as the jello effect, a blurring and stretching of objects. The jello effect is unacceptable in scientific research, including the embryonic field of pitch design.

The Edgertronic camera employs a global shutter, which captures every pixel at the exact same moment in every frame and at an extremely high frame-per-second rate, eliminating the jello effect. The Edgertronic also captures more light than many comparable high-speed, global-shutter cameras, enabling greater resolution. Sanstreak CEO Michael Matter named the Edgertronic after Harold Edgerton, or "Papa Flash," an innovator in the world of high-speed photography whose work published in *Life* magazine fascinated him as a child. "I've always been good at getting things to work faster than people thought possible," Matter says.

Matter knew there would be scientific and research applications for his product. When the first commercial version was released in

2013, he saw the camera show up in the footnotes of papers in a wide variety of fields. Rocket scientists used his high-speed camera to film exhaust and examine how mixtures were burning. A biomechanist in Riverside, California, used the Edgertronic to study kangaroo rats, which have unusually quick reflexes. In ultraslow, undistorted footage from an Edgertronic available on YouTube, a kangaroo rat narrowly avoids the jaws of a darting rattlesnake, leaping at perhaps ten times the quickness and speed of the snake. Matter never imagined which industry would become his biggest client: Major League Baseball.

That market opened with one order placed by one pitcher: Trevor Bauer. Many more orders followed; by the spring of 2018, the Astros had bought seventy-five cameras, outfitting every stadium in their system with a number of hard-mounted Edgertronic cameras in addition to equipping evaluators with portable units. (Boddy suspects the next-closest club was the Dodgers, with six.) Matter expected at least fifteen MLB teams to have purchased at least one camera by the start of 2019 and for baseball to represent more than half of his business.

After Bauer purchased his first Edgertronic, Warren began experimenting with it early in 2015 at Jim Wagner's ThrowZone Academy in Santa Clarita, a warehouse-like structure with a corrugated metal skin and artificial turf. He was astounded by its resolution and speed. To this point, high-speed cameras were only capable of illuminating larger body movements. But Warren conceived a new application: He could use the Edgertronic to see how the grip interacted with the ball as a pitch was thrown. The cameras the Bauers had previously employed offered video that was "too grainy to see the fingertips," Trevor says. Now Warren could see how the grip imparted spin and also the pitch's precise spin axis.

"You know how hard it is to keep your eyes on a hummingbird? How quickly it shifts?" says Trevor. "With the right slow-motion camera, you can see everything. The hummingbird can have a tattoo on its wing that tells you exactly how he uses his wing to fly, to create lift. . . . You don't even have to try and figure out how a hummingbird flies because he's just telling you."

The camera helped Warren win a long-standing argument he'd had with his son. Trevor believed pitchers decided when to release pitches, but Warren didn't believe this was a conscious action. The camera confirmed his suspicion. It showed that pitchers don't release the ball by moving their fingers. Rather, the hand accelerates the ball linearly, forcing the fingers to extend or open. This led to a key finding that would shape Trevor's future approach to pitch design: grips were best thought of as escape routes for the ball.

That winter, Bauer developed his first pitch with the camera, a two-seam fastball he called the Laminar Express. This was a reference to the principles of laminar flow, a property that can influence the movement of a thrown baseball or any sphere. If undisturbed, layers of air tend to move in parallel, or in a laminar fashion. But if, say, a spinning sphere is smooth on one side and rough on the other, the air it passes through will be less disturbed, or laminar, on one side and turbulent on the other. The ball will dart toward, or seemingly be pulled toward, the side with more turbulent air. This is why pitchers will sometimes try to scuff one side of the ball, even though it's illegal.

In the 1990s, Hall-of-Fame right-handed pitcher Greg Maddux perfected the comeback, two-seam fastball, which would start inside off the plate to a left-handed batter and then move into the zone. He wasn't scuffing the ball; rather, he was harnessing laminar flow, although he wasn't aware of it. No one had knowingly applied the laminar effect to design a pitch until Boddy stumbled upon a 2012 video by University of Sydney physics professor Rod Cross, who explained how laminar principles could be employed in cricket and baseball to create ball movement. Cross had been alerted to the laminar effect in baseball when a Freddy Garcia split-finger fastball broke the wrong way on its path to the plate during an April 30, 2011, game at Yankee Stadium. In demonstrating the effect with a Styrofoam ball in a YouTube video, Cross described it as "a little bit of magic." [3] Boddy immediately understood the significance of the science. "This," he believed, "is the most important video on pitching."

At Driveline in the winter of 2015–2016, Boddy used the video to help Bauer design a spin axis that would maintain a smooth spot at the front of the ball—uninterrupted by seams in its rotation—throughout its flight to the plate. Using the Edgertronic to provide constant feedback as he experimented with different grips, Bauer built a reasonable facsimile of Maddux's comeback two-seamer. It was a remarkably short period in which to acquire a skill that would be effective at the highest level of sports. Boddy believes that such rapid pitch acquisition will become the new norm. "Unbeknownst to me, multiple hitting coaches saw that video and then saw us develop the two-seam fastball and were like, 'That is why hitters could be fucked for basically the next ten years if they're finding out new ways to move the baseball,'" Boddy says. "And that's true."

Not only can new technology like the Edgertronic allow pitchers to quickly learn new pitches, it can also help improve the ones they already throw. As Bauer worked on developing a two-seamer in 2015–2016, he decided to examine *all* his pitches with the Edgertronic to better understand their underlying characteristics and determine whether he could improve upon them. Existing pitch-tracking technology measured how the pitch moved and how fast it traveled after it left the hand, but it revealed little beyond that. Each time he changed grips during that first winter with the Edgertronic, Bauer imported the high-speed video into Adobe Photoshop and used the software to count the revolutions of the ball. (Today, this function is widely available through Rapsodo, a tracking device that identifies spin axis and differentiates between spin type, unlike the radar-based TrackMan system.) Bauer was thrilled to see that by just spiking his curveball grip—raising his right index finger at the knuckle and digging its tip into the surface—he had added 250 rpm of spin, which meant more movement. "It's a huge, huge deal," he says. And in the winter of 2017–2018, he trained the camera on his nascent slider.

While the Edgertronic is a powerful tool that offers a shortcut to expertise, designing a new pitch begins with first principles. There's a wide array of pitch labels—fastball, changeup, slider, and so forth. But what is a pitch? It's a combination of velocity, spin rate, and a spin axis. Creating a pitch is not magic; it's physics. Boiling pitches down to their underlying properties, as Bauer had done with his Laminar Express, unlocks the power of pitch creation. Designing pitches from scratch begins with understanding the spin that governs how a baseball moves.

There are two types of spin that affect a ball: transverse spin and gyroscopic spin. The spin type is determined by the spin axis of the ball, which in turn is determined by the pitcher's grip. Transverse spin makes a pitch move, a slider swerve. That's because transverse spin is sensitive to the Magnus effect.

In 1852, German physicist H. Gustav Magnus was perplexed about why artillery shells shot out of smooth-bore cannons often curved in unpredictable ways. He discovered a shell would deviate from a straight path because of pressure differences around the object that increase with the rate of its spin. As a baseball (or any sphere or cylinder) travels, it drags a thin layer of air with it, causing a difference in pressure on each side of the ball. The ball moves toward the area of lower pressure. The faster the spin, the greater the pressure differential, and the greater the movement. A curveball breaks downward because its topspin creates a downward Magnus effect. A fastball with a high spin rate appears to rise—even though it really just falls less than a lower-spin pitch—because its backspin produces a Magnus effect that pushes the ball up, opposing gravity.

A football thrown in a spiral or a bullet shot out of a rifled barrel demonstrates *gyroscopic* spin. Objects with gyroscopic spin are immune to the Magnus effect, and thus they travel straight. (It was the advent of rifled muskets—those with grooved barrels to impart gyroscopic stabilization—in the mid-nineteenth century that made the American Civil War so deadly, as increased accuracy and range overpowered outdated tactics.)

In a projectile moving with gyro spin, the spin axis is in line with the movement of the object rather than perpendicular to it. But the vast majority of pitches spin on a slightly tilted axis. In other words, the majority of pitches have an element of each type of spin: in the jargon of a pitch designer, they do not have 100 percent spin efficiency. Bauer knew his future—and the future of pitching in general—was tied to understanding and enlisting the power of physics to design and refine pitches.

We saw Bauer's pitch-design process in action during the winter before the 2018 season, when he worked to add a slider to his arsenal of pitches. It began in mid-October 2017. The Indians had just been eliminated by the Yankees in the division series, and Bauer flew home to Los Angeles. In his childhood bedroom in a colonial-style home in Santa Clarita, he and his father spent six hours formulating the concept of the pitch.

What Bauer wanted that off-season wasn't just any slider, but the perfect slider: a pitch with zero vertical movement aside from the effect of gravity, but one that darted laterally away from right-handed batters and toward lefties. He hoped to attain ten inches of horizontal movement or break—an elite level. (In 2017, the Dodgers' Yu Darvish led baseball with an average of nine inches.) Break like that required a specific spin axis, one with its poles oriented nearly north and south on the ball. The perfect slider would also be disguised to look like his fastball but would appear to break at the last moment, with a different shape and speed from his curveball and a direction opposite that of his two-seamer and changeup. There was also a compounding benefit to adding another pitch: it was another variable that would make it exponentially more difficult for the batter to anticipate or identify what was coming.

Bauer placed push pins into two baseballs to simulate the spin axis and visualize how to produce it with his grip. The objective sounded simple, but because of the biomechanics of the hand and wrist, creating a north–south spin axis was much more difficult than an east–west one, like that of a four-seam fastball. With a laptop open, Warren looked at old Edgertronic footage of Bauer throwing a slider with his thumb up on the side of the ball, wondering, how does it come off the hand? How do we adjust the grip?

Trevor and Warren looked at slow-motion video of sliders whose movement Trevor wanted to emulate, like those of teammates Corey Kluber and Mike Clevinger. He and Warren captured their slider grips via the Edgertronic, which they occasionally set up in Progressive Field or spring training stadiums.

Having conceptualized the pitch, father and son made their way to Wagner's facility, the ThrowZone. For six hours after ThrowZone had closed for the night, Bauer experimented with different grips, the Edgertronic camera and pitch-tracking technology recording every pitch. Even in that first session, the slider showed hints of promise, occasionally darting more horizontally than vertically. On December 4, Bauer traveled to Seattle, where he had purchased a number of condos—many he rented out and one that he inhabited in the winter—enabling him to embed himself at Driveline, his off-season head-quarters.

Almost since the beginning, Driveline has been associated with velocity training. But Boddy is interested in researching and improving all areas of pitching and baseball performance. Although the pulldown, max-intent throws and the radar-reading boards scattered around the facility speak to the importance of speed, pitch design became a greater focus after the 2015 season, when Warren introduced Boddy to the Edgertronic camera.

Initially, Warren had refused to show Boddy any Edgertronic video, treating it as something of a proprietary secret. Boddy continued to challenge Warren: "Let's see what film you've got." Finally, Warren acquiesced. He and Trevor flew to Driveline, carrying the camera in a special hardened case to protect it in transit.

At Boddy's facility, Warren filmed Weathers, by now a Driveline regular. They sat down to watch the footage. When Warren pressed play on his laptop, Boddy saw every aspect of Weathers's delivery at several thousand frames per second, including the ball coming off his hand in unprecedented detail. Boddy had never seen anything like it. The only two people in baseball who had were Warren and Trevor.

Boddy dropped his head into his arms, which were resting on the table. He was not on the cutting edge of pitch design. He stood up and went to his computer. Five minutes later, he returned. "I bought one," he said. Although he wasn't awash in cash at the time, it had taken just one throw to convince him that the camera was a game changer. "That meeting changed the entire landscape of professional baseball," Trevor says.

Along with tracking technology like Rapsodo, the camera represented the Rosetta stone of pitch design, a language that Bauer and Boddy believed was the future of baseball. "The next thing is, how do you develop individual pitches?" Boddy said at the time. "And I guarantee you no team's been doing that. Not the Astros. Not the Indians."

Bauer and Boddy were.

Not all of Bauer's pitch-design experiments succeeded. Many fizzled, and even those that did work were preceded by a multitude of microfailures before the big breakthrough. During the previous winter of 2016–2017, Bauer had tried to develop another pitch, a split-changeup, in much the same manner. But there were two differences that time.

One problem was that development began later in the off-season. Bauer threw only fifteen innings of live batting practice with the split-change at Driveline that winter. When he set out to design his slider in the winter of 2017–2018, he threw forty innings of live batting practice with the slider, along with more pitch-design sessions.

The other factor was that Mickey Callaway was no longer the pitching coach in Cleveland. Callaway was often against Bauer expanding and experimenting with his pitch arsenal. The relationship between pitcher and pitching coach had grown combative, fueled by differences in philosophies and approaches to pitching.

"My Overlord was not happy with it," Bauer says of Callaway. "Mickey always wanted me to shrink my arsenal. . . . Ultimately, I did what I wanted to do, but it was always with fear or expectations of backlash."

By the spring of 2018, Callaway had been hired as the manager of the Mets and replaced as pitching coach by Carl Willis, whom Bauer suspected would be less overbearing. Bauer's intention was to show up to spring training with a new, polished pitch, not a work in progress. He was always working, always throwing, maintaining his velocity. On one pulldown throw that off-season, he set a new facility record by hurling a three-ounce ball 116.9 mph, which was greeted by oohs and aahs.

In live at-bats throughout the winter, Bauer had thrown only fastballs and sliders. He knew that by limiting himself to two pitches, he was turning amateurs or minor leaguers into "fringe big leaguers" because they could rule out his other offerings. "They were teeing off on him," Boddy says. But Bauer wanted to fixate on the fastball and slider because he was trying to make them look as similar as possible for as long as possible on their paths to the plate.

After at-bats, Bauer would ask for feedback on the movement of the pitch. In this laboratory of data and cameras and pitch-tracking technology, players' opinions were still valued. The hitters told him his slider still looked too much like his curveball, not breaking laterally enough.

Bauer could have trained in Los Angeles or elsewhere. But the Driveline culture was important. The other athletes there pushed him, which was crucial for skill development. Driveline had created a culture of urgency, born of motivated (and/or desperate) athletes clawing for a way into professional or college baseball. Boddy turned away clients he didn't think fit. One day in the winter of 2016–2017, Bauer complained to Weathers about their weight-room workouts.

"You think this is fun?" said Weathers in response, while adding weights to a bar. "I'd rather be home with my wife. You're being a bitch."

The surest way to anger Bauer is to call him a bitch. He stormed out of the gym. Whenever someone called Bauer a bitch, he thought back to *Lone Survivor*, the book by former US Navy SEAL Marcus Luttrell, who suffered multiple gunshot wounds and a broken leg in a Taliban ambush in the mountains of Afghanistan. If Luttrell could survive that, Bauer could finish a workout.

When he reentered the gym, he was surprised to find Weathers taking weights off the bar.

"What are you doing?" Bauer said.

"Oh, I banged it," Weathers answered. He had quit for the day.

Recalling this incident, Bauer broke out into laughter. Weathers went home, but Bauer had been spurred to finish his workout.

By late January 2018, Boddy asked Bauer when he would expand his pitch mix. He was nearly done with his live at-bats and had still limited himself to just the two pitches. The hitters, knowing the quality of the curveball, asked, then demanded, then challenged Bauer to throw it.

"You don't want that. That's not gonna be good for anyone," Bauer said again and again.

The demands continued. "Come on! On your last day, throw all your pitches!" the hitters beseeched him. Bauer relented. "All right, all five? I'm gonna throw five innings against you guys," he said. A cheer went up.

A number of pro hitters stepped in against Bauer, including independent leaguer Don Comstock and Marlins minor leaguer Gunner Pollman. They flinched. They whiffed. They left the cage in awe. Bauer faced the minimum fifteen batters in his five fake innings. He struck out thirteen of them. Boddy watched and laughed.

"It was ridiculous, 'cause they're just not gonna be able to hit a big leaguer with five pitches," Boddy says. "The first time he threw a curveball, it was fucking like, 'oh!'"

Although a January session against low-level hitters wasn't an accurate reflection of what Bauer would face in the big leagues, it was the first hint he got of the power of his expanded arsenal, which included his new slider, his Myelin Express.

While the camera helped create a shortcut to skill acquisition, there was no substitute for deliberate practice. There's no official record of Bauer's winter workload, but he guesses that he threw more pitches that off-season than any other pitcher in professional baseball. (He did record his workload at Driveline during the 2018–2019 offseason: 8,820 throws made, and $3,000 lost in training bets against hitters.) And it was intense, focused practice.

"[Bauer] yells at himself all the time. It's terrifying and funny," Boddy says. "I'll be in [the office at Driveline], he'll just throw a pitch and be like, 'Fuck!' Like, 'What the fuck, dude? What are you talking about? Your strike percentage is good today.' . . . He's like, '[I'm] not focused.'"

Bauer confirms. "If I am not focused about everything in the moment, if you take away my training time or cause a distraction, I get super pissed off."

Bauer is an extreme example of single-sport specialization at a time when many front-office executives blame specialization for the rise in pitcher injuries. ASMI and other organizations recommend that pitchers take an extended break from throwing in the off-season. But Bauer never stops throwing. And conventional training wisdom might be wrong: March is the month with the most reported injuries that lead to Tommy John surgery, which could be because pitchers have a hard time handling the 0-to-60 stress of spring work after throwing only lightly in the winter. Sixty percent of Tommy John surgeries occur from January to May, according to researcher Jon Roegele.

The idea that "specialization is dangerous or bad" strikes Boddy as paradoxical, considering that the more a person deliberately practices a task or skill, the more adept he gets. "Kids should do lots of things, because no one knows what they want to do when they're thirteen. . . . I like it from that point of view," Boddy says. "But increasingly it made no sense from a specialization standpoint because the single largest growing sect of players in the majors [is] Dominican Republic players. All they do is play baseball. Their injury rates are not [higher]."

"People are reversing causation," he continues. "'Everyone in the big leagues played multiple sports, therefore playing multiple sports leads to being a big leaguer.' No, everyone in the big leagues played multiple sports because they're the best athletes in the world. When you're fourteen and you run like Carl Crawford, you play every sport because you fucking dominate all of them. And the coaches are greedy. Whereas by the time Trevor is thirteen or fourteen, he knows he's not going to be a pro unless he does something. He recognized that early."

Bauer learned intent and worth ethic during his youth. He didn't often play catch with his dad. Rather, he threw balls as far and hard as he could. He taught himself velocity. Now he was determined to teach himself a slider.

"You cannot name a pitcher in the big leagues, or probably from Double-A and up, who is a worse athlete than Trevor," Boddy says. "There is probably not a single person. He doesn't belong in professional baseball. And that is an unbelievable story."

Boddy can say this objectively because he's tested a wide range of professional players in his lab. He notes that Bauer has pathetic jumping and running ability. "His vertical is probably two standard deviations under a standard [pro] athlete and probably a standard deviation under an average man," Boddy said. "He can barely jump twenty inches." He has a slow arm and low testosterone. "He has a bad bod," Boddy says. "It leads people to believe that he doesn't lift weights, but that's not true. He deadlifts 540 pounds and he benches 100-pound dumbbells. It just doesn't matter because he has no testosterone so his body doesn't change."

In discussing the most recent *The Body Issue* of ESPN: *The Magazine*, someone joked with Bauer that he wouldn't have the guts to put his unaesthetic body on display for the world.

"I've been telling everyone in the clubhouse in 2019 I'm going to be in *The Body Issue*," Bauer says. "They are like, bullshit! They just laugh at me. Next year when I get a life-size picture of my ass, I will slap it [up] in the weight room so I can tell you, 'I told you so.'"

Boddy says Bauer's poor athleticism helps him in one regard: His slower arm speed places less stress on his elbow and shoulder. He can and needs to endure a great volume of work.

Bauer is "at least one standard deviation away and probably two" from a typical pro pitcher in arm speed measured in angular velocity, Boddy says, adding, "He's the most efficient 95–97 [mph] pitcher in the big leagues. He expends the least amount of arm stress to get the greatest amount of velocity."

Bauer would seem to be an embodiment of the 10,000-hour rule, living proof that anyone can become an expert if they practice the right way and practice enough. But Boddy rejects this suggestion. "No strategy matters at all in skill development unless it's your passion," he says. "If you tell someone all you have to do is ten thousand hours of work, deep practice—I think that is all correct, but we are starting very much with a symptom of the thing. And the thing is Trevor is obsessed with competing. When other people say that they want to win the Cy Young Award and think that anything short of that is a failure, they think it sounds good in the media. When he says it, he actually means it. That's the stupid shit he thinks. That's a very dumb goal to have. But because of it, he's been able to achieve some of those things, like being drafted in the first round and winning the Golden Spikes. Those were very dumb goals, too." Dumb as in unrealistic—but for Bauer, they weren't.

Bauer's example proves that everyone can get better with focused, deliberate practice. But not every pitcher can or should try to be Bauer from a throwing-volume standpoint.

"Trevor being the poster boy for 'No such thing as overuse' is something I think he fears and I fear very much," Boddy says. "He was throwing every day to the fence without his father. He threw weighted balls at a young age. I know Trevor does not think that is the right thing to do for everyone. . . . The Trevor Bauer story is the one every nerd in America who can't throw over 55 [mph] at the county fair should read. It is not the one that Zack Greinke at twelve should read, the nerds that are young that have a good arm. They should stay away from that story. . . . What Trevor's biggest weakness is, he's turned into a strength. He's not that athletically gifted, but he's nearly unbreakable when it comes to volume. That's a blessing and a curse."

Boddy adds that the idea that Bauer is some sort of eccentric genius is also off base.

"He's actually not that intelligent when it comes to analyzing stuff," Boddy says. "To me, intelligence is picking up skills quickly. He's really shitty at [that]. But he's *really* good at brute-forcing things. . . . He doesn't belong in the big leagues, but he's there because he's delusional. I wish that was the story that could go out there, but it's not that popular. It sends kids a different message rather than 'You can do anything.'" The message, Boddy suggests, is that achieving lofty ambitions requires maniacal obsession. "To me, that is true skill acquisition. He gets the most out of who he is."

Like his confounding idol Elon Musk, Bauer is obsessed with work and often expresses what seem to be far-fetched, unreachable aspirations. Musk wants to go to Mars and build a Hyperloop; Bauer wants to win three Cy Young Awards. "There are ten three-time Cy Young winners," he says, rattling off names and numbers. "Seven are in the Hall of Fame, two are still playing [Clayton Kershaw and Max Scherzer]. One is Roger Clemens [who was tarnished by a connection to steroids]. . . . If I want to win three Cy Youngs—I'm twenty-seven, but at thirty-three my window will be closing. My skill will be in decline.

"I have no idea what drives me, to be honest. I've spent ten to fifteen years trying to figure out why I want to be elite. Is it personal achievement? Is it to throw a middle finger up in everyone's face? Is it to be right? I don't know, exactly. I don't know. It all comes back to I want to be the best, period."

The clock is ticking. There is no time to waste in achieving those goals. When Bauer left Seattle in early February for the Indians' spring training facilities in Goodyear, Arizona, he had the foundation of a new slider. While he had not perfected the pitch, he felt he was close. He told reporters at the start of spring training that he thought he was as close as he had ever been to maximizing his ability. But those were just words. All that mattered was the way he would pitch.

7

THE CONDUIT

You don't take a photograph. You make it.

—ANSEL ADAMS

"He's got two pitches!" a livid-looking Chris Sale screamed in the Red Sox dugout during Game 4 of the 2018 World Series, dissing the Dodgers' starter, Rich Hill. Already on their heels after their eighteen-inning Game 3 loss to Los Angeles early that morning, the Sox had just fallen behind by four in the bottom of the sixth inning and were three innings away from losing their lead in the series.

Boston subsequently came back to tie the game on two homers and won in the ninth, setting up a series victory the next night. "Chris Sale's shouts rally Red Sox to brink of title," the Associated Press's headline said. Maybe—but they came back against the bullpen, not against Mr. Two Pitches.

What Sale shouted was true. The thirty-eight-year-old Hill threw 92 pitches in Game 4, 53 of them four-seam fastballs and 39 curveballs. Hill had no need for a third pitch. He left with a 4–0 lead after allowing one hit and three walks over 6 1/3 innings, with seven strikeouts.

Oddly enough, the man largely responsible for Hill's mastery was wearing a Red Sox uniform: Brian Bannister.

Bannister, Boston's vice president of pitching development and assistant pitching coach, watched the game unfold from the clubhouse because MLB rules limit teams to seven coaches in the dugout. "As a baseball fan I can enjoy it and hate it simultaneously," Bannister texted us right around the time that Sale was expressing his slightly less nuanced emotions nearby. "Cheer for the human being and root against the different name on the front of the jersey."

The Red Sox hired Bannister, a former major-league pitcher who retired in 2011, as a pro scout and analyst in January 2015. That August, he and Hill crossed paths. Hill, who was then thirty-five, had started the season in the bullpen for the Nationals' Triple-A affiliate, but the Nats released him in June. It was the third time a big-league team had cut him loose in a sixteen-month span; even the Red Sox, for whom he'd pitched in Triple-A and (sporadically) the majors from 2010 to 2012, had released him the previous March. So Hill sought the last refuge of the unwanted journeyman: the independent leagues. In July, he joined the Atlantic League's Long Island Ducks, making two impressive starts before the Red Sox signed him for the third time and sent him back to Triple-A Pawtucket on August 14.

On the same day, Red Sox manager John Farrell announced that he was taking a leave of absence to undergo treatment for lymphoma, which activated a coaching carousel. Triple-A pitching coach Bob Kipper was called up to the big leagues, and a lower-level coach was requisitioned to take his place. During the brief window before that replacement arrived, Bannister was dispatched to Pawtucket. He had spent his first season with the Sox scouting, submitting written recommendations for ways that the organization could improve its pitching development, and wishing he weren't so far from the field. Here was a chance for him to be hands-on and make a difference directly. He had one man in mind.

Hill, a native of Milton, Massachusetts, had already made his first start with Pawtucket on August 15. He'd held the Phillies' affiliate scoreless for 6 1/3 innings, but he hadn't dominated, walking three and striking out two. Bannister, who's a year younger than Hill, met with Hill for about an hour and a half on back-to-back days, laying out a roadmap to reinvention. "I took one of my ideas that I'd always been wanting to test out on somebody and pitched that idea to him," Bannister says. Bannister could tell from TrackMan that Hill had a potent curveball that was hard to distinguish from his high-80s to low-90s fastball. "When I pulled up his numbers, it was just incredible how talented he was with the ability to spin the ball," Bannister says. If Hill varied how he used his curve, he could throw it much more often.

Weeks earlier, Hill had been out of affiliated ball, and now he was talking to a team official who was making comparisons to Clayton Kershaw, Max Scherzer, and Sale in explaining how Hill's curve came out of his hand. Eight years, five teams, one shoulder surgery, and one elbow surgery removed from his only one-hundred-inning season in the majors, Hill was willing to listen. "He just opened my eyes up to the creative side of pitching," Hill says. "Being creative with my curveball. Changing the shape of it. That was really the first time that I had heard anything about that."

Bannister explained that Hill could vary the pitch's speed, spin, and location, throwing it higher to make it look like his fastball. Hill heard him and thought, "OK, I can throw my curveball more than what I had been told throughout my career." He dropped his two-seam fastball from his repertoire and put the new pitching plan into place. In his next four Triple-A starts, he struck out twenty-seven and walked six.

On September 8, the Red Sox made their last round of expanded-roster additions. Hill was one of them. Five days later, he made his first big-league start since July 2009. It went well: he held the Rays to one hit and no runs over seven innings, striking out ten. The next time out, he struck out ten Blue Jays, and the game after that, he struck out ten Orioles in a two-hit, complete-game shutout. Only six other pitchers all year had struck out ten batters or more in three consecutive starts, and Hill had done it in his first three starts after a six-year hiatus. He finished the season by holding the Yankees to two runs over six innings, with six more strikeouts.

Throwing curves 39 percent of the time—second-most among starters with at least twenty innings pitched on the season—Hill had taken on every other team in the AL East and emerged with a 1.55 ERA and a 34 percent strikeout rate. Among the ninety starters who threw at least ten innings between Hill's comeback and the end of the season, only four struck out more batters, and only NL Cy Young winner Jake Arrieta allowed a lower opponent batting average than his .141 or a lower WHIP (walks plus hits per inning pitched) than his 0.66. "It was one of the most amazing [four]-game runs I had ever seen in my life," Bannister told us the following year.

To that point, all of Hill's guaranteed major-league contracts combined totaled $3.9 million. Less than three months after meeting Ban-
nister, he topped that with one signature, inking a one-year $6 million
deal with the A's. The *Six Million Dollar Man* jokes were almost too easy
to make.

With the A's—and the Dodgers, who traded for him mid-season—
Hill continued to deal in 2016, producing a 2.12 ERA. That year, he
threw curves 47 *percent* of the time, the highest rate on record for
any pitcher with at least one hundred innings pitched. Despite his
age, that season earned him a three-year, $48 million deal from the
Dodgers. Repeated problems with blisters ate into his innings totals,
but among pitchers with at least four hundred innings pitched from
2015 to 2018, Hill's 29.3 percent strikeout rate ranked fifth in the majors, and his 2.98 ERA ranked sixth, between Arrieta and two-time Cy
Young winner Corey Kluber.

Even prior to his work with Hill, Bannister had believed that careers could be saved with the right type of intervention. "It always fascinated me that with a few changes or giving the guy the right mental
approach, the right physical approach, the right pitch mix, the development of a new pitch, you can completely change his projection or
his future ceiling," Bannister said in 2016. Prior to 2015, though, that
kind of conversion was only theoretical. Hill's incredible career turnaround was both a proof of concept and a galvanizing force. "He just
did something that I'd never seen before, and that got me excited,"
Bannister said. "It also was exciting because it was kind of like the
lightbulb going on, like, hey, this stuff can work."

A lot of lightbulbs went on around baseball after Hill's ice-breaking,
trend-setting run. "You see a lot of guys now, since that time, using
their breaking ball a lot more," Hill says. "It used to be . . . you were labeled as soft if you didn't throw your fastball. [Now] it's like, 'No, your
job is to get hitters out. I don't care how you do it.'"

Players are taking it further every year. In 2017, the Astros' Lance
McCullers Jr. slightly surpassed Hill's record curveball rate. From 2008
to 2017, five 100-inning pitchers threw sliders at least 40 percent of
the time; in 2018 alone, six did. One of them, Diamondbacks starter
Patrick Corbin, upped his slider use into that range at the team's rec-

ommendation, after years of getting good results with the pitch but still throwing it only about a quarter of the time. He had a career year at twenty-nine and landed a six-year, $140 million contract with the Nationals in December. "Philosophies have changed over the years," says Diamondbacks pitching strategist Dan Haren, a pitching contemporary of Bannister and Hill. "Really, it's about how many times a pitcher can throw his best pitch in a game."

This growing trend toward breaking balls is reflected in league-wide rates. In 2010, pitchers threw 75 percent more sinkers than sliders. In 2018, for the first time on record, they threw more sliders than sinkers. "To me it's a very simple concept," Bannister says. "It's harder to hit something that's traveling along a curved path than a straight path."

In 2018, batters whiffed on 36 percent of the swings they took against sliders and only 14 percent of the swings they took against sinkers. When they made contact, they produced a .263 wOBA on sliders and a .351 wOBA on sinkers. The difference persists across counts. "I think every team will push for performance in the direction of what's working," Bannister says. "It's very tough to be a sinker-baller right now." In light of the stats, that seems obvious, but the combination of Bannister and Hill helped snap pitchers out of their anti-breaking-ball bias.

It's dizzying to think, as Hill has, of how many things had to happen for his resurrection to occur. First, he had to sign with the team that had recently hired Bannister. Then Bannister had to be at Pawtucket because of Farrell's illness. Then Hill had to get called up in September, which likely only happened because Red Sox pitcher Steven Wright had suffered a concussion in August when he was hit on the back of the neck while running sprints during batting practice. And, of course, technology that could track Hill's spin had to be available, both so that Bannister could recognize his hidden potential and so other teams could be confident that his four-start success wasn't a small-sample fluke. "If we push it back maybe even [to 2013], maybe people don't look at those numbers because they're not out there," Hill says, adding, "It's giving guys chances, [compared to] before where scouts were pretty closed-minded . . . they were just like, 'What does the radar gun say?'"

There's another compelling case for promoting so-called second-ary stuff. Recent research has shown that contrary to long-held be-liefs about breaking balls inflicting the most stress on pitchers' arms, fastballs actually do the most damage. "When you see there's not a spike in injuries with guys throwing more secondary pitches—and in fact it might even be the opposite—it opens up this whole world of op-portunities that was never there before, because people were afraid," Bannister says. The unfounded bias against breaking balls, he adds, "prevented thousands of pitchers from pitching at a higher level." One wonders how many Hill-like soft tossers fell by the wayside before teams had the tools to find them and the willingness to let them work in the ways that would benefit them the most. Without those things, Hill says, "you'll never know the potential of the player."

Technology, and the right interpreter, arrived just in time to make Hill a poster boy for this period. Now Bannister and a growing number of fellow athlete-stathead hybrids are making it their mission to en-sure that no more players will have to wait until they're thirty-five to tap into their talents—or worse, never unlock them at all.

In his 2018 book *Quantitative Hitting*, investment analyst turned swing mechanic D. K. Willardson pointed out an intellectual divide that's stunted progress in player development even since the game got smart about stats. "The analytical side focused on the data has steered clear of mechanics, while the 'traditional' coaching and player-development side has steered clear of the data," he wrote. "The result is fertile and untrodden turf in the middle of the two polarized camps."[1]

In theory, the teams that tread on that turf first should derive a real advantage. "The challenge," Willardson continued, "is that there is no career path and, consequently, no available talent pool that en-compasses experience on both sides—data analysis and mechanics. It is clear, however, that value will not be maximized without those two sides thinking together." The right message existed, but the messen-gers were missing.

A farm system is essentially a school for players, and as technol-ogy and statistics suffuse the sport, even the big-league level is increasingly looking like a continuing-education course. If decades of ineffective attempts at top-down, data-driven school reform have taught educators any lesson that baseball teams can learn, it's that communication and cultural awareness are overlooked keys.

The late Seymour Sarason, Yale professor and father of the field of community psychology, unwittingly anticipated the problems impeding player development in one of his seminal studies of school reform, the 1971 book *The Culture of the School and the Problem of Change*. The conundrum, Sarason explained, is that "the agents of change from outside the school culture are too frequently ignorant of the culture in which the change is to be embedded, or if they are part of the culture, they are themselves victims of that very fact." On one side of the process, the outsiders evince a "too frequent tendency to underestimate the complexity of the school system as a social system, and how this adversely affects what one hopes to accomplish." Meanwhile, many members of the insider group "do not seek change or react enthusiastically to it." That mutual ignorance polarizes relationships. In baseball, that polarization produced the not entirely untruthful stereotypes of backward baseball men and arrogant numbers nerds who *never played the game*. The only thing the two camps had in common was that both thought they had the answers and resented interference from the other.[2]

Until very recently, most players, on the subject of stats, sounded similar in tone to 1930s ace and Hall of Famer Dizzy Dean, who said, "I hate statistics. What I got to know, I keep in my head." Nonathlete analysts had plenty to teach them. Yet in their haste to tip sacred cows, sabermetric reformers were sometimes overzealous in dismissing received wisdom.

In his 1914 manual *How to Play Baseball*, John McGraw wrote about "shaping the ball" by subtly pulling pitches toward the plate to get borderline calls, yet sabermetricians ninety years later denied pitch-framing existed and scoffed at managers who chose defense over offense at the catching position. The importance of all forms of fielding, the merits of makeup and clubhouse chemistry, the existence of the hot hand: all were staples of baseball wisdom until statheads looked askance at them. In all cases, later research—based on better data or a grudging acceptance that existing stats were too imprecise to settle every question—rescued the original concepts, at least to a certain extent. Statheads once mocked people who praised pint-sized infielder David Eckstein's "heart" and "grit," but Eckstein was a five-foot-six nineteenth-rounder who fashioned a ten-year career during which he was worth more than all but 13 of the 1,224 players selected the same year. Grit, a quality that new schoolers now see as a secret to successful practice, probably *was* why Eckstein got good.

Add drastic changes in established player performance to the list. Statheads once dismissed any drastic uptick in an established player's performance as a small-sample fluke and another reminder of Voros's law, which sabermetrician Voros McCracken laid down in 2000: "Anyone can hit just about anything in 60 at-bats."[3] In September 2014, months after the Astros undervalued J.D. Martinez, Baseball Prospectus cofounder Joe Sheehan tweeted, "Narratives about mechanics aside, J.D. Martinez is the same player he was before, plus some power. Can't be a #5 hitter in a real lineup."

Four years later, Sheehan issued a mea culpa in his newsletter. "I was, not long ago, prone to dismissing talk of how this player had tweaked his stance or his swing or his position on the rubber. . . . Now, though, I'm less certain." Sheehan acknowledged the potentially transformative power of revamped pitches and swings. "I've long been an advocate for the use of statistics in the evaluation of baseball players," he continued, "but I simply missed how this new category of information would render a lot of my priors moot."

As Sheehan's reversal revealed, the complex interplay of unseen forces at the field level can make big data seem simple by comparison. Statheads had to learn to listen too. More information, or better data, usually isn't enough to change minds because people are so attached to their beliefs that rebuttals actually make them dig in deeper—the so-called backfire effect. But MIT political scientist Adam Berinsky, who has studied the spread of misinformation, found that partisan subjects with preconceived positions believe one type of messenger to be particularly credible: the unlikely source.

Among athletes, the unlikely source is the stathead who's spent time in uniform, satisfying Sarason's condition that the ideal go-between be embedded in the community, "rendering some kind of service within the schools, requiring that in some way they become part of the school." These rare birds of baseball, fluent in front office and dipped in dugout wisdom, are "perfect conduits to get a message from high theoretical guys down to guys who are just used to grinding it out on the baseball field," San Diego Padres manager Andy Green said in 2017. "Unless that message gets translated where a guy speaks both languages, it usually ends up falling on deaf ears. It can be the perfect game plan laid out by the front office, but if it doesn't run through one of those conduits, it tends to, one, not be understood, or two, not be implemented at all or maybe even spurned altogether."[4]

When Hill heard he'd been approaching pitching wrong, it mattered to him that the message came from someone who had walked in his cleats. For the Red Sox, signing Hill was just a prelude to the really smart part. "The effects on contracts and free-agent signings are a very small part of what makes a new-school front office smart," says Mike Fast. "It's the [conduit] stuff that's huge. And the technologies that undergird that work."

The last mile is a term used by engineers to describe the disproportionate difficulty of delivering network services—broadband Internet, for instance—to an end user. It's relatively easy to build a network that travels three thousand miles from coast to coast, but the final leg, into houses and offices, is where bottlenecks occur. Baseball's last mile is the divide between the front office and the dugout, which stops stats from flowing to the people who can put them to use. Bannister became a conduit who could cross that divide in 2015, but he began preparing for the role long before baseball knew it needed him.

Bannister belongs to a family of pitchers. His father, Floyd, was the first-overall pick in the 1976 draft and pitched for fifteen years in the majors. Floyd's brother-in-law was a second-round pick a year earlier and topped out at Triple-A. Brian is the eldest of three brothers, one of whom pitched at Stanford and the other of whom, like Brian, was drafted out of USC, although he never advanced beyond Rookie ball. They grew up in Scottsdale, where Floyd settled after attending Arizona State.

Floyd's career lasted until Brian was eleven, and he pitched with a lot of legends who succeeded in distinct ways: Tom Seaver, celebrated for his perfect mechanics and pinpoint command; Steve Carlton, renowned for his unorthodox training routines and devastating slider; Gaylord Perry, practitioner of the spitball; Nolan Ryan, pure power personified. Brian asked questions and absorbed baseball knowledge. He wanted to know why pitches moved and what made each pitcher's delivery different.

Although Floyd lasted a long time in the league, his career park-adjusted ERA was exactly average, which was seen as underwhelming for a first-overall pick. Perhaps people overestimated the predictability of prospects: Floyd's 26.6 career WAR tops the 22.3 average for first picks from 1965 to 2003. But he was known for his fastball and urged to "establish it" by most of his pitching coaches, and now he wishes he'd made more use of his above-average breaking balls. "I should have thrown a lot more [curveballs], and I probably would have had a much more successful career," he says.

Floyd, who grew up working on cars, liked to design things in his head and bring them into being with his hands. Brian inherited his father's mechanical mind. "He liked to create things," Floyd says. "He would spend hours in the playroom working on Legos or Lincoln Logs or Construx. It seemed like his goal a lot of times was to use up every piece. It was amazing what he would create. He would sit there for hours." Later, he graduated to SimCity.

When Brian was about ten, Floyd bought a new piece of software: Photoshop. Brian became enthralled. He could faithfully sketch what he saw, and he was quick with numbers; he missed only one math question on his SAT. Eventually, he gravitated to photography, which like pitching allowed him to fuse his artistic and scientific sides.

In 2002, a year before Brian graduated from USC, he proposed that he and his father start a photography studio in a building Floyd had bought as an investment. Floyd labored to turn the space into a nine-thousand-square-foot professional facility, Loft 19, which he still operates in Brian's absence, renting out equipment and doing photoshoots and video shoots. "When we built the studio, [Brian] would sit out there on the computer and just study different photographers that he liked, and he would get online and see exactly how they set up their lighting," Floyd says.

Brian, mostly serious, says, "Everything I learned about pitching development, I learned from Ansel Adams." He likens his process to Adams's zone system, a technique for ensuring optimal film exposure and development that Adams explained in his second book, *The Negative* (1948). "What the zone system attempted to do was understand the physical limitations of the chemicals in a negative piece of film and then, knowing those limitations, be able to, essentially, optimize them or cheat them in order to create a better image," Bannister says. Adams, Bannister says, would visualize his ideal image of a scene from, say, Yosemite National Park. Knowing the specifications of his film and camera and the physical properties of light, the photographer could calculate the perfect settings for a certain moment, given the tools he was working with.

"I believe coaching baseball players is the same thing," Bannister says. "Half of it's art, it's experience, it's creativity, and then half of it is just knowing the pure science and knowing the data you're working with and being able to manipulate it in the direction that will benefit the player the most." When Bannister works with a pitcher, he visualizes him as the perfect form of himself, with optimal mechanics and an optimal pitch. He understands the limitations imposed by the physics of the body and the baseball, and he tries to work around them by tweaking an arm slot or wrist angle or grip to get to the goal. Adams seeking the most striking shot of Yosemite, Bannister says, was "no different [from] us trying to create perfect baseball players, or at least as close to perfect as possible."

Bannister was far from a perfect pitcher. His face looks like his father's, and at six foot two, 202 pounds, he boasts a slightly bigger build. But unlike the left-handed Floyd, a flamethrower who twice led his league in strikeout rate, the right-handed Brian threw a four-seamer that averaged less than 90 mph. Drafted by the Mets in the seventh round in 2003, it took him seventy-four minor-league games to make the majors, compared to Floyd's seven. Brian wasn't a top prospect, and he pitched only thirty-six innings for the Mets as a twenty-five-year-old rookie in 2006 before being traded to the Royals.

In 2007, Bannister made the Mets look silly, making twenty-seven starts, posting a 3.87 ERA, and finishing third in AL Rookie of the Year voting—one spot higher than Floyd finished in 1977. But Bannister was too statistically savvy to believe it would last. While with the Mets, Bannister had been introduced to sabermetrics by pitching coach Rick Peterson, and he'd immersed himself in the stats with the same single-minded intensity he'd brought to Lincoln Logs, Photoshop, and Ansel Adams.

Before Bannister, the closest the statistical community had come to influencing a major-league pitcher's performance was what came to be called the "Félix Incident." In June 2007, future FanGraphs managing editor and Padres analyst Dave Cameron—then a full-time corporate cost analyst for Hanes and a part-time blogger for the Mariners site U.S.S. Mariner—posted "An Open Letter to Rafael Chaves," the Mariners' pitching coach. Cameron observed that the Mariners' ultratalented but mercurial ace-in-waiting, Félix Hernández, was far too fastball-reliant early in games, and he pleaded with Chaves to make him mix it up. Soon after, a fan in the stands handed a printout of the post to Chaves. Chaves, who claimed that he'd already been trying to persuade Hernández to vary his pitch selection, relayed the post to the pitcher to prove that his pattern was well known. "Chaves gave me a report," Hernández said in early July, after his second consecutive strong start. "On the Internet, they say when I throw a lot of fastballs in the first inning, they score a lot of runs. I tried to mix all my pitches in the first inning."

The Félix Incident was a milestone moment, but it was also an isolated event in an era when teams still banned bloggers from the press box, to say nothing of inviting them into the decision-making process. Asked if he'd read the Internet more often, Hernández laughed and said no. Bannister had a fraction of Félix's talent, but the blogosphere couldn't afford to be picky with its champions. He established himself as an Internet hero by becoming the first big leaguer to out himself as a sabermetrician and profess his devotion to PITCHf/x data. Even then, he was thinking like a conduit, saying, "The truth is coming out that [outsiders] have some interesting things to say. If I can bridge that gap a little bit, I'm happy to do that."

The irony of Bannister being a statistical trailblazer was twofold. First, Bannister played for a defiantly old-school team led by a scouting-centric GM, Dayton Moore. Second, Bannister was one of the pitchers who looked far worse via advanced statistics than he did via traditional ones. The best pitchers decrease their dependence on defense and luck by controlling the "three true outcomes": strikeouts, walks, and home runs. Bannister didn't do that: among the ninety-four pitchers with at least 150 innings pitched in 2007, his strikeout rate ranked eighth-lowest. He'd been bailed out by the third-lowest BABIP (batting average on balls in play), which at .261 was more than forty points below the AL average. He knew that number was bound to climb, taking his ERA with it.

To try to forestall the coming correction, he sought more strikeouts in 2008, and he did increase his strikeout rate slightly. But just as anticipated, his BABIP rose to .308, and his high fly-ball rate came back to bite him as more of his flies left the park. Bannister's underlying performance was almost the same as it had been the year before, but his ERA inflated to an untenable 5.76.

Bannister exhibited a post-Moneyball mindset in an era when his own employer was still resisting Moneyball. "Most guys are using [stats] for the purpose of projection," he told the *Seattle Times*. "I'm using them for the purpose of changing the future projections. I want to find my weaknesses and find which stats will help me do that, and change my pitching style accordingly."[5]

Bannister's weakness was an inability to miss bats. Having tried and failed to fix that, he steered into the skid. If he had to allow contact, he'd try to make it *weaker* contact, getting grounders and keeping the ball in the park. PITCHf/x data told Bannister that his four-seamer was holding him back, so entering 2009, he went away from the four-seamer in favor of his cut fastball, a more grounder-oriented pitch whose movement resembles a cross between a slider and a sinker. Compared to 2008, Bannister increased his cutter rate by 30 percentage points, throwing it almost half the time. He also designed a power changeup, mimicking the grip of right-hander James Shields to give him greater sink.

Bannister's self-directed reconstruction worked remarkably well. He started the 2009 season in Triple-A, but he soon made it back to the majors and looked like a new man. His ground-ball rate increased by 12 percentage points, a single-year spike surpassed—among pitchers from 2002 to 2018 with at least 150 innings thrown in back-to-back seasons—only by Johan Santana in his 2004 Cy Young year. Getting grounders didn't make Bannister a Cy Young contender, but it did make him a major-league pitcher again. He lowered his ERA to 4.73, and his FIP (fielding independent pitching) fell to a career-low 4.14.

The comeback could have been even better. Through his first twenty starts, Bannister sported a 3.59 ERA, a 4.00 FIP, and an even higher ground-ball rate. But just as it seemed that Bannister had found a way to make himself as perfect as possible, a new imperfection appeared. In the twentieth outing, a 117-pitch, seven-inning shutout in Tampa Bay on August 2, Bannister partially tore his rotator cuff. He tried to pitch through the injury, making six more starts, but he got shelled, allowing thirty-four runs in thirty-one innings before the Royals mercifully shut him down in early September. The following season wasn't much of an improvement; Bannister's smarts couldn't help him if his arm wouldn't cooperate, and his ERA ballooned to 6.34. He planned to pitch in Japan in 2011, but he and his wife were trying to have a second child, and in the aftermath of the Tōhoku earthquake and tsunami, they thought it safer to stay home. Bannister had just turned thirty, but his pitching career was complete.

In a November 2011 interview at FanGraphs, Bannister's Kansas City pitching coach, Bob McClure, suggested that Bannister had committed a cardinal sin of old-school baseball: overthinking things. "Banny got a little overboard and tried to do more than he was capable of doing," McClure said, adding, "He got into things like how the ball was turning, and to me, it's not that complicated." McClure, a pitching contemporary of Floyd's, was a baseball lifer who harbored some reservations about the role of data; elsewhere in the interview, he spouted the age-old advice that had held back Hill: "Establish your fastball, if you can, to as many hitters as you can." McClure became Boston's (and Hill's) pitching coach the next year but was fired in August, as the last-place team's pitching staff posted the worst park-adjusted FIP in franchise history.

Bannister, who thought he had made the most of modest abilities that were further reduced by his injury, was stung by the criticism. "I felt like it was a little unfair," Bannister says. Trey Hillman, Bannister's manager from 2008 to 2010, says that like McClure, "I thought at the time that he was a little too analytical in his approach." But Hillman, who has since worked for the analytically advanced Dodgers, Yankees, and Astros, among other teams, has realized that Bannister was "way ahead of the curve." Bannister is still close to McClure, who's since grown more receptive to the new tools at players' disposal, but back then, Bannister says, "it was so new, and he'd been in the game so long, that when he connected the dots, it felt to him like I had let this information get in the way of my performance." That "pushback moment," as Bannister calls it, contributed to his decision to temporarily withdraw from the sport. Baseball wasn't ready to change.

To play a part in pushing it forward, Bannister needed to know more. When he was with the Royals, Bannister had an accomplice in his pitching explorations: Zack Greinke. Like Bannister, Greinke saw pitching as a science experiment. In 2007, Bannister's first season in Kansas City, Greinke recorded a 5.71 ERA through his first seven starts and was banished to the bullpen. There, Bannister says, Greinke learned that although he had great command, he didn't need to nibble; he could get creative and blow batters way. At the end of the season, Greinke returned to the rotation for seven more starts and posted a 1.85 ERA, launching the peak of a Hall of Fame–caliber career.

"We used to try to come up with the nastiest sequences Zack could throw," Bannister says. One favorite from 2009 was the slowest curve Greinke could throw for a strike—something in the 60s—followed by an upper-90s fastball up and in to a righty, tunneled out of the same slot and often fouled off, and then a coup de grâce 90 mph slider down and away. "That three-pitch sequence alone took him to a Cy Young Award that year," Bannister says. Greinke was worth 10.4 WAR in 2009, the highest pitcher total in the fifteen years following Randy Johnson's fourth consecutive Cy in 2002. When he won the award himself, Greinke told the New York Times, "I'm also a follower, since

Brian Bannister's on our team, of sabermetric stuff and going into de-tails of stats about what you can control," adding, "That's pretty much how I pitch, to try to keep my FIP as low as possible."[6]

Unlike Bannister, Greinke was a virtuoso who threw five pitches with stuff to spare. Not only could Greinke easily outstrip Bannister's loftiest radar readings, but when he and Bannister challenged each other to see who could throw the slowest curve for a strike, Greinke won that competition too. In 2009, he threw pitches at every mile-per-hour increment from 60 to 100. He and Bannister were testing the limits, consulting their PITCHf/x archives to see what worked. "It was getting into the concept of sequencing, of tunneling, maximum contrast between pitches, throwing pitches to the parts of the zone where they moved the most," Bannister says. "It was really fun to see somebody that was one of the best pitchers in the world really start to get into the forefront of information and leverage some of those concepts."

Serving as Greinke's sabermetric spirit guide helped Bannister em-brace his calling as a conduit. "I realized that my future was not about me ever competing for a Cy Young Award or being an All-Star . . . but about taking that information, studying it more than anybody, and using it to help the best players in the world become even better," he says. "Or to identify, in a predictive way, inefficiencies in other players where they're drastically underperforming their ceiling and helping them understand why they're underperforming."

Bannister's breakthroughs are a testament to one constant in the story of player development: human beings' ability to be wrong about things they think they understand. During Bannister's career, he'd been fascinated by pitchers who succeeded despite underwhelming stuff—like his 2006 teammate Tom Glavine, an All-Star at age forty with an 85 mph fastball—or underperformed despite seemingly over-powering stuff. The more he watched and listened, the more he real-ized that "nobody really knew what created pitch quality." "I thought to myself, are we throwing all of our pitches wrong?" Bannister says. "Have all of our pitches been taught incorrectly for decades? Is there an optimal way to throw every pitch? How close are we, right now, to that optimal way?"

For the next three years, Bannister spent eight to ten hours a day browsing the public PITCHf/x site Brooks Baseball, "recreating from the ground up what I believed good pitchers did." If he could isolate their attributes, he could recreate them in others, just as he'd reproduced 3-D figures from Photoshop. One pattern he picked up on was pitchers' tendency to throw their fastballs in the wrong locations. With two strikes, they would almost invariably aim down and away, which made sense in a pre-pitch-tracking era, when umpires could be coaxed to allow a little leeway at the edge of the zone. As umps began to get graded based on their adherence to the zones specified by tracking systems, though, pitchers stopped getting strike calls on balls that batters couldn't hit. At the same time, technology revealed how high-spin fastballs, which appear to rise, could coax batters to whiff when elevated.

"That was a revolutionary thing for me, in that we were indoctrinated to throw it down and away," Bannister says, adding, "You see so many pitchers throw their fastballs to locations where it continues to underperform, maybe because of tradition, or outdated philosophies, or just a lack of knowledge of what the data says."

Unlike Trevor Bauer and Kyle Boddy, Bannister isn't brash; he doesn't take Twitter potshots or call out coaches who don't see things the same way. "My goal was always to be the most coachable guy on the team," he says. Yet his studies drew him to the same conclusion: baseball was beset by beliefs that didn't stand up to scrutiny in the more illuminating light of the post-PITCHf/x era. Right-handers have to throw from the third-base side of the rubber to maximize deception; pitchers should come to a balance point during their deliveries; changeups must be at least 10 mph slower than fastballs; pitchers need to pitch on downhill planes. "I've pretty much debunked all of those pitching concepts that are just rehashed over and over again to every pitching prospect that comes along," Bannister says. "And I disagree with almost all of them completely. . . . I think those things, as innocent as they seem, have destroyed more pitchers' careers over the years than anything else."

Bannister tentatively planned to found a Driveline-like independent facility where he could instill the new principles of pitch quality in impressionable pitching minds. In a 2014 interview, he described his vision as "Moneyball but on the player side," a means of "promoting stats instead of steroids." Unexpectedly, though, MLB beckoned: a few years after his last professional pitch, at least one team was ready to receive his ideas.

In 2013, Brooks Baseball proprietor Dan Brooks had invited Bannister to speak at Saber Seminar, where he delivered a prescient presentation on sabermetrics on the field. In 2014, Bannister returned to conduct a live, outdoor demo of a TrackMan system. Among the onlookers was Red Sox senior analyst Tom Tippett, who approached Bannister and asked if he'd be interested in interviewing for a vacant assistant farm director role.

Bannister hadn't gone to Boston with the intention of trying for a team job, but Fenway was in the neighborhood. A day later, he and Tippett walked to the club's historic home and sat in the seats on top of the Green Monster, where Bannister interviewed with assistant GM Mike Hazen. Over the course of the conversation, it became clear that assistant farm director wasn't the right role for Bannister, whose passion was pitching-centric and who wanted to work closely with players. "I don't think they quite knew what to do with me," Bannister says. He didn't fit the profile for any preexisting position, so they agreed to get together and feel their way forward. The player-stathead was a new breed, but the Red Sox knew they wanted one.

Adams wrote that "to photograph truthfully and effectively is to see beneath the surfaces and record the qualities of nature and humanity which live or are latent in all things." Replace "photograph" with "develop pitchers," and you've described Bannister's job with Boston: perceiving what pitchers potentially could do and helping them do it. The day after Hill made it back to Boston in 2015, Bannister was promoted to director of pitching analysis and development. The next July, he joined the major-league staff as an assistant pitching coach; in November, he was elevated again to vice president of pitching development, while retaining his role as assistant pitching coach.

"Most guys have the potential to pitch in the big leagues," Bannister says. "You just have to give them the right ingredients." Not everyone wants them. Selling a player on a particular approach, Bannister says, is "almost like an ad agency pitching a company on a campaign." When Bannister approaches a player or coach for the first time with an analytical recommendation, he often encounters one of four reactions. Some guys get defensive, because by suggesting a way in which they could do something differently, Bannister is implicitly critiquing the way they work now. Some get scared, hesitant to tamper with whatever propelled them to pro ball. Some get angry and rant about technology ruining the game. And some buy in too much, developing such an insatiable appetite for information that even Bannister thinks they might be in too deep to perform freely. "It's very rare to just get a casual, normal reaction where they process what you're telling them, don't have an emotional reaction, see the upside of it, [and] they're willing to try it out," he says.

Bannister makes a medical analogy to describe how the front office and field staff function. The analysts upstairs are the radiologists who dissect the data and relay it to the surgeons (coaches), who operate on the patients (players). Bannister, who's inhabited all three roles, likens altering players without using technology to performing surgery without ordering an MRI.

To stick with the surgical theme: years passed between Joseph Lister's nineteenth-century discoveries about the infection-fighting effects of sterile surgery and the advent of universal, routine handwashing in the operating room. In the time it took for Lister's ideas to be adopted, lives were needlessly lost. Baseball decisions aren't life or death, but teams are still trying to reduce that delay. In the absence of better information, experience and a history of trial and error were competitive advantages. Now they can be constraints, unless they're accompanied by a healthy humility. "People upstairs are learning faster than you can ever learn, and so you can't fight it," Bannister says. "You have to be the conduit."

Coaches who can stomach that status get something back in the bargain: they don't have to worry that doing their jobs will cost them their jobs. As a former No. 1 pick, Floyd knows better than most that tampering with top prospects has historically been a career-jeopardizing proposition. "Most pitching coaches are fearful that if

they tweak anything and they hurt you or make you even less effective, then all the eyeballs come looking at them," he says. "I saw that
a lot." The consequence of cover-your-ass coaching was that players
with the most talent received the least instruction. Today, the wisdom
of any tweak a coach wants to make can be tested and backed by data.
That doesn't guarantee the tweak will work, but it ensures the coach
won't be crucified if something goes south.

Naturally, technology has changed the type of tweaks that teams
tend to make. In the 2011 interview where he verbally brushed back
Bannister, McClure said, "You don't have to have great stuff in order to
be a good pitcher. You just need good command and good feel." Bannister's research has led him toward a different emphasis. "I'd rather
have a pitcher with a 70 or 80 [pitch on the 20–80 scouting scale] that
really has no idea where it's going than a pitcher with a 50 pitch that
can throw it exactly where he wants to every time," he says. "I'll always err on the side of pitch quality."

A tweak as subtle as reorienting a slider's spin axis by 15 percent
may translate to more efficient movement, more whiffs, and the difference between foul after foul and a true putaway pitch that can replace a weaker weapon. "It's just almost like Christmas when you see
a guy with all the right physical characteristics to throw a 70 or 80
pitch, and then you realize he's gripping the ball wrong, and you're
just like, yes!" Bannister says. "That's the final puzzle piece, that he
doesn't know that that's making his pitch a 50 or a 60 instead of a 70
or 80."

There's an art to that insight, but it's nothing ineffable. "Pitching is
not mysterious, it's just physics," Bannister says. "[We're] trying to get
away from, 'This pitcher has this quality that we can't teach anybody
else.' . . . It's not magic. He's just doing something better than everybody else." Once a team deciphers that "something" and identifies the
components of pitch quality, it can automate much of the process of
finding players who are ripe for repackaging. A program combining
machine learning and basic artificial intelligence can comb through
data on mechanics and pitch characteristics and flag anything that
seems suboptimal: a great pitch that's barely being thrown, or an underperforming pitch with high spin but poor spin efficiency, which

Bannister compares to a car with a powerful engine but bald tires. Then the pit crew of coaches and communicators can come in and devise the best strategy for fixing the flaw.

In his current role, Bannister says, "99 percent of the work I do is standing out in the outfield during batting practice or during a bullpen session, holding my phone and showing it to a pitcher, showing him what the data says and then telling him why I think he should make an adjustment and backing it up on the spot." Before Bannister, no one on the Red Sox staff needed to deploy data that way. Boston's old internal information repository dated back to before the iPhone-iPad era, and it wouldn't work on mobile devices. After joining the Red Sox, Bannister learned SQL (Structured Query Language)—a programming language that's become a prerequisite for front-office work—to retrieve information from the database more quickly, but the queries he created weren't powerful enough for his purposes.

Enter a new application called PEDRO (pitching, evaluation, development, research, and optimization), a nod to Red Sox legend and onetime Bannister teammate Pedro Martínez. PEDRO, which was built by R&D analyst Spencer Bingol, a former baseball blogger hired by Bannister, functions as a "sandbox of ideas on the player-development and scouting side." It also enables Bannister to do with one click what once would have taken him hours or days, applying his custom pitcher evaluations on a "mass scale" and allowing him to exchange computer time for face time with players.

Much of that time also takes place in the company of cameras. Bannister's affinity for photography isn't just a rich source of analogies. It's also a skill he draws on daily as he works with a suite of optical tools that includes Edgertronic, Rapsodo, and KinaTrax, a six-figure markerless, long-distance motion-capture system whose eight to sixteen high-speed cameras mounted in the stands from the first-base side to the third-base side record the movements of twenty-five joints on athletes' bodies and enable its clients (including four MLB teams in 2018) to dissect the mechanics of players who appear in their parks.

Bannister has used that technology to satisfy some lingering curiosity about his own career. Although he didn't throw hard, he knew there was more to his fastball's ineffectiveness than velocity alone. After diagnosing himself the same way he diagnoses new pitchers, the mystery was solved: his fastball suffered from low spin efficiency. "Knowing what I know now, I would never have pitched the way I did," he says. Instead of compensating with command and his cutter, the only measures he could take at the time, he "would have completely redesigned my biomechanics and how my arm worked."

Bannister isn't crying over spilt spin efficiency. "You only get one short career, and we just didn't have the data available," he says. The latest technology arrived too late to help him, but not too late for him to help others.

During games, Bannister typically sits in the clubhouse, consulting Statcast to monitor pitch selection, spin, and speed changes that might indicate injuries. If a pitcher encounters command problems, Bannister checks KinaTrax for mechanical misalignments, and when other issues arise, pitchers (or pitching coach Dana LeVangie) walk through the tunnel to ask for advice. But much of the magic occurs before games, when Bannister turns the outfield or the bullpen into an interactive pitching lab, setting up cameras and tracking devices and inviting pitchers to ask each other questions, share information, and experiment in a more focused way than they can while playing catch casually. "I've found that kind of coffee-shop environment builds a lot of culture, because you get pitchers talking about their craft more openly," he says, adding, "There's all kinds of little miracles that happen with guys that pump their game up a little bit."

One of the most obvious outward manifestations of Bannister's influence is the rate at which the Red Sox throw their four-seamers in the upper third of the zone or above. Shortly after bringing Bannister on, the Sox became the kings of the elevated four-seamer. "It was a fun way to take an analytical concept and exploit it and surprise teams," he says.

After a twentieth-place showing in park-adjusted ERA in 2015, Boston's MLB ranks climbed to fifth, then third, then second from 2016 to 2018. But any advantage the Sox derive from their onslaught of high heat won't last long. Bannister believes Boston is about two

PERCENT OF FOUR-SEAMERS THROWN HIGH, 2015–2018

Year	MLB	Red Sox	MLB Rank
2015	40.0	39.4	16
2016	39.9	48.6	2
2017	45.3	59.1	1
2018	45.9	59.1	1

years ahead of public awareness on analytical topics, but no team ever builds a big lead on its most progressive rivals. Tactics that work well soon inspire copycats, and teams that get lapped by the field resort to a policy of "If you can't beat 'em, hire 'em." In late 2016, the once defiantly traditional Diamondbacks hired Hazen as their new GM; Hazen, in turn, brought Sox executive Amiel Sawdaye with him as an assistant GM and also hired Boston bench coach Torey Lovullo as Arizona's manager. Not long after, a newly slider-reliant Corbin became the club's ace.

To cope with that cutthroat environment, Bannister takes a cue from the stock market, which he watches closely. "I can't beat the league long term, but if I find an idea, I can beat it in the short term, and that's all I'm looking to do," he says. By the time a team could test a good, data-driven idea at one affiliate or with a small group of minor-league pitchers, assess the results, and get the green light from leadership, the advantage would have dissipated. Bannister believes it's better to employ people who'll go rogue but not reckless, Jack Bauers of baseball-skill acquisition who can cut the red tape, take ideas directly to the big leaguers who are most likely to benefit, monitor the effects, and expand the approach to the rest of the roster as confidence in its efficacy increases.

The second he thinks he's beaten other teams to a developmental tactic, the clock starts counting down to the day it slips away. "You always have to come up with the next thing, and then it's like, 'Aw, we could have been way ahead of everybody if we just did this last year, but I didn't think about it that way.' It's a never-ending cycle. The rabbit hole goes very deep."

Boston's conduit count is now up to two. While Bannister travels with the big club, one of his past pitching opponents, Dave Bush, serves as his counterpart in the minor leagues. The more modern development becomes a way of big-league life, the more minor leaguers want to mimic it. "They want to look like a big leaguer, they want to act like a big leaguer," Bush says. "They're gonna want to use data like a big leaguer too." Especially if the people telling them to have been big leaguers themselves.

Given Bannister's concerns about the league catching up, it's not surprising that other clubs have hurried to hire their own conduits. At least eight non-Boston teams now employ cerebral, recently retired players in positions that task them with funneling information back and forth between the front office and the field. With the exception of Haren, who was one of the best pitchers in baseball for a few years in his twenties, there are no former all-stars in the group. Most of the hitters had short careers as part-time players, and most of the pitchers threw fastballs that sat below 90 mph: eventually even Haren morphed into a homer-prone finesse pitcher in his thirties and now tweets from the handle @ithrow88. To a man, they all had to *think* about what they were doing rather than relying on pure power and speed. "There's definitely a class of players that ha[s] to work very hard and be very good at other parts of their game in order to stick around," Bush says. "And I'm not surprised that those are the kind of guys that are gravitating toward this type of job."

It also helps that, Haren and the Rangers' Brandon McCarthy aside, none of the players made bank by big-league standards, which makes them more willing to keep working. "I'm sure a lot of it is correlated to what your bank account looks like," says former outfielder Sam Fuld, whose account was boosted by about $7 million over an eight-year MLB career that ended in 2015. Fuld joined the Phillies in 2018 as major-league player information coordinator, a nebulous label for a broad role. "I'm trying to figure out as simple a question as, am I a coach or a front-office member?" he told us in May. The answer is obviously "both." Some days Fuld spends a few hours upstairs and then changes into uniform like Clark Kent and dashes down to the field. On different days, it's the other way around.

When Fuld was five, his father gave him *The Complete Handbook of Baseball*, an annual tome stuffed with stat lines that he studied obsessively. After majoring in economics at Stanford and being drafted by the Cubs in the tenth round in 2004, he discovered *Moneyball* in 2005, his first professional season. "That was when I got so much confirmation of these things that I had thought about," he says. "It felt really comfortable and cool to know that there were other people out there in the world that thought like that."

As a former fringe player who had to scrap for roster spots, Fuld understands the thought process of a middling major leaguer who's afraid to jeopardize a big-league gig by making a change that could help him in the long run. "'I'm making seven figures. I don't want to make $50,000 at Triple-A next year.' How can you blame a guy?" he says. One of a conduit's duties is trying to coax players past that sticking point. In spring training and at the All-Star break, Fuld joins manager Gabe Kapler, GM Matt Klentak, and other coaches and front-office members in individual, data-driven meetings with every player, designed to reinforce what's working well and offer concrete goals for improvement. "It's almost emotional support, knowing there's somebody there to explain things to you," he says. Over the 2018–19 offseason, the Phillies hired two more recently retired players, Ed Lucas and Rob Segedin, as player information assistants for the minor leagues.

Kapler, a conduit himself, is a former outfielder and farm director. Exposure to so many aspects of progressive development makes conduits sought-after manager material. Gone are the days when much of the minor-league system was outside the skipper's purview; a modern manager is expected to be plugged into player development. "When I got called up [by the Cubs], [Manager] Lou Piniella had no idea who I was," Fuld recalls. "He was like, 'Can you play left field?' [I thought], 'Sure, but why don't you know this?'" In late 2018, Fuld interviewed for the Blue Jays managerial job and reportedly impressed, but out of satisfaction with his current role and a reluctance to relocate his family, he withdrew from the running.

Advanced development, and its conduit accomplices, are even starting to spread overseas. In Nippon Professional Baseball, Japan's major leagues and the second-highest-level league in the world, conduits have come to the Tohoku Rakuten Golden Eagles. Rakuten was the first NPB team to develop its own internal database, installed TrackMan in 2014, tested a Statcast-like system in 2018, and has acted aggressively in enlarging its strategy office to ten members. One of those members is Norihito Kaneto, a lefty reliever who retired in 2017 after a ten-year career, the last half of which he spent with the Eagles.

Kaneto wasn't stat-savvy as a player, but since he joined the strategy office, he says (with director of team strategy Shingo Murata acting as interpreter), "my perspective has changed 180 degrees." Murata adds, "He regrets that he didn't really use [data] before. But now he doesn't want the younger guys to make the same mistakes. He wants to let them know that there are all kinds of resources available to them. I call him the sales guy of the strategy office."

In NPB, player development may be even more vital than it is in the majors. Players don't reach free agency until after their eighth year in the twelve-team league, which restricts player movement, and organizations control far few players. Aside from several draft picks per year and some shuffling of each club's complement of (at most) four foreign players, rosters are mostly static, so teams have to enhance what they have.

Japanese culture's hierarchical relationship between *senpai* (elders) and *kōhai* (junior colleagues) promotes deference to seniority, which makes it harder for young players to buck tradition. "Whatever coaches say is pretty absolute," Murata explains. It's crucial, then, that some of Rakuten's coaches are saying the same things as Murata. It's not just Kaneto, who's insisted that players meet with Murata personally in the locker room, but also Tatsuya Shiokawa, a former Eagles infielder who retired in 2011 and worked in the strategy office before returning to the clubhouse as a strategy/infield coach. Twenty-eight-year-old Eagles ace Takahiro Norimoto, who led Pacific League pitchers in WAR in 2018, was the first player to meet with the analytics team and adopt TrackMan as a tool to experiment with his pitches. "His goal is to throw one pitch that confounds us in each game," Murata says. Eagles closer Frank Herrmann, a former major leaguer who gained an appreciation for the finer points of player development while in the Indians' system, says the Eagles "have a blueprint" and are "taking the proper steps." He credits Murata with helping him trust his slider, which he threw almost five times as often in his second season abroad as he did as an NPB rookie.

Dr. Tsutomu Jinji, a biomechanics expert who worked for Rakuten, left the team in 2016 to join a company called Next Base, the Driveline of Japan. Founded in 2014 by IT executive and former varsity player Shinichi Nakao, Next Base offers a web application called BACS (Baseball Analytics and Coaching System) that recommends adjustments based on TrackMan data. The company also conducts motion analysis, imaging almost 70 pro pitchers so far. Jinji, who's now Next Base's director, says the company's philosophy is that "tracking data is useful for the development of players, so the players themselves should use it." Although Jinji acknowledges that few NPB players do, he's worked closely with one of Japan's top pitchers, Yusei Kikuchi. Kikuchi, a Seibu Lions starter who signed with the Mariners after the 2018 season, sought Next Base's help with pitch design, pitch selection, and tunneling in preparation for his move to MLB.

What Willardson wrote about there being no talent pool with experience that spans stats and mechanics is growing less true all the time. Bannister started a virtuous circle: a few stathead players became conduits, who are minting many more stathead players, some of whom will turn into conduits when their playing days are done. As conduits and data-driven coaches become expected parts of the player-development process, the days of having to persuade players to accept stats will come to a close.

"Each new wave of players is more open to it than in the past," Bush says. And the guys who are against it? "Honestly," he says, "they're weeding themselves out."

8

PERFECT PITCH

What's a perfectionist? Someone who puts the responsibility of
mastering the task at hand ahead of all social considerations,
who would rather be right than liked.

—**MALCOLM GLADWELL,** *Revisionist History*

The sun rose above the Superstition Mountains to the east on a quiet
morning in Goodyear, Arizona. Spring training days start early, with
players arriving at complexes before 7 a.m. As the hour grew later, the
quiet was interrupted by the thwacks of baseballs meeting gloves as
pitchers tossed. In recent years, that age-old sound had been joined
by the more resounding one of weighted balls thumping against pads
hung from the chain-link fences around the backfields. And on this
particular morning, Goodyear was also less tranquil because Trevor
Bauer was pissed off.

Bauer's elevated voice bounced off the raised ceilings of the spa-
cious modern clubhouse. He wanted to know what teammate Mike
Clevinger had done with his weighted balls, which Bauer had loaned
him. Clevinger explained he had forgotten to return them to Bauer's
locker. Bauer condemned Clevinger for getting in the way of his routine. He forbade him to use his equipment again. Some nearby teammates were laughing, amused by Bauer's outrage.

"He was upset about me messing with his routine, blah, blah,
blah," Clevinger says. "We had a pretty good disagreement. I had
choice words I shared with him as well. We made up. . . . We are like
brothers. I get mad at my brother and tell him to fuck off all the time.
It's no different with [Bauer]."

Clevinger is one of those closest to Bauer in the Cleveland clubhouse. The two can often be seen during games leaning on the dugout

railing, talking side by side. Yet Clevinger doesn't dispute that Bauer can be demanding and difficult.

"He is. That's just him. It's just learning to know him. . . . He's vocal about his difficulties, as some might say. He's very up front about it," Clevinger says. "I appreciate the honesty even if I think you're a dick or a piece of shit. If you're honest, I appreciate that."

The Indians' front office knew that working with Bauer could be challenging.

In the February after the infamous drone accident in the 2016 playoffs, Bauer unleashed a daylong flurry of politically fueled tweets. It began when Bauer complained that Apple and Twitter "continue to flood my phone with liberal slanted anti trump articles. fair and equal reporting, no?" The tweet invited a wave of criticism, totaling hundreds of responses. Bauer sparred with some users. He wrote in one response that "almost all" of his teammates had supported Donald Trump in the November election. Indians second baseman Jason Kipnis "liked" a tweet that challenged that assertion. Tiffany Otero, the wife of Bauer's teammate Dan Otero, was so appalled by the pro-Trump tweets that she responded with a link to a story about Otero's grandmother defecting from Cuba.

Bauer tells us he didn't actually vote for Trump or, for that matter, anyone else, since he felt his vote was meaningless in the red state of Texas. At times he just enjoys trolling. In the back-and-forth that day on Twitter, Bauer went on to question the human impact on climate change and wrote that he'd never encountered a Native American offended by the Indians' Chief Wahoo mascot. Bauer often brings a puerile brand of humor to social media, specializing in "420" and "69" jokes, but the tone on this day became uncivil. One user wished cancer upon Bauer, and Bauer suggested another critic "quit life."

After the episode, Bauer says, he was called into the office of baseball operations president Chris Antonetti. Indians officials had asked Bauer to be a better teammate. Bauer asked them to define what it meant to be a good teammate. To Bauer, being a good teammate wasn't about being one of the guys; it was about sharing useful information and helping teammates get the most out of their abilities. The Indians gave him an outline of how they defined being a good teammate. The list included expectations like showing up to stretch on time and meeting workout requirements. Bauer checked off all those boxes. "Then, highlighted in bold, italicized, circled, with arrows pointing to it, was, 'Don't do anything that might make someone mad,'" Bauer says. The conversation with Antonetti, as Bauer recalls, focused on his Twitter account, which Bauer was asked to surrender voluntarily for the 2017 season.

Despite his social-media missteps, Bauer had become more comfortable and accepted in the Cleveland clubhouse by the spring of 2017. With the Diamondbacks, and early in his years with Cleveland, Bauer earned a reputation as a loner. He spent much of his time in the clubhouse editing video, researching photography or drones, and keeping to himself.

Bauer has since found a way to engage more often with teammates and in locker-room banter.

"Would I rather be doing something else? Probably," Bauer told Travis in 2017. "But it's more beneficial for me to do that. Little things like that I've had to learn. Sometimes it's tough because I don't think I can truly be myself a lot of times. I joke with people that two years ago, when I kept all my feelings inside about my teammates, I was a bad teammate. Now I tell them how much I think they suck and I'm a good teammate. It's so backward."

Whether or not he met the club's expectations of being a "good teammate," he'd become a valuable teammate in helping some of those in the clubhouse become better performers on the field. Upon joining the Indians, all Clevinger really knew about Bauer was the "dirty hat" he wore at UCLA. In his first spring in Goodyear, in 2015, he approached Bauer to discuss pitching mechanics.

"At first I was like, this guy is out of his mind," Clevinger says. "I saw him doing all these different drills and these weird workouts with bands and stuff and thought, 'What's he doing?' . . . But then I started watching and doing my own research and looking at all the Driveline stuff and talking to Kyle [Boddy]."

Bauer introduced Clevinger to Boddy. Clevinger said the Indians had adopted some Texas Baseball Ranch weighted-ball programs when he arrived via trade, but he was doing "three little drills" with weighted balls while Bauer had an extensive routine. Boddy sent Clevinger PDFs on why Driveline employs weighted balls.

"I read through that. He has proof to back it up. I'm a huge science guy. I want to see the facts. I want to see the proof. I don't want to throw shit against the wall," Clevinger says. "Since I've been up here, [Bauer] has been a huge help."

Clevinger took time to understand why Bauer did what he did, why he was the way he was. Bauer took the time to teach Clevinger his weighted-ball practices. Bauer helped Clevinger become "more of an athlete" in his motion, through implicit-learning-based drills.

What Clevinger came to understand is that Bauer has a low tolerance for disrupting his routine (including missing weighted balls) and perhaps a low "threshold," as defined by renowned sociologist Mark Granovetter. Granovetter was investigating why people do things like riot or protest when he came up with what he called the threshold model of collective behavior. Granovetter theorized that everyone has a threshold score, which is sensitive to peer pressure. Gladwell explained the theory on his *Revisionist History* podcast: "Your threshold is the number of people who have to do something before you join in." If you have a low threshold score, Gladwell added, "you're someone who doesn't need the support or the approval or the company of others to do what you think is right." If you have a low threshold and your high-school teammates refer to your shoulder tube as a penis pole, you keep using it. When it came to development, Bauer might have a threshold score of zero.

Gladwell has observed that former NBA great Rick Barry likely had a very low threshold score. Barry was a great free-throw shooter (89.3 percent for his career). But he shot free throws underhanded, a motion derided as a "granny shot," even though its biomechanical simplicity could lead to improved success for struggling shooters. Virtually no NBA players have adopted this iconoclastic method—including notoriously poor free-throw shooter Shaquille O'Neal (52.7 percent). Shaq once told Barry he'd rather shoot "zero percent" than shoot underhanded. Another poor free-throw shooter, Wilt Chamberlain (51.1 percent), did adopt the underhand method for one season in 1961–1962, the best free-throw-shooting season of his career (61.3 percent). But

Chamberlain stopped using the approach the next season. He wrote that using the "granny shot" made him look "like a sissy." Shaq and Wilt had higher threshold scores. Of course, those with lower thresholds are not always easy to be around. They can be perceived as arrogant, uncompromising, and unwilling to adhere to social norms. Billy Paultz was a teammate of Barry's with the New York Nets and famously said of him, "Half of the players disliked Rick Barry. The other half hated him."[1]

Barry told Gladwell, "It's almost incomprehensible to me that someone could have that attitude, to sacrifice their success over worrying about how somebody feels about you or says about you. It's sad, really."

The low-threshold life can be a lonely existence. But as Gladwell concluded, "Rick Barry was the best basketball player he could possibly have been, and Wilt Chamberlain could never say that." Bauer wants to be able to say he was the best pitcher he could possibly be.

Falvey, the Indians' former conduit to Bauer, says, "[Bauer] is willing to experiment. Fail. Learn from it. That cycle is real and beneficial. Lot of guys are afraid to do that because they don't want to look bad. He doesn't have that fear. He is not afraid."

While Bauer is also frustratingly uncompromising, he's willing to do something else that is perhaps underappreciated. "He's willing to share," Falvey says.

In 2013 at the Texas Baseball Ranch, Dutch athletic trainer Frans Bosch delivered a guest lecture in which he referred to University of Georgia kinesiology professor Karl Newell's theory of constraint training in motor learning. Bosch told the audience that altering one of three variables during practice improves the pace of progress. Bauer was listening closely.

"It turns out the quickest way to acquire a new skill is to force yourself to do that skill with a constantly changing environment, implement, or activity," Bauer says. "If you can vary one of those [elements] every single time, with the same goal, then your body acquires that skill a lot more quickly."

Weighted balls—and differential weighted balls that are of slightly different size and weight—are an example of an implement constraint. "You throw thirty-two bullpens a year, not including spring training, and practically all of them are wastes of time because you are not forcing your mind to be active the entire time," Bauer says. "Your mind goes, OK, yeah, I'm throwing a bullpen. You tune out after the second or third throw, especially because most guys throw five fastballs here, three curveballs, etc. There is no skill acquisition."

A more effective way to learn, Bauer says, is to change the task by throwing a series of different-sized or weighted balls. Each throw feels a little different, which forces the player's mind to be active and his body to adapt. If he struggles with command or the feel of a pitch, his next bullpen session will often include work with those nonstandard balls. The value of what Driveline calls differential command balls goes beyond velocity training. "All of a sudden, in the next outing, that pitch is back," Bauer says. In the off-season he will further randomize practice by shooting a basketball, swinging a bat, or kicking a soccer ball between throws.

Falvey says Bauer introduced the Indians to the concept of differential training, which has been well documented to provide benefits in a number of pursuits, including memorization and recitation. Bauer shared a research paper with the front office on the benefits of random practice (a type of differential practice) in typing.

Baseball has traditionally employed the opposite type of training: block practice. Consider batting practice. Every day, batters take on-field BP, which consists of a coach lobbing the same types of pitches again and again at much slower speeds than they see in games.

A 1994 study conducted by California Polytechnic State University tested random batting practice versus block batting practice.[2] The study divided thirty junior college baseball players into three groups: control, blocked practice, and random practice. The hitters faced three types of pitches—curveballs (CB), fastballs (FB), and changeups (CU)—in fifteen-pitch sets. The random group's hitters faced the three pitch types in unpredictable fashion: FB, CU, CU, CB, FB, CB, and so on. The blocked group's list of pitches came in segmented groupings of fifteen consecutive pitches of identical type: FB, FB, FB; CU, CU, CU, CB, CB, CB, and so on. In the testing phase, the researchers found that "the random group performed significantly better than the blocked group" in quality of contact under game conditions.

The Indians had become more open to new development practices and had expanded and changed their staff. In addition to the rise of Falvey, they hired Eric Cressey disciple Matt Blake to be their pitching coordinator in 2016. In October 2016, Cleveland hired James Harris—who had one year of experience in professional baseball and had never played the game at an organized level—to be their farm director. He had spent one year with the Pirates after coming over from the NFL and the Philadelphia Eagles, where he'd been an assistant under Chip Kelly. Kelly was on the cutting edge of player-development practices in football. Each morning a plastic cup waited at the Eagles players' lockers. It was a urine test, part of a daily assessment that included heart-rate tests and soreness and mood surveys conducted via iPad. The Indians even brought on author and ten-thousand-hour disciple Daniel Coyle as a consultant.

And with Mickey Callaway gone, Bauer felt he was more welcome to share his ideas and information and throw his weighted-ball bullpens. But while the Indians were among the most aggressive teams in changing their player-development practices, and while Boddy thought they were a great club for Bauer, Bauer wanted them to be even more forward thinking, quicker to implement change, and open to the ideas he shared.

"I think he wants to advance pitching forward. He thinks about it beyond himself," Falvey says. "I think that's the part that's misunderstood."

Bauer always wanted to push, including in the brand-new field of pitch design. But he was learning that creating a new pitch doesn't always follow a smooth, linear path.

On March 7, two weeks into spring training, Bauer's slider began to run into trouble.

During a night exhibition game against the Cubs in which he'd already allowed five runs, Bauer threw a slider to center fielder Albert

Almora. The pitch did not break sharply and stayed out over the middle of the plate, and Almora smashed it for a three-run homer, the ball landing on a grassy berm where fans fought each other to retrieve it. Bauer shook his head immediately after contact, disgusted with his execution.

Bauer was frustrated both with himself and with the Indians as the spring went along. One source of friction with the club was that it had not heavily invested in Edgertronic cameras. Bauer says the Indians had only one camera available at Goodyear, and scores of pitchers. Boddy was on hand to observe Bauer's next start on March 12 and set up an Edgertronic in the center-field camera area to get an updated look at Bauer, but access to Edgertronic video was inconsistent, depriving Bauer of the immediate feedback loop he enjoyed at Driveline. One would think that Bauer could have used his own camera, but when he had his father come film him one spring on a complex backfield, they were later called into the "principal's office" to talk to Indians manager Terry Francona. Some coaches were irked that Bauer was turning the complex into a pitching lab.

Bauer's fastball was sitting at 95 mph. His curveball was breaking sharply. He completed the spring with a satisfactory pitching line, leading the team with thirty-nine strikeouts in 29 1/3 innings, although he also allowed five home runs. But as Opening Day drew closer, the slider's movement profile was becoming less horizontal and more vertical, and he didn't have the information he needed to reverse its decay. In his second-to-last start of the spring on March 22, he allowed a home run to San Diego's Manuel Margot on another imperfect slider.

There was another problem, too.

"My delivery changed slightly," Bauer says. "My delivery is different in the off-season compared to the regular season just because of how loose I am and how much I am throwing. Early in spring training the slider was good. As spring training was finishing, the movement profile changed. It wasn't breaking laterally."

As the Indians loaded their equipment trucks at the end of March and headed north to begin the season, Bauer's new pitch was headed in the wrong direction.

As April went on, Bauer became increasingly frustrated with his slider. Each time he sat in front of his locker after games and pulled up the pitch's horizontal movement on his smartphone, he noticed it declining. His off-season project was failing. Although he'd had a fine first month (2.45 ERA, 46 strikeouts and 16 walks in 40 1/3 innings), he was frustrated with the pitch's lack of improvement and doubted he could sustain success without it.

On April 1, his slider averaged 6.7 inches of horizontal movement. In his second start on April 7 versus the Royals, the horizontal movement fell to 6.2 inches, and then to 4.5 inches on April 12 at Detroit. He wanted 10 inches. Although he was pitching relatively well, he was also facing some of the weakest teams in baseball. In terms of performance against extra-divisional opponents, the 2018 AL Central was the second-weakest division of all time, and Bauer didn't have to face its best team. On April 20 at Baltimore, the horizontal movement averaged 5.1 inches. He also wanted the slider to have zero inches of vertical depth to keep it on the same plane as his fastball for as long as possible, creating deception. Instead it was breaking 3 to 4 inches. The slider was behaving like a less effective version of his curveball.

The Indians did not travel with their Edgertronic camera, Bauer says, and its use at home was sporadic. There were occasions when the camera wasn't used because a Fox Sports TV camera occupied the camera well behind the plate. "The TV guys were down there," Bauer recalls the club explaining. "I don't give half a fuck," he responded. "Tell the TV guys to get out of there."

The Indians' video personnel also lacked familiarity with the device, and as a result, some bullpen sessions were not recorded properly. It was all maddening to Bauer.

There was another potential use of the camera that the Indians weren't fully exploiting, although the Astros—and Bauer before them—had done so previously: intelligence gathering. Bauer didn't just want to study himself; he also wanted to study the other best pitchers in baseball. The ironic thing about criticism from past teammates like Miguel Montero was that Bauer *didn't* believe he had all the answers. He was always searching for better information and practices. On his own team, Corey Kluber and Clevinger had two of the best sliders in baseball. As Bauer designed his slider in the winter, he had studied their grips, which he had filmed the previous season. And on April 13, there was another pitcher he wanted to study: Toronto's Marcus Stroman.

Stroman and Bauer had long admired each other from a distance. Prior to being selected in the first round of the 2012 draft, Stroman called Bauer a "pioneer to the pitching world" on Twitter. Stroman said he used to watch tape of Bauer's UCLA starts in his Duke dorm room. Bauer cited Stroman as his favorite non-Cleveland player to watch.

Now Bauer wanted his elite slider.

Leading up to that start on a frigid April evening, Bauer hounded the video staff and its coordinator, the white-haired and studious-looking Bob Chester, to make sure they got Edgertronic footage of Stroman. But in the first inning, as Clevinger pitched for the Indians, neither Chester nor the camera was in the camera well behind home plate. If this start wasn't filmed, Bauer would be livid. Between innings, Chester and the Edgertronic appeared in the camera well. As Stroman started pitching, Chester attached the camera to a tripod directly behind home plate. He then left the area. But the camera view was obstructed. This was Bauer's one chance to get a look at Stroman and his slider on the Edgertronic. The first inning was over, and there was no usable footage. But Chester, realizing the error, returned in the second inning and repositioned the camera more to the left of the plate, allowing for an unobstructed view of Stroman. It was perhaps the most important repositioning of a high-speed camera in the brief history of pitch design.

After the game, Bauer immediately dove into the video: eleven minutes and fifty-one seconds' worth of Stroman throwing pitches, a global shutter capturing every detail in thousands of frames per second. In May, he shared the video with Travis and motioned to Stroman's right hand.

"You see his thumb?" Bauer said. "It slips really early."

That was the key. As Stroman's upper body rotated and his right hand came through to throw, his thumb lost contact with the ball first, with his index and middle fingers still in contact before release. The middle finger was on the far side of the ball, the index finger behind the ball. Bauer paused the video.

"His middle finger never gets to the front of the ball. It just kind of brushes the side of it," Bauer said. "Then you can only see his pointer finger appear once there is separation between the ball and his hand. . . . The pointer finger pushes the ball [to Stroman's left], which puts more of a sidespin component on the ball. When I saw this video I was like, I have to find a way to get my thumb to slip earlier while my hand is still behind the ball."

Two days later, Bauer threw his bullpen indoors, in something of a concrete bunker in the depths of Progressive Field. He commandeered the Edgertronic and filmed the session. One of his first throws resulted in a nearly perfect gyroball, a pitch immune to the Magnus effect; not what he wanted. His index and middle fingers wrapped too much around the ball. His thumb was still in the way. To get his thumb to leave the ball earlier, he tried tucking it under the ball. This would push the axis up, he hoped, creating more sidespin and resulting in more lateral movement. One of his first attempts resulted in a pitch that got away from him; had a right-handed batter been in the box, it would have hit him in the helmet. He adjusted, applying more pressure with his index and middle fingers on the far side of the ball, running along the wide part of the figure-eight seam. Progress. The axis tilted up slightly, but not enough.

Bauer took his experiment to the mound over the following four starts at Baltimore on April 20 (5.1 inches of horizontal movement), against the Cubs at Wrigley Field on April 25 (4.8), at home against the Rangers on April 30 (5.4), and at Yankee Stadium on May 5 (4.4). It still wasn't working.

A day before his May 11 start at home against Kansas City, Bauer discovered something while lobbing balls back toward the infield during batting practice. Instead of gripping the "horseshoe" part of the seam with his middle finger as he had since the winter—and as most pitchers do when throwing a slider—he tried throwing one with a two-seam fastball grip, only tucking his thumb like Stroman. He spread his index and middle fingers over a narrower stretch of parallel seams and tucked his thumb and locked his wrist as he always did.

"I was like, holy shit," Bauer recalls. "I could definitely see that the axis was different. I'm throwing the ball toward the collection bucket. I just flipped a couple. I saw a left-handed turn. . . . I said, 'I'm going to try that tomorrow.'"

The grip allowed his thumb to get out of the way, to create a pitch with a more vertical axis. His index finger made the last contact with the ball, just brushing it, to create an element of sidespin. He had the gyrospin and sidespin mix he was seeking. He knew he couldn't get a perfect north–south axis. He was hoping to create an axis pointed toward him at about 60 degrees.

Most pitchers don't experiment in games. They save experimentation for bullpens. But Bauer doesn't mind failing before thousands. That's one benefit of having a low threshold. You don't care what anyone thinks if you are doing what you believe is right. If Bauer listened to his pitching coach and was always agreeable, he argues, he would not have a career. "And people wonder why I have the reputation of not listening to coaches," he says.

On May 11, Bauer used the new grip for two innings, the second and third. His slider began to dart horizontally. As he examined the data after the game, he saw that one slider had moved eight inches. He was thrilled, at least until he learned that only one inning had been captured on the Edgertronic. While the pitch moved like he desired, he couldn't control it.

"I switched back [during the game] because I had no idea where it was going," he says. "I was in self-preservation mode. I switched back to my old grip, which was more comfortable, but it didn't have the profile."

The start was a disaster: he allowed five runs and eleven hits in 4 2/3 innings. But it may have been his most important start of the season. The grip had given him the movement he wanted.

The Indians next traveled to Detroit, where Bauer threw his bullpen. He felt he was able to replicate the grip and axis. Those watching the bullpen session had their doubts that it was an improvement. "In my head I was throwing a freaking party," Bauer says. "I went with it exclusively, and the movement profile was drastically different."

With greater confidence in his new slider grip, Bauer took the mound on an afternoon getaway day at Comerica Park in Detroit. The stands at the home of the rebuilding Tigers were mostly empty.

With two outs in the first inning, Bauer faced a 2–2 count against Nick Castellanos. Bauer threw a slider with the new grip. Behind the plate, catcher Roberto Pérez held his glove outside and just below the strike zone. The pitch appeared to make a left-handed turn as it neared the plate, darting into Pérez's glove. Castellanos swung and missed. In the second inning, Bauer threw another two-strike slider to the Tigers' John Hicks. Again, the slider appeared to be headed for the center of the plate before breaking to the left. Hicks also swung and missed.

One reason Bauer had longed for a slider was to pair it with his two-seam fastball, the Laminar Express. Because they both have little vertical movement, the two pitches could share the same path, or tunnel, for much of their journeys toward the plate but break horizontally in opposite directions too late for batters to adjust. To start the fourth inning, Bauer threw a 95 mph, two-strike two-seamer to the right-handed-hitting Pete Kozma. The pitch's axis allowed for a smooth spot to develop near the nose of the ball. As it neared the plate, the turbulent air on its backside compelled it to break back toward the plate and catch the outside part of the strike zone. Kozma gave up on the pitch, thinking it was outside. Instead, he stared at strike three.

With two outs in the seventh, Bauer again faced Hicks. On a 2–2 count, Bauer threw an excellent slider. It held its plane, masquerading as a fastball bound for the outside corner before darting away. Hicks whiffed to end the inning. Bauer looked businesslike as he walked off the mound, as if he had done this before. But he hadn't, and inside his head he was celebrating. It was arguably the finest start of Bauer's career: eight innings, four hits allowed, no runs, no walks, and ten strikeouts. All ten of the Ks had come via whiffs on sliders or batters looking at his comeback two-seamer. That day, Bauer threw his new slider sixteen times and induced eight swings-and-misses: an outstanding 50 percent whiff rate, the best of all his pitches in the outing.

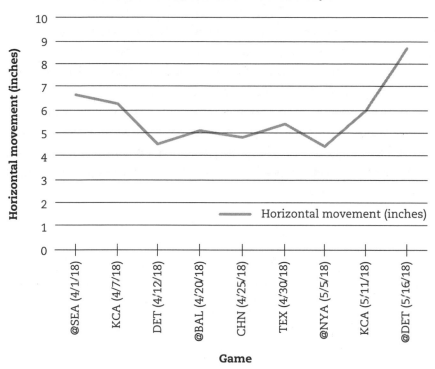

Trevor Bauer's Horizontal Slider Movement by Start

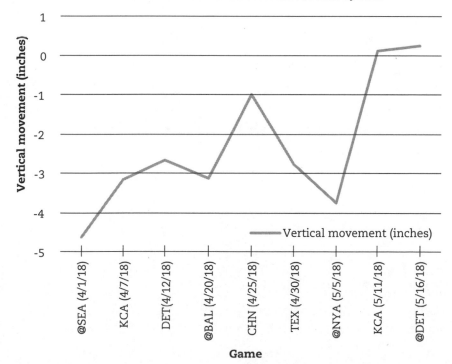

Trevor Bauer's Vertical Slider Movement (inches) by Start

The pitch had an average horizontal movement of 8.6 inches, nearly what he wanted and roughly double where it had been in the previous six starts. The slider also averaged 0.3 inches of vertical movement relative to gravity. It was nearly perfect.

Through his first nine starts, Bauer owned a 2.59 ERA and a 2.82 FIP. He had struck out sixty-seven batters in fifty-nine innings and allowed just forty-five hits, and only in his last outing had his pitches felt fully operational. He was as close as he'd ever been to becoming what he thought he could be.

9

WE'RE ALL ASTRONAUTS

Pilots devoutly believed that it was necessary to fly out to the edge
with regularity in order to maintain proficiency or 'decision-making
ability.' On one level it was a logical enough equivalent to an athlete's
concern with staying in shape; but on another it had to do with the
mysteries of the right stuff and the ineffable joys of showing the world,
and yourself, that you had it.
—**TOM WOLFE,** *The Right Stuff*

Ryan Pressly was at best the fifth-most-famous of the six major
leaguers traded on July 27, 2018, the day he joined the Astros and
his trajectory changed. An eleventh-round Red Sox draftee in 2007,
Pressly scuffled on the farm as a starter before finally being moved
to the bullpen in 2012. He pitched a bit better in relief but not well
enough for Boston to add him to its 40-man roster. That left him exposed to the Rule 5 draft, an annual farm-system flea market in which
players who've been stuck with one organization for several years can
be rescued by another. The Twins took Pressly, and he made the majors in 2013, pitching well enough to stay there but not well enough
to stand out. From 2013 to 2017, the first five seasons of Pressly's career, MLB relievers recorded a collective 3.80 ERA. Over the same span,
Pressly's ERA was 3.81.

Pressly's 2017 season had started so disastrously (nineteen runs
in eighteen innings) that he'd actually been demoted to Triple-A. His
first half of 2018 was much stronger, and through July 26, he trailed
the major-league leader in appearances by a single game. But no one
was expecting second-half heroics from a twenty-nine-year-old, generic right-hander with a respectable but not otherworldly 3.40 ERA
on the year.

Although the trade was disorienting for Pressly, there were benefits to being uprooted. The Dallas native was returning to Texas. He was also upgrading from a 1.2 percent chance to qualify for the postseason to a 99.9 percent chance, according to FanGraphs' playoff odds. He flew from Boston to Houston and arrived at Minute Maid Park in time for the following day's Lone Star Series game against the Rangers.

No more than fifteen minutes after he finished unpacking in the clubhouse, Pressly was summoned into a meeting. In attendance were Astros pitching coach Brent Strom, bullpen coach Doug White, and multiple analysts from the front office. The Astros, Pressly learned, had a plan for him to be better, and the analysts launched into the details. "They sat me down and they put up all these x, y charts and all this other stuff," Pressly says. "It almost sounded like they were speaking in a different language. I just raised my hand and said, 'Guys, just tell me what to throw and not to throw.'" They told him his two-seam fastball to lefties was ineffective but that they loved his curve and hoped he'd throw it more. They also suggested he elevate his four-seam fastball and throw his slider slightly more to make his fastball more effective.

The newest Astro was open to input. With the Twins, he had wondered, "Why is it not clicking for me?" Now someone was offering answers. And it wasn't just anyone; it was the Astros, who had won the World Series the year before and had a history of acquiring and improving much more accomplished pitchers, including former Tigers ace Justin Verlander, the best AL pitcher of his era. "I was just curious to see if this works," Pressly says. "Let's buy in. Obviously, you have a Hall of Fame guy over there," he says, referring to Verlander. "He's [having] the best year of his career, and he's thirty-five. It's like, maybe I should pay attention over here."

That night, Pressly got into the game in the seventh inning, and the first batter he faced was Rangers second baseman Rougned Odor. Pressly threw six pitches, following the Astros' recipe: four four-seamers (three of them high), one curve, and one slider. Odor pulled pitch number six, the slider, over the right-field fence for a home run. "I'm like, OK, this is bullshit. You guys are lying to me," Pressly remembers thinking. "But at the same time, just give it some time."

Pressly stuck to the blueprint. With the Twins from 2017 to 2018, Pressly had thrown his sinker 13 percent of the time against lefties. Only once in that span had a southpaw swung at it and missed. With the Astros, he threw the sinker to lefties less than 1 percent of the time. With the Twins in 2018, Pressly had thrown the curve 24 percent of the time. As an Astro, he threw it 39 percent of the time. With Houston, he also elevated his four-seamer and threw his slider slightly more often. "In baseball in general, there's a sort of macho [feeling] of, I've gotta throw my fastball, I've gotta throw it inside if I'm gonna be a man," says Mike Fast, the Astros' research and development director when they traded for Pressly. "And that turns into, I'm gonna throw my fastball even if it's not my best pitch. The Astros have not, for a while now, had any hesitation about just, 'Throw your best pitches.'" The 2017 and 2018 Astros threw curveballs and sliders more than 34 percent of the time, the highest rates on record; in their 2017 pennant-clinching performance in ALCS Game 7, Charlie Morton and Lance McCullers threw sixty-five curves in 108 pitches, the highest single-game rate.

Pressly remembers one moment that drove home how well the new formula was working. On August 31 in Houston, he entered in the eighth inning and faced the best player of the decade, Angels center fielder and two-time MVP Mike Trout. Pressly started Trout off with a fastball inside. Then he threw back-to-back sliders, one for a foul and one for a ball. On the 2–1 count, he threw a curve that appeared to defy physics, starting inside and breaking over the outside corner, where it was framed for a strike. And on 2–2, he went back to the slider, throwing it slightly higher than the curve and freezing Trout for strike three. Trout didn't argue: As he stood at the plate and removed his elbow protector, he nodded slowly several times, acknowledging how thoroughly he'd been beaten.

"[Astros pitcher] Collin McHugh came up to me after the game and goes, 'I have never seen Mike Trout do that before,'" Pressly says. "He didn't know what was coming. That's an unreal hitter up there, and to get a guy to do that, it's kind of, OK, this might be working."

It wasn't working only against Trout. Among the 130 major-league relievers with at least twenty innings pitched from July 28 on, Pressly ranked fourth in ERA (0.77), third in FIP (1.49), third in OBP (on-base percentage) allowed (.179), fifth in strikeout rate minus walk rate (34.5 percent), and fifth in wOBA allowed (.171). He also ranked eighth in ground-ball rate (60.4 percent) and first in soft-contact rate (31.3 percent). "He lit the league on fire," Astros catcher Max Stassi says.

Pressly led the Astros with twenty-six regular-season appearances after being acquired, and only Héctor Rondón, who served as the club's closer for most of the season, had a higher average leverage index—a measure of the importance of the situations when he entered the game—during Pressly's time with the team. He also pitched in five of the Astros' eight postseason games, allowing one run and striking out seven batters in five innings. With one trade and one meeting, Pressly had become one of baseball's best relievers.

"If you had told me all of that last off-season, I probably would have laughed you out of the room," he says.

Pressly cost the Astros their tenth- and fifteenth-ranked prospects, as assessed by MLB.com—not nothing at the time, but a steal for what turned out to be an elite late-inning arm under team control through 2019. "He fits how we like to pitch," Astros manager A.J. Hinch said when the trade was made. One way in which Pressly fits the Astros' profile: he possesses almost unparalleled spin. The Astros led the majors in overall average spin rate in 2018, besting the second-place Indians. Of the 134 pitchers who threw at least 150 curveballs in 2018, no one had a higher spin rate than Pressly's 3,225 rpm. (The league average was 2,493.) Pressly's slider and four-seamer are also among the fastest-spinning pitches of their type. In fact, of the 506 pitchers with at least four hundred pitches of *any* type thrown in 2018, Pressly's average spin rate across all of his offerings was the highest.

Pressly still doesn't know *how* he spins pitches so fast, but after the Astros helped him optimize his mix, that high-spin, three-pitch approach made him almost unhittable. It's rare and unfair for a reliever to throw multiple breaking balls so well and so often. In 2018, two hundred fifty pitchers threw at least thirty innings out of the bullpen. Only Pressly threw both a curve *and* a slider at least a quarter of the time each. Thanks to its spin, Pressly's curve had the second-biggest side-to-side break of any AL pitcher who threw the pitch at least two hundred times, trailing only his Houston teammate Morton, who threw the second-spinniest curve behind Pressly. Pressly's slider, meanwhile, was by one definition the majors' most unhittable pitch: by locating it lower and throwing it more often on two-strike counts, he transformed it into a weapon that induced a whiff roughly a third of the time he threw it—the highest rate of *any* pitch thrown two hundred times in 2018. It almost seems like an afterthought that Pressly's four-seamer averaged nearly 97 mph, topping out just shy of 100.

Excising the sinker from his repertoire and throwing each of his remaining pitches between 29 and 39 percent of the time helped Pressly keep hitters guessing and, often, flailing. Houston hitters who had faced Pressly told him his high-spin fastball up in the zone looked like it was rising, and his breaking balls looked like his fastball, usually until it was too late. "They were like, 'Dude, your pitches look the exact same and then they just go different ways on all of them. It's like we can't sit on anything,'" Pressly says.

Pressly had always possessed high spin, and if all the Astros had done was move more quickly than other teams to collect pitchers who'd exhibited that ability elsewhere, their strategy wouldn't be fundamentally different from the Moneyball Athletics' embrace of OBP. But spin alone didn't make Pressly so hard to hit; what helped him reach what he describes as "a whole 'nother level" were the adjustments he made at Houston's behest. For Pressly, being traded to Houston was akin to Harry Potter arriving at Hogwarts. For the first time, he was fully aware of and encouraged to use his powers, and he finally felt like himself.

Pressly learned from watching his new teammates more than from anything they said. "If guys are pitching up in the zone and throwing curveballs off fastballs up in the zone, you can clearly see it," Pressly says, adding, "It starts to click—I have that same exact stuff. So if *they're* having success . . ." The montage of fruitless swings Pressly admired from the pen was a better sales pitch than any analyst's graph. "It's just the Astros' philosophy," he says. "They just have a different kind of mindset over there."

Mindset is a psychological concept that's already earned its own TED Talk. As noted earlier, Stanford psychology professor Carol Dweck turned "mindset" into a business buzzword when she codified an attitudinal difference that could help explain the separation between high and low achievers. "Individuals who believe their talents can be developed (through hard work, good strategies, and input from others) have a growth mindset," she wrote. "They tend to achieve more than those with a more fixed mindset (those who believe their talents are innate gifts)."[1] The Astros value a growth mindset in their players, and more than anyone else, they also embody it as a franchise. They're baseball's best proof that even elite performers possess untapped talents.

From 2009 to 2014, the Astros won 382 games, MLB's fewest by 47. Splitting that six-season sample in two reveals a difference in degrees of despair. From 2009 to 2011, they won only the fourth-fewest games, posting a bad-but-not-abysmal .424 combined winning percentage. From 2012 to 2014, though, they won 24 fewer games than any other team, managing only a .362 winning percentage. The first of those three-year chunks came under owner Drayton McLane and GM Ed Wade. The second came under new owner Jim Crane—a billionaire businessman who made his fortune in shipping and logistics—and former Cardinals executive Jeff Luhnow, whom Crane hired as GM in December 2011.

The outgoing administration had allowed the Astros to grow old, leaving Luhnow with little talent in the majors and a fallow farm system. In 2011, the Astros finished 56–106, easily the worst record in the majors, and *Baseball America* rated their minor-league system twenty-sixth. As constituted, the Astros were neither competitive nor promising, so Luhnow decided to do something drastic: strip the roster down to the studs and accept a lot of losses in order to stockpile prospects. Although the players on the field would do their best from game to game, the front office would, in the short term, essentially not try to win.

For the first few years of Luhnow's tenure, the Astros were unwatchable. And unwatched: from 2013 to 2014, Astros games sporadically drew 0.0 ratings, indicating that no Nielsen household was masochistic enough to tune in. By Opening Day 2013, Luhnow had slashed the team's payroll to $26.1 million, the lowest figure any team had committed to its active roster in five years. That season, the club bottomed out at fifty-one wins. In those years, the Astros' most memorable, emblematic on-field moment was an extra-innings, run-scoring, Keystone Kops sequence in a game against the Nationals in August 2012, which featured two throwing errors and a collision between two Astros fielders, all precipitated by a bunt. That came toward the tail end of a 4–34 stretch for the team, a run of ineptitude unsurpassed in a sample of that length since 1916.

Many teams had rebuilt and been bad before, but few, if any, had intentionally taken the strategy to such an extreme. Luhnow and Crane passed the MLB equivalent of the marshmallow test (another product of the Stanford psychology department), rejecting short-term satisfaction in favor of long-term gain. That forbearance led to Little League–looking plays, the worst record over a three-year stretch of any team since the expansion '60s Mets, and a fifteen-game losing streak to end the 2013 season. But it also paid dividends via top draft picks, prospects gained through veteran trades, and money allocated to amateur signings and saved for future seasons. The Astros' uncompromising rebuild was a manifestation of a relentless, stay-the-course conviction that sometimes makes them hard to root for as well as tough to beat. That same mentality would give them the will to take on the last bastion of hidebound baseball thinking and construct an unprecedented player-development machine, although that wouldn't come without human costs.

Precisely as planned, the Astros emerged from their years in the wilderness with one of the game's richest arrays of talent. In 2015, the Astros won a wild card, returning to the playoffs for the first time in a decade. In 2017, they won the first World Series in franchise history and boasted Baseball America's third-ranked farm system. In roughly six years, the Astros had transformed from the worst team in baseball with one of the worst farm systems to the best team in baseball with one of the best farm systems.

From 2015 to 2018, the Astros won 374 games, the most in the AL. From 2017 to 2018, they won 204, the most in the majors. Even though the 2018 squad won "only" 103 regular-season games, it was, by some measures, one of the most dominant teams in decades. The 2018 Astros boasted the third-highest run differential (+263) since 1954, trailing only the 1998 Yankees and the 2001 Mariners, two of the three winningest regular-season teams of all time. They also posted a .679 Pythagorean winning percentage—an estimate of what a team's record "should" have been based on its runs scored and allowed and the league-wide run environment—which was the second-highest since World War II. Although they lost to the Red Sox in five ALCS games, they actually outhit Boston in the series.

Alex Bregman, the fruit of one of the high draft picks the Astros had gained by being so bad, was the best player on that 2018 team. Shortstop Carlos Correa, the No. 1 pick from 2012, was the second-best player on the 2016–2017 teams and the third-best player in 2015. The other three of the four best players on the 2015 team that ended the Astros' dark days—José Altuve, George Springer, and Dallas Keuchel—were additions that predated the Luhnow regime. Focusing on that core makes what the Astros accomplished seem simple: inherit a few future stars, lose a lot, and reap the rewards. But neither holdover prospects—who once weren't seen as rising stars—nor lofty draft picks were a renewable resource. Rather than rely on them, the Astros implemented a model for finding and developing players that would be self-sustaining, outlasting both the leavings of Luhnow's predecessors and the immediate payoff of top picks that was bound to disappear as soon as the team got good again.

As a result, the Astros are dominating the *minors* even more than the majors. In 2018, four years removed from the franchise's last No. 1 pick, Astros pitchers led their league in strikeout rate at six successive levels, from MLB down to short-season A-ball. (At the seventh level, Rookie ball, their rank sank all the way to second.) At those top five minor-league levels combined, Astros pitchers struck out 26.5 percent of the batters they faced. The gap between them and the second-place Yankees (2.4 percentage points) was as big as the gap between the Yankees and the *nineteenth*-place Cubs. And it's not as if Houston had veteran arms on the farm inflating the stats: weighted by playing time, the average age of those minor-league pitchers above Rookie ball, 22.9, was the third-lowest of any organization and the lowest of any AL organization. Astros *hitters* above Rookie ball, meanwhile, were eighth-youngest in age, second in walk-to-strikeout ratio, and—despite not playing in any notably offense-friendly parks—fourth in home-run rate, behind three organizations with at least one bandbox or team at altitude apiece. And as for wins—well, Astros minor-league teams led all organizations in combined winning percentage above Rookie ball (.585), short-season A-ball (.587), full-season A-ball (.589), and High-A (.592).

The *way* they did that is telling, too. According to TrackMan data obtained from another team, Astros hitters led the minors in pull percentage and the percentage of balls hit in the air, while also recording the seventh-highest rate of balls hit 95 mph or harder. Despite that power-centric approach, they chased balls at the third-lowest rate and maintained an above-average contact rate. On the pitching side, Astros minor leaguers led all teams in fastball velocity, breaking-ball spin rate, off-speed-pitch percentage, percentage of four-seam fastballs thrown in the upper third of the zone, and whiffs per swing, in addition to inducing pop-ups more often than all but two other teams. Name a data-driven developmental trend in today's game, and the Astros aren't just at or near the forefront of it at the big-league level, but they're also grooming the current roster's replacements from Triple-A down to the Dominican Summer League.

In August 2012, a few days after the bumbling bunt play, Luhnow wrote a letter to Astros season-ticket holders. "In order to compete consistently, the Astros must develop and maintain a world-class scouting operation and farm system," the letter said. "Through the scouting and player development function, we will be able to produce and keep winning players. Teams that excel in these areas tend to win championships in baseball." Five years later, the Astros won the World Series, proving him right. And by then, the Astros' scouting and player-development process looked like no other team's had before.

Like most teams that have embraced novel methods of player development, the Astros aren't led by lifelong baseball men. Luhnow was a

McKinsey consultant before Cardinals owner Bill Dewitt Jr. hired him as a scouting executive to help the Cards catch up to the sabermetric movement. Sig Mejdal, a *Moneyball* disciple Luhnow hired to head up the team's newly formed analytics department in 2005, was a former part-time blackjack dealer who went on to collect a long list of degrees and work as an engineer for Lockheed Martin and NASA. Mejdal's amateur-player projections, which were based on painstakingly assembled college stats, helped the Cardinals draft more major leaguers over the next several seasons than any other club, many of them late-round finds.

Although Luhnow oversaw St. Louis's player-development process, he and Mejdal intervened less in that area than they did on the draft side. "There was much less effort and energy put into player development than we later did in Houston," Mejdal says. "We were much more observers than participants."

When Luhnow left for Houston, he brought Mejdal with him as the Astros' director of decision sciences. (Another thing the Astros do differently: job titles.) Mejdal recreated and deployed his draft model, expecting to unearth underappreciated players at the same rate he had in St. Louis. But it soon became clear that other clubs had caught on. Suddenly, the players Mejdal's model liked were being snapped up earlier than they had been before. Potential draftees the Astros thought would fall to the fifth round were hearing their names called in the second or third, and sleepers who might once have been available from rounds 10 to 15 were off the board by then. "In hindsight, I was naïve," Mejdal says. "I thought that our advantage in the draft was going to remain there for quite a few more years, but I think the steepness of the innovation adoption curve hit me. . . . The processes that probably only a few teams were doing in 2005 to 2010 are more table stakes now."

With the Astros' edge in the draft shrinking, the front office refocused its efforts on an area where the frontier wasn't so settled. "Organizations that embody a growth mindset encourage appropriate risk-taking, knowing that some risks won't work out," Dweck wrote. The Astros were one of those organizations. "Working for Jeff, there is always a culture of innovation and searching for the next thing that could perhaps improve us," Mejdal says. "There's no problem with bad ideas and false alarms. And so that culture probably led us to focus on player development."

The Astros' string of spectacular successes in data-driven player development started in earnest in 2013, propelled in part by the 2012 hiring of Mike Fast as a front-office analyst. Fast, a tech engineer with a physics degree, started producing baseball analysis on his personal blog in 2007, then climbed the hierarchy of sabermetric sites. His pioneering PITCHf/x analyses soon drew the attention of teams, and the Astros spirited him out of the public sphere not long after Baseball Prospectus published his most influential article, a September 2011 piece that conclusively demonstrated the impact of pitch-framing.

Fast had first gotten a taste of the potential for tech-aided player development in 2008, when he wrote a three-part series at the baseball analysis website Stat Speak breaking down comments Brian Bannister had made about his efforts to suppress his BABIP. Bannister left a long comment on the third post, praising Fast's work, then emailed Fast to ask how he could allow fewer home runs. Fast spent twenty-seven hours studying data and producing a fifteen-page PDF file featuring almost fifty charts. At the end of the document, he made a few recommendations but also acknowledged the limitations of his work. "I believe the most effective method would combine the various tools, such as the pitcher's own insight, traditional scouting and video tools, and the query power of PITCHf/x trajectory information, into a tighter feedback loop," Fast's report concluded. He was describing a process that wouldn't work without direct access to a team. Four years later, he had that.

Once on the inside, Fast began to collaborate with coaches and players, funneling his insights to the field. "When I came there and saw our player-development goals, I was like, oh my word. This is stuff you can't work on," Fast says. "It was stuff like, 'Improve your command.' How's a pitcher supposed to go into the off-season and improve his command? He needs a drill. He needs to know how to measure if he's getting better." Branch Rickey had understood this, forbidding his managers from criticizing a player's mistakes without telling him how to correct them. "It isn't enough to tell a youngster

that he strikes out too much—he knows that as well as the manager,"
Rickey's comrade Fresco Thompson wrote. "What he must be told is
how to reduce his number of strikeouts."

As it had in the case of Craig Wright and Jim Sundberg, the first
breakthrough came with a catcher: Jason Castro, the Astros' first-
round pick from 2008. Castro made the majors to stay in 2012 and hit
well enough to earn a plurality of the playing time at the position. But
he was severely limited on defense, costing the Astros runs in every
way a catcher could, particularly with his subpar pitch-framing.

Fast's previous research made that flaw a logical place to start,
and in the spring of 2013, he, Castro, and Astros coach Dan Radison
met every morning to review video and refine Castro's technique in
ways that would help him improve his performance on pitches the
stats suggested he wasn't presenting properly. That tighter feedback
loop paid dividends: according to Baseball Prospectus, Castro's framing performance improved from well below-average in 2012 to average and then well above-average in 2013 and 2014, respectively. After
costing the Astros twenty-four runs on defense in his first two partial
major-league seasons—which had made him a subreplacement-level
player—Castro *saved* them forty-one runs over the next four years.
Although Castro later left via free agency, he first passed along what
he'd learned to an understudy, Stassi. In Stassi's early years in the organization, he didn't rate as a standout receiver, but encounters with
Castro convinced him to refine his framing craft. "He was the first one
to teach me," Stassi says. "He really understood." In 2018, Stassi led
all AL catchers with fourteen framing runs saved despite starting only
sixty-four games.

The next early victory came the following year. Altuve had been an
All-Star in 2012, his first full season, but even then he'd barely been
a league-average hitter. At twenty-two, he'd been named to the team
mostly because *someone* had to represent the woeful Astros. The next
season, his bat went backward. The tiny Altuve, who'd signed out of
Venezuela for only $15,000 and had never appeared on top-prospect
lists, had defied the odds and flummoxed scouts just by getting to the
big leagues, but his five-foot-five-ish head seemed to be bumping up

against a low power ceiling: through more than 1,500 MLB plate appearances, he'd slugged just .377.

Over the 2013–2014 off-season, he worked with the team to implement a more forceful approach. "That was [hitting coach] John Mallee," Fast says. "And it was based on data that I shared with him (from his questions) about the value of getting the ball in the air. He told Altuve to meet the ball out front and helped him retool his swing to do that." Altuve slumped in spring training and went homerless through his first twenty-three regular-season games as he perfected the timing of a new leg kick, and at the end of April his slugging percentage still stood in the .370s. After that, though, the new swing clicked: he batted .355 and slugged .471 the rest of the way, winning a batting title, leading the majors in hits, and finishing third in doubles. He was on his way to double-digit home-run totals and a 2017 MVP award.

As Altuve was working on his swing over the winter, the Astros were evaluating the then twenty-six-year-old Rockies swingman Collin McHugh, who to that point had allowed fifty runs in 47 1/3 MLB innings for the Mets and Rockies from 2012 to 2013. "After another disastrous season . . . it's time to ask what McHugh really offers a major-league team," Baseball Prospectus wrote in its annual guide. The Astros asked themselves that question and thought the answer was "a lot." Unbeknownst to the public, McHugh had a high-spin curveball and a sinker he threw too much. The Astros claimed McHugh off waivers, advised him to ditch the sinker and trust the curve, and installed him in the starting rotation. The righty recorded a 2.73 ERA, struck out more than a batter per inning, and finished fourth in Rookie of the Year voting. The next year, he received down-ballot Cy Young votes.

Within one year, the developmental trinity of Castro, Altuve, and McHugh provided powerful proofs of concept. All three went from subreplacement level—less valuable than a theoretical fringe player promoted from Triple-A—to cornerstone-type players. Even more encouraging, the tweaks affected every aspect of performance: fielding, hitting, and pitching. Based on those early returns, there was no facet of the game the Astros couldn't optimize.

The Astros' developmental trend line didn't climb continuously. Amid those early successes, the franchise suffered two spectacular failures to cultivate talent.

J.D. Martinez made the majors alongside Altuve in 2011, and from 2011 to 2013 he outslugged the second baseman by only ten points. When he reported to spring training in 2014 claiming to have remade himself, the Astros didn't give him an opportunity to prove it. Under manager Bo Porter, who'd be fired later that year, Martinez got only eighteen at-bats in fourteen spring games before the Astros released him.

Granted, no other team realized what Martinez was about to become; the best he could do was land a minor-league deal with the Tigers, who sent him to Triple-A and didn't promote him until after he'd hit ten homers in seventeen games. But the Astros had wildly underestimated a player they should have known better than anyone. "When you have arguably the best hitter in baseball and you let him go, and no other team puts him on the forty-man, it's a wonderful anecdote of how finite our knowledge is," Mejdal says. "The lesson is as giant as the numbers he puts up."

Improbably, the Astros experienced perhaps an even more infamous failure in the same season. Their prize for enduring the indignities of 2012 was the No. 1 pick in the 2013 draft, which they used on right-handed starter Mark Appel. Appel, a six-foot-five native Houstonian, had posted a 2.12 ERA with eleven strikeouts per nine innings as a senior at Stanford. But he got off to a catastrophic start the following season at High-A Lancaster, where he allowed fifty-one runs in 44 1/3 innings while also surrendering nine homers. After Appel amassed middling numbers the next year, the Astros traded him in a package for Phillies closer Ken Giles in December 2015. By then, Appel's stock had fallen so far that he was more of a throw-in than the trade's main attraction. His next two Triple-A seasons went no better, and he ultimately retired in 2018, joining the injury-impaired Steve Chilcott (1966) and Brien Taylor (1991) as the only No. 1 draft picks not to make the majors.

From the front office's perspective, Appel's arrested development was a symptom of inefficient information transfer. "Part of the problem was that every coach and every coordinator and every special assistant in the org had their idea of what was wrong with Appel, whether it was mechanical or mental or something else," one Astros source says. "And so in the midst of struggling at Lancaster, he was getting all sorts of conflicting advice about what was wrong with him." The Astros were plagued by the same problem Rickey had designed Dodgertown to solve. "There would be different things said," Appel acknowledges, adding, "It's something that I've thought about because I can always sit back and look and say, 'Man, if certain coaches didn't say certain things . . .'"

The Astros learned from both errors. Their reluctance to change their prior opinion of Martinez highlighted the need for technology that could quickly determine—and, when proactively applied, alter—a player's true talent. As for Appel, Fast says, "That failure was a huge impetus for what happened the next spring training, which was getting a pitching-development plan, including TrackMan data, in front of every pitcher in the minors and having a front-office person present to explain it to them."

According to counts culled from team media guides, the pre-Luhnow Astros employed an exactly average-sized 51-member player-development staff in the spring of 2011, including all coaches, managers, and front-office executives devoted to player development. By the spring of 2015, that headcount climbed to 78, mirroring the rapid growth in PD departments around the game. Between the springs of 2011 and 2018, the average size of the staffs assigned to player development by MLB teams increased by 51 percent, from an average of 51 in 2011 to an average of 77 in 2018. (The deep-pocketed Yankees led all teams in 2018 with 102 PD personnel.) Those totals have kept climbing since.

The Astros helped spur that expansion in the spring of 2015 by pioneering the position of development coach, a role that other clubs subsequently copied. The development coach wouldn't replace any of the existing coaching positions. It would be an *additional* job designed to cope with the growing data demands facing minor-league coaches. The new kind of coach, Mejdal says, would be, "more technologically

[and] quantitatively savvy than a conventional coach . . . someone who can throw [batting practice] and also write a SQL query."

The Astros couldn't add the latter task to their regular coaches' duties because many of them already had their hands full. "Usually a pitching coach gets to the ballpark 3 to 4 p.m., dillydally, have a throwing session," a former Astros scout says. "Astros pitching coaches get to the ballpark at 9 to 10 a.m., they prepare video, they prepare classroom work. These guys friggin' *work*. That's the future of coaching. It took five years and 90 percent turnover to get everyone on the same page."

Across baseball, the coaching ranks are increasingly reflecting the emphasis teams are placing on nondogmatic development. As Mariners director of player development Andy McKay says, "Your number one tool as a coach in 2018 is not playing experience, it is a growth mindset that allows you to be curious and take advantage of all of the information that is readily available. . . . So while for years and years the first question asked in an interview was, 'Where did you play?', the question is becoming, 'How well do you learn?'"

This shift isn't confined to the farm. In the past, big-league coaches tended to be buddies with the manager, who traditionally has selected his staff. Today's development-focused front offices are less willing to let managers make decisions that could compromise the consistency of the message the players hear from one level to the next. "Young, prospect-laden teams want to continue to develop players [in the majors], so they want the hitting and pitching coaches to actually coach the players," an Astros source says. "It's a radical idea, by the standards of Major League Baseball."

Like the rest of PD departments, MLB staffs are expanding: at the start of 2019, the thirty teams listed a combined eighty major-league coaches *other* than the previously standard six (bench coach, hitting and pitching coaches, first- and third-base coaches, and bullpen coach), including twenty-five *assistant* hitting coaches, six assistant pitching coaches, and several dedicated catching and/or quality control coaches. (Some teams, including the Dodgers, White Sox, and Angels—who've hired several cutting-edge coaches who'd gained attention on Twitter—employ *three* hitting coaches.) With the average

MLB player's salary now upward of $4.5 million, it's only logical for teams to make much smaller investments in the right support staff to ensure that those players fulfill their potential. "You have coaches who want to be the filter—'Oh, don't show that to them, that might mess with their head,'" Fast says. "And then you have the coaches who are not afraid of the data and say, 'Oh wow, this is really helpful. I've got a drill that'll help the players with this.' That latter kind of coach is really valuable."

It's no coincidence, then, that progressive teams tend to target young, inexperienced managers. That's partly because recently re-tired managers may be better at relating to young players and because front offices want to dictate in-game tactics like batting orders and bullpen moves, which longer-tenured managers may consider their domain. But the Astros source says it's also because one way to en-sure the front office can appoint its handpicked coaches "is to hire a manager who doesn't *have* a lot of coaching buddies—isn't part of the whole coaching favor-trading network, doesn't owe a bunch of coaches for getting to this point, and will just let the front office name the coaches they want."

Pressly's old team, the Twins, is one recent, instructive example. Minnesota's front office knew about the power of Pressly's curve. That Pressly didn't make those changes until he *left* the Twins, baseball operations director Daniel Adler told the sports website The Athletic in October, was "a very hard lesson."

At the end of the 2018 season, the Twins fired sixty-two-year-old manager Paul Molitor and jettisoned most of his staff. "We just feel a change in voice and potential style with some of these younger play-ers could be of benefit to us," Falvey said at the press conference, not-ing the need to "put the best possible resources around" the team's young talent. Weeks later, Falvey hired a rookie manager, poaching thirty-seven-year-old Rocco Baldelli from the Rays. "Not only does he understand the information and how it can impact players, but he champions it with players," Falvey said.

The Astros fought this battle, too. In 2014, Luhnow and then man-ager Bo Porter beefed about Appel being brought to Houston to throw a bullpen session for big-league pitching coach Brent Strom without

Porter's approval. Porter, who could be closed-minded and resented challenges to his authority, was appalled that Strom was reporting to the front office and not to him. Later that season, Luhnow made clear where his loyalties lay, firing Porter and retaining Strom, who had been a fixture at the Texas Baseball Ranch. And with good reason: Strom, a former major-league pitcher and, at seventy, the oldest active pitching coach in the big leagues, is exactly the kind of coach the Astros covet. "Stromy is probably one of the most underappreciated persons in the analytics movement," Mejdal says. "He has as much experience as anybody, but he also has an insatiable curiosity and competitive desire to find something to give him, and the Astros, an advantage."

Dweck identified another attribute of organizations with a growth mindset: "They support collaboration across organizational boundaries rather than competition among employees or units." In September 2014, the Astros hired a manager who wouldn't stand in Strom's way. The then forty-year-old A.J. Hinch, a former big-league catcher—and a Stanford psychology major—had been a farm director and manager for the Diamondbacks and then a pro scouting vice president and assistant general manager for the Padres before Luhnow invited him to return to the dugout. Having done every job, he understood that the manager is just the steward of the final leg of a long-term process of player development. "I am pretty open-minded," says Hinch, whom the Astros extended through 2022 in the summer of 2018. "I was hired by an organization that demands it."

Gradually, awareness of Anders Ericsson's research and the power of deliberate practice "permeated our system," Mejdal says, and the front office applied that philosophy not just to players but to itself. "The player-development organization made leaps and bounds over the last three years or so," Fast says. "Every year things got much, much better."

The development coaches helped. So did the Astros' unflinching commitment to putting the people they wanted in place, no matter how high the turnover rate. Kyle Boddy consulted for Houston on pitching mechanics in 2013 and 2014 and visited the Astros' spring training complex in Kissimmee, and the experience gave him an appreciation for Luhnow's implacability. "His commitment level to whatever he does is at the maximum," Boddy says. "He just goes all in when he makes decisions."

Boddy recalls hearing about how the pitching coaches for the Astros' minor-league affiliates had defied Luhnow's orders to implement long-toss training in 2012. In hopes of softening their resistance, Luhnow sent one of the skeptics, his sixty-something first-year minor-league pitching coordinator and former major leaguer Jon Matlack, to the Texas Baseball Ranch to learn more about the controversial technique. "Matlack comes back and he's like, 'It's stupid. They're gonna hurt their arms,'" Boddy says. "And Jeff's like, 'All right . . . I can believe that. What's your report? What's your backing behind that? What's your reason?' Matlack's like, 'It's just dumb.' And Jeff's like, 'You're fired, just leave,' and canned him. And canned all the pitching coaches. And one of the other people in the organization was like, 'Did you set out to fire all the pitching coaches?' And Jeff said, 'No, but I'm not gonna tolerate insubordination.'"

The Astros replaced the coaching casualties with more malleable instructors, many of them recruited from colleges. Of the fifty-three people in player development in the spring of 2012, Luhnow's first full year with the team, only two remained in explicitly PD-related roles for the Astros six years later. Even player-development director (and later director of player personnel) Quinton McCracken, who left the team in 2017, was dropped because he wasn't cutthroat enough for the front office's taste, too reluctant to let go of players and coaches who didn't deliver. "The story of a lot of people who got pushed out in that time frame is people who wouldn't push their people to do what the front office wanted," one Astros source says, adding, "I don't know if anyone has ever so thoroughly turned over a front office down to the coaches and scouts."

Although that purge established Luhnow's authority, it didn't destroy the surviving staff's ability to innovate. Russ Steinhorn was a coach at Delaware State University when Mejdal saw an item in *Sports Illustrated* about DSU batters shattering the all-time Division I hit-by-pitch record during the 2012 season. Steinhorn had made his players so hungry to reach base that they were willing to take 1 (or 152) for the team, an ethos that appealed to Houston's whatever-it-takes brain trust. The Astros hired him as a minor-league hitting coach in 2013, and he served first in that role and then as a minor-league manager until October 2017, when he left to take over as the director of player development at Clemson.

Steinhorn had the latitude to implement the practices he wanted. Anything, he says, to foster intent and continual learning and avoid an unchallenging environment where "the cream's gonna rise to the top . . . but you're not gonna be able to produce mass development in players at any level because you're basically just going through the motions."

An essential source of the trust and rapport between front office and farm—and, with all due respect to Altuve, Springer, and Keuchel, one of the most valuable prospects the Luhnow administration inherited—is Pete Putila, whom one former Astros employee labels "more valuable than almost anyone in that organization" and another describes as the most deserving future GM in the Astros' executive branch. The precocious and personable Putila, who was hired as a baseball operations intern in January 2011, played a pivotal role in creating a culture of collaboration between coaches and analysts and rose rapidly to his current role as director of player development by August 2016.

As the quality of coaching and communication improved, so did the data. Investments in wearable sensors and high-speed video allowed the Astros to assemble more pieces of the performance puzzle. "It wasn't very long ago that even in the Astros organization it was sort of accepted that 'Hitters hit,'" Fast says. Since then, he notes, "We've learned a ton about what separates good hitters and bad hitters and how we can train that." In minor-league games, Astros pitchers began to wear harnesses made by Catapult, an Australian sports-performance-tracking company. The data the Catapult devices generated allowed the front office to make inferences about the pitchers' movements and mechanics. The team also uses Catapult GPS trackers that attach to players' backs beneath their jerseys to monitor how much ground they cover and how much energy they expend.

In practice, Astros minor leaguers also started wearing sensors from K-Vest and 4D Motion, two wireless motion-tracking companies. And using "deep learning" techniques, the Astros could ingest high-speed-video footage and convert it into data that could help coaches and analysts classify, quantify, and correct mechanical shortcomings.

Houston's capabilities increased again in 2016 when the organization invested in Edgertronic cameras, which Putila discovered independent of Bauer and Boddy. In his penultimate piece for the Hardball Times, "A digital salute to pitch grips," Fast had conceived a kind of pitch-grip cartography—a notation system that would allow a researcher to describe a grip based on how the ball is held in the hand, which part of each finger is touching the ball, and where on the ball each finger is touching. In the public sphere, it was hard to come by high-quality images of pitchers' hands holding the ball, but that existing framework made diagnostics and adjustments more manageable once Fast and the front office could easily obtain images of the grips of any pitcher they pointed a camera toward. Subtle tweaks could then alter an inefficient high-spin pitch into one that channels that spin to create more movement. "It's not 'high-spin breaking ball equals good,' but 'high-spin breaking ball is the raw material, along with the delivery, to turn that into an effective weapon,'" Fast says.

Dweck wrote that organizations with a growth mindset "are committed to the growth of every member, not just in words but in deeds, such as broadly available development and advancement opportunities." That's the case in the Astros system, where upon entering pro ball even the lowliest prospects receive biomechanical evaluations using the team's suite of tools. Reggie Johnson was an undrafted free agent signed in 2016 out of tiny Hampden-Sydney College, a Division III school that hasn't sent a player to the big leagues since 1962. As a right-handed reliever with an 88 to 90 mph fastball who'd allowed seventeen runs (seven unearned) in twenty-four innings in Rookie ball in 2016, Johnson was at the bottom of the pro-ball barrel when spring training started in 2017. Yet even he worked with TrackMan and an Edgertronic. "My first year, I was just wondering why that stuff really mattered because I felt like if you get outs, you get outs," he says. "But after going through the system for a year and then going to spring training and seeing how the team really benefited from it [and] how players benefited from that stuff, it made more sense."

Although the Astros' high-tech tools helped Johnson nearly double his 2016 strikeout-to-walk ratio in higher-level leagues, they also helped hasten his departure from pro ball. Between 2017 and 2018, the Astros downsized from nine farm teams to seven, eliminating their second DSL team and their Greeneville team in the Appalachian League, where Johnson had spent most of 2016. The resulting roster crunch forced out fringe players like him. It might seem strange that a team that holds a huge developmental advantage would want to reduce the size of its farm system, but it was precisely *because* of that advantage that the Astros slimmed down. "That was driven by feeling we were better at evaluating our players," a former Astros staffer says, although he acknowledges that ownership didn't mind the monetary savings. "We had less need to let them play a full season or two or three in order to know if they had major-league potential." With smaller samples required to come to conclusions and less talent easily obtainable through the increasingly competitive amateur markets, the organization opted to concentrate its coaching time on more promising players. The Astros were replacing Rickey's developmental maxim, "Out of quantity comes quality," with one of their own: "Out of *quantification* comes quality."

The Astros' new toys gave them PD powers they previously hadn't possessed. Take Appel: he now believes that his loss of stuff was a symptom of undiagnosed and largely unacknowledged arm issues that took a toll when he tried to pitch through them. Shoulder and elbow problems eventually drove him into retirement, which made him rethink how long his health had been compromised. "Being able to look back, I wasn't at the same health in pro ball that I was in college," he says.

One former front-office member says an injury would be consistent with what he saw from Appel: the pitcher suffered from poor fastball command, which hinted at problems with his delivery, but the team wasn't systematically gathering data on that then. By 2017, the Astros were establishing clear, individually tailored goals for their pitchers in spring training and giving them feedback based on TrackMan data after every outing, with portable and mounted Edgertronics—seven of which the Astros have installed at Minute Maid Park, with seven more at each minor-league park in their system—available for more detailed looks. "I'm not saying we could have diagnosed an injury from that process, but we could have made a more specific diagnosis about what was being executed and what wasn't," the former front-office member says. Data can overcome machismo by pinpointing a problem a pitcher can't pretend not to notice. "Saying his arm isn't 100 percent sounds like an excuse for bad performance," the source adds. "Saying, 'Your arm is late getting up after stride-foot contact,' and working on drills for that specific thing and not having them help, can give him an avenue to say, 'I can't do that because X hurts.'"

Advancing technology also altered the Astros' conception of what was possible on the offensive side. In late 2013, the year before Springer made his MLB debut, his strikeout rate topped 27 percent between Double-A and Triple-A. If he whiffed that much in the minors, he might swing and miss *more* often in the majors, limiting his offensive ceiling. But that was outmoded thinking. In the post-Moneyball era, Springer's strikeout rate wasn't set in stone. The Astros could help him make more contact.

Only seven hitters who made as many major-league plate appearances as Springer from 2014 to 2016 recorded higher strikeout rates than his 26 percent. During that period, the Astros featured Springeresque strikeout rates up and down the order: the team led the AL and ranked second in the majors in strikeout rate in 2014 and 2015, and its K rate climbed again in 2016. But even though the stigma surrounding strikeouts had decreased as teams realized that Ks weren't worse than other outs and often correlated with walks and homers, the Astros thought they could do better. What they'd learned would allow them to have their walks and homers and keep their contact, too.

Armed with Blast sensors and high-speed video, the Astros had set out to determine analytically what works at the plate. Belatedly, they realized that someone had beaten them to that territory: Charley Lau, an influential hitting coach who conducted groundbreaking video analysis at the Royals Academy and became baseball's first coach with a six-year contract and a six-figure salary on the strength of his success with George Brett and other high-profile hitters. "A lot of what we discovered from Edgertronic cameras in 2016 was just a rediscovery of things Lau had discovered thirty-plus years earlier," Fast says. "We ended up teaching almost exactly what Lau taught in terms of swing mechanics." Lau, who stressed the importance of balance, weight shift, rhythm, fluidity, and finish, "got associated with hitting it on the ground, but the swing he teaches doesn't actually do that," Fast says.

The Astros applied their new knowledge by acquiring hitters whose power swings didn't preclude contact and helping them keep their bats in the zone longer. They devised an app-based scoring system to promote smart swing decisions and encourage laying off pitches away until they got to two strikes. They also reconstructed Springer along Lau's lines. In 2017, the former frequent strikeout victim made *more* contact than the typical batter and also added power (ISO), culminating in a career year. "Players just don't do what Springer has done. Not to such an extent," wrote FanGraphs' Jeff Sullivan, in a post titled "Baseball's Improbable Contact Hitter." Nor do many whole line-ups look like that one did: the championship Astros finished with the major leagues' lowest strikeout rate *and* highest isolated power, yielding baseball's best offense on a per-plate-appearance basis since Babe Ruth and Lou Gehrig were batting back-to-back. "Everybody looks at Correa and Springer and Altuve and Bregman now and says, 'Well sure, you can do that with elite hitters,'" Fast says. "But none of them were doing that to that extreme before we worked with them."

When an organization embraces modern development, the internal appetite for information tends to snowball as players pass it along. But when a team is *trading* for someone it thinks could be better, it's difficult to forecast his willingness to tinker. The odds are better with players who fear they're running out of rope. "You try to do whatever reconnaissance you can when you're making a trade," Oakland's David Forst says. "You just don't know. We've certainly had guys who've come, and we've said, 'Hey, if you do A, B, and C, it may make a difference,' and he's said, 'Nah, I'm good with what I'm doing.'"

Houston hears a "nah" from time to time, but every success makes the next sell simpler. In a 2018 article about Charlie Morton's improvement in Houston, the *Boston Globe* observed that the Astros "have a way of sprinkling pixie dust on pitchers," but there's nothing supernatural about their track record. In November 2016, the Astros signed the free-agent spin king to a two-year, $14 million deal, despite his spotty history of health and performance and a career WAR of minus 0.5. "1st evidence of nuttiness of SP market," tweeted national newsbreaker Jon Heyman. "Insane!" Less than one year later, as Morton mowed down the Dodgers in World Series Game 7, Heyman sent another tweet noting Morton's "nasty stuff" and complimenting "a great free agent signing by Jeff Luhnow." What a difference one meeting makes.

"I had a reputation as a two-seam guy that threw a lot of sinkers and tried to get the ball on the ground," Morton says. "And then when I got [to Houston], they told me that they wanted me to try and get swings-and-misses, which was something I'd never heard before." As with Pressly and McHugh, the Astros asked Morton to trade sinkers for four-seamers and double down on his curve, which helped him handle lefties. He soon started throwing it more often than ever. "In retrospect, I wish I had thrown it a lot more throughout my career," he says. Two strong seasons in Houston, which included an All-Star selection in 2018, opened Morton's mind, ridding him of his impulse to pitch to particular spots and stay within the strike zone. "When I look in, I'm not looking at this rectangle that I need to throw to," he says. "I'm just looking at areas where guys are aggressive." In late 2018, a thirty-five-year-old Morton reached free agency again and more than doubled the size of his previous contract, signing with the Rays for two years and $30 million.

In terms of career accomplishments, Justin Verlander couldn't have been further removed from Morton when Houston traded for him seconds before the waiver deadline in August 2017. Yet the former MVP was also eager to learn. "What they're good at is telling you what *you're* good at," Verlander says. His new employers reassured him that he had an elite four-seamer with incredible ride and informed him that he was only hurting himself when he used a different fastball. "I didn't realize that my two-seamer was an ineffective four-seamer, basically," he says. Verlander also used an Edgertronic to tweak his slider, and in Houston he's thrown the pitch at career-high rates, locating it lower and getting more whiffs with it than he had in years. That altered arsenal helped him finish second in AL Cy Young voting in 2018.

In the spring of 2018, Verlander spent hours throwing with and talking to another trade acquisition, Gerrit Cole, who would be his biggest competitor for the title of Astros ace. Cole was drinking tempranillo with his wife at a California winery a month before spring training when he learned he'd been traded to the Astros from the Pirates, the team that had drafted him over UCLA teammate Trevor Bauer in 2011. "I [drank] a whole lot more of it right after I got off the phone," he says. At first, Cole had lived up to his promise in Pittsburgh, finishing fourth in NL Cy Young voting in 2015, but at twenty-seven, his career seemed to have stagnated. Like Morton, he was a fastball-curveball beast miscast as the type of pitch-to-contact sinkerballer the Pirates prefer. The Astros wanted to free him from Pittsburgh's pitching template, which had helped suppress his powers, turning him into a league-average pitcher in 2017. "Individualized development and individualized attention is one of the most powerful things you can have as an organization," Hinch says. "It's not one-size-fits-all in this game."

When he reported to spring training, the Astros pulled him into a conference room for an hourlong, personalized pitching pitch. Seated at the head of the table, Cole listened as the brain trust told him they'd been watching and trying to trade for him for almost two years. They laid out what they liked and what they thought could be better. "You don't scare the player by telling them there's this massive overhaul," Hinch says. "Certainly not Gerrit Cole." Every recommendation was backed up by video, heat maps, and clear explanations. Houston's presentation had the intended effect: Cole describes his reaction as "mind blown" and says, "I'd never experienced any meeting like that, at all."

By now, the next part is predictable: Cole threw more four-seamers and fewer sinkers and recorded a career-high rate of curveballs en route to his second All-Star season and top-five Cy Young finish. Among regular starters, only Chris Sale, Verlander, and Max Scherzer had higher strikeout rates. The Astros, Cole says, "highlighted the fact that my curveball's my best pitch for me, which took six years for someone to finally tell me." He'd always had a top-of-the-rotation toolbox, but until the trade, he says, "I was just sometimes pulling out the wrong tools."

The Astros' collection of post-trade true believers supports Dweck's contention that "when entire companies embrace a growth mindset, their employees report feeling far more empowered and committed." We're a long way from April 2013, when Astros pitcher Bud Norris said, "I understand they have a philosophy, but we are unfortunately the test dummies for it." Today's Astros are willing participants in the front office's experiments, and the resulting team no longer looks like a car crash.

Tyler White, a thirty-third-round pick from 2013 who's used Blast to blossom into an above-average big leaguer, has been an Astro long enough to watch the organization go from a laughingstock to a leader and his friends in other organizations become curious and envious about "what [the Astros] are teaching, what they're doing to make us as good as we possibly can be as players." White takes pride in playing for the team that's making the most of data-driven development. "We've been the ones that have taken off with it," he says. "I want it to make me better than I already am."

When Steinhorn says that "there's no separateness" between the Astros' front office and field staff and that "there's always conversation" between the two, he's describing a setup dramatically different from the way player development has historically worked.

In the past, "you ha[d] these silos," says former Padres analyst Chris Long. "Player development, those guys are working on players in completely different cities and states. . . . They're part of the organization, but they're going to be a thousand miles away from you. So the interaction was minimal." That geographical divide produced an informational and philosophical fracture. "We had no idea what the training regimens were for the players," Long says. "It was completely offline. . . . All that stuff was just completely inaccessible unless you visited [the team] or called the guys and hassled them."

Technology has reduced that divide. Thanks to TrackMan and rapid video transmission, the front office can monitor its minor leaguers' performance virtually in real time. What's more, the whole staff is accessible via the workplace-communication software Slack, and the development coaches and performance apprentices—a new position focused on strength and conditioning that the team put in place for 2019—provide plenty of points of contact. In 2017, the Astros front office went one step further than communicating with coaches: Mejdal *became* a coach, spending the summer in short-season A-ball with the Tri-City ValleyCats, who didn't yet have a development coach. "A part of me going there was for the front office in general to become a bit smarter about the constraints of minor-league ball," Mejdal says. "It's easy for us to imagine ways of improving it, and sometimes the ideas are great. Other times they fall flat on their face, and we weren't very good at predicting which way some of these ideas were going to go."

Mejdal wasn't confident that he could predict how *this* idea was going to go, either; he hadn't worn a uniform since Little League, and while he was capable of throwing BP, even deliberately practicing his fungo-hitting skills improved them only from "godawful to really bad." As Mejdal recalls, "There was initially an anxiety of how the players were going to perceive me. . . . Like, 'Shit, we could have a real coach, but instead we have this guy from NASA. Thanks a lot, Astros.'"

Johnson, who pitched for Tri-City, confesses to some skepticism on the part of the players, saying, "At first we were wondering what he was doing here . . . is he up to something?" But both Mejdal and Johnson say that Mejdal soon settled in and became almost indistinguishable from a regular staffer, coaching first base and spending time with the players at meals and on the bus. He emphasized the importance of pitching ahead in the count, worked with hitters on using swing sensors, and always had his laptop on hand to dig up data and present it to the players in a digestible way.

Mejdal's minor-league odyssey is symbolic of the centrality of player development to every other initiative in the post-Moneyball era. For the all-in Astros, development is everything, and everything is development. But the technology that's powering that revolution has one clear casualty: scouts. "Traditional scouting could be dead in about five years at some clubs," one Astros source says. In Houston, it's already on life support.

In *Moneyball*'s immediate aftermath, traditionalists feared that stats would force scouts into extinction. Over the next decade, the opposite happened: teams hired *more* scouts, as front offices' appetites for information intensified and international markets bore richer fruit. Now, though, it's looking like those gains were akin to a dying star expanding before its core collapses. If old-school scouting is extinguished, the cause of its death will be the same thing that birthed the development revolution: better data, derived from technology, that does most of a scout's job better than a human can.

Like most teams, the Astros have eliminated in-person advance scouting, using Statcast and video instead. More recently and radically, though, the Astros have virtually eliminated *any* form of in-person scouting of professional players, even in the minors. One scout the Astros recently let go mentions a directory of pro scouts that's circulated around the industry. On the Astros' page for 2018, he says, "It just says Astros, and it has a picture of [Special Assistant] Kevin [Goldstein] at the top. One photo." In his new job with another team, the scout says, "I wore my [World Series] ring a lot to the big-league park. Each night, people would say, 'Can I see that? I haven't seen an Astros scout all year.'"

In August 2017, when the Astros informed eight scouts that they would not be brought back, Luhnow called the cut a "reconfiguring," telling MLB.com, "the overall number of people in the scouting departments [is] going to be roughly the same, if not increased" and characterizing the news as "normal" and something "that happens every year." As one of the scouts let go at that time says, "It rubbed us the wrong way when he said that." In 2009, the Astros employed 55 scouts, above the MLB average of 41.5. As of spring 2016, they still had 52, although the MLB average had climbed by close to 10. By early 2019, multiple waves of layoffs had trimmed that total to fewer than 20, less than half the size of MLB's next-smallest scouting staff. The Astros didn't have to fire everyone they deemed dispensable; following the first culls, some scouts read the writing on the wall and left or retired of their own accord. "It's very calculating, and none of it happens by chance or coincidence," another former Astros employee says. "They're very cerebral and Machiavellian."

Even before the mass layoffs, one scout says, "Any kind of gut feel or any type of subjective portion took a huge back seat to the numbers." Often, the stats determined where a scout would be sent. "You wouldn't scout a guy who didn't have a good stat score," one former amateur scout says. "They weren't going to take him." The scout recalls one incident from his first year with the Astros that hammered that home. "I got laughed at, like literally laughed in my face, because I turned in a fifth-year senior catcher who could catch bullpens," he says. "Maybe if somebody went down, there's value in a guy who can catch, right? It doesn't have to be a big leaguer, but there is organizational value. So I turned that guy in . . . and they just laughed at me. 'This guy's got a minus fifty stat score.'"

Unfortunately for scouts, the human eye just isn't as perceptive as a high-speed camera or a device that measures spin, and experience matters only so much. When the Astros acquired Morton, Cole, and Pressly, it wasn't because they'd sent scouts to see them; instead, they'd sought the opinion of their scouting analysis group, a compact crew in Houston that studies athletes from afar. "I think their vision for scouting is gonna be maybe having only a couple scouts and a lot of video guys running around," another ex-Astros scout says. "And a bunch of tech people in their scouting analysis group and their front office that can just crunch numbers, crunch data, crunch the video."

One might think scouts could save themselves by being more open-minded and reaching across the analytical aisle, but the Astros' ultrasecretive front office tended to keep them in the dark. One former scout says, "They'd be like, 'When you can, put this little Blast [sensor] on the guys' bats, because we think we're pretty good at identifying what is important.' They didn't say what it was. And I was like, 'What is it? What are we looking for? Why am I putting this on?' . . . I was trying to learn, [but] I didn't really get any direction."

Some adaptable scouts tried to indicate their openness, to no avail. "I'm actually really into the tech aspect of what the Astros do and was proactive in trying to incorporate that into my work," another scout says. "I'm not like a lot of the other scouts that are sensitive to being told what player to see via a model. I know that stuff works." He asked to be exposed to TrackMan and trained on Edgertronic, but his willingness to learn didn't save his job. It's cheaper to send a cameraman or a video intern to tape someone than to send a scout, and if anything, the Astros prefer that their remaining scouts abstain from technology so as not to be biased by the data.

There are still analog-only locations where scouts are essential, but those schools and international markets are dwindling by the year. For a time, the Astros tried to disguise their gear and preserve their video advantage by placing strips of tape over the Edgertronic logos when they dispatched personnel to film players. They dropped that counterintelligence tactic when the company protested, but even so, many teams' scouts still film on their phones, giving the Astros an edge. "You see the Astros using the Edgertronic cameras in the international market a lot," Brian Bannister says. "You'll have twenty scouts standing behind a backstop, and you'll have one guy with a pole with a high-speed camera on it, and you know which team he's with without even looking at his bag tag."

In the days leading up to the 2019 draft, the Astros will hold a series of amateur workouts across the country. At each one, six to eight Edgertronics will capture every movement, and TrackMan will be trained on the field. Why send scouts to the kids if the kids will come to the cameras? Although the expansion of international scouting raised the average team's scout count to 54.6 in spring 2019, up from 41.5 in spring 2009, other teams are starting to follow the Astros' lead and make their own pro-scouting subtractions, and the MLB Scouting Bureau—a league-operated entity founded in the 1970s to supplement teams's internal efforts—was shuttered in 2018.

Some technological blind spots persist: stats still don't do a great job of judging pitchers' deception, and they can't judge mental makeup, although scouts' efforts in that area are always imprecise. The Astros know they may miss a player here or there who slips through the statistical net, but they think they'll make up for the few who get away by more efficiently targeting the players whom they can confidently project and develop, with no annoyingly fallible humans to muddy their analytical outlook. Even most of the scouts who've lost their jobs with the club see some wisdom in the Astros' restructuring—and that's what concerns them. "It's hard to argue because they've been so good," one scout admits, continuing, "If it goes well, then scouts in general should be worried because you aren't going to need them anymore." Still, he says, "I think over a longer term that will come back to bite them a little bit." So far, so good for the Astros; so far, so bad for the scouts.

The death spiral of old-school scouting is closing a chasm that until now was endemic to teams. Historically, the scouting department signed players, and the PD department did its best with what it was given. In the draft room, one former farm director says, "you'd have the scouting director arguing with the farm director or vice versa." That changed at the predraft meetings in Houston in 2017, when the Astros introduced a different, development-centric model of draft prep, unbeknownst to the scouts.

"It was such a surreal thing," one Astros source says. "A huge group would sit in the draft room . . . during the day. The scouts would talk. The front-office people would mostly stay quiet." The team was at home, so at the end of the day, the scouts were excused to watch the game. After they left, though, the meetings went on. Putila and assistant GM Mike Elias had analyzed the Edgertronic video that the team had harvested from amateur games, and a few other front-office members had scrutinized the available college TrackMan data. As the smaller group reviewed each pitcher, a member of the R&D department would explain how the stats said his offerings graded out, and Putila would weigh in on what could and couldn't be fixed on the farm. "The scouts would come back the next day, and the whole draft board would look different, and nobody would know why," the source says.

In 2018, that prep work fell to the scouting analysts, who were well versed in the Astros' PD process. The traditional scouts' influence continued to decline. "Player development and scouting are two different entities across baseball, but the Astros don't view it like that," a former Astros staffer says. If the Astros can't improve a player, they won't take him in the first place.

The Astros' powers of player development are relative. Only 13.6 percent of all players who entered the minors in any organization from 2006 to 2008 ended up making the majors. Like any team's, Houston's record is marred by mistakes, and even in the Astros' case, many more minor leaguers miss than hit. They're just currently the leaders at a predominantly losing game.

Much as they try to keep a low profile, the Astros can't conceal their results: every other team can tune into their games and dissect their TrackMan data. But most of the developmental process still happens outside the spotlight. And just as players have a hard time improving if all they're told is a desired outcome, teams have a hard time aping the Astros just from watching them win. "I think there's an interest in the league of, 'What the hell, how are they doing this?'" Mejdal says. Luhnow isn't interested in answering their questions, or ours. The GM declined to be interviewed, saying, "You say it yourself, that PD is now the game's greatest source of innovation and the big leagues' most closely contested battleground. Why would any team willingly choose to talk about the things they do that may be considered proprietary or innovative?"

The Astros found out firsthand how hard it is to keep secrets in baseball when Luhnow and Mejdal's former Cardinals colleague Chris Correa was prosecuted for repeatedly hacking into Houston's database, dubbed Ground Control, over an extended period that began in 2013. Correa went to prison for his intrusion, but there are plenty of perfectly legal ways to learn about competing teams. "One thing I've heard from other teams is that when [the Astros] send our minor-league players somewhere else in a trade, the first thing that's always remarked about in an organization is that these guys know what their goals are and what they're working on," Fast says. Players talk—not just to each other, but to pesky reporters, too.

Even though NDAs bar analysts and coaches from taking team property with them, they can't forget what they know. That presents a problem, because although the Astros have modernized player development by breaking down barriers between baseball worlds, they aren't indivisible. The pursuit of a championship acted as a unifying force, but in the wake of the 2017 title, even some nonscout Astros sources grew disgruntled, believing that Luhnow was becoming too cost conscious and overly reliant on numbers—criticisms that *external* sources once lodged during the Astros' no-holds-barred rebuild.

Front-office members have clashed over a series of subjects, including how much information to share with scouts, how many scouts to employ, and whether to trade for reliever Roberto Osuna, whose 2018 acquisition in the midst of a domestic-violence suspension—followed by Luhnow's convoluted attempt to square the swap with a supposed "zero-tolerance policy related to abuse of any kind"—caused a public backlash. According to multiple sources, most or all of the front office was strongly opposed to that trade, but Luhnow—who had earlier been talked out of drafting Oregon State pitcher and convicted child molester Luke Heimlich, who has trained at Driveline—rammed it through regardless, with Crane's support. The same pursuit of inefficiencies that prompted the GM and owner to strip-mine the roster and revamp player development convinced them to cross a line that many of their own recruits considered morally reprehensible. "They don't give a shit, to be honest, what people think about them," one former Astros staffer says, adding, "Jeff's gonna do what he wants to do." Houston has a low threshold, too.

Even if public opinion is a secondary concern, internal discord could derail the Astros' efforts. "I do feel like things on a human level have, sadly, gone downhill since the World Series," says another source, who felt "disgusted" by Luhnow's public justifications of the Osuna trade. The constant turnover and clandestine nature of the Astros' operations also seem to have taken a toll on morale; as one Astros source says, "Slack accounts being deactivated is how anyone knows who's leaving. Nothing gets announced."

It would take a lot to puncture the pipeline Houston has in place. "Throughout the minor-league system, there's so much consistency from top to bottom that you can't try to copy it," Steinhorn says. "You won't be able to do it." Nonetheless, other teams *are* trying to. And many of them will have help from former Astros employees.

Several Astros Slack accounts went silent late in 2018. The Orioles hired Elias as their new GM. Fast opted to leave the Astros rather than renew his contract at the end of October. After fielding overtures from sixteen teams, he joined the Atlanta Braves, reuniting him with another recent Astros émigré, former scouting analyst Ronit Shah. Mejdal and assistant pitching coordinator Chris Holt joined Elias in

Baltimore. Minor league field coordinator Josh Bonifay took a job as the Phillies' farm director, replacing an outgoing director of player development who reportedly resisted a data-driven approach. Ryan Hallahan, the team's senior technical architect and the person primarily responsible for building Ground Control, left his full-time role to pursue nonbaseball work. Every member of the original analytics team that occupied the Astros' "Nerd Cave" in 2012 has departed. "Approximately 20 percent of the [off-season] openings for senior-level talent across all areas of baseball operations were filled with Astros employees," Luhnow told writer Richard Justice in February 2019. "Jeff says that happens to all successful organizations, but I don't buy that," one ex-Astros employee says, adding, "People look for reasons to stay if it's a good place to stay."

The coaching exodus has happened even faster. After 2017, the Giants hired Astros assistant hitting coach Alonzo Powell as their primary hitting coach, the Phillies hired Astros scout and scouting supervisor Chris Young as their assistant pitching coach (now pitching coach), and the Red Sox hired Astros bench coach Alex Cora and bullpen coach Craig Bjornson (whose contract Houston hadn't renewed) as their new manager and bullpen coach, respectively. In Boston, Cora beat the Astros at their own game, using starters in relief in the playoffs and emphasizing air balls and a blend of power and contact, as he'd learned to do in Houston. Another flurry of departures and promotions came after 2018: the Yankees hired Astros minor-league hitting coach Dillon Lawson and elevated him to hitting coordinator, and four other minor-league managers or coaches left or were let go. The Rays hired Astros Triple-A manager Rodney Linares as their MLB third-base coach; the Cardinals hired assistant hitting coach Jeff Albert as their hitting coach; the Blue Jays hired hitting coach Dave Hudgens as their bench coach; and the Angels hired bullpen coach Doug White as their pitching coach. Strom and third-base coach Gary Pettis are the only remnants of Hinch's staff from 2014.

"One of our advantages has been not being afraid to be the first to try (and probably fail) to implement new methods," Putila says. At a time when so much can be measured, it's fair to wonder how many more new methods are out there and whether the Astros—or any team—can keep planting flags so fast. But those who've been at baseball's bleeding edge don't foresee a slower pace. "I realized after a few years in Houston that I kept thinking, well, now that we have got TrackMan digested and understood, things will slow down," Fast says. "And then, OK, now that we have Blast Motion digested and understood, things will slow down. Now that we have Statcast—etc., etc. The pace keeps increasing. The tilt keeps getting bigger." And the old methods of development are falling further and further behind.

University of Missouri pitching coach Fred Corral remembers attending an arm-care meeting at an ABCA (American Baseball Coaches Association) convention in Nashville in the 1980s. During the meeting, longtime Miami-Dade coach Charlie Greene stood up and spoke, full of remorse for the obsolete developmental practices he'd once espoused. "I'm sorry, because we taught all wrong, and the things that we're teaching right now are so much better than what we taught back in the day," Corral recalls Greene saying. Corral continues, "I couldn't take it anymore because I respect him and care for him a lot. I interrupted him and said, 'There's no reason to apologize because you were the astronaut who took Apollo 1 up to the moon. . . . We're all astronauts, and there's nothing wrong in that.'" Appropriately, the Astros have been baseball's most adventurous astronauts for the past several seasons. And if a player doesn't have the right stuff when he gets to Houston, he may well when he leaves.

10

SPINGATE

I reckon I tried everything on the old apple but salt and pepper
and chocolate sauce topping. . . . I'd always have grease in at least
two places in case the umpires would ask me to wipe one off. I never
wanted to be caught out there with anything, though. It wouldn't
be professional.

—GAYLORD PERRY, Hall of Fame pitcher and spitball enthusiast

Bauer began his pregame routine in preparation for his May 27 start
against the Houston Astros as he typically did, unleashing high-arcing
throws that traveled three hundred feet, nearly from foul pole to
foul pole on the sun-soaked Progressive Field outfield grass. Then he
worked back toward his throwing partner, eventually shrinking the
distance to near sixty feet, with pulldown throws that must have terri-
fied those on the receiving end. Bauer, the player who epitomized the
idea of growth mindset, was preparing to pitch against the team that,
more than any other, incorporated the strategies he espoused into its
organizational fabric. In many ways, Bauer respected the Astros. He
thought they were the game's model organization. But in 2018, the
Astros loathed Bauer.

Bauer eventually made his way to warm up on the mound in the
home bullpen at Progressive Field, where both bullpens are tiered behind the right-center-field wall. Warming in the visiting pen, parallel
to and situated above Bauer, was his former college teammate, Gerrit Cole. It was one of the more awkward pregame throwing sessions
in baseball history. Cole and Bauer threw alongside each other, but
neither acknowledged the other. There had never been much of a relationship between the two, even as they pitched UCLA to the 2010

College World Series, and weeks earlier their relationship had become embroiled in controversy. An already compelling matchup between two of the top pitchers of early 2018 had grown more intriguing.

On April 10, Travis wrote an article for FanGraphs entitled "The Astros Might Have Another Ace," which chronicled Cole's breakout in Houston. Cole's underlying traits showed something more curious than the usual Astros intervention. While his velocity held steady from 2017 to 2018, Cole's spin rate jumped.

From 2015 to 2017, Cole's four-seam spin rate averaged 2,163 rpm with a 96.1 mph velocity. Through April 14, 2018—a period encompassing three dominant starts in which Cole allowed three runs in twenty-one innings, striking out thirty-six batters and walking only four—his four-seam spin rate averaged 2,322 rpm and 95.9 mph. His fastball's whiff/swing rate of 41.3 percent led the majors, nearly double his 2017 rate (21.6 percent). (On the season, Cole's four-seamer averaged 2,379 rpm and 96.5 mph.) That increase in spin rate produced an extra inch of vertical movement.

According to those most familiar with the nature of spin—Driveline Baseball researchers, Bauer, and perhaps University of Illinois physics professor Alan Nathan, an MLB consultant—such a sizeable increase is unlikely to occur naturally with such consistent velocity. "It's probably pretty hard to change that [fastball spin] ratio for an individual," Nathan told FiveThirtyEight. "A fastball is pure power. There is no finesse." While spin increases with velocity, Driveline discovered that pitchers have natural rpm/mph fingerprints, which they dubbed Bauer Units in order to normalize and compare pitches and performance. Only Diamondbacks and Cubs reliever Jorge De la Rosa had a greater year-to-year rpm/mph improvement on his fastball (+2.31 rpm/mph) than Cole (+2.01) in 2018.

The only method that Bauer and Kyle Boddy identified of increasing rpm/mph rates on a fastball was applying a sticky substance to a pitcher's hand or ball to improve the pitcher's grip, thereby increasing spin. Boddy responded to a tweet Travis sent to publicize the story on Cole by accusing Cole of applying such a substance. "Fuck it, I'll say it," Boddy tweeted on April 11. "It's pine tar and/or Firm Grip. Use them if you want a higher spin fastball or slider."

Bauer, in turn, tweeted that "pine tar is more of a competitive advantage in a given game than steroids." It sounded hyperbolic, but he had data to support his claim, showing the league-wide difference in results on four-seamers bucketed by spin. During the 2018 season, batters hit .270 with a 7.5 percent whiff-per-pitch rate against fastballs with spin rates ranging from 2,000 to 2,299 rpm, .245 against fastballs between 2,300 and 2,599 rpm (9.8 whiff percent), and .226 against fastballs with a spin rate of 2,600 rpm or greater (11.9 whiff percent).

MLB Rule 6.02(c) states that applying a "foreign substance of any kind to the ball" is prohibited. In theory, pitchers who violate it receive an automatic ten-game suspension. But the rule is rarely invoked unless the offense is egregious, as in cases like that of former Yankees pitcher Michael Pineda, who was ejected and ultimately suspended for having pine tar visible on his neck in a 2014 start. Managers rarely ask the umpire to check an opposing pitcher, partly because they know they likely have offenders on their own roster. It's mutually assured sticky destruction. (Red Sox manager Alex Cora did ask umpires to check the glove of Astros catcher Martin Maldonado during the 2018 ALCS, and Maldonado's glove was cleared.) Sticky-stuff usage is believed to be widespread in the majors.

In the past, pitchers have justified their use of sticky stuff on safety-related grounds, arguing that it gives them better control, thereby preventing hit by pitches. But the advent of spin-tracking technology revealed its considerable impact on movement and performance. Spin started to become king, more prized than even velocity.

From 2015 to 2018, the Astros ranked third in rpm/mph gains as a staff (+0.90), trailing only two fellow analytical powerhouses, the Yankees (+1.47) and Dodgers (+1.12). It was clear that some teams were hoarding and/or teaching spin; the Astros targeted pitchers with extreme spin rates, like spin-rate outliers Justin Verlander and Ryan Pressly. Pressly's spin rate didn't increase in Houston, although that doesn't mean he wasn't benefiting from a sticky substance. In August 2018, television cameras caught him spraying a substance on his left forearm in the visiting bullpen in Oakland. He then touched the forearm between nearly every pitch after he entered the game. It's common to see pitchers touching their caps, gloves, forearms, and pants while they're on the mound, but this was a more brazen display.

On May 1, a Twitter user asked Boddy about the Houston spin-rate increases of Cole, Verlander, and Charlie Morton. Boddy tweeted that the findings were "a weird coincidence," accompanied by a "thinking face" emoji that suggested he thought it was anything but. Bauer replied with many emoji of his own and then added, "If only there was just a really quick way to increase spin rate. Like what if you could trade for a player knowing you could bump his spin rate a couple hundred rpm overnight. . . . Imagine the steals you could get on the trade market!"

Boddy and Bauer's May 1 tweets lit the fuse on SpinGate, perhaps the nerdiest controversy in baseball history—not least for being conducted largely on Twitter. The festivities started when Astros third baseman Alex Bregman, who trains with Bauer in Texas for part of the off-season, fired back at Bauer with a taunting tweet that said, "Relax, Tyler [sic] . . . those World Series balls spin a little different."

Then, Astros pitcher Lance McCullers Jr. suggested that Bauer was envious of Cole's success. "Jealousy isn't a good look on you my man," he wrote. "You have great stuff and have worked hard for it, like the rest of us, no need for this."

Bauer responded that his issue wasn't with any Astros pitcher, but with "the hypocrisy of MLB for selectively enforcing rules when it suits them." Bauer said he would be perfectly fine with everyone being allowed to use sticky stuff if baseball would just legalize the practice and place, say, a can of Cramer Firm Grip on the back of the mound next to the rosin bag. He acknowledges that the rule is difficult, if not impossible, to enforce.

During the Indians-Astros May series, Cole told Travis that his four-seamer improvement was tied to working with the Astros' analytical staff on how to optimize the pitch's effectiveness, as well as help from Verlander.

"I remember a day playing catch with Justin," he said. "And we were talking about the four-seam, 'cause [the Astros] showed me videos of ones that they liked, and I told him that. He obviously is the four-seam master . . . so he knows what he's looking for. . . . He's like, 'I'm gonna look out for true rotation and hop. . . . And I threw him like three or four, and he nods his head yes. I call him over and I'm like, 'Dude, I'm yanking those.' And he's like, 'No, you're not.' . . . I'm like, 'OK, so that's what I need to [get] chase?' And he's like, 'Yeah. That's what you need to [get] chase.'"

That's Cole's story. As for suspicions that only a sticky substance can create spin-rate gains?

"Other people's opinions aren't my business," Cole said.

And the issues between him and Bauer?

"I'm not going to talk about personal issues," he said.

In a meeting with reporters, Bauer acknowledged that he and Cole "had a rocky relationship in college, because he told me that I had no future in baseball and he insulted my work ethic as a freshman. I don't take kindly to those couple things, so we had our issues." But he added that those feelings "have long since faded."

In the middle of May, Bauer said Cole had brushed off his theories when they were college teammates.

"I'm not shy about telling people that they are wrong," Bauer said. "Or that they are behind. I get a lot of arrows. I could very easily not advertise that I go to Driveline. I could not advertise that I do anything differently. Not talk about it with the club. Just talk about it privately. Play the game. No one would have any clue that I'm any different than anyone else. But that's not who I am. That's not true to myself."

Before the Astros traveled to Cleveland, Terry Francona apologized to A.J. Hinch for the SpinGate controversy. Hinch also addressed the controversy with reporters leading into the May matchup.

"I roll my eyes at it," Hinch said. "I do think people need to sweep their own front porch and deal with their own situations more than throw allegations around that are unfounded. I don't know if it's a personal vendetta or if he's got a problem with things. . . . It's time to get to baseball."

But Bauer *may* have conducted an experiment that confirmed the claims he made about the power of sticky stuff.

In the first inning of his April 30 start against the Rangers, Bauer threw nine fastballs. They were unlike any fastballs he'd thrown before or would throw after in 2018.

The spin rate of those first-inning fastballs against Texas averaged 2,597 rpm (at 93.5 mph). During the rest of that start, the figure fell to a much more typical 2,302 rpm (93.2 mph). For one inning, Bauer had increased his fastball spin rate nearly 300 rpm. What happened?

"No comment," Bauer told reporters the next day, when people pointed out the rpm spike and asked if he'd applied a substance to the ball.

Bauer went on to make additional comments to a swarm of reporters that gathered around him as the SpinGate controversy blossomed.

"There is a problem in baseball right now that has to do with sticky substances and spin rates," Bauer said. "We know how it affects spin rate and we know how spin rate affects outcomes and pitches and movement that have a big difference in a game, a season, and each individual player's career. . . . The people who choose not to do it are at a competitive disadvantage."

So why doesn't Bauer cheat if so many others are?

"At the end of the day, I want to know that everything I achieve is 100 percent me," Bauer told us.

Major League Baseball declined to comment on whether it was investigating the issue. But in contrast to the steroid era, MLB now has a tool in Statcast that can identify rule breakers or at least raise red flags. Bauer blew the whistle on a subject that everyone seemingly wanted to keep quiet. And in the process, he proved again that by understanding the factors that result in success, players can get more out of their ability, whether by legal or illegal means.

In June 2018 in Seattle, we enlisted the aid of Matt Daniels, Driveline's then pitching coordinator—who was hired by the Giants to fill the newly created position of coordinator of pitching analysis in January 2019—to test sticky substances to see firsthand whether they make a measurable, immediate impact on spin. For the sticky-substance experiment, Daniels turned on an iPad and connected to the Rapsodo. Before applying any substance, Daniels delivered a dozen pitches from the mound in the R&D building at Driveline. This was his control sample.

He threw at perhaps 80 percent effort, registering velocities in the low 70s mph range. After several throws, he examined the velocity and spin data. His natural rpm range is 1,700–1,750, and his natural rpm/mph range is between 24.0 and 24.4. The MLB average in 2018 was 24.2.

After establishing those baselines, Daniels tested two products. First, he sprayed his right hand with Firm Grip. He laughed, amused at its sheer stickiness. Then he fired off several more 80 percent throws. The Rapsodo data said his spin rate had spiked. His first three throws with the Firm Grip resulted in Bauer Units of 26.3, 25.7, and 26.7. His raw spin rate jumped up to the 1,850–1,900 rpm range, and the vertical movement of his pitches increased due to the greater Magnus effect generated by the ball's faster revolution.

Daniels tried to remove most of the Firm Grip. Then he dipped his right index and middle fingers into a jar of Pelican Grip Dip, some of the stickiest goo ever concocted. It had been a while since he'd tested the product. "Holy shit!" he said. "This is so bad."

With the Pelican applied, we could actually *hear* the ball come off Daniels' hand with a sound akin to a Band-Aid being ripped off skin. Daniels spiked some of his next pitches into the ground as the sticky substance dramatically changed the angle at which his fingers released the ball. With help from Pelican, Daniels' rpm/mph readings spiked to 27.5 and 27.9.

"Dude, I literally have baseball on my fingers!" he said. The small crowd gathered around his outstretched hand for further inspection. Sure enough, traces of white residue—baseball leather—had adhered to his fingers. He'd been pine-tarred and leathered.

The following November, Bauer further experimented with sticky stuff at Driveline. On one series of throws, he threw five pitches for the Rapsodo tracking optics at about 80 percent effort, applying Pelican before each one. The results:

82.6 mph/2,500 rpm (30.2)
82.8 mph/2,428 rpm (29.3)
81.3 mph/2,421 rpm (29.7)
80.5 mph/2,518 rpm (31.2)
80.5 mph/2,561 rpm (31.8)

Those were extreme spin rates.

Bauer then applied Pelican once before a set of pitches, as if apply-ing it between innings in the dugout (or in the tunnel) during a real game. He did not apply Pelican again.

78.4 mph/2,486 rpm (31.7)
78.8 mph/2,412 rpm (30.6)
80.3 mph/2,401 rpm (29.9)
81.5 mph/2,444 rpm (29.9)
80.9 mph/2,312 rpm (28.5)
80.8 mph/2,409 rpm (29.8)
81.8 mph/2,334 rpm (28.5)
81.6 mph/2,278 rpm (27.9)
81.1 mph/2,228 rpm (27.4)
82.8 mph/2,223 rpm (26.8)

His rpm/mph units declined as the substance gradually wore off his hands. This was another way that MLB could potentially identify substance users. Some pitchers are thought to apply substances be-tween innings, which wear off as they perform. A dramatic decline in rpm/mph over the course of an inning would be another red flag, indicating an artificial peak followed by a return to the natural rpm/mph footprint. Although pitchers could claim, if anyone asked, that Statcast was mislabeling pitches or that they had found a natural way to improve their spin rates, explaining away mid-inning Bauer Unit declines is more difficult.

After the test, Bauer shared a picture of his index and middle fin-gers. Like Daniels', they were covered in white baseball leather.

In the absence of an MLB investigation, Hardball Times writer Bill Petti analyzed publicly available Statcast spin-rate data from 2018. According to his previously unpublished research, the team with the biggest average intra-inning drop-off in four-seam fastball Bauer Units between the first and last four-seamer of an inning was—plot twist—the Indians, at 2.6 standard deviations above the mean. The Astros ranked 10th, although admittedly Petti's method wouldn't de-tect more regular application between pitches, and it's impossible to isolate the impact of sweat on mph/rpm rates within an inning. (In 2017, the Indians and Astros ranked 2nd and 18th, respectively.) According to Petti's numbers, Bauer ranked 169th out of 178 pitchers with at least 50 five-fastball innings in 2018, more evidence that he was pitching a clean (nonsticky) game. Cole ranked 27th, up significantly from previous seasons.

There was nothing abnormal about Bauer's spin rate on May 27. He struck out thirteen Astros in 7 1/3 innings. The Indians won in extra innings. Through the season's first two months, Bauer had established himself as one of the best pitchers in baseball—and he was doing it without bending the rules.

11

AMATEUR BALL

I ain't afraid to tell the world that it don't take
school stuff to help a fella play ball.
—SHOELESS JOE JACKSON

In the spring of 1948, each morning at Dodgertown brought the same curious sight. Long before most of the Dodgers' prospects reported to practice, the sixty-six-year-old Branch Rickey sat on a stool next to home plate on one of the facility's fields, wearing his habitual bowtie and chewing an unlighted cigar. With him was hitting coach George Sisler, a Hall of Famer who had broken into both college ball and the big leagues on teams managed by Rickey. On the mound was instructor and scout John Carey, a retired minor-league pitcher, and behind the plate was a player recruited to catch Carey's pitches. At the plate was the reason for the ritual, a twenty-one-year-old, left-handed-hitting center fielder who would, more than thirty years later, join Rickey and Sisler in Cooperstown: Duke Snider.

Snider, like Jackie Robinson, had debuted in the big leagues the previous year. But unlike Robinson, who had won the Rookie of the Year award, Snider had struggled in his forty games with Brooklyn. Of the 245 players that year who made at least eighty trips to the plate, only 6 recorded a worse strikeout-to-walk ratio than Snider's eight-to-one. Five were pitchers, and the other never played in the majors again. "Many players who come up to the big leagues but don't stay are failures because they never learn the strike zone," Snider wrote in his 1988 memoir, *The Duke of Flatbush*. In 1947, it looked like he might be one.

As a raw rookie, Snider found curveballs and high fastballs too enticing to let pass. So Rickey went to work, devoting an hour a day to Snider's instruction. For the first fifteen minutes of each hour, Snider recalled, Rickey had him stand at the plate and call each pitch—where it was and whether it was a strike or a ball—without taking the bat off his shoulder. For the next fifteen minutes, Snider would swing at every pitch he thought was a strike and, whether he swung or not, tell Rickey where it was, after which Rickey would ask the other three to say where *they* thought it was. In the third fifteen minutes, Snider hit off a tee with the ball placed in the strike zone. And for the final fifteen minutes, he swung at pitches again, but Carey threw only curveballs and changeups, and (like Hornsby before him) Snider was forbidden to pull the ball to the right side of second base.

"Branch Rickey was the one who taught me the strike zone, and how to lay off bad pitches," Snider wrote, adding that Rickey "made it possible for me to become a major-league hitter." Like a lot of power hitters, Snider never stopped striking out: from 1948 to 1961, he hit more home runs than any other player and struck out more than all but two. But he also exhibited patience, walking more often than he struck out in 1955 and leading the league in ball fours in '56. In the seventeen seasons after Rickey made him his "personal project," Snider struck out only 1.25 times per free pass.

Almost seventy years later, an even younger hitter needed a similar lesson. Fortunately for him, amateur ball became the latest locus of modern development just in time for a high-tech intervention to turn his career around.

Trey Harris was once the second-best high-school second baseman in the country, according to the amateur-scouting service Perfect Game. But Harris struggled in his first two seasons at the University of Missouri from 2015 to 2016. In 369 combined at-bats as a freshman and sophomore, Harris hit only five homers, slugging .333, and he struck out more than 2.5 times for every walk, posting an OBP barely over .300. Like his stat line, his build—listed, perhaps generously in more ways than one, at five foot ten, 215 pounds—didn't look like that of a future professional player. The big leaguer Harris aspired to play like wasn't a superstar: Pirates super-utility man Josh Harrison, who had a similar swing and compact frame. But even Harrison's career would be beyond reach unless Harris started hitting.

In the summer of 2016, after Harris's sophomore year, Mizzou hired a new head coach, Missouri native Steve Bieser. Bieser had a brief big-league look in the late '90s as a pinch-hitter and outfielder for the Mets and Pirates, and he played professionally for thirteen seasons. His first job after retiring as a player was as a high-school head coach and math teacher, a dual role in which he won two state championships while also instructing students in algebra and geometry.

When Bieser arrived, in the midst of Missouri alum Max Scherzer's second Cy Young Award–winning season, the program had a reputation for specializing in developing pitchers. One of the first questions the administration had for Bieser, he says, was, "What are you going to do to enhance our offensive production?" Bieser had an answer: he was going to get a TrackMan system. By the time the 2017 season started, the radar was installed. No longer would the school's hitters have to go by gut feel in practice.

Bieser secured funding from the school for the TrackMan hardware, but he didn't have a full-time staffer to break down the data. Fortunately for him, his first year at Mizzou was also the first for freshman Matt Kane, a sabermetrics-obsessed economics, mathematics, and statistics triple major in search of a sports-related research opportunity. When Kane called the baseball team, hitting coach Dillon Lawson said he was looking for someone to design a TrackMan database. Kane's programming skills, which he'd developed to indulge his own interest in baseball stats, gave him the expertise to help implement Bieser's and Lawson's vision of a progressive program.

For Mizzou, becoming a developmental laboratory was a matter of survival. Prior to the 2012–2013 academic year, Missouri moved from its former athletic home, the Big 12, to the Southeastern Conference (SEC). Not only is the SEC the most cutthroat region in NCAA Division I baseball, but Mizzou is its northernmost school. "While Florida is practicing in 60 degree weather in January, we are up here getting snowed out in March," Kane says. Snow is not only an impediment to practice, but also a recruiting handicap. "That definitely is what other schools in our conference use against us, is our weather," Bieser says.

Mizzou's baseball facilities are subpar, and the program competes for attention with the Royals to the west and the Cardinals to the east. Its games average about eight hundred fans, dead last in a fourteen-team conference that also includes LSU, which draws bigger crowds than MLB's Miami Marlins. These disadvantages force Mizzou to be smart. "Our whole goal is really just about player development," Bieser says, adding, "We're trying to look for those small things that maybe other people don't do to give our guys an advantage."

Kane's most crucial contribution was a way to quantify and improve plate discipline. The first rule in Ted Williams's treatise *The Science of Hitting* had nothing to do with the swing: "Get a good ball to hit." As Williams wrote, "Giving the pitcher an extra two inches around the strike zone increases the area of the strike zone 35%." Even college pitchers can exploit an undisciplined hitter's poor plate judgment, so Bieser believed the most powerful application of the program's new tech would be helping hitters learn the zone.

Williams had also promoted the power of deliberate practice. In *The Science of Hitting*, he recalled correcting the purposeless practice of Washington Senators first baseman Mike Epstein. "He practiced as much and as hard as anybody on our club, but he wasn't practicing the right way," Williams wrote. "He was having the pitcher in ordinary batting practice tell him what was coming, rather than make a game of it." Williams modestly noted that Epstein "had better results" after he heeded Williams; in fact, after the first month of Williams's tenure as Senators skipper in 1969, during which Epstein batted .231, Epstein posted a .990 OPS for the remainder of the season, the fifth-highest mark in the majors behind four Hall of Famers.

Mizzou also embraced that facet of Williams's wisdom. In their quest to optimize the team's offensive results, Kane and Lawson—who had worked as a coach for the Astros during the 2016 minor-league season before joining Missouri—read *Peak*, Ericsson's book about deliberate practice. Lawson wanted to turn plate discipline into a points system, post the leaders' scores on a board in the clubhouse, and work with the laggards on an individual basis. With Kane's help, the coaches could "keep track of good swings, bad swings, good watches, bad watches."

The metric Kane created gamified discipline, assigning negative or positive points to the hitter for each pitch, depending on the count, the pitch location, and the batter's decision. If a hitter swung at an outside pitch on a 3–1 count, when a ball would have resulted in a walk and he should have been sitting on something more centered, he'd lose points. If he took that pitch, or swung at one that was in the zone (regardless of whether or how well he hit it), he'd gain points. Hitters could see their scores rise or fall in response to their decisions, and Lawson could monitor each player's progress and intervene as needed. In Missouri's first season under Bieser—and with TrackMan and Kane—the offense improved by fifteen points of OBP and forty-three points of slugging, generating 30 percent more extra-base hits and almost 70 percent more home runs despite losing the top three hitters from the 2016 squad.

Harris, who hadn't heard of TrackMan in his first two years at Mizzou, was the biggest beneficiary. As a sophomore, he had failed to hit his weight, batting only .213 with one homer. At that career nadir, he was willing to try something new that might make him into the hitter he still believed he could be. As his junior year began, he grew intrigued by Kane's system, which produced a report that plotted each pitch location in red or green depending on whether the hitter's decision on that pitch was bad or good. "My goal every game was to get in the green," Harris says. "And then once I started noticing that I was in the green, I started noticing I was getting more hits." The hits were welcome, but going green in game after game became an end in itself: "A big deal," Harris says, "like a battle within the battle."

Harris pored over his hot and cold zones, which revealed that he was adept at distinguishing strikes from balls on the outside part of the plate but struggled to tell them apart on the inside corner. Once he'd diagnosed that problem, he could work on correcting it by paying particular attention to pitches in his problem area and looking closely at his results. "That was all because of TrackMan," Harris says. "Being able to tell me exactly where the pitch is, what the pitch was, was really helpful for me."

TrackMan did for Harris what Rickey did for Snider, without the subjectivity of having humans call out pitch locations and without requiring three other people to devote an hour a day to a single player's practice session. In his junior year, a TrackMan-enhanced Harris struck out twenty-seven times, walked thirty-two times—more than he had in his first two seasons combined—and upped his OBP by nearly ninety points. No one on the team with more than one hundred at-bats reached base at a higher rate. And that was only half of Harris's improvement.

As Harris practiced his hitting on the field, an iPad connected to the TrackMan system displayed the angle and exit velocity of each batted ball, along with the estimated odds that a ball hit at that trajectory and speed in a game would turn into a hit. The team turned that into a competition, too. "We would play games with it all the time," Harris says. "Like how many times can you get it between this degree and this degree above this launch angle, and you got points for it." The first time Harris took TrackMan for a test drive confirmed that power wasn't his problem. "I could hit the ball hard, but my launch angle seemed to be straight into the ground," he says. With help from Kane and Lawson, who told him to aim for the top of the batter's eye in center field, Harris worked on angling up his downward swing.

Harris's resurgence required both him and his head coach to reject their past practices. "I look back at my early coaching career and think, gosh . . . I was really teaching and coaching some of the swing mechanics wrong and different," Bieser says. He believed in the "swing down, chop down on the ball to create backspin" mentality he was taught growing up, and he taught it to his players. Harris had heard it too. But TrackMan told him that on balls between 15 and 25 degrees, the league batted roughly .700, which sounded good to a .213 hitter. As a junior, he upped his average to .268 and slugged .508 with twelve bombs, more than double his dinger total from his first two collegiate seasons combined. Big-league teams weren't yet convinced that his improvement was real, and Harris went undrafted in 2017. But as a senior, he launched another eleven long balls and batted .316. Suddenly, more scouts expressed interest.

It takes a certain belief in one's abilities to become a professional athlete—to trust that you can get good wood on an opposing pitcher's best fastball or blow the ball by an imposing power hitter. Up to a point, that arrogance is advantageous, inoculating competitors against the doubts that might otherwise hamper their performance. But it can also convince players who need to change that they're perfect as they are, or—if they *do* make a data-driven adjustment—that the numbers were a minor factor in their success. Harris has no such delusions. He credits 30 percent of his metamorphosis to his natural ability. The other 70 percent he attributes to TrackMan.

Harris graduated from Missouri in May 2018, but his baseball graduation had to wait until June. As expected, his name wasn't called during the first two days and ten rounds of the draft. On the third day, when he hoped it would be, his mother had to work, and his father took his sister out to eat. Harris stayed home alone, not wanting to risk losing service and missing a fateful call. Eventually, it came, and the voice on the other end told him he'd been drafted by his hometown Braves in the thirty-second round. It was later than Harris had hoped—his "bad body" label had come back to bite him—but any selection was cause for celebration, considering how inconceivable it seemed after his sophomore season. The odds are heavily against any thirty-second-round pick making the majors. Then again, the odds were also against Bieser. He was a thirty-second-round pick, too.

Success stories like Harris have helped Missouri compete in spite of its uphill climb in the conference. Although the team hasn't qualified for the NCAA tournament since it left the Big 12, it recorded better winning percentages in its first two seasons under Bieser than in any season since 2008. Just as important, player-development successes send a signal to potential recruits that Mizzou can help amateur athletes improve, prepare them for the data-rich environment of affiliated ball, and provide data to MLB teams that may help them get drafted.

When potential recruits come to visit Mizzou, Bieser and his subordinates present Astros-style development plans tailored to each player, mapping out paths to pro ball. Kane confesses that he's become an attraction on the tour; occasionally, he says, a coach will purposefully walk by his workstation with a recruit in tow. Qualities that once might have been turnoffs to jocks are now considered selling points: the presence of nerds, a laundry list of technological tools, and a promise to tinker with the way they play.

Missouri's story is not unique. That's the biggest hitch in Mizzou's plan to ride its development edge to contention: other programs with rosier records and greater resources are just as invested in modern development. UCLA was the first school to install a TrackMan system, and according to TrackMan, fifty-seven colleges (all but one in Division I) had their own systems installed by Opening Day 2019, including eleven of the fourteen teams in the SEC. It's difficult for an underdog to triumph when the dominant dogs are using the same smart methods.

One obstacle to even wider use is that college teams don't typically have huge R&D departments, which limits the tech's power as a player-enhancement asset. Some programs resemble miniature MLB baseball-operations departments, while others, says TrackMan's Zach Day, receive the system and wonder, "OK, what are we going to do with this?" Day expects to see an "army of college students" dissecting NCAA data and subsequently getting hired by MLB teams; Kane already interns for the Pirates. About fifteen college programs and five MLB teams are using an app called PitchGrader to turn the data into an intuitive, automated tool for development; the app's developer, Wayne Boyle, has already used it to engineer his son Sean, a right-handed pitcher, into a 2018 twenty-fifth-rounder, and in January 2019, the two independently published a coauthored book called *Applied Technology in Pitching*.

At the University of North Carolina, which returned to the College World Series in 2018 for the first time in five years, stats major Micah Daley-Harris is the Matt Kane equivalent, and pitching coach Robert Woodard is the open-minded accomplice. "I have a bunch of shoulder impediments, so I came up with this herky-jerky windup that disrupted timing with hitters because I would rather win with an unconventional windup than be smooth, effortless, and clean and get beat," Woodard says. "Unfortunately, there's a tendency that people would rather lose conventionally and not be questioned." Although the more talent-rich UNC has primarily applied data toward in-game tactics, it's begun dabbling in development. "Once you bite into something that tastes good, you're going to keep going," Woodard says.

At the University of Iowa, former pitching coach Desi Druschel retweeted Trevor Bauer, Kyle Boddy, and Doug Latta and shared images of his screen-strewn workspace and Hawkeyes players being put through their paces in gadget-filled settings straight out of *Rocky IV*. "A lot of people have seen us on social media—that's a big deal," Druschel told us. The school also drew attention for former assistant coach Pete Lauritson's "Great Wall of Groundball Prevention," a ring of screens arrayed around the infield to encourage hitters to aim up. Not long after the wall went viral, the Indians hired Lauritson as a minor-league hitting coach, and the Rays tried the same tactic in spring training.

The honor roll of advanced development programs contains many more names: Dallas Baptist. Wake Forest. Vanderbilt. Coastal Carolina. Clemson. Michigan (where Rickey's coaching career began). And both of 2018's College World Series finalists, Oregon State and Arkansas—the former filled with Driveline disciples. At the amateur level, where wins matter more than they do in the minors, every team feels an urgency to make the most of its talent before the draft takes it away.

Harris made his pro debut less than two weeks after the 2018 draft, playing center field for the Golf Coast League Braves. He started slow, got hot, and was bumped up to A-ball in time to spend the final month of the minor-league season playing close to home in Rome, Georgia. In fifty-three combined games, he hit .302 with a .409 OBP, walking more often than he struck out. He couldn't check TrackMan in Florida, but his radar love was rekindled in Rome, where he reviewed his swing decisions daily. Harris hit eighteen doubles in only 189 at-bats, but he drove only one ball over the wall, which he blames on his average launch angle: 7 degrees, a little lower than he'd like. Over the off-season, he planned to trim some wasted movement from his swing and fifteen to twenty pounds from his frame with the goal of reaching High-A, hitting .280 or higher, and popping five to ten homers in 2019. If he doesn't keep climbing, it won't be because he hasn't chased every chance to be better.

Players used to come out of college not knowing much. Doug Jones, a third-round pick in 1978, didn't pitch his first full season in the majors until 1987, when he was thirty. Jones became an All-Star closer at thirty-one and pitched into his forties, but before he broke out, he muddled through 246 minor-league games, learning through failure and gradually paring down a five-pitch mix to a trusty fastball-changeup combo. "I've learned that in baseball, a lot of adjustments are made on your own," Jones told the *Newark Star-Ledger* in 1989. "People will tell you a lot of things, but no one really tells you how to do it. It's something that you've got to develop for yourself." The only advice Jones offered to future minor leaguers who were similarly stalled was, "Don't give up."

Harris exemplifies a new type of player that's permeating pro ball as more schools obtain sophisticated tech. "As you see more kids come from Division I college programs that have TrackMan, that have an in-house analyst . . . they're coming into the pro ranks with a pretty solid knowledge of their pitch physics or what their data are saying about them," Bannister says. "So it actually might get us part of the way toward accelerating their development." In baseball, multiple clocks are always ticking, counting down the time until the end of a team's contractual control, the end of a player's prime, and the end of his career. The tools available to teams and players today are adding more productive time to the clocks.

The most analytically advanced college coaching staffs are suffering from brain drain, thanks to teams poaching player-development prospects just as they do the top talents in the draft. "I'm not of the belief that the only people that [can help in] professional baseball are in professional baseball," says the Twins' Derek Falvey. In November 2018, Falvey's organization—which already employed three minor-league coordinators plucked from colleges—hired Arkansas pitching coach Wes Johnson as its MLB pitching coach. Johnson was the first in recent years to make that jump, but as teams prioritize results over pro-ball pedigrees, it will become more common. In December, Russ Steinhorn left Clemson to work for the Phillies, and the Rangers came close to hiring Woodard as their minor-league pitching coordinator. (A late push by UNC convinced the coach to stay.) And in early 2019, the Cardinals convinced Coastal Carolina coordinator of video and analytics Michael McDonald to join their minor-league staff, and the Yankees hired Druschel as their manager of pitch development. The only thing preventing this poaching from happening more is that college coaches often make more money and enjoy more job security than their minor- and major-league equivalents.

In late 2017, Lawson, who helped remake Harris, was rehired as a minor-league hitting coach for Houston. Missouri replaced him with Matt Lisle, a disciple of J.D. Martinez mentor Craig Wallenbrock. But only five months into his Mizzou tenure, Lisle was hired by the White Sox to serve as their hitting analytics instructor, a newly created position on the minor-league side. The professional plundering of the amateur coaching ranks continues.

That raiding may soon extend to even lower levels. "It wouldn't surprise me if they got TrackMan in high school too," Harris says. At least two high schools, JSerra Catholic in San Juan Capistrano and IMG Academy in Bradenton, already have. Like any first mover, JSerra head coach Brett Kay has encountered criticism, in his case for extending data-driven development to a level it hadn't penetrated previously. "A lot of people frown on it in a high-school realm," Kay says. They say it's too soon for kids to get so serious, or they worry that every player will adopt a robotic, cookie-cutter swing, or they fear that impressionable players will be overwhelmed by the flood of information before they're fully formed physically. But none of that resistance stems from the team. Among the players, Kay says, "Everybody is interested and excited." And even at the high-school level, the allure of improvement is a powerful draw. "If we can educate an eighth grader who wants to make a decision, we want to be able to help him get better," Kay says. Some eighth graders grow up to be big leaguers. And these days, it doesn't take long.

Neither of us played past eighth grade, so we're perfectly qualified to experience modern development as any other amateur would. We decide that one of us should be a technological tourist, personally sampling and subjecting himself to the latest tools, and I, Ben, take on the task.

If I'm going to write about how real players are using data to detect and eradicate their weaknesses, I should at least try to catalog mine.

It's summer in Seattle, and I've arrived at the bland-looking industrial park that houses Kyle Boddy's Driveline Baseball. It seems unlikely that a baseball laboratory is hiding here until I hear the resounding, distinctive ping of metal bat on ball. I follow the sound and soon start to hear others: a blaring stereo, the thud of dropping barbells, and occasional laughter. It's all emanating from a single-story prefab building that bears the orange Driveline logo. On a sweltering, un-air-conditioned day, the facility is a sweat lodge where actual athletes congregate to conquer their insecurities and I've come to magnify mine.

I'm here to experience the same three-part intake process that any paying player goes through on his first day at Driveline: a hitting or pitching performance evaluation, a mobility screen, and a strength test. These exams produce a picture of the player's physical abilities and baseball skills, a baseline by which the player's progress can be judged. In my case, of course, the workup will quantify precisely what separates someone with no postchildhood playing history from the people with professional experience or aspirations.

My sherpa for part one is Joe Marsh, Driveline's lead engineer. When he was nineteen, Marsh showed up at the fledgling Driveline and added 13 mph to his crow-hop throws in five months by following the facility's MaxVelo Program. (Driveline's official Facebook account trumpeted Marsh's success to its followers but also appended what it described as a standard disclaimer: "Results not typical. Mostly because typical baseball athletes are a bunch of soft-bodied weak-willed complainers who don't push themselves hard enough.") When Driveline purchased fifteen cameras built by the motion-capture company OptiTrack, Marsh, who by then had finished school and joined the staff, established himself as the resident master of biomechanics, overseeing both a permanent motion-capture installation in Seattle and the construction of a "fully mobile biomechanics lab" that enables the company to make house calls to team clients.

Marsh works with all of Driveline's pro clients, which means he's slumming it by working with me. He suggests that I warm up, an unappealing prospect on the hottest day of Seattle's summer. Then he

tells me to take my shirt off, which immediately makes me twice as
anxious as I already am about performing physical feats in front of
people who train athletes for a living (as well as some actual athletes;
the current crowd at Driveline includes Kyle Zimmer, a formerly top-
ranked Royals prospect who ran into arm trouble and is here to rehab).
The act of stripping down completes an uncomfortable role reversal.
One of the occupational hazards of writing about baseball is the periodic requirement to lurk fully clothed in clubhouses, surrounded by
ballplayer bodies in various states of undress. Now, though, I'm finding firsthand that being a buttoned-down writer in a roomful of partially undressed athletes is infinitely easier than the inverse: being a
partially undressed writer in a roomful of fully clothed athletes.

I'm asked to strip down not to make me more nervous but because
Marsh needs to place forty-seven bulbous gray markers all over my
trunk and limbs. The cameras will pick up the markers and track my
movements, translating each flaw into figures and forces and angles.
"We basically make you into a video game and then do analysis on
that," Marsh says. Some of the markers refuse to stick to my skin, as
if they're rejecting a host who isn't up to their standards, so Marsh
sprays me with an adhesive that mostly makes them comply. Soon
I'm studded with small bulbs and on my way to the same mound
where Trevor Bauer blew away batters with his lab-grown breaking
ball months earlier.

Marsh asks me to face home plate and stretch out my arms in a
T-pose to calibrate the system. Then he gives me the go-ahead to throw.
Even if I can pass for a baseball player when I'm standing still—which
isn't saying much if you've seen some baseball bodies—I definitely can't
fool fifteen tracking cameras once I'm in motion. When I was a player,
I spent most of my time at second base, where one's arm doesn't matter much. I've never pitched, apart from Wiffle ball. I muscle up and
manage to hit 60 mph at the maximum, which in the most positive
possible light means I'm about two-thirds of the way to a mediocre major-league fastball. I repeat the process a few times, and Boddy, who's
observing from the side, asks if I throw any breaking balls. I laugh.

When the session is over, Marsh helps me hunt for and remove the
markers. At the workstation where Marsh was monitoring my throws,

Boddy shows me a computer-generated model with the same inef-
fectual motion as me. Although I felt like my urge to avoid embarrassment was making me throw as hard I could, I can see now that I
definitely do not throw with intent, for three reasons: first, I've never
needed to; second, I'm afraid of hurting myself physically; and third,
I'm afraid of hurting myself *psychologically* if I really air it out and the
radar reading is still extremely low. It's prettier to pretend that there's
a little extra in my arm if I ever need it.

Boddy later sends me a six-page PDF of my results, and Marsh
translates the technical terms into plain language that lays out, as
he says, "the sciencey reasons you're not a big leaguer." Science, evidently, has a lot to say on this subject. My maximum shoulder external
rotation—a key to creating velocity—should be about 160 degrees, but
it's only 128 degrees. At foot contact, my trunk is angled 25 degrees.
"The best throwers are around zero degrees, which is perpendicular
to home plate—closed off," Marsh says. "You leak open early." I have
little separation between my hips and shoulders or between my peak
pelvis rotation and my peak torso rotation. "Your hips and shoulders
basically rotate at the same time, rather than on a delay," Marsh says.
My lead leg block is "soft," and without that base to brace me, the
rest of my readings are slow and low; if my motion were a whip, it
wouldn't crack. When I release the ball, my trunk is angled 11 degrees
*back*ward, rather than forward toward the plate, which means that my
extension is subpar; my stride length should be about 75 percent of
my height, but it's only 62 percent.

Almost the only encouraging news—aside from Boddy reporting
that I did "much better than Travis" (who says he "developed the yips
in real time")—is that my weak-sauce mechanics don't place much
strain on my arm. My elbow extension speed and shoulder internal
rotation speeds are only 70 to 75 percent of a real pitcher's, and as a
result, my joints incur about 40 newton metres of pressure, compared
to the typical 100. As Marsh sums me up, "You're in worse positions
and move slower than pro players, but hey, your torque values are really low, so you probably won't get injured!" Not apart from my pride.
At least Bauer and I have one thing in common: neither of us has ever
had an arm injury.

If I have a (relative) strong suit as a player, it's hitting. When I'm playing with friends—most of whom, granted, are no more jocks than I am—I can almost always make contact. So it's with slightly more panache, and less exposed skin, that I meet with Driveline's lead hitting instructor, Jason Ochart. Ochart's standard hitter evaluation process spans one week and hundreds of batted balls, but I'm not in town that long, so he hands me a thirty-three-inch, thirty-ounce bat with a Blast sensor attached to the knob.

Because it's attached to the bat, the sensor can't discern anything about the movement of body or ball; instead, it provides info solely on the swing, measuring bat speed, peak hand speed, attack angle, and time to contact. (According to Driveline research, changing a hitter's attack angle by one degree typically produces a corresponding quarter degree change in launch angle.)

Ochart sets up a tee and atop it places a hitting Plyo, a sand-filled, weighted training ball. The ball deforms on impact, giving the hitter better feedback on quality of contact than a baseball can. Strike a hitting Plyo off center, and it spins away on an oblique course that reveals the mistake in the swing. These particular Plyos are motionless, so I manage not to mishit them. After a few swings, Ochart shows me how my Blast stats stack up to the Driveline pro averages. My average bat speed at impact, 54.4 mph, is almost 20 mph below the 74.2 mph standard. My average peak hand speed, 17.4 mph, is off by 5.7 mph; my attack angle of 7 degrees is 5 below the typical 12; and my time to contact, .22 seconds (which *sounds* fast), is considerably slower than the .14-second standard. "Hate to break it to you, but you have a lot of work to do if you wanna play pro baseball," Ochart says.

After my throwing and swinging sessions, Driveline hitting trainer Max Gordon puts me through a TPI (Titleist Performance Institute) assessment, a program designed by the golf equipment company to identify deficiencies in movement that can impede the swing and increase risk of injury. (The more often golfers get injured, the less time they spend swinging, and the fewer golf balls they buy.) Gordon makes me contort my anatomy in numerous ways to test my flexibility and balance and records the results on an app that grades me on a stoplight scale. The TPI tells me that I'm not great at rotating either my left or right lower extremities on their own or my entire lower body independent of my upper body, and it also reveals that my shoulder flexion is limited to roughly 120 degrees instead of the ideal 170.

After Gordon is finished putting me through my paces, he passes the embarrassment baton to lead trainer Sam Briend, who subjects me to a range-of-movement screen and a strength test. Briend has me lie on a padded table, first supine and then prone, as he pushes and pulls parts of me until they can't move any farther without something snapping. A few times, he has me push back to gauge my strength. Then it's on to the weight rack for a round of back squats, deadlifts, and bench presses, *exactly* what I want to do next. Briend says I can skip this part, but Bauer's Navy SEAL lodestar wouldn't shy away from a little lifting, so I guzzle some water and courageously continue.

Driveline practices velocity-based weight training, which is more concerned with the speed or explosiveness of athletes' movements than the maximum weight they can lift. Briend runs me through a few reps of each exercise, placing more weight on the bar each time to match predetermined percentages of the optimal max lift for my height and weight. A clip attached to the end of the bar trails a wire that in turn connects to a sensor; when I complete a rep, the sensor beeps and records how quickly I completed the lift. (Two months later, Boddy will buy Briend's high-performance department a new toy: an eighteen-camera rig from OptiTrack capable of tracking movements like weight lifting and jumping.)

Although my lifts aren't as fast as they should be—I've never tried to train for speed—Briend doesn't detect any mismatch in the strength or rotation of my right and left elbows and shoulders, which would point to impending injury and force him to shut me down to prevent further damage (as if being "shut down" would be distinguishable from my normal daily life). But Briend unwittingly echoes Marsh and Gordon by informing me that I exhibited low overhead shoulder flexion, especially on my nondominant side. All signs point to an anterior tilt in the musculature of my upper body. "We might have some serratus issues, or some of that rotator cuff might not be functioning properly, or the [thoracic] spine might be rolled forward a little bit," he says, making me worried about parts of my body that I've never even thought about before. This self-esteem-sapping knowledge won't help me be a better writer, but for a serious hitter or pitcher, insights like this could be the secret to attaining peak performance.

After Briend explains my results, he e-mails me a summary. The header of the document contains my name, the date of the assessment, and then three chilling words: "NOT AN ATHLETE." I *think* this phrase refers to the fact that I'm a member of the media, not an actual client; it's not a commentary on my abilities. But I now have a whole lot of data that says the statement is accurate either way.

Three-time All-Star John Kruk once said, "I'm not an athlete. I'm a professional baseball player." It's getting harder for high-level players not to be both. One new tool designed to accelerate strength training is Proteus, a product of the startup Boston Biomotion, which was established in 2016 and is confusingly headquartered in Queens. The company claims that its product "fundamentally alters and improves the way athletes rehab and train." In late 2018, the Dodgers became the first MLB team to partner with Boston Biomotion and install a Proteus system.

I meet founder and CEO Sam Miller—and Proteus, an angular piece of equipment that looks like the large robots that build cars—at Boston Biomotion's lab in Long Island City. Proteus waits patiently while Miller tells me how his father conceived and partially developed the product in the basement of Miller's childhood house. He'd imagined a machine that would be capable of providing three-dimensional resistance, unlike most exercise machines, which can only move one way at a time. He eventually abandoned the idea, believing it was impossible, or at least beyond his abilities. Much later, Miller realized its time had come. "I saw a lot of other technologies come out that were really focused on [the] quantified self," Miller explains, but few of them were focused on training and measuring strength.

Miller recruited experts in robotics, mechatronics, and full-stack software development. The machine they made, which features a long metallic arm attached to a rotating handle, moves on three axes, utilizing the magnetic brakes used on trains, as well as sensors and algorithms that detect the arm's position in space, to smoothly supply the desired resistance. Its capacity for rotation makes it an obvious sidekick for athletes in baseball and golf.

While Miller mans the screen that controls the exercise selection and resistance level, I grab the handle and start pushing and pulling Proteus's arm in and out, up and down, and side to side—as many dimensions as advertised. Proteus is set to freestyle mode, which means I can perform any motion I want. I windmill my arm, mimic a throw, and, holding the handle with both of my hands, swing it as if it were a bat. Proteus grudgingly goes along with whatever I do, but even at a low level of resistance, it makes each movement more taxing, as if I'm moving through water without getting wet.

Much like aquatic therapy, a staple of pitcher rehab, a workout with Proteus provides concentric-biased training. In weight lifting, the concentric phase occurs when one lifts the weight, and the eccentric phase follows when one lowers it. The latter phase does more damage to muscle fibers, which maximizes muscle growth but also increases the risk of injury and lengthens recovery. Proteus focuses on the former phase, which confers many of the explosiveness-enhancing and muscle-building benefits without the costs of eccentric training. And because the resistance is exerted in more than one plane, each rep is more capable of pumping you up. "This resistance can produce two to three times the muscle activation compared to the same exercise and the same load with a free weight or a cable machine, and do that with lower strain and mechanical stresses—so, lower load on the joints and tissues and ligaments," Miller says.

Proteus won't replace deadlifts or bench presses, but it could be ideal for rehab programs and in-season work, when players are trying to stay in shape without taking themselves out of action. In Miller's vision of baseball's future, players will use Proteus for arm-care programs, full-body workouts, and pre- and postgame warm-ups and cooldowns. Cable machines won't exist, free weights will be used in limited ways, and each team will employ five to ten Proteus systems. (Cha-ching.) "I think the focus of a lot of the training is going to be on moving and moving well," he says.

Prior to each exercise, Proteus's screen asks me how I'm feeling; afterward, it asks me how hard it was. Proteus isn't just being polite.

Naturally, it's tracking everything: when one completes a session, summary statistics appear on the screen, along with 3-D, color-coded graphics that trace the trajectory of each movement and indicate when and where the user was applying peak power. All of the stats are saved to the cloud, enabling long-term progress reports.

As of late 2018, only four Proteus systems existed in the wild, including the Dodgers' unit. Miller says that when he pitches Proteus to teams, he consistently hears that "nobody's ever seen anything like this." If the product delivers, it won't be unfamiliar for long. Although he's primarily marketing Proteus to teams and professional facilities until costs come down, Miller envisions a world where every gym welcomes one or more of his machines as virtual personal trainers. We could all use a helping hand, even if it's attached to a telescoping arm.

"Winning baseball games is quickly becoming as much a high-tech pastime as it is an art and science," wrote *Popular Mechanics* in a May 1984 feature entitled "Science Goes to Bat," which quoted rookie Mets manager Davey Johnson calling computers "a sixth coach." Eight years later, the magazine took another hack at the same subject in a new article with a slightly tweaked title, "Technology Comes to Bat." Some of the then cutting-edge tech documented within those pieces seems dated decades later: VHS video that allowed players to study their swings; boxy computers that could call up basic batted-ball data or batter versus pitcher stats; twin-wheel pitching machines that weren't limited to fastballs; radar guns that could definitively establish who threw hard (in an era when 90 mph was considered speedy). Other ideas sound far-fetched for the mid-'80s, like a "revolutionary TV system" that would supposedly project a laser beam that would register when a hitter swung an electronic bat at a 3-D holographic image of a ball "thrown" by a videotaped pitcher. A few products, though, don't sound so different from items in use today, including an experimental Diagnostic Bat that could graph the length and strength of a swing and the Quick Bat II, a bat-speed meter that used optical sensors to time the swing.

The successors to those objects, of course, are more accurate, easier to use, more widely available, much more highly valued, and more comprehensive. One of those training tools is a biofeedback device called the K-Vest, developed by a company called K-Motion that, like TrackMan, began in golf and adapted its sensors to baseball. The K-Vest provides a different piece of the performance puzzle than ball-trackers like TrackMan or bat-trackers like Blast. "Those technologies measure results," says K-Motion CEO and president Brian Vermilyea. "What K-Vest does is tell you, what am I doing to *create* that bat speed or to *create* that bat angle or exit velocity or whatever. It's the input that drives results." That makes for an appealing pitch, and at least eight big-league teams—the Astros, Red Sox, Yankees, Cardinals, Cubs, Athletics, Giants, and Mariners—were K-Vest clients in 2018, with more in active discussions.

The K-Vest, which costs $5,500, consists of four small, lightweight, wireless inertial sensors that capture the speed, direction, and acceleration and deceleration of a hitter's major movements. One sensor is attached to a batting glove on the hitter's lead hand, one is strapped to the upper arm, one hangs on a harness worn around the chest, and one is clipped onto a belt-like loop at the pelvis. Readings from each sensor are recorded as colored lines on a graph that charts what each body part is up to over the course of the swing, enabling more accurate appraisals of players' mechanics.

Ochart, a K-Vest convert, says that some hitters excel at certain parts of the swing but squander their energy on others: their hips rotate as fast as Mike Trout's, but the potential power they generate gets lost along the way to contact. "Being able to measure hip speed, shoulder speed, arm speed, hand speed, and bat speed and look at the relationship between all of them, you can find out exactly where a particular hitter is lacking," Ochart says.

Now it's time to measure me. K-Motion 3-D performance consultant Jim Beadle, a former college baseball player and golf pro, pays me a personal visit in Manhattan with the tech in tow. Beadle gives me an indoor demo, and then we head outside. There isn't much space to swing a baseball bat on 42nd Street, so we walk to my building's terrace and set up facing a wall. We use tennis balls instead of baseballs to reduce the risk of smashing something, and we definitely don't dent the façade of the building, if anyone from my condo board asks.

Beadle helps me put on the sensors, and I take a few warm-up hacks. Then he tosses a few balls from a squat at my side, and I let loose at each one, trying not to be too mindful of the fact that every move I make is being beamed to Beadle's phone. The sensors report my position about two hundred times per second; the one on my hand detects when I make contact, and the app dings once when it saves a swing and again when it's ready for another. Later, he sends me the graphs and breaks down the data. The good news is that my four tracked regions reach their peak speed in the desired sequence: pelvis, then torso, then upper arm, then hand. "I like that the pelvis is reaching maximum velocity before the middle of the forward swing," Beadle says. "I like that the pelvis then decelerates nicely and gets down to right around zero when we're getting ready to hit contact. . . . That means the transfer from pelvis to torso tends to be OK." I preen, unreasonably proud of my pelvis.

But even though I'm reaching my max speeds in the right order, those speeds are subpar. K-Motion includes pro speed ranges for each tracked part of the body, based on data gathered from hundreds of hitters on participating teams. My hand/bat speed is only 1,344 degrees per second, below the typical pro range of 1,500 to 2,230. (Mariners hitting adviser Edgar Martínez, a newly elected Hall of Famer, clears 3,000 even in his fifties.) My torso moves 1.5 times as fast as my allegedly exemplary pelvis, and my lead arm moves 1.5 times as fast as my pelvis, but instead of extending the pattern, my hand moves 1.9 times as fast as my arm, which Beadle says indicates that I "swing the bat a little bit too much with the hands." Speaking of my hands, a line on the graph suggests that mine start, stop, and start again as I swing; maybe I'm a trailblazer, but it's probably not a good sign that Ochart says, "I've actually never seen that before."

As Beadle scans the rest of my results, which compare me to pro ranges in dozens of categories, I'm gratified (and surprised) to see that while my peak speeds are slow, my positioning is almost on point. There's just one problem: my pelvis—the one part I thought I could count on—has betrayed me. For one thing, while it's reaching its max speed at the right time, its starting position is too "straight up and down." It should be angled forward, which would "engage the glutes, engage the core, so [I] can drive a little bit harder." Nor is it rotating sufficiently; my torso-pelvis separation at contact is too small, just as it was when I "pitched" at Driveline. Beadle says this may mean that I have a "girdle issue" or "something wrong with the hip joints or [my] ability to tilt [my] pelvis," which joins poor shoulder flexion on my growing list of physical faults. Now I have an excuse for not knowing how to dance.

The K-Vest comes with a package of training routines that isolate certain deficiencies and drill them until they improve. A hitter who doesn't move well in one way or another can follow an exercise regimen that targets a given weak point and then, once it's stronger or more flexible, reinforce the right motion by performing it over and over again while wearing the sensor. An on-screen display reveals when the player has entered the right range, and a ding confirms it via a second sensor. "I can tell somebody if I'm giving a golf lesson, 'Hey, I need you to be more rotated. I want you to feel like your pelvis is going underneath you at impact,'" Vermilyea says. "Well, they may not understand what I'm saying or have the same feeling or sensation I'm feeling when I'm trying to explain it. This breaks down all of those barriers. . . . It just shortens the learning curve for training mechanics." I'm feeling more rotational already.

I'm not the first unhip hitter to have a pelvic epiphany courtesy of K-Vest. Vermilyea gives me more confidence by mentioning an Oakland A's player who suffered from a similar problem and broke out after correcting it. "They tweaked his pelvis by 3 degrees, and he started lighting it up in spring training after that," he says. Later I learn his name: Eli White.

White, who turned twenty-four midway through the 2018 season, was the Athletics' eleventh-round pick in 2016. Entering 2018, his calling card was versatility; as a professional, he's played five positions, including the most exclusive noncatcher spots, shortstop and center field. It's a good time to be a budding super-utility player: as bullpens get bigger and benches get smaller, defensive subs are increasingly asked to be positional polyglots, fluent in all forms of fielding. As a consequence, 2018 was the first season in major-league history in which teams averaged at least one player per game stationed somewhere other than his full-season primary position (not counting DH and lumping the three outfield spots together). And more Ben Zobrist-esque super subs are on the way: 29 percent of minor leaguers with at least one hundred games played in 2018 spent time at more than two positions, and 13 percent, including White, spent time at more than three positions. Both of those figures are record highs dating back to at least 1984, when Baseball Prospectus's comprehensive minor-league database begins.

But even an aspiring super sub, like Justin Turner circa 2013, has to hit. And prior to 2018, White—a willowy six foot two, at 175 pounds—had never hit more than four home runs in any single season in the minors or in college at Clemson, where he slugged a career .379. In the spring of 2018, though, White was one of a group of A's prospects who experimented with the K-Vest as the A's evaluated the tech. "I guess we were just kinda like guinea pigs," he says. White wore the vest a few times while he hit off a fastball machine, and the A's relayed what the ensuing report revealed. "They thought that I had a little hip slide, and they could see that my hips weren't engaging right away as my front foot was landing," White says, adding that on inside pitches, his bat path was "coming across it a little bit instead of staying through it."

White and his hitting coach targeted the deficiencies the sensors had exposed. After spring training, he was bumped up from High-A to Double-A to start the season. And despite the stiffer competition—plus the additional burden of a ballpark in Midland that suppresses right-handed home-run power—he hit five long balls by the end of May, surpassing his previous single-season high. He finished with nine homers and a .450 slugging percentage, and he led all Oakland minor leaguers in hits and runs scored. White credits the data with helping him approach his power potential. "There's always been power in there, but I think once we [were] able to clean up some of my bat-path and hip-rotation issues . . . that definitely helped me have a good season."

Before he wore the K-Vest, White wasn't listed by MLB.com as one of Oakland's top thirty prospects. By the end of the season, the site had upgraded him to seventeenth in the system, and he'd been invited to play in the off-season Arizona Fall League, an MLB-operated, six-team circuit that caters to the cream of the prospect crop. In December, he was traded to the Rangers, with whom he ranked twelfth. "A host of mechanical adjustments have helped White blossom offensively, as he's now consistently in a good position to hit, with a better bat path that yields more line-drive and fly-ball contact and allows him to get to his modest raw power," White's MLB.com capsule said. His ETA in the majors was listed as 2019.

The last stop on my humbling baseball walkabout brings me to the Ball Yard, Doug Latta's Los Angeles headquarters, which is hidden behind an unassuming storefront on an aggressively unsporty street, Business Center Drive. Even though it's a summer Saturday and Latta says he's cleared his schedule to work with me, his small facility is still abuzz with baseball activity. A high-school student who's recovering from a leg injury and wearing a knee brace visits, parents in tow, to take some swings; a polished-looking recent graduate who's committed to Harvard for the fall stops by for a final hitting tune-up; and Latta's phone rumbles repeatedly as clients text to schedule appointments or relay mechanical emergencies. Everyone wants to be the next Turner, and Latta is the oracle they call.

Compared to K-Motion and Driveline, Latta is low-tech. Instead of fifteen high-definition cameras, he has one, standard-definition, black-and-white model that he's been using for more than two decades. Black-and-white, he says, provides better color contrast and doesn't strain his eyes when he spends hours dissecting swings. Nor does he think the lower resolution holds him back, as it did when Warren and Trevor Bauer were trying to study how the ball left Trevor's fingers. "I don't need to see what this pinky is doing," Latta says. He advocates a hitting style that's supported by the data, but he doesn't inundate his hitters with angles and exit speeds. For him, hitting is all about balance.

"Your weight should be balanced, distributed evenly on both feet and slightly forward on the balls of the feet, with the knees bent and flexible," Ted Williams wrote in *The Science of Hitting*. "If you insist on resting back on your heels, find another occupation." Williams went on to mention balance five more times in the text, a total that Latta exceeds within the first few minutes of our conversation. Latta employs the Socratic method when we talk about hitting, and I soon discover that the safest response when I'm unsure of an answer to one of his not-quite-rhetorical questions is usually something about balance or an absence thereof. A sample exchange:

LATTA: Watch your front shoulder. Which direction is your front shoulder going?

ME: Is it . . . backward?

LATTA: Backward. Pitch going this way, your shoulders are going that way. What does that mean to me?

ME: I guess I'm gonna be . . . out of balance?

LATTA: Out of balance!

After quizzing me for a while in a way that causes uncomfortable flashbacks to being called on in class, Latta hands me a black Louisville Slugger and has me hit in his cage for a few minutes as he feeds me balls from his seat on a bucket behind an L-screen. Then we retire to the TV to examine my swing from a side angle, sometimes pausing to study something in detail and then advance frame by frame. "Actually, not bad body movement," Latta says, possibly buttering me up. "There's good things in there." But he spots plenty of problems, too. The first flaw, as the Blast sensor also suggested, is that my bat's trajectory is too flat and, like White's, takes too long to get to the point of contact. I'm "swinging around the ball," which is bad because there's no room for inefficiency against high-level pitching. Most people who hit like that, Latta says, end up "working for the post office."

As Latta explains, though, my issues start before my swing does. My shoulders are too tense, and I'm leaning backward slightly with my weight on my back leg, as if I'm headed uphill. "If you see a balance point, you're behind it," Latta says. My head is off plane, and my front foot is open, preventing me from "containing energy." As I swing, my shoulders pull away from the pitch, my hands are loaded back behind my body, and my front foot drifts off to the side. By the time I'm actually in position for bat to meet ball, my initial misalignment has doomed me to weaker contact. "You're at the point where it's blind squirrel finds nut, or I'm just gonna try and force contact or block the ball, or do things because I'm no longer really in control," my tutor tells me. That hasn't stopped me from hitting my low-velocity friends, but against good pitching, Latta warns, I'd soon find myself in "scuffle city."

I'm still mulling over my inadequacies and trying to keep track of defects to fix when Latta mercifully stops listing new ones. After tearing me down, he tries to buck me up again. "Believe it or not, there's a little athlete in you," he says. It's just "being choked off."

I may be inept, but no one can call me uncoachable. Back in the cage, I consciously loosen my shoulders and shift my weight so I'm not leaning back. I bring my hands forward and watch where my front foot falls. It takes me a few tries to synthesize a new swing from Latta's instructions, but before long I go from making a mental checklist of prepitch adjustments to adopting a different alignment naturally. It feels like I'm moving less but each motion is mattering more. My swing seems less looping and more forceful. And that's when I realize: relative to my usual stroke, I'm *raking*. It's not as if I was whiffing before—Latta isn't throwing hard—but suddenly I'm striking everything with what seems like authority. The *crack* of contact is a lot louder, and the ball keeps whistling away on a line.

I'm beaming, because no matter how many road-to-Damascus moments I've heard actual athletes describe, it's euphoric to feel it myself. If *I* can improve so significantly in such a short time, small wonder that an actual athlete might make massive strides with a sustained effort. I try unsuccessfully to suppress my smile, because I feel silly swinging a bat while wearing a big, dumb grin. It also strikes me as silly that I'm so excited about being a bit better at hitting a ball covered in cowhide with a wooden stick, an ultimately meaningless activity that American culture collectively decided would be worth many millions of dollars when performed with a certain skill. Rational or not, though, the fulfillment is real. After years of nibbling at baseball, I'm actually "letting it eat," ballplayer lingo for holding nothing back. I hadn't known how hungry I was.

"Ten minutes in, and we're in a better place," Latta says when we review the tape. "Now your body's working a little differently. Looks more athletic, felt easier, but results are stronger. . . . You've got more extension through the ball."

We go through this process—hit, review, revise—multiple times. I'm getting a form of feedback from Latta and from my own perception of how hard I'm hitting the ball, but as a new disciple of deliberate practice, I lament that my progress isn't being quantified. I tentatively ask Latta how much he thinks my launch angles and exit velocities have increased in this single session, which sets off another Socratic exchange.

LATTA: When you started hitting the right way, how many balls
     did you hit in the air?
ME: More.
LATTA: A lot more. How well did you hit the balls in the air?
ME: Much better.
LATTA: OK. Did I tell you to hit the ball in the air?
ME: No.
LATTA: Did I try to force you to hit the ball to the top of the cage?
     No? Then what happened? What was the miracle?

I consider saying "balance," but instead I mumble something about making more natural motions. Latta says he doesn't want me to reduce what we did to a number; better numbers are the by-products of better body movement. "If I have a good swing and I can square up a ninety-mile-an-hour fastball, what am I going to have?" he asks. I know this one. "Higher exit velocity," I say. "Higher exit velocity," Latta echoes, satisfied.

"I did nothing more today than just try to get your body in line with what it's designed to do," Latta says. Maybe my mostly sedentary pursuits are more my choice than my destiny. "Believe me," he adds, "for a writer, you weren't that bad." That's all I've ever wanted to hear.

It's not too painful for me to confront my physical failings, because I never wanted to (or thought I could) be a big leaguer. Andy McKay wasn't one either, but building big leaguers is his job. To do that, the Mariners' director of player development has wholeheartedly embraced the latest tools. "[The Mariners] are our biggest powerhouse user in baseball right now," says Vermilyea, who notes that the M's have eight K-Vest systems—one for Seattle, one for each farm team, and a mobile unit.

In 2008, when McKay managed the La Crosse Loggers of the Northwoods League, a collegiate summer circuit, he insisted that his players show up at the park by 1 p.m. for 7 p.m. home games. That extra time, a rarity in a laid-back league where "It's just summer ball" was a frequent refrain, would be allotted to deliberate practice of player-specified skills. "If a second baseman wants to work on his double-play turn, you do it right for fifteen minutes per day and the results after three or four days would astound you," he said at the time. McKay's mindset hasn't changed, but his ability to put that time to good use has. "In terms of evaluating, is this player getting better, we've never had the ability to say, 'Yes, it's absolutely better' or 'No, it's not,' the way we can now," he says.

McKay estimates that the Mariners have had seven or eight "key breakthroughs" on the pitching side, and just as many (if not more) on the offensive side, that were "completely the result" of their utilization of technology like K-Vest, Blast, and Rapsodo. "If all of these tools and technologies help one player help you win one game in the big leagues that wouldn't have otherwise have done it, then it's absolutely worth it," he says. Although the details are different, in McKay's mind the impulse to measure every aspect of player performance is similar in spirit to the way any evaluator would assess, say, a forty-yard dash. "They would never just watch the guy run and go, 'That's really fast' or 'They're kind of slow,'" he says. "They would take a stopwatch. Well, we now have a stopwatch for all of these other parts of the game."

Just because a team can identify a problem doesn't mean that a player can correct it. But the odds are better than they would be if the issue went undiagnosed—or worse, misdiagnosed. Some players look good being bad, and others look bad being good, but objective measures, McKay says, are "separating the efficiency from the style." The tools tell him the difference, and he tells players, who can't dismiss the message as merely one man's opinion. "It's not my opinion, it's hard data, which I think everybody appreciates," McKay says.

"Everybody" is a slight exaggeration. But McKay doesn't mind dissenting opinions. "I would have no problems debating anybody who wanted to stand up and tell me how their naked eye and twenty years of experience would be more valuable than getting real data points that told the truth," he says. "No other business in the world would be run like that. It was perfectly acceptable when we didn't have the tools, but now we do." It's true. I've tried them. And unfortunately for my ego, they definitely told the truth.

12

THE ALL-STAR PLAYER-COACH

You spend a good piece of your life gripping a baseball, and in the end it turns out that it was the other way around all the time.

—**JIM BOUTON**, former pitcher and author of *Ball Four*

On the evening of Sunday, July 8, 2018, at his Westlake, Ohio, apartment, Trevor Bauer learned he'd been named to the American League All-Star team.

He led the majors in pitching WAR (5.2), and his 2.24 ERA was second only to Chris Sale's (2.23). His first-half ERA was the lowest by an Indians pitcher at the break since Tom Candiotti's in 1991. He'd allowed just six home runs in 136 first-half innings and had struck out 175 batters. Although Bauer was not pleased to have made the team as an injury replacement for the Astros' Justin Verlander, which he took as a slight, he had crossed off an item on his personal achievement list: he had made himself an All-Star. He had greater aspirations, though. He was now squarely in contention for a Cy Young Award.

On July 10, a week before the All-Star Game, he returned to the mound as the Indians hosted the Cincinnati Reds at Progressive Field. There was a game within the game. One of the sport's most cerebral pitchers (Bauer) would match up against its most cerebral hitter, the Reds' star first baseman Joey Votto.

"They are pretty much the same guy," Indians catcher Roberto Pérez said.

In the first inning, Bauer began Votto with this sequence: four-seam fastball (ball), four-seam fastball (called strike), changeup (ball), four-seam fastball (called strike), two-seam fastball (foul), and a big-bending curveball that broke from Votto's belt to his heels that he fouled off to stay alive. Votto stepped out of the box and broke into a grin. He and Bauer had briefly spoken at a UFC match they had attended the previous winter. Each respected how the other approached the game. Votto was one of the most difficult players to strike out, and now he had seen most of Bauer's pitches. With two strikes, Votto choked up on his bat dramatically, as he always did. Votto didn't care that few players choked up so dramatically. He didn't care about looking silly. Like Bauer, he wanted to be the best he could be. Bauer shook off Pérez once. Pérez put down two fingers for a curveball. Bauer shook him off. Pérez put down three fingers for a slider. Bauer again shook him off. Pérez then gave a three-finger sign but moved it to his left thigh. It was a combination of pitch type and location Bauer had rarely thrown: a comeback slider.

"He was fouling off great pitches," Pérez said. "I didn't know what to call. [Bauer] just shook until I got to the backdoor slider."

The pitch began in the right-handed batter's box and broke back over the plate. Votto looked at it for strike three. The inning was over. Bauer had executed a perfect pitch. As Bauer walked off the mound he looked back toward Votto, and Bauer pointed at his own cap. Votto didn't see him.

"I was like, gotcha," Bauer said of his motion toward Votto. "That's the second [comeback slider] I've thrown this year. . . . It's just a matter of avoiding what he happens to be looking for at that moment in that count. You can't do one thing to him and be successful. He has hot zones and cold zones, whatever, but you go [to a cold zone] repeatedly, and he's obviously going to figure it out. There are people that have a cold zone that just can't hit it. Like with [Reds outfielder Scott] Schebler, I can tell him a curveball is coming, he is not going to hit it, which is basically what I did for three at-bats. But with Votto, if the report says he doesn't hit curveballs and you throw him three consecutive curveballs, he's going to whack the third one."

After this episode, Rob Friedman, who creates pitching GIFs on social media, made a GIF of Bauer shaking off calls and superimposed it over a bobblehead figure on Twitter—the world's first bobblehead that shakes its head side to side. It isn't easy to catch Bauer, whom Pérez has worked with since 2013.

Before every Bauer start, Indians pitching coach Carl Willis brings him the scouting data the front office has harvested on that night's opponent, along with his own insights. They go over the intel several hours before first pitch. The catcher is usually part of the meeting. But if Pérez isn't around, they usually don't bother to find him.

"Where's Roberto?" Bauer says Willis will ask.

"Well, it doesn't really matter, Carl, because I'm going to throw what I want to throw anyways," Bauer says.

"Yeah, I know," Willis says.

"Just tell me and I'll shake off," Bauer says.

Says Pérez: "There's not a plan. He knows how to attack guys, and I follow him. . . . He knows a lot about the game. We go through the scouting report, but he knows what he wants to do. . . . It would be nice not to be shaken off. I think any catcher would like that. But I am used to him. It's his game, man. I am back there suggesting signs. . . . He knows how to attack guys."

For Pérez, it's not personal. And Bauer says it's not a one-way relationship. He values Pérez's ability to get a closer read on hitters' swings, as well as his opinion on how pitches are playing.

"It's gotta be really hard to call pitches for me," Bauer says. "You can call the right pitch, and a lot of times I will say no to it because I have some other thought. . . . My idea on pitch sequencing is centered around the fact that I don't want to do the same thing too often. . . . You work based upon the hitter's timing."

Bauer's start against the Reds was one of the best of his career. He threw eight shutout innings and struck out twelve, allowing seven baserunners. He also had his best slider of the year: it averaged 10.2 inches of horizontal run and 0.6 inches of vertical movement. He had built exactly what he wanted. In July, the pitch averaged 9 inches of horizontal movement. (Clevinger led the majors on the season with 9.6 inches of horizontal slider movement.)

Bauer finished the start with a 2.23 ERA. He'd developed a new, elite pitch. His slider's whiff-per-swing rate of 41.4 percent ranked eighteenth among all sliders in 2018, and its run value per one hundred

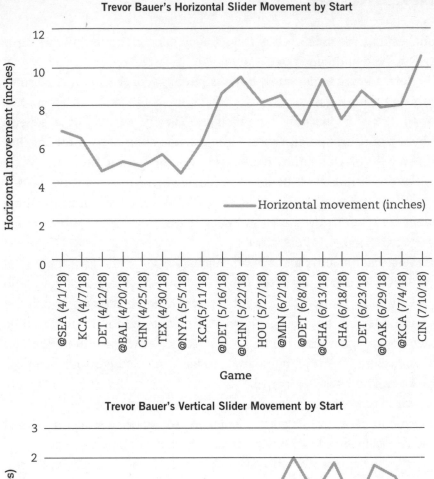

Trevor Bauer's Horizontal Slider Movement by Start

Trevor Bauer's Vertical Slider Movement by Start

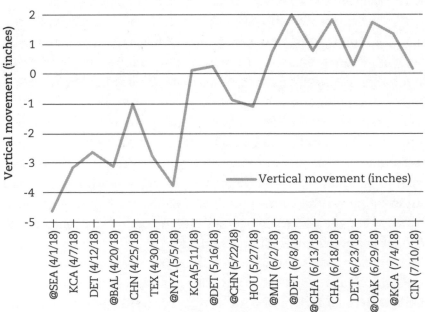

pitches ranked third in all of baseball at 2.8 runs above average, trailing only the sliders of Blake Snell and Miles Mikolas. His velocity was at a career-high level, averaging 95.4 mph. His command had never been better. But the start was also something of a high-water mark.

On Sunday, July 15, he joined four other teammates on a charter flight from Burke Lakefront Airport to Washington, D.C., for the All-Star Game. Bauer's All-Star experience was mixed. He mostly kept to himself in Washington. He didn't talk to many people. But he was invited onto the set of MLB Network a day before the game to talk about his pitch grips. On live TV, he measured his hand size against that of Pedro Martínez, one of his childhood idols. Martínez's hand engulfed his. Asked on the broadcast if he knew his WAR, Bauer quipped, "Of course." In the visiting AL clubhouse, he was given a cold shoulder by the Astros contingent, still angry over his accusations earlier in the season. He made a point of saying hello to Bregman when Bregman was around his Astros teammates. There was only awkward silence. Having pitched on the Sunday before the game, Bauer wasn't eligible to appear in the exhibition. He flew out after the game, ready to get back and begin the stretch run of a Cy Young chase.

Bauer not only changed his performance on the mound in 2018—improving from perhaps the worst pitcher in the majors at the end of May 2017 to an All-Star—but he altered his reputation as a teammate. Bauer wasn't only adding value through his own pitching ability; he was adding value to some of his clubhouse peers. He was particularly interested in assisting with one area: command and control.

In late July, Indians pitcher Josh Tomlin sought out Bauer in the trainer's room in the depths of Progressive Field. Over the previous few years, Tomlin had possessed the best command on the staff. He had walked no more than 1.2 batters per nine innings, or 3.2 percent of all batters faced, in every season since 2014. But in the summer of 2018, he was off. He had walked 2.5 batters per nine innings in June, a 6.7 percent overall walk rate, and he had been missing badly within the strike zone all season. He had to be ultrafine to survive in the majors with his sub-90 mph fastball. Tomlin had been placed on the injured list on July 10 with a hamstring pull, but he knew he was soon expected to rejoin the team. He needed help, and quickly. He sought out Bauer, who was receiving a routine treatment. He had come to Bauer with questions before, but this time was different. Bauer recalls Tomlin saying he had no idea what was going on with his command, which, Bauer says, "created an opening."

"All you've been focused on the last two weeks is worrying about your mechanics," Bauer told him. "You've gotten all robotic: leg lift is this, etc. You're thinking everything inside. You're internal. You need to go play shortstop."

Tomlin did a double take. What?

Bauer was interested in all aspects of sport science, including psychology. He was particularly interested in finding better ways to train and improve the mental aspects of command because it was the part of the craft he felt was most confounding to master.

"If you took a normal person, nonathlete, and you gave him a big leaguer's physical ability for a day and put him on a mound for a game, it wouldn't matter what big leaguer's ability he had," Bauer says. "The mental side of it would crush him."

Bauer was interested in Robert Nideffer's "Theory of Attentional and Personal Style" as it related to athletic performance. In 1976, Nideffer had published and theorized something of a Punnett square of performance mindsets. He found that at any one time, an athlete's focus is determined by two dimensions: width (broad or narrow focus) and direction (internal or external focus). There were four possible mindsets: narrow-internal, broad-internal, narrow-external, broad-external. An internal focus meant an athlete was consciously thinking about their movement, which is detrimental to pitching. A broad focus meant the athlete was aware of much of their surroundings. What Bauer was after was a narrow-external focus. Narrow-external shifts one's attention outside oneself and upon a specific task. That was ideal for pitching or, say, shooting in basketball or sinking a putt in golf.

After his treatment, Bauer and Tomlin went out to throw on the field in an empty, pregame Progressive Field. Tomlin had two days until his next start. Bauer had him throw long toss with different weighted balls. He then had Tomlin make each of his throws coming out of some athletic movement.

"Trust me, don't worry where the balls go today," Bauer recalls telling Tomlin.

Bauer had Tomlin throw fastballs and curveballs after pretending he was turning a double play as a shortstop, with the quick footwork required to pivot and throw taking his mind off mechanics.

"Just getting him to do something else to get him out of his head," Bauer says. "It cleared everything up."

Tomlin was sharp in his following rehab start at Double-A Akron, throwing three perfect innings. His walk rate in the second half of the season after rejoining the Indians was 0.84 walks per 9, or 2.1 percent.

Not every Bauer intervention worked, but he would help teammates and friends in the pitching field who approached him for advice. Tomlin had perhaps a very mild case of what is known as the "yips," the mysterious plight of athletes who lose the ability to do something—like throw a pitch or strike a golf ball accurately—they had accomplished thousands of times before. Bauer had experimented with more radical remedies to attempt to free players of more severe psychological blocks adversely affecting command.

Some pitchers with the yips recover their ability to throw the ball where they want, while others, like Steve Blass or Rick Ankiel, never regain their former command. At Driveline two winters earlier, Bauer had helped create a sort of sensory-deprivation bullpen to help his friend Cody Buckel, who was struggling through a career-threatening case of the yips.

Bauer and Buckel had met when they were thirteen and bonded over their big-league goals. "He's almost my mentor," Buckel said about Bauer in 2012. Buckel was the Rangers' second-round draft pick in 2010. As a teenager in 2011, he dominated in A-ball, and *Baseball America* credited him with the best control in the Rangers' system. The next year he was named the organization's minor-league pitcher of the year, and in the spring of 2013, the twenty-year-old Buckel earned an invitation to big-league camp. In his first exhibition outing against big leaguers, he walked five hitters and recorded only one out. In his second outing, he got two outs before being pulled. Rather than relaxing when he opened his minor-league season, he seemed to heap more pressure upon himself. Through May 1, he'd allowed a 20.25

ERA. Most disconcertingly, he'd walked twenty-eight of the sixty-six batters he'd faced.

"You just begin to see it piling up, piling up, and then pretty soon it's overwhelming," Buckel says. "I don't want to say appears, but it's just kind of there. . . . It's overtaking you."

He'd go on to meet with the Rangers' team psychologists and minor-league rehab coordinator Keith Comstock, who'd overcome his own case of the yips. He'd try Bauer-inspired practices like differential bullpens and tossing Plyo balls. Nothing worked.

Sian Beilock, a University of Chicago psychology professor and the author of *Choke*, says the yips are tied to a switch from subconscious to conscious thinking.

"When people are watching you, you start watching yourself," Beilock says.[1]

The problem may be more about the environment than the performer. So in the winter of 2016–2017, with Buckel having suffered through four years of not being able to throw strikes, Bauer turned the lights off in the Driveline R&D building. In the dark there would be no visible environment at all. The space was completely black save for a red laser dot, a command trainer, to throw toward. No one could watch Buckel throw. No one could see the results.

Driveline data showed that Buckel's strike rate rose from 50 to 60 percent during his time at the facility. Boddy sent video and velocity and spin-rate readings to teams, and in January 2017, the Angels saw it and signed Buckel to a minor-league deal. But when he returned to game conditions, when people began to watch him in the fishbowl that is the center of a baseball diamond, the mental block returned.

After twenty-one walks in 20 2/3 Double-A innings, he walked away, finished as a professional pitcher.

"It got to the point where I was basically enjoying training way more than I was competing," he says. But while his pitching career is over, his baseball career is just beginning: he's become a conduit in the minors, first for the Mariners and now for Cleveland.

Bauer knows the mindset that's required to execute a pitch. The challenge is training that mindset and consistently bringing it to a professional pitching mound.

At Driveline, Bauer and others play what he calls mini-games to hasten motor learning related to command. In one such game at Driveline, Kyle Boddy would stand about forty feet away, yell 'Go!,' and throw a large rubber ball up in the air. With his back turned, Bauer would pivot, try to locate the ball in the air, and hit it before it landed. The activity removed conscious thought. It was another drill designed to try to cure Buckel. Not every experiment was a success. But he had helped Tomlin in 2018. He was always talking to Clevinger. He educated Adam Plutko about spin axis. And after watching new reliever Neil Ramírez for several weeks after he joined the team in May, he approached Ramírez about developing a new pitch.

"I think we were just in the dugout, on the railing [watching a game]," recalls Ramírez. "[Bauer said], 'Hey, I was kind of looking at your numbers of your stuff.' I think I had approached him about a split-finger. [He said], 'I think curveball would be a better pitch.'"

Ramírez had a good fastball with above-average spin (2,436 rpm) and speed (95.3 mph), and an adequate slider. Bauer thought he needed a vertical breaking ball.

"If you add an elite breaking ball and you tell [Ramírez] to throw his fastball 40 percent of the time, he becomes an elite pitcher," Bauer says.

There are many coaches in professional and amateur baseball who doubt the viability of creating an above-average breaking pitch from scratch. Some think the feel for spin is innate. Bauer's own experience suggests that fixed mindset is wrong.

Ramírez was perhaps more open-minded compared to other pitchers, as he was desperate to remain in the majors and had added 2 mph to his fastball (93.1 mph in 2017 to 95.3 mph in 2018) the previous winter through a weighted-ball program led by Caleb Cotham, who then worked at The Bledsoe Agency. Cotham, a former professional pitcher and Driveline alumnus, suggested that Ramírez reach out to Bauer when the Indians called him up from Triple-A in May to reinforce their tattered relief corps.

"I like Bauer, man. I will come in after a game and he'll [joke], 'You were only throwing 94 mph tonight, you pussy,'" says Ramírez, who chuckles. "I don't put anyone into a label or box until I get to know them. Bauer is a guy that goes out there and competes every five days and competes his butt off. That's what I saw on the outside and that's what I've seen [in Cleveland]. . . . People fear what they don't understand."

They had begun to work on the pitch prior to the All-Star break, including training an Edgertronic camera on Ramírez's nascent curveball grip. Ramírez played catch with Bauer, experimenting with grips. To help with the pitch creation, Bauer also taught Ramírez about the concept of elbow spiral to improve his arm action.

Bauer's delivery is different from most pitchers'. It almost looks like he's throwing a football. As he takes the ball from his glove to begin his delivery, he does not extend his pitching arm away from his body toward second base. For Bauer, that's all wasted movement causing unneeded stress. Rather, when Bauer takes the ball from his glove, he keeps the ball close to his body by moving his throwing elbow back toward first base, his forearm parallel to the ground. As his left foot strikes before the mound, his forearm pivots upward to a 90 degree angle so his hand and the ball are in a position not too different from a quarterback holding a ball near his ear. It's *compact*. It's efficient. It's called an elbow spiral because the elbow takes a spiral-stairwell-like journey to a readied throwing position.

Boddy and the Driveline crew stumbled upon the idea of the elbow spiral in a book on pitching mechanics by Japanese instructor Kazushi Tezuka, with a title translated as *The Identity of Pitching*. There was no English-language translation of the book available, so Boddy paid to have one done. Driveline staff modified Tezuka's idea of the elbow spiral but believed the underlying concept of "marrying external rotation to supination" was unique and "led to a more efficient arm path." Bauer shortened his arm action through drills he picked up at Driveline, including the pivot pick, but he says he had arrived at this arm action mostly naturally, "likely because of my high volume of throwing from a young age. Natural adaptation to handle the workload." Bauer calls that lack of backward movement with the ball a "neutral position." He felt the movement kept him healthier than most pitchers. He'd never been placed on the injured list or missed a start.

Conversely, Ramírez had an exaggerated arm action that was negatively affecting his ability to throw a quality curveball. When he extended his pitching hand toward second base, he was pronating his arm, then supinating it, before going through pronation again as he moved forward to release.

In other words, Bauer explains, "There's a lot of moving parts there." But with the elbow spiral, a pitcher never reaches a pronated position until he's releasing the pitch.

The new breaking ball was getting close, Bauer believed. But the project was shut down because the coaching staff believed it could have a negative effect on Ramírez's slider. (If anything, Bauer felt it would be useful differential training.) Ramírez acquiesced to the club's request. He didn't want to go against the Indians' coaching staff. But Ramírez says he made the development of a curveball, and mastering the elbow spiral, off-season priorities at the Bledsoe pitching lab.

Bauer's assistance extended beyond teammates. That summer, he also met with Indians front-office officials who were interested in outfitting Progressive Field with Edgertronic cameras in 2019. They wanted to know where and how to employ them in the stadium. When the Indians sent minor-league pitching coordinator Ruben Niebla to the major-league clubhouse to talk to Bauer about pitch design and some minor leaguers who could benefit from new pitches, Bauer spent nearly the entirety of a game along the dugout railing discussing pitch-design principles. He felt more and more that he was having productive dialogue with the team and that what he had to say was valued.

Bauer thought he could teach Ramírez the curveball relatively quickly. He believed the concept behind velocity creation was simple. "Try to throw the ball hard and your body figures it out," Bauer says. The summer of 2018 supplied more evidence that this was true.

In the spring of 2016, the Dodgers wanted to experiment. They gave Boddy, who was consulting for the club, guinea pigs to work with: ten of their lowest-regarded minor-league pitchers held back from affiliated ball. The pitchers were invited for an involuntary extended stay at the Dodgers' Camelback Ranch complex just west of Phoenix to see if Boddy's Driveline team could add velocity. Two of the experimentees were Andrew Istler, the 702nd player taken in the previous draft, who had produced an 8.38 ERA in Rookie ball, and Corey Copping, the

942nd player in the same draft, out of Oklahoma University. Istler had topped out at 88 mph in college, Copping at 90 mph.

"We were in our own little world, pretty much," Copping says. "They told me I wasn't going to make an affiliate and that I was going to be in extended spring training. . . . [Driveline] came down. They made us use these wrist weights and weighted balls, which I've never in my life done before. That was definitely new to me."

After their extended spring with Boddy, they had enjoyed velocity and performance jumps that continued through the summer of 2018, when they become something more: prospects and trade deadline assets.

On July 31, the Dodgers traded Copping to Toronto for reliever John Axford to bolster their bullpen with an eye on October. On August 31, the Dodgers traded Istler to the Nationals for Ryan Madson, who would become Dodgers manager Dave Roberts' most trusted setup man.

"It was free money," Boddy says of the velocity improvement.

Boddy and Bauer had proven velocity could be bolstered and pitches could be taught. Command was trickier. While Bauer had slowly and steadily improved, cutting his walk rate from 10.6 percent in 2015 to 8.6 percent in 2016 to 8 percent in 2017 to 7.5 percent in the first half of 2018, there hadn't been a breakthrough like he'd had with his slider or with his velocity gain in 2014. In August, Bauer's command would begin to waver, and he would experiment with a more forceful remedy.

On August 6 at Progressive Field, Bauer's narrow-external focus was slipping into something more internal.

"I'm getting close to Ken Giles-ing myself," said Bauer while at breakfast with his parents a day after the appearance, referencing the Houston Astros reliever who punched himself in the face after a poor outing earlier in the season. "Last night it happened twice, where I completely lost the ability to throw strikes."

The first occasion was in the second inning against the Twins. Bauer walked Max Kepler on five pitches, with the fourth ball, a fastball, sailing high and outside. Bauer proceeded to throw three straight pitches out of the zone against the following batter, Logan Forsythe. Bauer stepped off the mound. He took off his hat, wiped his brow with his jersey sleeve, and stepped back on. He threw three straight strikes, including a perfectly placed 95 mph fastball on the corner that Forsythe swung at and missed for a strikeout.

How did he lose his command and then so quickly regain it?

"I started spraying balls and then all of a sudden I throw three straight in the same damn spot," Bauer said. "A lot of times I have to literally slap myself to distract myself . . . from whatever is going on. The body gets out of its parasympathetic nervous system. Or is it the sympathetic nervous system? One of them shuts down. It's complicated."

If Bauer loses feel for pitching in an inning, he'll sometimes leave the dugout during the next half inning and throw some Plyo balls to try to remove the feeling of throwing a baseball and get his feel back on track. He's also explored the benefits of slapping himself in the face to reorganize his mental focus.

Kathy Bauer, Trevor's mom, explains the sympathetic nervous system in more relatable terms, saying it's responsible for fight or flight, controlling the body's responses to a perceived threat.

She says there was another recent example of Trevor's subconscious at play. At home against the Pirates on July 25, Bauer threw a first-inning, 94 mph fastball to the Pirates' Gregory Polanco. The pitch was supposed to be down and in to the left-handed-hitting Polanco, but it drifted out over the plate. In the first-inning afternoon sunlight, Polanco stung a ball right back at Bauer, who barely avoided taking a line drive to the face. Indians shortstop Francisco Lindor was positioned behind Bauer in an infield shift, and he fielded the one-bouncer to end the inning.

But when Bauer came out for the second inning, his velocity was down as far as it had been since an April start in frigid weather against the Royals. He threw a 91.7 mph fastball to Josh Bell and another one at the same speed to Colin Moran. His fastball averaged 94.6 mph for the season.

"[Polanco's hit] goes between my glove and my face. It was the last pitch I threw," Bauer says. "I go down to the dugout. I remember feeling extremely tired. Feeling not all there. I felt great the first inning. I go out for the second inning and I am throwing 90. I felt sluggish." The game's velocity plot reveals the sudden dip. "Carl [Willis] thought I was hurt. After the inning he goes, 'Hey, are you OK?'" I say, 'Yeah, my body went to sleep for some reason.' Your body freaks out. Something happens. . . . I'm just starting to play around with this."

After the second inning, Bauer went into an area behind the dugout hidden from cameras and slapped himself in the face—what he calls a velo slap (short for velocity).

"I literally slapped myself across the face," Bauer says. "You have to get out of that mindset."

After the top of the third inning, Bauer approached Mike Clevinger in the home dugout.

"Where were you after the second inning?" he asked.

"I was in the clubhouse," Clevinger says. "Why?"

"Well, you missed your chance to velo slap me," Bauer told him.

Clevinger seemed sincerely disappointed to have missed the opportunity to slap Bauer across the face.

In the off-season at Driveline, if someone is just shy of challenging his velocity record, a training partner will slap him forcefully. "[You] slap the shit out of them," Warren says.

"You get an immediate adrenaline rush," Trevor explains. "A lot of times you will jump 2 mph."

The velo slap might also be useful to hone command.

On August 6, the Indians were leading the Twins 6–0 with two outs in the sixth inning as Bauer prepared to make a 3–1 pitch to Miguel Sanó. For the second time in that outing, his command left him. Bauer threw a 97 mph fastball that missed low below the zone. He walked off the mound in his white game jersey with his red socks pulled high, covered his mouth with his glove, and screamed "Fuck!" The word was uttered loudly enough to be audible in the press box. Willis made his way to the center of the mound. Bauer was seething. Although the game was essentially over and the AL Central was all but decided, the AL Cy Young race was not.

"I was thinking, 'I have a great FIP going on right now. Goddammit. It just cost me,'" Bauer says.

Approaching the mound, Willis saw the rage on Bauer's face. He understood why he was upset. Willis laughed.

"I'm super mad," Bauer says. "He comes out, sees it, he just kind of laughs and says, 'Well this guy is a low-ball hitter, well, just stay behind the ball.'"

We ask Bauer if he's thinking about FanGraphs' version of Wins Above Replacement in real time during games. FanGraphs' WAR formula uses FIP to determine a pitcher's run-prevention ability independent of the defense behind him. Walks are a significant part of the formula.

"Of course, always," Warren interjects with a laugh. "The only thing he thinks about more is strikeouts, because strikeouts preceded FanGraphs WAR."

Was there value in a mound visit? Especially when a pitching coach with a traditional background like the gray-bearded Willis visits Bauer? Warren answers again.

"Most really good pitching mound visits have nothing to do with pitching," he says. "If you are going out there to talk about pitching, you might as well take him out of the game. . . . Mechanical [adjustments] are taking them out of the mindset they need to compete out there."

Trevor speaks up.

"I will tell you about the best mound visit I ever heard of, courtesy of Brent Strom," he says. "He's the pitching coach somewhere. They have a rookie out there who is making his second start in the big leagues. Walk. Walk. Hit. It's one of those types of innings. He loads the bases with one out. The manager is like, 'Brent, go talk to him.' Brent thinks, 'I don't know this kid at all. Can't talk about approach.' So I pinch my ass cheeks together, and I walk out to the mound. I go, 'Hey, kid, I am going to shit my pants if you don't get out of this inning, but I can't go to the restroom until you get out of this. So I need to get out of this real quick.' He pinches his ass cheeks together and walks back to the dugout. Two pitches later, a double play gets [him] out of it."

Strom had flipped the focus back to narrow-external.

Maybe Willis's amusement at Bauer's FIP-tallying against the Twins had refocused him and broken a mild mental block. Bauer went to 3–2 on the next batter, Max Kepler. On the full-count pitch, he dotted the outside corner for a strikeout: his last batter of the outing. Bauer had entered the game neck and neck with Chris Sale for the AL WAR lead. He left the start with a 5.7 to 5.6 edge.

Bauer threw seven shutout innings, striking out eleven, including his two hundredth K of the season. He reached that landmark in the third inning, when he got Twins catcher Bobby Wilson looking at a comeback Laminar Express. He received a standing ovation from the crowd, which Warren was on hand for as he sat in the scout seating behind home plate. He had traveled with the Edgertronic camera to film the start. Before the game, he mounted it on a railing behind home plate, in front of the first row of seating. During the game, he monitored and edited video in real time on his laptop in the scout section. We asked Warren how often scouts have approached him and asked what he's doing and what type of camera he's using. "One guy a few years ago wanted to know," Warren said. That was it.

In the midst of his best season, after arguably the best month of his professional career, Bauer knew what he needed to get back: consistent feel for command. He had to get his subconscious in order, and his focus—more specifically, his narrow-external focus. He needed a good differential bullpen. He wouldn't get the chance.

13

PERFORMANCE-
ENHANCING DATA

Somebody once asked me if I ever went up to the plate
trying to hit a home run. I said, "Sure, every time."
   —MICKEY MANTLE

Justin Turner spent most of the pregame June morning at PNC Park
in Pittsburgh seated on a pleather couch in the center of the open,
windowless visiting clubhouse, working through a crossword puzzle.
It's a common way to kill time in major-league locker rooms, at least
among cerebral players. Athletes have a lot of downtime, and that
means many hours to obsess over their successes and failures. Turner
needed the distraction.

Near the end of 2018 spring training in Arizona, A's starting pitcher
Kendall Graveman had broken Turner's left wrist with an errant fastball. Turner missed the first five weeks of the season. Since coming
back from a broken hand, Turner had struggled, batting .243 with .325
on-base and .343 slugging marks, well below his recent high standards. In his eighty plate appearances, he had homered only once.
The Dodgers were expected to be one of the best teams in the National
League but were just 30–30, third in the NL West as they arrived in
Pittsburgh.

Doug Latta tries to watch every Turner plate appearance, live if he
can. Maintaining a successful swing requires constant attention. And
Latta had noticed some problems since Turner had returned. The effects of his weakened wrist were cascading throughout his body, as
other parts compensated. The imbalance would result in a groin strain
later in the season. Latta and Turner worked to find a solution.

Repairing a swing is something of an art form. Nearly every day Latta and Turner would talk or exchange ideas through text message. "It's a constant dialogue back and forth with him," Turner says. "Just talking about different ideas, different things to try, different things to think about to get in a better spot."

There were principles that remained constant amid tweaks, Turner says. He wanted to gain ground toward the pitcher, find his balance, and swing underneath his shoulders. But after going through that checklist, there was room to tinker. They experimented with different fixes, different hand placements. By early July, Turner's hands were lower in his setup. Latta felt his hands needed more "space to work," more room between his body and the plate.

Turner made some improvement throughout June, hitting four homers and posting a 139 wRC+. But his struggles extended into July, when he went homerless in forty at-bats (89 wRC+). The tinkering continued. In early August, Turner debuted a conspicuous adjustment: He opened his stance dramatically, meaning his front (left) foot went from near parallel to the mound to pointing toward third base. This tweak was designed to give his hands more room and freedom to work.

For the first half, Turner hit .258/.354/.393 with a 110 wRC+. In the second half, he was the second-best hitter in baseball, recording a 190 wRC+ and a .356 batting average, both marks trailing only those of Milwaukee's Christian Yelich (220 wRC+, .367), the NL MVP. Turner's line-drive rate spiked from 20 percent in the first half to 31.4 percent in the second.

Prorating Baseball Prospectus's WARP (Wins Above Replacement Player) over six hundred plate appearances, Turner was the most valuable player in the NL on the season (8.9 WARP per six hundred PA) and trailed only Mookie Betts (10.9) and Mike Trout (10.8) overall. To get there, Latta and Turner had gone back and forth on creating subtle adjustments.

"I see people say, 'Do this drill, do this and that, you're going to get better,'" Latta says. "Does that actually translate to the cues a high-level professional hitter needs?"

He has evidence that his method works. Latta helped turn Turner into an MVP-level player. Betts's swing change helped him win the AL MVP Award in 2018, fueled by career bests in home runs (32), slugging (.640), and wRC+ (185). Betts dropped his ground-ball rate from 40.4 percent in 2017 to a career-low 33.9 percent in 2018 and increased his HR/FB (home run to fly ball) rate from 10.1 to 16.4 percent in converting to the Hyers-Latta philosophy.

The fly-ball revolution is spreading, bolstered by the young and old players adopting it, the coaches (and organizations) preaching it, and the technology and feedback making it more effective for all. And the next phase of the revolution could be its most momentous.

In 2014, then Rays manager Joe Maddon noted that the rise of tracking technology was disproportionately helping teams *prevent* runs instead of score them. "The hitter's at a total disadvantage right now," Maddon said. "And there's no advantages on the horizon. I don't see it. That's why it's going to take a lot of creative thinking. . . . Right now, offense is going south, and it's going to continue going south based on pitching and defense. Everything—data, video, all the information—benefits them over offense."

Offense actually increased in three consecutive seasons after Maddon made those comments, but that was largely attributable to changes in the ball that spurred the surge in homers. Maddon's observation about the imbalance of power on the analytical end still applied. "It's easier to use information and change your game if you're a pitcher and you have the ball in your hand," Sam Fuld says. "It's just easier to control the decisions that you make. Obviously, hitting is very much reactive."

No one knows this better than former Driveline hitting director Jason Ochart, who was hired by the Phillies as their minor-league hitting coordinator in December 2018. At Driveline, Ochart was trying to play catchup at the same place that's helping make life harder for hitters. "It's actually frustrating for me, because I'm right in the belly of the beast where I'm seeing all these progressive things happen on the pitching side," Ochart said in the summer of 2018. "Then I talk to hitting people in baseball, and they're still arguing about, like, hitting ground balls, whether it's a good or bad batted ball. Like, guys, we're getting crushed."

Ochart lamented that "we just know so little about hitting in general." But batters *are* belatedly reacting, and the defense-offense imbalance is beginning to look less extreme. At Driveline, the company that upturned the training of pitchers, rethinking hitting is now arguably the greatest growth opportunity.

Like so many new-age coaches, Ochart's coaching career had humble origins.

A Glendale, California, native, he was admittedly a lousy player at Glendale Community College and, after transferring, San Francisco State. Ochart, who majored in kinesiology, was interested in all aspects of sports science and biomechanics. His younger brother, Adam, played at Menlo College, a business school in the Silicon Valley town of Atherton. The program had lost a coach, and Adam asked his brother if he wanted to help out as the hitting coach. Ochart applied and got the job. Menlo College became his first laboratory.

"I was willing to try different stuff because, A, I wasn't very good, so there was no ego there, and, B, it was just kind of a test, something that was just fun for me," he said. "So I was applying theories of motor learning and sports science in general."

In 2013, Menlo College set a program record with thirty-four wins and advanced to the NAIA national tournament. While the team had an excellent pitching staff and defense, it also out-homered opponents 32 to 6, outslugged them .415 to .305, and out-on-based them .378 to .328. The environment was ideal for experimentation. The players were lab mice without egos.

"I was like, maybe this stuff actually, like, works," Ochart said.

Ochart began to post some of his unorthodox practices to Twitter. "Hitting Twitter" is a derisive term for the questionable coaching and tips that can often be found on social media and YouTube. It can be difficult to distinguish between expert instruction and wayward advice. But amid the sea of unqualified coaches are some good ideas, or at least ones worthy of exploration. Boddy was curious about what

Ochart was doing with data tracking, underload/overload training with weighted bats, and discussion of launch angle before launch angle became a big thing. Boddy reached out to Ochart, and Ochart read Boddy's 2014 book about building velocity, *Hacking the Kinetic Chain*.

"It just blew my mind," Ochart said. "Nothing in player development up to that point, in my opinion, was structured in a way that was as scientifically sound as his book. No one's talking about baseball like this. Like most of the baseball books, [they're] just, like, so bad. So I was really intrigued, and then he asked me if I had any interest in joining the team. They were thinking about going into hitting in the future. And I was, like, yeah, absolutely."

Ochart moved to Seattle.

"It went from literally having a budget of, like, fifty dollars [at Menlo] and one cage at a small college with holes in it and messed-up baseballs to Kyle saying, 'You have a company card, get whatever you want. Just track everything . . . I'll check back in six months,'" Ochart said. "It was, like, *whoa*. So it was intimidating. I was paralyzed at first, like, God, I don't know. Like, where do I start?"

Staying true to the ethos of the company's pitching program, Ochart began measuring and questioning everything. The numbers show that balls in the air to the pull side are the best outcome a hitter can hope for. Yet pulling the ball is discouraged by many coaches and has been for decades. "Most of our amateurs have a negative launch angle to their pull side, and being able to pull the ball well is a skill that is very rare and something that the best hitters in the game can do pretty well," Ochart said. "And [pulling the ball] is also not *taught*. Never. I don't know about you, but in my youth, in high school, even college baseball, no one ever practiced pulling the ball. It's always go oppo. Practice hitting the ball oppo, practice using the whole field. The vast majority of hitters that I work with that are amateurs, they just suck at pulling the baseball."

But the most valuable batted ball *can* be taught. Latta has taught it. And there are examples of the skill being acquired elsewhere, fueling far-fetched talent transformations. Consider Francisco Lindor and José Ramírez, who in 2018 became two of the unlikeliest power hitters in baseball history.

According to Baseball-Reference.com, there have been 462 individual seasons of thirty-eight or more homers in major-league history, produced by 178 different players. There have been only 46 such seasons by players five foot eleven or shorter, by 22 players. Lindor, who is maybe five foot eleven, and Ramírez, who probably isn't five foot nine, are the two most recent additions to the list. More improbable yet, they are teammates.

While Ramírez and Lindor are coy when asked about their hitting approach—Lindor insists he's not a power hitter—Cleveland, as an organization, is challenging old-hat hitting wisdom. The club's hitting coach, Ty Van Burkleo, was once a part of Latta's think-tank sessions at the Ball Yard. The Indians have appointed outsiders to minor-league coaching positions. They've replaced coaches with pitching machines that toss balls at near-game velocity during on-field batting practice at their minor-league affiliates. In their indoor batting cages at places like Low-A Lake County, they have hitters compete against each other—complete with leaderboards—to see who can produce the best exit velocities and launch angles. It's not just the Indians rethinking batting practice. The Astros' Tyler White noted on social media that the Astros engaged in differential-style training at extended spring. In each batting cage, and in on-field batting practice, were a fastball machine and a breaking-ball machine. A coach would hold up pitches in each hand so the batter wasn't sure if he would face a breaking ball or fastball.

Lindor hit thirty-eight home runs in 2018. Ramírez hit thirty-nine. No scouting report ever projected anything more than average power for Lindor, and most foresaw even less for Ramírez, who never hit more than five home runs at a minor-league stop. (Lindor never hit more than six home runs for a farm team.) Ramírez slugged .340 as a rookie.

"Nobody thought I could do this," Ramírez told ESPN. "I was too small."

Even in 2018, neither was particularly powerful in terms of exit velocity. Ramírez ranked 166th out of 332 qualifying batters in average exit velocity of fly balls and line drives (92.4 mph). Lindor ranked 80th (94.3 mph). What they did do was begin eschewing pitches they could not drive and instead seek pitches in certain zones where they could make contact out in front of the plate. "When I try and cover the whole plate, that's when I get in trouble," Lindor says. "I can cover the whole plate if I want to. I can put the ball in play anytime I want. That's not going to do any good for me or the team."

If you're hitting the ball out in front of the plate, the angle of the bat will yield a hit to the pull side. With the Indians and the data advocating that approach, Lindor and Ramírez began lifting the ball to their pull sides.

In 2018, Ramírez had the 11th-lowest ground-ball percentage to his pull side (43.7 percent). Betts was 28th (46.3 percent), and Lindor 68th (50.9 percent). The league-wide average was 58.7 percent. (Turner posted the 10th-lowest mark among qualified batters, at 43.4 percent.)

All of those numbers represented massive steps forward. In 2017, Ramírez had recorded a 48.8 percent ground-ball rate on pulled balls, ranking 48th. Lindor ranked 94th at 52.8 percent, and Betts ranked 70th at 50 percent. And in 2016, Ramírez had posted a 57.1 percent ground-ball rate on pulled contact, ranking 132nd. Lindor ranked 246th at 64.6 percent, while Betts ranked 88th (54 percent).

It was a remarkable transformation. These three undersized sluggers hadn't suddenly learned how to hit the ball 450 feet. Rather, they optimized their swings, and in doing so learned to create more optimal batted balls.

The first phase of the fly-ball revolution was getting balls off the ground. Both Lindor and Ramírez did that, increasing their average launch angles (and home-run totals) by the year.

But the second, and arguably more important, phase was pulling those balls in the air. And in the teammates' mutual evolutions, they made no trade-off at all in swing-and-miss, which one would expect to be a detrimental side effect of trying to lift more balls in the air.

The MLB leaderboard in pulled home runs in 2018:

1. Ramírez   32
2. Lindor   27
3. Betts   26

In terms of total fly balls hit to the pull side, Ramírez was 2nd in baseball in 2018 (251 batted balls), undersized Astros MVP candidate

LINDOR

Season	Avg. Launch Angle	HRs	Swinging Strike %
2015	3.8	12	8.6
2016	7.6	15	7.7
2017	13.6	33	6.4
2018	14.5	38	7.4

RAMÍREZ

Season	Avg. Launch Angle	HRs	Swinging Strike %
2015	9.5	6	4.2
2016	12.9	11	4.9
2017	14.8	33	5.4
2018	18.8	39	4.7

Alex Bregman was 3rd (246), Lindor was 8th (226), and Betts was 18th (205). In learning to pull and lift, they'd *all* become MVP candidates despite standing at seventy-two inches or shorter. In 2013, following a nineteen-year-old Betts's homerless half-season in Low-A, *Baseball America* had labeled him the thirty-first-best prospect in the Red Sox system alone, sniffing, "The question is whether he has a true plus tool because he's not physical and doesn't really impact the ball." But in 2018, the correlation between height and Isolated Power among hitters with at least 250 plate appearances fell to its lowest point (.23) since 1954. Smart hitters don't have to be big to go yard.

For Latta, teaching the optimal batted ball is an art form. It comes from his eye and years of experience. He talks incessantly about "balance" and "timing." Latta doesn't try to teach increased exit velocity. He never talks about launch angle. Yet he's transformed careers.

There's also a data-based approach to optimizing the swing undertaken at places like Driveline and within professional and college clubs. In a conversation with Ochart, the words *timing* and *balance* did not appear once. It's not that he doesn't believe in those concepts, but unlike Latta, for whom they form the core of his belief system, Ochart's revolves around measuring and quantifying everything. He'll split the strike zone into nine subsections and scrutinize batted-ball performance in each one. Ochart showed us data generated by amateur hitters and diagnosed them at a glance: one had too low a launch angle, another did damage in the middle of the plate but struggled to adjust to pitches in and out. "His programming would be tinkered to try and work on that," Ochart clinically concluded.

Ochart measures his hitters' hand speed and bat speed, as well as the efficiency of the relationship between the two, a homebrew stat of his own devising. "[Efficiency] is bat speed divided by hand speed," he said. "Often, we'll have two hitters who have the same exact hand speed, they're able to generate the same amount of velocity with their hands, but one guy can turn that into bat speed better than the other. So that has to do with a number of things, like how well can you decelerate your hands to accelerate the barrel. Also, your grip. I've toyed with different grips with guys, and numbers jump up. Increasing wrist mobility with some guys is an issue. Some guys lack the ability to get into supination."

Some of the science jargon sounds a lot like that of the pitching world Bauer and Boddy inhabit. But the art-to-science ratio is still higher on the hitting side.

"There's just a basic understanding of what good pitchers do, and what things correlate to success . . . whereas in hitting it's still a lot of gray area and it's a lot of guesswork," Ochart said. "So I think we're really at rock bottom, and I think that hitting is in a place now where the best natural athletes are succeeding in spite of the training."

It's not uncommon to hear Driveline staffers say that they can do more good for the game there than they'd be able to with one team. "I think there's more general ability to impact the field," says Driveline quantitative analyst Alex Caravan. "If I worked for a team, I would basically be engineering how those pitchers could get out next week's batters, which will help that team but can only help baseball so much."

In the summer of 2018, Ochart expressed a similar sentiment. By the end of the year, however, he had joined the Phillies, though he will retain a working relationship with Driveline. Maybe he can begin to build better hitters at the pro level. They could use his help.

"A guy like Trevor Bauer, if he wanted to become a hitter and just did traditional hitting training, he never would have made it," Ochart says. "A guy like Trevor had to exhaust all resources and really push it to become the best version of himself because he wasn't exactly the most gifted athlete naturally. Whereas in hitting, it's kind of sink or swim: let's see who makes it, who's going to be the people at the top."

14

JUST BE BETTER

So this is how a person can come to despise himself—
knowing he's doing the wrong thing and not being able to stop.
 —DANIEL KEYES, *Flowers for Algernon*

For all his powers of player development, Branch Rickey believed some flaws were unfixable.

Take Tom Winsett. Winsett was a left-handed slugger in the Cardinals system, nicknamed Long Tom because six foot two was tall for a player in the 1930s. Winsett was a lousy left fielder, but in each of his minor-league seasons from 1934 to 1936, he batted at least .348 and slugged at least .617. In the last of those years, he slugged .731 in the American Association, launching a league-leading fifty home runs in 536 at-bats.

Publicly, Rickey described the slugger as a "coming Babe Ruth," intoning, "Woe unto the pitcher who throws the ball where the Winsett bat is functioning." Yet for some strange reason, Rickey couldn't find room for this Ruth on his roster, giving Winsett only twelve big-league at-bats in his Cardinals career.

That reason was later revealed. In August 1936, Rickey traded the twenty-six-year-old Winsett to Brooklyn for three players and cash. Although Winsett had a "beautiful swing," Rickey said, he "sweeps that bat in the same plane every time, no matter where the ball is pitched." Most major-league pitchers proved capable of throwing the ball where the Winsett bat *wasn't* functioning. Over parts of three seasons with the Dodgers, he batted .241 and slugged .357 with seven home runs in 465 at-bats. During his years in the majors, only one other player with at least six hundred combined MLB plate appearances struck out at a higher rate. Unable to repair Winsett's beautiful, broken swing, Rickey had sold Brooklyn a good-looking lemon.

Rickey had one other baseball bête noire: hitters who took too long a stride, costing them their balance and power. As a college coach, he tried placing a shot-putter's guard rail at the front of the batter's box so that hitters would stumble if they strode too far. Some of them wouldn't *stop* stumbling, so he stopped subjecting them to sprained ankles and tried tying ropes around their ankles instead. That felt too confining. "You can't cure an overstrider," Rickey conceded to the *New Yorker*'s Robert Rice in 1950.

Except that someone could. By 1986, outfielder Dave Gallagher, a 1980 Indians first-rounder, was in his seventh minor-league season and his third at Triple-A. His OPS was stuck in the .700s, and he blamed an excessive stride. "I was jumping at the ball, throwing my balance off," he told *Sports Illustrated* in 1989. "I figured that if I could control my feet, the rest of my body would follow suit." Gallagher didn't know about Rickey's rope, but he made something similar with more modern materials, including plastic chain and Velcro. The device, which he dubbed the Stride Tutor, inhibited his stride without getting in his head.

Using the Stride Tutor during drills, Gallagher upped his Triple-A offense, and in 1988, at age twenty-eight, he got to the big leagues for good, finished fifth in AL Rookie of the Year voting, and played seven more major-league seasons. He patented the Stride Tutor and sold five thousand units in 1988, making more in sales than he made in salary. In a 2012 interview, he credited the Stride Tutor—a superior implementation of an old idea—for making his career. Maybe a K-Vest could have made Winsett's swing more adaptable, or TrackMan training could have taught him to lay off the high pitches he tended to chase. Maybe Gallagher could have helped history's overstriders.

Then again, while Gallagher is a good story, most players still stall somewhere on the way to the majors. Plenty of prospects flop despite playing for teams that are well equipped to help them. That's why one of baseball's biggest questions is where the limits of development lie. "What everybody's trying to diagnose," Brian Bannister says, "is what attributes are almost set in stone and what attributes are pliable."

When the Red Sox released Rich Hill in March 2014, they opted to keep Craig Breslow, another slow-throwing lefty reliever who, like Hill, had pitched for the team in each of the previous two seasons. Breslow, who's five months younger than Hill, was forced to start the season on the injured list with a shoulder strain, but his roster status was never in doubt. From 2012 to 2013, he'd tied for the sixth-lowest park-adjusted ERA in the game among relievers with at least 120 combined innings pitched, trailing only All-Star closers. From 2005, his rookie year with the Padres, through 2013, he'd tied for the eighth-lowest park-adjusted ERA out of more than three hundred pitchers who'd thrown at least four hundred innings, ranking right alongside Clayton Kershaw and single-season saves record holder Francisco Rodríguez.

The five-foot-eleven Breslow was a twenty-sixth-round draftee who was never a top prospect, an All-Star, or a closer. The Brewers, who drafted him, released him after two years. Like Hill, he briefly landed in independent ball and then tried out with the Padres, who signed him for a one-dollar bonus. San Diego let him leave after one season, so he signed with the Red Sox. In subsequent seasons, he was selected off waivers three times and traded twice. He didn't post sterling strikeout or walk rates, and some ERA estimators suggested that he should have allowed many more runs than he did. No one wanted to lock him up long term. Yet he kept getting outs by inducing soft contact, preventing pulled pitches, and limiting both his BABIP and his home-run rate. In his first eight big-league seasons, Breslow's ERA never reached as high as 3.80.

Because Breslow threw in the low 90s and didn't miss many bats, he didn't have much margin for error. In 2014, his long-running high-wire act stopped working. Perhaps hampered by the shoulder strain, his four-seamer speed dipped into the 80s. His walk rate climbed, his home-run rate skyrocketed, and his ERA soared to 5.96. The next year was better, but still far from his heyday. The Sox had seen enough, so in 2016, he signed with the Marlins just before spring training. They cut him in July. The Rangers picked him up, sent him to Triple-A, then released him weeks later, the day before his thirty-sixth birthday. It looked like the end of the line.

Breslow was determined that it not be. He didn't want to walk away. "I think there's this assumption that because I *can* do other things, that I *want* to be doing other things," Breslow told us in 2017. Breslow had always seemed almost too smart to be a baseball player. He'd double-majored in molecular physics and biochemistry at Yale, and despite that daunting course load—not to mention his commitments as captain of the varsity team—he'd maintained a 3.5 GPA. When he'd been between baseball gigs after Milwaukee cast him loose, he'd taken the MCAT, applied to medical schools, and been accepted by NYU. The Padres probably prevented him from becoming Dr. Breslow.

A beat writer dubbed Breslow "the smartest man in baseball" in 2008, and the sobriquet stuck. To outside observers, baseball seemed somehow beneath Breslow, a youthful pursuit he'd one day abandon to do something serious. That wasn't how he felt. Nothing else made his heart beat harder and his adrenaline flow faster while also engaging his brain. The combination of "the intellectual component of critical thinking and problem solving, alongside the physical preparation and the competition, is one of those things that's really unique to sports," he says.

Despite his background, Breslow went years without trying to apply his scientific training to pitching. In an interview with Baseball Prospectus in 2006, a twenty-six-year-old Breslow drew a distinction between his studies and his sport. "Biochemistry is such a specific science," he said. "It's so analytical and methodical, and that kind of mentality can actually hurt in baseball." Eleven years later, looking back on the young player he'd been, Breslow said, "While I was having success, I was probably naïve and assumed that would last into perpetuity." The thought process of a pitcher who's sailing through a season, he added, is, "Am I risking taking myself out of this successful zone by becoming interested in things that I currently am not, or by using information that I don't think about right now?'"[1]

The first time Breslow strayed far enough from the success zone to consult advanced stats was 2011, when his ERA was over 4.00 as late as September 12. "I kept thinking to myself that my stuff was the same, my command was the same. I felt like I was striking out guys at the same clip; I was walking fewer guys," Breslow says. "It just seemed like every time a ball got put in play, it found a hole."

Breslow realized he didn't need to rely on feelings and impressions to assess his season. He could see what the stats said. To his relief, the numbers backed him up: he was pitching just as well as before, if not better, but his BABIP had spiked as a passel of singles snuck through. The apparent rough patch was just a random bout of bad luck, not an indication that Breslow's lease on major-league life was about to expire. He could carry on as before and wait for better bounces.

Five years later, though, the stats had nothing reassuring to show him. Even in Triple-A, Breslow was getting hit hard. Unlike in 2014, he couldn't pin his problems on an injury, and he had to face facts: he was three years removed from his last vintage season, at an age when players don't typically bounce back from decline. "I could no longer claim I was simply going to be better than I had been before for unknown reasons, which is kind of a nice myth to tell," he says. "I felt like my options were: drastically overhaul my repertoire, my skill set, my mechanics, or be out of the game, at least on the playing side. And for me that was a pretty simple decision."

Breslow reached out to as many team talent evaluators as he could. He knew there wasn't much interest among teams in retaining his services for 2017. His question was: Why? What was he missing, and what could he do to make himself more appealing to potential employers? Over and over, the answer came back: he had to be better against southpaws. Breslow had never been a true lefty-killer, the kind of pitcher a manager might summon with the other team's top same-sided slugger due up in a do-or-die spot. But there was sometimes space in a big-league bullpen for a southpaw who could be counted on to come in and record a quick out or two against his own kind.

"My limiting variable was always going to be velocity," Breslow says. He did some weighted-ball work and considered going to Driveline to boost his sagging radar readings, but he figured even going from the high 80s to the low 90s—below average to average, which would be a big jump in a short time frame—wouldn't be the best use of his time. "No matter what I did, no change . . . was going to take me from 88 mph to 98 mph," he says.

What Breslow did have, though, was "this incessant drive to be better today than I was yesterday." Figuratively speaking, he adds, "*That's* my fastball." And if his literal fastball was flagging, his figurative fastball was just finding its pace.

Breslow decided the most meaningful and manageable way for him to be more effective against fellow lefties was to create more deception against them. And the best way to do *that*, he believed, was to lower his arm slot from over-the-top to low-three-quarters, which would give lefties less of a look at the ball and make them more likely to whiff. If he then refined his breaking ball—which he'd barely been throwing, relying largely on four-seamers, sinkers, cutters, and changeups—he'd have the makings of a pitching profile that could catch teams' eyes.

With his career clock ticking, and with one winter to internalize "a new approach, a new delivery, a new repertoire," Breslow had to find the most systematic, efficient form of feedback to accelerate his overhaul. For that, he turned to technology. Seeking something affordable and portable that could help him monitor his movement and spin, Breslow bought a $3,000 Rapsodo device and a $500 cloud account with the company to store the information from his practice pitches. He then threw a bullpen session in September 2016, using his standard delivery and repertoire to establish baselines that he could use to track his progress.

Back in 2006, Breslow told BP, "For me to lower my arm slot—and I have tried—feels as foreign as throwing right-handed." The first time he tried it in 2016 felt similarly unnatural; when he reviewed video of the tentative attempt, he was surprised to see that what had felt like a drastic change amounted to a two-inch drop, probably imperceptible to anyone else. Eyes on the prize of employment, he pressed on, playing limbo with an invisible bar.

As he experimented with lower release points at Boston College and other local facilities, Breslow wore a motusTHROW, the first wearable device approved for in-game use in the majors. The small sensor, which is embedded within a compression sleeve, contains gyroscopes and accelerometers that record arm angle, speed, and stress. "As I lowered my arm angle, I actually decreased the stress on my elbow, but increased the velocity with which I could throw," Breslow says.

"And so the obvious question became, 'Why wasn't I throwing like this for the last thirty-five years?'" After frequent repetition, Breslow's brain rewired itself to make the new motion feel natural. Four months into his makeover, he reported, "The idea of throwing from my old slot feels more unusual than this current one does."

Lowering his arm slot was only half of Breslow's battle. Like Trevor Bauer sincerest-form-of-flattering Kluber and Stroman, Breslow looked for gold-standard pitches whose traits he could try to adopt. "When you talk about a left-on-left breaking ball, you think about Andrew Miller's slider; when you think about a left-on-left sinker, you think about Zach Britton's," Breslow says. Here, too, Breslow ran into limitations. Not only could he not throw nearly as hard as Britton or Miller—his friend and former teammate—but he lacked their extension toward the plate and ability to manipulate the ball. "I'm not six foot eight, with incredibly long arms and fingers," he says. "I can't make my fingers longer; I can't make them more flexible. I don't have the levers that [Miller] has."

Although he couldn't expect to replicate those best-in-class pitches, he could come closer to them. "The shape of the breaking ball, the axis that it spins at, those are things that I can attempt to mimic," he says. His baseline readings revealed that the spin on his sinker and slider was inefficient. By changing his arm angle, grip, and finger pressure and consulting Rapsodo after each pitch to see whether he was getting warmer or colder with respect to his left-handed lodestars, he harnessed his spin to generate more movement, developing what he believed to be "the optimal breaking ball for me."

Breslow made his movement gains quickly. He could see them with Rapsodo, but they were also detectable with a less sensitive instrument—the human eye—by the time his regular throwing partner returned to New England after his late-October loss in the NLCS. That partner's name: Rich Hill.

In the past few years, the former teammates' positions had switched: Breslow, who had made Boston's 2014 team, was out of work, while Hill, who'd been cut in 2014, was making NLCS starts and was six weeks away from landing a lucrative deal with the Dodgers. "Rich gives everyone hope," Breslow says. Hill gave him more hope when he told him that because of his new arm slot and movement, he'd become uncomfortable to catch. If he was hard to catch, maybe he'd be hard to hit, too.

Discussing the contrast between baseball and chemistry in 2006, Breslow said, "The specificity of what you do in the lab is something you can't take to the mound with you." He continued, "On the mound you need to make adjustments . . . you can't do that in the lab."

Breslow spent late 2016 and early 2017 in a baseball lab of his own devising, searching for the compound that would make him good again. Technology told him he'd found it, but to make his off-season experiment more than an academic endeavor, he *would* have to take it to the mound.

On January 23, 2017, representatives of roughly fifteen teams flocked to an indoor facility in Waltham, Massachusetts, where Breslow's agent had invited them to see the results of his client's labor. Any down-on-his luck pitcher can claim to be better, but Breslow had data and video that his agent had disseminated to document his claims. Even so, the scouts and executives wanted to see for themselves. Throwing his first high-pressure pitches in months, Breslow strutted his new stuff. His velocity still stood in the 80s, but in January, that didn't mean much. What mattered more were the new arm angle and revamped sinker-slider combo. This was a different Breslow than the one teams knew and no longer loved, and a different Breslow could be a better one.

Breslow's one-man metamorphosis made him a prospect in multiple capacities. Teams wanted his mind as much as his arm. Even if he never regained his old form on the mound—or, more accurately, his old performance in a new form—he might have value as a mentor to other players in need of their own reboots, or even as a future front-office member. And in the wake of Martinez, Hill, and other out-of-nowhere player leaps, teams were taking the possibility of a Breslow bounceback seriously.

In the days after his showcase, Breslow received ten offers. Although they were minor-league deals with invitations to spring training, not guaranteed tickets to the majors, that low-dollar Breslow bidding war was still an improvement over the previous summer, when no one was calling at all. He picked the Twins, not necessarily because they gave him the best chance to be a big leaguer again or even offered the most money, but because the team's newly hired top baseball official, Derek Falvey, spent hours on the phone with him, discussing data-driven development over the course of several conversations. Falvey described the team's relationship with Breslow as a "partnership," one in which the Twins would help support the work-in-progress pitcher.

Breslow's experiment was already a partial success: he'd made his new arm slot second nature; he could tell from Rapsodo data that his slider and sinker had moved closer to where he wanted them to be; and better yet, he had a job. "The only thing [the data] doesn't show is whether I can get hitters out," Breslow joked to the Minneapolis *Star Tribune* just before spring training. In Florida, he pitched nine games and allowed only one run, although he also walked as many batters as he struck out (seven). Breslow broke camp with the Twins and was back in the big leagues for the twelfth season.

Breslow's MLB data from 2017 paints a picture of a very different pitcher from the one he was before. His cutter—which he lost the feel for from the lower slot—was gone, replaced by more sinkers. His slider (sometimes classified as a curve) was a staple instead of a rarity. His average release point was more than nine inches lower, falling from the thirty-seventh percentile to the fifth percentile in height among lefties with at least two hundred pitches. His sinker and changeup dropped by about four inches more than ever before, and they also added an extra couple of inches of sweeping, side-to-side break.

There was only one problem: those redesigned pitches still weren't getting guys out. Breslow's stats with Minnesota were worse than they had been in Boston or Miami, and on July 29, thirty games (and an IL stint for rib-cage soreness) into his trial, the Twins released him and his 5.23 ERA. On August 7, the Indians signed him and sent him to Triple-A, then promoted him in September, reuniting him with Bauer, his teammate for a brief time during Bauer's debut year in Arizona. "I think we both approach new pursuits similarly: analytically and methodically," Breslow says. "But obviously, he has been far more effective."

The good news about Breslow's season was he'd held lefties to a .580 OPS (albeit without many strikeouts). The bad news was that righties, against whom he was now extra vulnerable, had demolished him, recording a .934 OPS—and he'd faced twice as many righties as lefties.

Undeterred, Breslow signed another minor-league deal the following February, this time with Toronto. The thirty-seven-year-old started the season in Double-A, pitching at that level for the first time in a nonrehab appearance since 2005, his age-twenty-four season. He missed a month and a half with a hamstring strain, then made it to Triple-A. That's where he spent the rest of the summer, riding buses and waiting for a call that never came.

The buses didn't bother Breslow, who says he was too consumed with his quest to care about the low salary or the lack of big-league luxuries. What frustrated him was not knowing why his process wasn't working. He struck out thirty batters in 28 1/3 innings, but he walked twenty-four. He allowed an .865 OPS to lefties, and his ERA finished at 5.40. Breslow spoke to Toronto's front office regularly and monitored his TrackMan info after each outing, looking for some secret of tunneling or deception or sequencing that he might have missed. "The pitch profiles that [are] objectively measured indicate that I should have success as a left-on-left reliever," he says. "And so when I'm not having success, what is the reason?"

One non-Toronto front-office analyst who's analyzed Breslow's minor-league TrackMan data from 2018 says there isn't really much of a mystery. He agrees that Breslow made his breaking ball better, but only from a 35–40 pitch to a 45–50 pitch on the 20–80 scouting scale. "With a fastball at 88, that's going to get hit," he says. Losing his cutter and his hopping four-seam fastball gave Breslow fewer weapons to work with, and aging took a toll. "I think by hurting himself against [righties], he offset whatever he did to help himself against [lefties]," the analyst says. "But with the velo loss and all the walks, whatever repertoire changes he made pale in comparison to how much worse that made him."

The analyst questions whether Breslow's strategy of targeting left-ies alone was sound. He also notes that pitchers often run into trouble when trying to talk themselves through transformations, especially without the aid of an Edgertronic, which Breslow considered invest-ing in but ultimately opted not to. "Doing pitch design well is still a competitive advantage for teams because it's not obvious how to do it right," the analyst says. He suggests that trying to boost his velocity might have helped Breslow more, but even that wouldn't necessarily have helped, because ultimately, "It's Father Time that's hurting him more than anything he did wrong."

On the surface, Breslow had all the ingredients of a modern make-over success story. At minimum, he was one of the smartest men in baseball. He was well-attuned to technology, with a commendable work ethic and access to Hill himself. But the hope Hill's example gave him may have been false. Not only did Breslow not throw hard, he didn't have a brilliant breaking ball yearning to breathe free.

"[I] certainly have recognized both the excitement and promise and also the limitations of creating a new pitcher in a lab," Breslow says. So have the Blue Jays. A member of Toronto's front office ac-knowledges that previous tech-enabled breakouts affected the team's belief in Breslow. "Now that there have been enough positive versions of this, you want to look at [players] with fresh eyes and try to eval-uate what might be there as opposed to what was there two years ago, three years ago," the source says. The chance of buying low on the next career rehabilitation, the source admits—coupled with the prospect of working with a player who promised to be ultrareceptive to front-office input—may have clouded the club's thinking.

Although failing to make the majors for the first time since 2007 was disappointing, Breslow says it "didn't really change how I feel about the process or undertaking the endeavor." But Breslow's path is finally diverging from the field. He's father to young twins, and he and his wife welcomed a third child in December. As long as he lingered on the mound, he was missing moments with them. And shortly after the season, it became clear that lingering longer might not be an op-tion. "I've become more of a highly sought-after postplayer than cur-rent player," Breslow acknowledged in December. It was bittersweet, he said, but also, perhaps, the right time to turn the page. "What I've learned about teaching analytics, what I've learned about myself as a pitcher, and also what I've learned about trying to implement or pitch to certain data points . . . should help me tremendously in my next life."

That life began quickly. In January, the Cubs hired him as director of strategic initiatives for baseball operations, a wide-ranging conduit role in which he'll play a part in pitcher development. Breslow tried to rebuild himself to recapture an old career. Instead, he started a new one.

In an on-air discussion on MLB Network in February 2018, Reds star Joey Votto was asked to speak about the significance of launch angle. Votto, a former MVP and perennial on-base machine who's famed for his ability to avoid pop-ups, is an authority on the subject; in 2018, he led all regular hitters by concentrating 45.9 percent of his batted balls in the launch-angle sweet spot of 8 to 32 degrees. "I think a lot of the hitters that have made the change in their hitting style from more of a line-drive, gap-to-gap approach to attempting more fly balls and benefiting from it, I don't think we've told the story about how complete they are as hitters," he said.

In other words, some of the hitters who've joined the elite by adopting a data-driven swing change may have benefited because their preexisting skills allowed them to make that adjustment successfully. Twins assistant director of player development Alex Hassan, a former outfielder hired as a conduit in 2018, makes a similar observation. "The point that could get overlooked here is that Chris Taylor made it to the big leagues prior to making these adjustments," Hassan says. "So did Justin Turner, J.D. Martinez. These guys were big leaguers before they did these swing overhauls and became these household names." They weren't *good* big leaguers, but even with counterproductive approaches, they had big-league ability.

Because the players whose adjustments pay off get to stay in the majors and in the public eye, Hassan says, "There's a huge survivorship bias." We're much more likely to talk about those guys than we are the ones who never turn into impact players or never make the majors at all, provided the latter aren't well known enough to be busts like Mark Appel. "Those stories aren't as apparent because those guys, nobody knows who they are," Hassan continues. "No one's going to keep asking, 'Oh, let's go find all those guys who flamed out in Double-A, get their story.'"

Hassan would know because he basically was one of those guys. A twentieth-round Red Sox pick out of Duke in 2009, he worked his way up through the minors roughly one level per year. In 2013, his age-twenty-five season, he repeated Triple-A and didn't get the call despite an .891 OPS. His offense that year was inflated by a high BABIP, and he hit only four homers in 210 at-bats, not ideal for a six-foot-three corner guy. Hassan had a good eye, but he decided he'd have to power up to cross the last barrier between him and the majors.

That off-season, he entrusted himself to a well-known hitting guru (he won't say which one). Hassan, a right-handed hitter, tried to make adjustments geared toward elevating the ball to left field, including shifting his weight forward aggressively and tipping the bat à la Barry Bonds, who would point his barrel at the opposite batter's box before starting his swing. Instead of helping, the changes fouled him up. "It just didn't work," he says. "I was not myself. . . . I was swing-and-missing in the zone a ton, which I didn't do prior to that. And I wasn't driving the ball."

The same winter the remade Martinez was lighting up the Venezuelan Winter League, Hassan was stinking up the Dominican Winter League. He then took his act to Triple-A and managed only a .621 OPS through May, with one homer and an uncharacteristic 30 percent strikeout rate. Ironically, that's when the call-up came. Hassan, who grew up twelve miles from Fenway Park with a family-built replica of the Green Monster in his backyard, was summoned as an injury replacement and singled to center in his first start. Getting the major-league monkey off his back gave him the confidence to restore his old swing, and when he returned to Triple-A, he raked the rest of the way.

Hassan never made it back to the big leagues after 2014. He retired at twenty-eight with one big-league hit on his career record. "[I] spent the rest of my career making adjustments to see if there was something I could tweak in my swing to help me," he says. "I ultimately never really found those answers like some guys had. Those adjustments seemed to click right away for some guys."

Hassan won't say that the guru's recommendations were wrong, only that he wasn't able to follow them. It didn't help that the process wasn't as data driven as he would have liked, occurring as it did just before swing- and ball-trackers became ubiquitous. "More measurable outcomes would've helped me get a little better direction as I tried to make those adjustments," he says. Maybe better tech would have made a power-hitting Hassan happen, but we'll never know.

Not every hitter *should* hit more flies, and aiming up can backfire if the flies aren't hit hard or lead to less contact. The hitter with the highest career fly-ball rate on record, the Padres' all-or-nothing infielder Ryan Schimpf, batted .158 with a 35.5 percent strikeout rate in 2017, then got demoted to the minors, traded three times in four months, and released. Many of the hitters who've benefited from angling up were in need of a change. Those who are already mashing, meanwhile, risk an Icarus ending by trying to fly higher.

In 2016, the Orioles' Mark Trumbo led the majors with forty-seven homers, but in 2017, his power cratered. The following January, Trumbo explained that he'd allowed himself to get "too distracted last year with a lot of different numbers, analytics, launch angles." He resolved to get "back to getting a good pitch and squaring it up," and he did, posting his highest average exit velocity and sweet-spot percentage (but lowest average launch angle) in 2018. A 2018 study by MLBAM senior database architect of stats Tom Tango showed that "hitters are more likely to maintain their launch angle if it was followed by an increase in performance," noting that hitters who slump tend to revert to what was working before.

In 2018, the Brewers' Christian Yelich won the NL MVP Award without chasing flies, even though his high ground-ball rates had identified him as a hitter who might benefit. Despite leading all non-Rockies NL hitters in homers, he hit more than half his balls on the ground, and his average launch angle was unchanged. "There has been no conscious change on my part, no buying into launch angle," Yelich told

MLB.com in October. Yet by making more subtle changes—swinging at more hittable pitches and attacking outside pitches farther in front of the plate—he raised his sweet-spot percentage and average launch angle on hard-hit balls without actually overhauling his swing.

Even when swing changes work wonders, those wonders do sometimes cease. After 2016, Yonder Alonso was a former seventh-overall pick who was about to turn thirty and who'd been a below-average offensive first baseman for more than two thousand major-league plate appearances, hitting only thirty-nine homers in seven seasons and topping out at nine in any one year. After watching other veteran hitters transform their careers and reading about fly balls at FanGraphs, Alonso decided to transfer more of his strength into his swing. "I was kind of hitting like if I weighed 150 pounds, instead of getting my 225 to 230 pounds into the ball," he told us. He watched video, sought Votto's advice, added a leg kick, and engaged his lower body to lift and drive the ball.

It worked. A career .387 slugger entering the season, Alonso slugged .501 with twenty-eight homers in 2017 and made the All-Star team. He raised his fly-ball rate—which had stood at 32.6 percent for his career—to 43.2 percent, and while his strikeout rate unsurprisingly spiked, trading contact for power was well worth it. FanGraphs' Dave Cameron dubbed him "the new poster boy for the fly-ball revolution."

After that season, Alonso signed with Cleveland. And while he continued to hit for more power than he had before 2017, other aspects of his performance slipped as he seemingly got greedy: he walked less, swung more, and chased the breaking balls below the zone that teams began to throw him more often, yielding weaker contact. In a sequence of rapid reversals, Alonso went from posting a combined 97 wRC+ from 2015 to 2016, up to 133 in 2017, and then back down to 97 again in 2018. In December, the Indians traded him to the division-rival White Sox for an unranked prospect.

It's easy to be seduced by the successes without factoring in the flops. It's also easy to oversimplify what should be an individualized process. "There is no one way to hit," Yelich said in October 2018. Nor is there one way to develop players.

Optimizing development is as much about knowing a player's weaknesses as it is knowing his strengths. Some of those weaknesses can be corrected, but not all of them. "You're still limited by [the player's] genetic ceiling in certain areas," Bannister says.

On the pitching side, for instance, "some arm actions are capable of creating high fastball quality—essentially, very deceptive, high-velocity, high-swing-and-miss fastballs," Bannister says. "Some pitchers' arm actions can create very high-quality secondary pitches. But there are very few that can do both." Teams pay top dollar for those talents, snapping them up in the draft or on the amateur market. If they miss out on the few, they do what they can to make the many more appealing. "I'm still to a never-ending degree trying to identify how much we can manipulate the body to have these characteristics," Bannister says.

Velocity, Bannister believes, is primarily muscular, which means that it can be trained and improved to some extent. Even that aspect of performance, however, is subject to body composition because some muscle types are more adept at handling load versus speed; some people can lift heavy weights but can't lift even lighter weights quickly, whereas others lift quickly but can't lift a lot. Still, muscle is malleable beneath a certain ceiling.

Spin is a separate quality: some pitchers throw hard but straight, while others (like Hill) throw soft with spin. "Spin and the ability to shape pitches has a lot to do with both the range of motion of your individual joints and, really, the elasticity of connective tissue," Bannister says. Some players' ligaments and tendons are stiffer and less responsive, whereas others store a higher amount of potential energy in the milliseconds prior to performing a movement. "They actually have connective tissue that's really stretchy, so it's like prestretching a rubber band," Bannister says. "So when they go to throw, it generates a snap-back quality on top of what their muscles are doing." Bannister cites Chris Sale, who looks like Mr. Fantastic, as an especially stretchy pitcher.

Thus, there's an elasticity and spin ceiling, too. "It's largely genetic and not something that can be taught or trained," Bannister says. Maybe you can cure an overstrider, but you can't cure an understretcher.

When Hassan was stuck in the minors, he says, he "definitely heard, 'If you don't like it, play better' repeated ad nauseam." He regards it as a message "that was so simple and obvious that it became really easy to ignore, but that was probably really honest and good." For some players, "just be better" is actionable advice, a reminder to redouble their efforts or focus on the measures that are most likely to work. For others, though, "just be better" is an inscrutable command they can't obey, something they hear, Boddy says, "when [they] are repeating High-A for the third time." Everybody can be better, but in baseball, better isn't always enough.

On the evening of August 22, Trevor Bauer drives his used Chevy Silverado pickup—140,000 miles and counting—to Clague Park, a mostly open green space in a Westlake, Ohio, neighborhood. This is where he usually flies his drones, including the infamous drone of 2016 that sliced into his right pinky finger. He finds a vacant picnic table and places the drone's case atop it. Building and racing drones is Bauer's escape from baseball. He prints off some of the parts from his own 3-D printer. He creates the specifications for the carbon-fiber frames and has them cut at a local shop. "I fully designed this," he says proudly, brandishing one of two drones he's brought to the park.

Bauer named this particular drone Monkey Business because of the amount of time it spends stuck in trees. He's lost two drones in this park. He offered rewards on Twitter but never received a response. There's been an important evolution in his drone designs over time: the frame is essentially upside down. What would normally be the bottom plate is now turned up, which allows him to attach and charge its battery without the risk of slicing off a finger. It's an unusual place for a power source, and it might negatively affect performance by disrupting air flow. Managing these trade-offs isn't too different from the theory of pitch design.

The drone is fitted with a camera. Bauer has a couple of goggle-like headsets that link to the video feed, giving the flier the feeling of being airborne. The drones' four propellers begin to spin, emitting a sound like a high-pitched weed whacker. The drone begins its journey through trees, through a gazebo, and over a curious dog and a couple on an evening walk. It clips a tree branch, but it stays in flight.

Bauer's device is highly maneuverable. Its course is dizzying. Trees. Open lawn. Then, roof shingles. The video abruptly goes black.

"That happens a lot," Bauer says.

Monkey Business has crashed into the roof of the gazebo. Bauer walks about a hundred yards to the crash site. Some debris, a yellow plug, rests on the roof. He finds the body of the drone and investigates it.

"Uh-oh," he says. "This one is done for the day." He speaks in a dispassionate way, even though significant repairs are required. He points to a shredded cable.

"This is a fairly typical flight session," Bauer says. "You got to see a good representation of what it is. Generally, you do more fixing than actual flying."

A lot like pitching, at least the science-based branch Bauer practices. Bauer walks back to his pickup. He's limping along, his right foot encased in a walking boot. The drone, his hobby, is a way to get his mind off the reality that his season might be over.

When Bauer took the mound August 11, 2018, in Chicago, he was hoping to create separation in the Cy Young race. Cole had faded after a dominant first half, and Bauer's primary competition at the time, Sale, had already made one trip to the injured list with a balky shoulder; he'd make another on August 18 that would ultimately end his Cy Young chase. Bauer's statistics were strong. He led the AL in pitcher WAR (5.7), just ahead of Sale (5.6), and with a 2.25 ERA he trailed only Sale (2.04) and Blake Snell (2.18), who was creeping up on the Cy Young radar.

For the first six innings, Bauer dominated the White Sox. His command was the sharpest it had been in the second half. He didn't walk a batter, and he struck out eight, allowing just two hits and one run. He was rolling. Bauer threw one hundred pitches in those first six innings, the twenty-fifth consecutive start in which he'd crossed the century mark. The streak tied knuckleball pitcher Tom Candiotti for the longest in club history since pitch counts began to be tracked in 1988.

Bauer, who'd never been placed on the injured list, felt impervious to arm- and shoulder-related injuries because of the efficiency of his throwing motion. More innings would give him an edge in the Cy Young race, so he wanted as much work as possible. He'd even been pushing the club to start him once every *four* days. This wasn't just a short-term ploy. Bauer plans to enter free agency after the 2020 season, and intends to market himself as a pitcher who can throw every four days and exceed 250 innings in a season. He wants to sign only one-year deals.

Francona permitted him to go out for the seventh inning, holding a 3–1 lead.

Bauer's second pitch of the inning was an elevated 94 mph fastball. As he readied to deliver it, Chicago play-by-play commentator Jason Benetti told his TV audience that Bauer "will be in the discussion for the Cy Young Award." Bauer dealt. José Abreu swung, and a line drive left his bat at 92.3 mph, striking Bauer's right ankle, which floated just above the mound about fifty-five feet away. Bauer crumpled to the ground. Though he left the game under his own power, an MRI would later reveal a small fracture of his right fibula. The doctors said he would miss four to six weeks. There were fewer than six weeks left in the season. For the first time in his career, Bauer was headed to the IL. And to make the situation more frustrating, he was headed there thanks to a fluke injury that was not related to his pitching mechanics or training. He had transformed himself from an average pitcher into an elite one, but no amount of training could prevent the injury that threatened to cost him his best chance yet at a Cy Young Award.

Bauer's initial depression was short-lived. While still in a "constant state of being pissed-off," he channeled his energy into thinking about how to beat the doctors' timetable. Within days of the injury, Bauer began doing modified long-toss drills from his knees to try to keep his upper body and mechanics in shape while he rehabbed his lower body.

Immediately after the diagnosis, the Indians' team medical staff had placed him on Forteo, an injection drug that promotes new bone formation and is typically used to treat severe osteoporosis. "There's a ton of research that shows it quickens fracture healing," Bauer says.

The Indians also placed him on a topical blood thinner, but his skin became irritated, so he quit applying it. While his ankle was swollen and painful, he avoided anti-inflammatory drugs, as they were thought to possibly slow healing.

But the team was already beginning to frustrate Bauer with its approach to his rehab. Less than two weeks after his initial MRI, he desperately wanted to be reimaged to see how the bone was healing. The medical staff decided to wait. Bauer also called outside medical professionals he trusts, including his physical therapist John Meyer, his sports chiropractor Curt Rindal, and Los Angeles Angels strength coach Lee Fiocchi, who promotes innovative theories and exercises and had helped Bauer clear up forearm discomfort earlier in the season.

After those calls in mid-August, he ordered a laser.

Cold laser, or low-level laser therapy, is a treatment that employs specific light wavelengths to accelerate healing of tissue damage. Bauer learned that employing the laser in conjunction with a bone stimulator, which sends low levels of electromagnetic energy to the fracture, *might* allow the two devices to "play off each other" and help mend his fracture. It was more of an experiment than a sure thing. He began to use them in tandem every night. Inspired by Bauer's willingness to experiment, Michael Baumann, a writer for the website The Ringer, took the opportunity to create some satire on Twitter. What could go wrong?

"Trevor Bauer says that the doctors' timeline for his return is based on outdated mainstream medicine and he's begun a course of blood transfusions and colloidal silver to rid his body of CIA nanites. He anticipates missing two starts, three tops," Baumann wrote.

On MLB Network, an anchor reported and read aloud Baumann's tweet as if it were actual news. Bauer was furious. The misinterpreted tweet made him appear ridiculous.

What *was* true was that Bauer, who considered using a soldering iron to seal the wound on his finger during the 2016 postseason, would use any legal means to accelerate his return to the pitching mound. And as Sale was sidelined and Cole and Verlander failed to pull away, hope began to creep back in. If he could make three more starts, maybe he could keep pace with the Cy Young field. The team thought a late-September return was likely, but Bauer targeted September 10.

At lunch at First Watch, a café close to his apartment, on September 4, Bauer told his server he needed to modify his usual order. He's a regular there. He asked for four eggs scrambled, a cup and a half of fruit, and a quarter cup of walnuts.

"That's what I get to eat today," Bauer said.

As the waitress took his order, she noted Bauer's expression and said, "I've been doing quinoa on and off for a year. That's my exact face when I go out to eat."

Bauer laughed. "I just want a bowl of pasta sometimes," he said.

Bauer's brief optimism hadn't lasted long. His rehab had stalled, and his September 10 target now looked unlikely, if not impossible. One issue was his weight, which was decreasing quickly. He'd lost almost 10 pounds. Most of the missing mass was muscle, as he fell to 196 pounds, which would cost him velocity.

"I lost thirteen pounds in a month [in 2014]," Bauer says. "I went from sitting 96.5 to 93."

The club's strength staff assured him when he started lifting again at full capacity the muscle would come back, but he had to do lighter weight-room work to reduce the stress on his ankle. Bauer was frustrated. He thought the Indians were too conservative with his rehab, and he suspected his team-mandated diet was accelerating his atrophy. He hounded the training staff.

"It would be dishonest to say there is not some fault on my end on how I phrase things," Bauer said. "I can be abrasive: this needs to change; fix it. But a lot of times when I ask [amicably], nothing changes."

Bauer had a food scale, and he'd been measuring almost everything he put into his body. He eventually wore a heart-rate monitoring device for an entire day and estimated that he had a nearly 1,400-calorie deficit. He needed more calories, and he needed to lift more weight. His diet plan was eventually adjusted. Bauer also decided he was going to resume working out at full capacity to regain the muscle he'd lost.

The other problem was the range of motion, or lack thereof, in his ankle. Any stress on the ankle was still painful, which had curtailed an attempted bullpen session on August 28. He was sent in for another exam. A Cleveland Clinic doctor said Bauer was suffering from ankle impingement, meaning a swollen joint capsule was restricting his mobility. Bauer's ability to bend his ankle was far from his baseline. In spring training, he had rotated his ankle joint, or moved his foot upward, by 12.5 centimeters in each ankle. On September 1, he was at 8 centimeters in his right ankle and 12 in his left. The Indians decided against the cortisone shot, preferring an anti-inflammatory drug used for patients suffering from gout. "I need to come in at 12," Bauer said. "That's normal for me." He was told that might be impossible.

On September 3, with no change in his ankle mobility, he visited another doctor, who stuck a needle in his ankle, drained out seven cubic centimeters of fluid, and gave him a cortisone shot. The ankle's flexibility began to improve.

By September 18, his weight was inching up, and the Indians were ready to see him in simulated game action. On a late afternoon at Progressive Field, Bob Chester set up the Edgertronic camera. Many of the Indians' front-office officials gathered at the dugout railing. A number of position players were enlisted to hit. Bauer buzzed through them with little issue. His slider seemed to have retained most of its movement profile. His fastball velocity was down, but still in the low-to-mid 90s. There was little hard contact. Between simulated innings, Chester brought a laptop over to show Indians officials the Edgertronic video. Indians star José Ramírez had come out to the dugout to watch but was not participating. During a break in the action, Ramírez chirped at Bauer.

"Lot of talk, no action," Bauer responded, smirking. "Want to see if you can hit it?" After the throwing session, he decreed that he was "close."

On September 21, Bauer returned to the mound against Boston and Chris Sale, another pitcher working his way back from injury. Despite their extended absences, they had remained first and second on the FanGraphs WAR leaderboard through September 11, a testament to how far ahead of the pack they had been. But Bauer had suffered too many setbacks and missed his original, optimistic return date by eleven days. He'd made himself a major leaguer. He'd designed a devastating slider. He'd transformed himself into an ace. At every impasse, he'd found a way to beat his body's limitations and defy the odds. But Bauer couldn't make himself heal faster than the doctors had predicted. Even he had limitations.

Bauer's first pitch in thirty-one days was an elevated 94 mph fastball that Tzu-Wei Lin swung through for a strike. In the second, he got Steve Pearce to swing and miss at a sharp-breaking slider. But he also hung a slider to Brock Holt, who slashed it into right field for a single in the second on Bauer's thirty-fourth and final pitch of the night. Before the end of the season, he made two more appearances, each lasting four frames. He allowed two runs over his 9 1/3 innings in September, striking out seven against one walk. His fastball velocity was 93.2 mph, down 1.4 mph from its preinjury average after May 1.

"I'm down mass," Bauer said. "I need to maintain a high level of training specificity to keep my velo. I'm not in peak form."

He had made it back, but he knew he was out of the Cy Young chase. And that wasn't the worst of it. On September 26, Francona summoned Bauer to his office and told him he was not going to be used as a starter until possibly Game 4 against the Astros, whom the Indians would face in the American League Division Series. Bauer would begin the series in the bullpen, and the Indians would be without their best starter. The baseball gods can be cruel.

15

SOFT FACTORS

Rogers Hornsby, my manager, called me a "talking pile of pigshit."
That was when my parents came from Michigan to see me play the
game! Did I cry? No! No! Do you know why? Because there's no crying
in baseball. There's no crying in baseball. No crying!
— JIMMY DUGAN, *A League of Their Own*

When catcher-turned-conduit John Baker was in Triple-A, his manager, he says, acted like an "evil stepfather." If the pitcher walked the
leadoff man, Baker would be fined $100. If he failed to catch a ball
cleanly, the manager would yell that he didn't *want* to catch the ball.
"One time I'd had enough," Baker remembers. "I was in his office, and
I'm like, 'Who can I talk to to be better at this?' And he's like, 'Nobody.
You gotta figure it out yourself.'"

Baker is now a coordinator of the Cubs' Mental Skills Program.
Players come to him asking the same question he once asked his
minor-league manager. And when they do, he says, "We don't say
that anymore."

Baker isn't some wizened relic recalling ancient history. Drafted by
the Moneyball A's, he's in his late thirties, younger than some active
major leaguers. He reached Triple-A in the mid-2000s. Yet attitudes
have evolved even over the course of his career. "The overwhelming
paradigm that was pushed by the oldest generations of baseball was
you need to be a tough, gunslinging, beer-swilling, slump-buster-
finding asshole of a cowboy to be a good baseball player," Baker says.
"And what we're realizing now [is] that that's not necessarily a paradigm for anything . . . other than ruining a marriage and being unhappy." Over the last several years, Baker continues, a new paradigm
has appeared. "People are much more open to the softer side of things,"

he says. "They understand better that it's not necessarily about mental toughness or confidence as much as it is about self-compassion and mindfulness and being in the present moment so that you can execute the techniques that you've practiced."

In 2018, emboldened by the new paradigm, the Cubs' players adopted a practice that once would have been as unthinkable as technology tracking every pitch. "Starting in spring training, they were getting together as a position-players group, and they were talking about all of the times where they feel shitty on the baseball field," Baker says. "From [Anthony] Rizzo to [Kris] Bryant to the lowest guy in the minor leagues, they were opening up and expressing to each other, showing that they're actually real people that are vulnerable. That was a massive turning point for us because it gave people the freedom to not feel like they had to be perfect."

A funny thing has happened in baseball as the sport has embraced every quantifiable edge: teams and players have also grown more receptive to innovation in areas that in theory should confer advantages but aren't communicable in degrees, revolutions per minute, or miles per hour. Each advance in technology leaves fewer aspects of the sport that can't be captured and expressed statistically, but it also opens minds and makes the pursuit of any remaining uncharted territory more intense. "You think about things like spin rate and exit velocity and how they're changing how we view baseball—well, those things are effective because they have science behind them," Baker says. "And that opens the door to other things that have science behind them. Things like mindfulness or meditation practice, or what I'm trained in now, which is mindfulness-based attention training." As Jerry Dipoto explains, "Player development has become a more holistic endeavor."

Soft science came to baseball on March 2, 1950, when a Manhattan psychologist named David F. Tracy began working for the St. Louis Browns, whose athletic trainer had convinced owner Bill Dewitt Jr. that if psychology could improve other businesses, it could also benefit baseball teams. Tracy, who wrote in rather glowing terms about his contributions to the Browns in his 1951 book *The Psychologist at Bat*, offered optional psychology classes twice a day in spring training to accommodate split-squad practices. As Professors Mary J. Mac-Cracken and Alan S. Kornspan recounted in a 2003 article about Tracy, "To help the athletes improve performance, Tracy's classes consisted of teaching hypnosis, autosuggestion, relaxation, and confidence-building techniques."[1] Believing that the Browns were suffering from stage fright, "Tracy based much of his work [on] changing negative thoughts to positive thoughts. For example, he taught the Browns pitchers to step off the mound and take three deep breaths when they were feeling nervous."

Thanks in part to pioneering figures like Harvey Dorfman (author of *The Mental Game of Baseball*) and Ken Ravizza (author of *Heads-Up Baseball*), sports psychologists are much more commonplace and accepted today than they were in the '50s, when part of Tracy's task was convincing the players he had any part to play at all. But some of the concerns are the same—and, in fact, may be made more acute by players' awareness that eyes in the sky (and sometimes sensors on their persons) are recording everything they do. "We're living in a shifting technological landscape where technology is taking a larger and larger role in our lives, and as a result, the rates of anxiety and depression have skyrocketed," Baker says.

Fortunately, just as modern teams have more tools to optimize players' physical performance, they also have more ways to set their players' minds at ease. The Cubs have consulted with Dr. Amishi Jha, a neuroscientist and associate professor of psychology at the University of Miami, as well as Scott Rogers, who runs the mindfulness program at the Jha Lab. The lab has worked with the military and with football players to develop a variant of the University of Massachusetts Medical Center's Mindfulness-Based Stress Reduction, a nonpharmacological formula to deal with depression or anxiety.

The Cubs, who plan to conduct their own research with players in the instructional league, obtained data on Jha's program that Baker says "shows a cognitive increase when people do it seven days a week and just a stabilization of cognitive function at something as small as three times a week, twelve minutes a day." At the start of spring training, they present their players at all levels with a one-page summary of the scientific benefits of mindfulness practice, and they promote the regular use of free meditation apps. The resulting program is a mixture of hard science, Stoicism, and Eastern philosophy. "All the stuff that we do works great for the general population to bring them back to homeostasis," Baker says. "But when you put those things onto the elite athlete, our vision is that it elevates them beyond what they are now."

The goal, Baker says, is to get players to reset and dismiss distractions before each pitch, allowing them to "play thought-free and allow all of the years of practice and training that is based on all of these scientific measures now to just express itself." To do that, they have to "consciously and nonjudgmentally come back to this moment right now and go, 'So, that happened. Now what am I going to do about it?'"

Although each team implements its mental-skills program in a different fashion, Baker says he sees a lot of overlap. In contrast to tight-lipped R&D departments, mental-skills personnel across teams tend to pool their knowledge, both because the field is still new and unsettled and because, Baker adds, "there isn't anything proprietary about meditation." Baker's department does surveys in the middle and at the end of the year to find out how players think their mindfulness training has affected their mental state and on-field performance, but as Baker observes, "We can't quantify, 'Oh, you've meditated for ten minutes and got two hits.' That's not a direct correlation." As teams have learned lately, though, just because something can't currently be measured doesn't mean it won't be one day.

It's a sign of progress that players are getting in the habit of saying "serenity now," but to some extent, mindfulness addresses only the symptoms of the stress that they encounter. Teams are also tackling some—but not all—of the *sources* of that stress.

In 2018, 254 of the 750 players on MLB's Opening Day rosters were born outside the United States, and almost a third of all major-league players hailed from Spanish-speaking countries. Many of those players face an especially steep uphill climb through the minors because in addition to figuring out fastballs and breaking balls they also have to learn a second language, deal with culture shock, and adjust to the transition from sometimes poverty-stricken existences to life as professional players (though life in the minors often isn't far from poverty). Teams are increasingly invested in easing that transition instead of asking players from Venezuela or the Dominican Republic to parachute into Peoria or Pulaski without a support system, which can impair their performance and sometimes send them packing before they've fulfilled their potential.

Doris Gonzalez, the Astros' manager of player education, has led the club's education, acculturation, and language-development efforts since 2006, when she began teaching English to players part-time. A longtime ESL instructor, Gonzalez emigrated from Honduras at eleven and learned English as a second language herself. Because she understands the challenge of adapting to United States culture, she's well suited to the role. Although she wasn't a big baseball fan, she "quickly kind of fell in love with the [players] and the idea of helping them do better." Just as quickly, they grew attached to her and began calling her "mom."

As soon as Gonzalez got involved in teaching the youngest Astros English, she realized that speaking skills were just a starting point. In concert with ESL classes, she now oversees a Formal Education Program, whose graduates gain a high-school diploma. She provides instruction in American culture and the differences between American culture and Latino cultures, including how to behave in various settings and situations (such as being stopped by a police officer). She also places a focus on character education and social skills, one aspect of which involves introducing players to the concepts of growth mindset and deliberate practice. The curriculum continues: history lessons (both baseball and the world), the perils of substance abuse, sex education, driver's ed.

Another part of her program is financial literacy. When Gonzalez started, players were throwing away their W-2 forms, not knowing what they were. Now they learn banking, taxes, and managing whatever money they make, some of which they send home to support their families. She also works to secure host families for the players in her program, who historically have been harder to place because fewer families are willing to accept players who aren't fluent in

English. Meager minor-league wages make conditions tough enough; not having a host family exacerbates the problem and places even more disproportionate demands on the players who are already handling the heaviest loads.

No matter how much Gonzalez lightens those loads, most of her students won't make the majors. But the life lessons they learn in her program—and a growing number of similar programs with other teams, which she has helped promote—will prepare them for their next careers. That's the part she's proudest of: ministering to the "thousands and thousands of Latino players that are literally dropping everything in their life to pursue a dream that they're probably not going to reach."

Gonzalez's efforts may seem far removed from swing changes and pitch design, but they work hand in hand with the Astros' technological trendsetting. For one thing, nonnative speakers are less likely to receive the proper attention from English-speaking coaches, making it harder to implement the Astros' development program (although teams are putting a higher priority on employing Spanish-speaking coaches). Players who are homesick, isolated, and struggling to stay afloat off the field will be in no frame of mind to study spin rates. By removing those off-the-field impediments to on-the-field development, Gonzalez is making major leaguers just as surely as the latest high-tech tools.

Like Baker, Gonzalez acknowledges that the impact of programs like hers is difficult to quantify, but in this case, anecdotes are data. "Specific players have at moments in time told me, 'I want my letter of release, I want to go home,'" she says. "And those players I pulled into my office and worked with on a daily basis, mentoring them, counseling them, giving them a space for them to express themselves and to practice better communication." Some of them, Gonzalez says, are in the big leagues now, whether with the Astros or with other teams. "When I receive messages from them telling me, 'Thank you, Mom, I want you to know that I made it to the big leagues, I want you to know that you played a big part in this,' that right there tells me everything."

One of the people responsible for some of the same duties for a rival team was Leslie Manning, the Mariners' director of professional development and assistant director of player development. Like Gonzalez, the bilingual Manning educated players, but she also coached baseball-operations staff in effective practice and communication methods.

Although women are still severely underrepresented in virtually every facet of baseball operations—a Mariners scout, Amanda Hopkins, became the first full-time female scout since the 1950s when the team hired her in 2015—player development is among the most demographically lopsided areas, even though minor- or major-league playing experience is no longer a prerequisite for employment. According to a list provided by MLB in November 2018, Manning was at that time one of only three women working in nonadministrative roles in a major-league team's player-development department, and the only one ranking higher than the coordinator level. "As far as I know, there aren't any other women with a role this baseball-intensive at the decision-making director level," Manning said.

Manning, who resigned for undisclosed reasons in February 2019 but continues to coach independently, doesn't dwell on her field's extreme gender skew. "Being a woman is no concern to me," she said. "Being the best is my only focus." But if teams want to be the best they can be at developing players, they'll stop drawing the people doing that development from an unnecessarily narrow pool.

MLB franchises are worth billions of dollars. Most turn a pretty profit per year and are owned and operated by corporations that could easily afford the expense—or more accurately, the investment—of paying minor leaguers enough to shrink or remove some of the off-the-field obstacles that stand in the way of their making the majors. Yet for years they denied them those dollars, both because most owners preferred not to spend a penny more than they had to and because no one was was willing to risk other owners' displeasure by breaking ranks.

MLB spent millions successfully lobbying Congress to pass the laughably named Save America's Pastime Act in 2018. That legislation exempted minor-league players—who aren't unionized—from protection under the Fair Labor Standards Act by classifying them as seasonal workers. As long as they make at least $1,160 a month, minor leaguers aren't entitled to overtime and don't get paid during spring training or the off-season. Consequently, many minor leaguers have to scrimp and save during the season and work second jobs over the winter, when they could be devoting their time to getting better at baseball. Although Triple-A players average roughly $10,000 a month, minor-league salaries start at a maximum of $1,100 a month (plus a $25 per diem on the road), and only a small percentage of players earn draft bonuses big enough to live on.

In the past, one of the most obvious manifestations of minor leaguers' lousy pay was an ascetic diet composed of items from the peak of the food pyramid. "The most difficult thing for me was making $250 every two weeks while living in one of the most expensive cities in the world," says Brian Bannister, who started his pro career pitching for the Low-A Brooklyn Cyclones. "When my parents came to town, they took all of the guys on the team to Costco, and I bought a mountain of Gatorade, Top Ramen, and macaroni and cheese. I literally survived off of those three food groups for months."

Bannister's Red Sox sidekick, Dave Bush, remembers a similar experience. "When I was coming through the minor leagues, the food we got was barely sustainable," he says. "It was peanut butter and jelly before a game, and that was it, and in some cases there was no food postgame. And that was just how the minor leagues were. It was a kind of this mental proving ground where you had to show that you were tough enough to handle really difficult situations, and if you weren't, then the big leagues weren't for you." Like Baker, Bannister and Bush are both under forty. They're describing a very recent status quo.

Playing pro ball at a high level is inherently hard; there's no need to make it *more* difficult by forcing players to starve or spend their few funds on calorie-rich food with low nutritional value. "When the body is malnourished (or tired), the brain begins playing a game of triage with cognitive functions," wrote Russell Carleton at Baseball Prospectus in 2012. "The first ones to go are the higher neurological functions, like attention, pattern recognition, and planning/decision-making centers, followed by fine motor control . . . things that might be helpful in playing baseball." Carleton argued that spending money on minor-league diets would be one of the wisest investments teams could make, noting that "by placing players in a situation where they have access only to nutrient-poor food, teams are systemically depriving players of the materials that they need to fully grow and develop." The development machine couldn't run efficiently without fuel.

Belatedly, teams are filling up players with premium unleaded. With the Red Sox, Bush says, "Guys get the food they need all the way down the levels." That's increasingly the case across the sport.

Cubs minor leaguer Connor Myers, a center fielder who played the 2018 season at age twenty-four, has seen that change firsthand. Myers, a twenty-seventh-round draft pick in 2016, signed for a $5,000 bonus ($3,200 after taxes), which didn't last long. When he debuted in pro ball, his paychecks netted him $330 every two weeks; in 2018, he made it to Double-A, but his payouts were still only "five-something." Fortunately, food is less of a drain on his wallet than it once would have been. "Since the Cubs won the World Series [in 2016], they put a lot of money into nutrition at every level," Myers says. "Each level has a nutritionist. . . . You have your protein smoothies, your weight-gaining smoothies, your hydration smoothies. You pretty much have everything you possibly need."

Myers is also a proponent of breathing exercises that he learned from the mental-skills staff. Whenever he's under stress on or off the field, he breathes in for five seconds, holds it, and then breathes out for five seconds, which, he says, helps him "get myself locked into any situation." He studies his TrackMan readings and praises the Cubs' coaches, who he says, "always have something at your fingertips for you to take that next step in getting better."

Even so, Myers embodies the ways in which even relatively enlightened teams are still holding back. In Low-A, Myers lived in a packed, five-person apartment. He economizes however he can—staying with a host family at one level, borrowing a car from his parents at another—but he can't come close to making ends meet via baseball alone. In the off-season, he works as a UPS driver, another occupation in which every movement he makes is tracked and made more efficient. He still finds time to train at a facility equipped with HitTrax and Rapsodo, but it's not easy to juggle the job, practice, and sleep.

Myers relishes his underdog status, so he isn't complaining. When prompted, however, he acknowledges, "If I had more money I could get more machines that I could use, recovery tools, all that stuff."

"That stuff" could apply to a growing array of products and approaches. It's true that teams are investing more in technology that can optimize a player's performance within the constraints of his current physical form. But "if you want to be really forward thinking," Mike Fast says, "that stuff is all the past. And the future is with sports science and strength and conditioning."

Sam Fuld, who's even younger than Baker, Bannister, and Bush, says that during his minor-league career, teams "were just starting to hire strength coaches. Even at the Triple-A level . . . our athletic trainer was essentially 90 percent secretary or travel administrator and 10 percent athletic trainer." Although that isn't the case with the minor-league teams of today, it hints at how far the game had to go. "The strength and conditioning world in baseball, by and large, is still very backwards," Fast says. "There are people who will say, 'Oh, don't lift because then you'll get tight and your muscles won't be flexible.'"

Fast says when the Astros started moving into the realm of sports science and strength and conditioning, they noticed players "improving things that people thought, well, that's just your God-given base-ball ability." It's easy for a front-office analyst or a coach to advise that a player perform a certain movement to achieve a desired result, but "so much of those physical adjustments [is] dependent upon your body composition," says Fuld, who notes that integrating coaching with athletic training is "the next obvious step."

According to a Quartz analysis of annual statistics provided by colleges to the US Department of Education, the fastest-growing major in postrecession America (2008–2017) was exercise science, which showed a 131 percent increase in its share of all majors over that span.[2] Those throngs of aspiring degree seekers suggest that understanding how to improve performance is a growth market. That's the case in baseball, where sports science or high-performance departments are popping up all over.

Those departments differ by franchise, but their purviews typically encompass workload monitoring and recovery, injury prevention, and strength and conditioning, all of which utilize wearable, biomechanical, and tracking technology to offer feedback. The Blue Jays have been the most aggressive about building up in this area; their sprawling high-performance department, founded in 2016, includes everyone from mental-performance coaches to trainers, rehab specialists, nutritionists, chefs, and a "fueling coordinator."

One trait many sports science departments share is international leaders with nonbaseball backgrounds. The Astros' sports science analyst, Jose Fernandez (who was hired in 2016), had most recently worked in Premier League soccer and international basketball, and the team's head strength and conditioning coordinator, Dan Howells (who was hired in 2018), is a veteran of English rugby. Neither had worked in baseball before. The director and assistant director of the Blue Jays' high-performance department, Angus Mugford and Clive Brewer, are both from the UK, and before beginning his own rugby phase, Brewer spent several years as the national program manager for SportScotland, a government body devoted to athlete development. The Yankees' principal sports scientist, David Whiteside, previously worked with Tennis Australia.

Teams are recruiting internationally because domestic sports science research has tended to be academic, conducted by professors who get funding for research. "While the research is good, it's not meant for application," says Patrick Cherveny, the former innovation specialist for Callaway Golf and director of sports science for Blast Motion, who joined the Indians as a sports science analyst in November 2018. Overseas, he explains, sports-science work is "much more focused on talent-identification programs, and then that is directly related to player development."

That's partly a product of a disparity in the size of the talent pools. The large population of the United States creates a cornucopia of athletic talent, which leads to less emphasis on maximizing individual development. In places where the population is significantly lower, Cherveny says, "They actually focus a lot more on identifying talent [and] developing that talent so that they can get on the medal stand.

. . . Sports performance programs are [operated by] the national governing body in these overseas countries because they just have limited athletes in their pool, and so they're trying to optimize that."

The unusual nature of baseball injuries is another reason why the sport has been behind in this field. In soccer, rugby, football, basketball, and hockey, "a lot of [the] injuries are soft-tissue-based," Cherveny says. "That is a little bit easier to control now with wearable technology because you're really monitoring the true workload, the acceleration [and] deceleration." As some players' waistlines would indicate, baseball is much less aerobic-based, which means players' bodies break in different ways. "Baseball is still dominated by shoulder and elbow injuries, especially on the throwing side," Cherveny says.

"We know that velocity does predict success," says the Mariners' Andy McKay. "It also predicts injury So there's a yin and yang going on there that I don't have the answer to." There's ample incentive to find one: according to Baseball Injury Consultants, MLB players lost a cumulative 36,876 days to injury (including day-to-day ailments) in 2018, the highest total on record dating back to 2002. The website Spotrac estimates that teams spent more than $745 million on the 34,126 days players spent on the IL alone. Many of the most costly injuries involve pitchers' arms.

To prevent pitcher injuries, "you have to be able to get into areas where teams don't have data yet," Bannister says. "That's usually biomechanical information." In Boston's case, KinaTrax is one such source; several other teams are clients of a rival markerless-motion-capture company, Simi Reality Motion Systems. KinaTrax president Steven Cadavid, an expert in computer vision and machine learning, developed some of his techniques by tracking the interactions of infants and mothers in order to detect early indicators of autism. Later, he applied his learning to baseball. "There are definite differences that we can pick up between pre- and postinjury data and that can be used by the teams," Cadavid says, citing an example of one pitcher who returned to action too soon (and pitched poorly) even though his KinaTrax readings from a bullpen session prior to his premature comeback showed that he was still hampered by his injury. "Trade decisions are being made with the KinaTrax data," Cadavid says.

It's inarguable that the player-development revolution's breakthroughs have helped hundreds of players, with countless more to come. What's still uncertain is whether other players may be burned by those same discoveries.

There's little downside to devices that directly aid in recovery. Many of the Mariners, whose team traveled an MLB-high 40,783 miles during the 2018 season, wore the Firefly, an FDA-approved band that the user wraps around the leg beneath the knee. The device electronically stimulates the peroneal nerve, promoting circulation, reducing muscle soreness, and preventing swelling during travel. Some teams routinely use ultrasound machines to image muscles and stimulate muscle recovery, and others employ a tech cocktail to accelerate the rehab process.

In 2015, Marcus Stroman tore his ACL in March and was believed to be done for the year. Instead, he returned in time to make four starts in September for the playoff-bound Blue Jays, thanks to a trio of wearables: Catapult to measure his exertion and physiological strain, Polar to monitor his heart rate, and Omegawave to measure his heart-rate variability and other indicators of overwork. Those devices allowed support staff to push him hard enough to get better but not hard enough to cause setbacks. His timeline was determined by the data, rather than an athlete's, trainer's, or doctor's intuitions or expectations about typical recoveries, which may be misleading. "I'm in the best shape of my life," Stroman told Ben at the time, parroting a time-honored baseball cliché. "I know people say that, but I can prove it with numbers."

The data gets dicier when it follows players off the field, or when there's potential for information provided in confidence to adversely affect earning power or playing time.

The 2017–2021 collective bargaining agreement (CBA) established a Joint Committee on Wearable Technology, a five-member panel composed of representatives from the league and the Players Association, to regulate the use of wearable devices at the major-league level. Through 2018, the committee approved four devices—the Catapult sensor, the Zephyr Bioharness, the Motus biomechanics sleeve, and the Whoop heart-rate monitor—for in-game use, with four other bat sensors from Blast and Diamond Kinetics approved for on-field activity outside of games (and in-game use in the minors). An attachment to the CBA specifies that the use of wearable tech is "wholly voluntary" and prohibits teams from intimating otherwise. It also limits information access to certain team personnel and mandates that the data be kept confidential, be made available to the player upon request, be deleted upon the player's request, and not be used for commercial purposes. However, it doesn't seem to provide for any penalty in the event of a violation.

In the minors, meanwhile, teams can compel players to participate. "In the major leagues, I am like a menu of things to try, and it's up to [the players] to come to me, tell me what they want to do, and then I'll help them build that into their routine," Baker says. "Whereas in the minor leagues it's the opposite. I can come in and say, 'This is what you have to do; this is what we are going to do.' Like, 'We are going to run this study. You have to sit with me for twelve minutes a day over the next six weeks. You're not allowed to do anything else.'"

In the minors, the Cubs and other teams have issued Whoop straps and Readibands, which players wear even while they sleep, allowing teams to assess their rest habits and levels of fatigue. "If we find out that somebody hasn't been eating or this person's weight is going down, that information will come to the mental skills program, and we'll be tasked, sometimes, to go investigate what's going on," Baker says. "We're kind of the boots on the ground, and we are allowed to ask the tough questions to people."

That type of intervention *can* be beneficial to team and player alike; some players may not realize that their sleep quality is low or that it's impairing their performance. Astros pitcher Josh James went from a lethargic, low-ceiling thirty-fourth-rounder to a promising major leaguer after his roommate told him he snored and he visited a sleep specialist, who diagnosed him with sleep apnea and equipped him with a CPAP machine. There may be more minor leaguers like him.

But by its very nature, off-the-field monitoring is intrusive. Alan Milstein, a bioethics and sports law lawyer and litigator and an adjunct professor at Temple University Law School, sees it as a serious "privacy problem," stating, "I don't believe just because you're a professional athlete, that you should be treated differently. . . . These athletes are adults, and they have the right to make choices about their lifestyle when they're off the field without the ownership essentially criticizing them." In Milstein's mind, we're bound for a rebellion akin to the "medical mutiny" from *Apollo 13*, when the entire crew removes the biometric sensors feeding info to flight controllers, led by Jim Lovell (Tom Hanks), who declares, "I'm sick and tired of the entire Western world knowing how my kidneys are functioning."

Baker and his colleagues participate in regular conference calls with other player-development personnel, and at times, they'll learn that a player is having trouble with a mechanical adjustment that will help him in the long run. "That'll result in a text message or a phone call from one of us, and then somebody is showing up on site to make sure that they understand the purpose behind why they're practicing," Baker says.

In the course of conversation, though, mental-skills staff may learn sensitive information. Maybe a player is a party animal or has a drug or drinking problem. Confiding in a professional can help, but players are still taking a risk by opening up to a team employee. "Our players know that when they talk to me, not everything goes back to the organization," Baker says. "I'm not there to rat them out. . . . They trust us, because we don't get on the phone and call Theo [Epstein] and immediately go, 'So-and-so is doing this!'"

Baker sees his role as one of player advocacy and support, divorced from purely performance-driven decisions. Yet he also says, "Strength and conditioning, athletic training, neuroscience, nutrition, mental skills—we all have an open relationship where we communicate about the players." Maybe Baker, a former player, wouldn't divulge information that's supposed to be secret, but perhaps someone else would, especially if a sensor suggests a problem is present and a pennant race or many millions of dollars may depend on a player producing. By the time a player makes the majors and is protected by the CBA, teams will have learned a lot about him.

"The whole theory of this stuff is that we're going to help you be a better player," Milstein says. Jerry Dipoto, a former major leaguer, makes that argument. "It's good for both the player and the club," he says. "The club gets the best version of that player, and the player maximizes his value. . . . Players have been quoted as saying that this is information they're just gathering to hold me down. It's quite the opposite, actually." Yet Milstein isn't swayed. "It's just as possible that when the data comes in, they realize that the player has physical problems or problems off the field, and then it might be better to go elsewhere," he says. "There's no guarantee and there's no express promise that the information that is going to be used will be used only for the betterment of the individual player."

In the dystopian, darkest-timeline vision of the post-Moneyball era, teams could screen players for predispositions to certain conditions. That scenario may seem far-fetched: the 2008 Genetic Information Nondiscrimination Act prevents employers from compelling DNA testing or basing employment decisions on DNA information. In 2009, though, MLB admitted to asking some Dominican prospects to undergo DNA testing as a means of detecting identity fraud. Milstein warns that the union or individual players could someday decide to surrender DNA data voluntarily. "[If] it crosses over the DNA line, everybody should watch out," Milstein says. By then, though, some of the flaws that testing turns up may be fixable. And in a world with gene-editing technology, humanity will soon confront questions about being better that extend just a bit beyond baseball.

16

IF YOU BUILD THEM, THEY WILL COME

There are three types of baseball players: Those who make it happen, those who watch it happen, and those who wonder what happened.
—**TOMMY LASORDA**

In November 2017, a strange construction project began on St. Nicholas Avenue in Harlem, between West 124th and 125th Streets. Rockies pitcher Adam Ottavino had taken control of a vacant, narrow storefront flanked by a Dollar Tree and a Chuck E. Cheese. A delivery truck was parked before the entrance. Its trailer contained a portable pitching mound Ottavino had purchased, along with a roll of AstroTurf. Once they were set up inside, so many curious onlookers peered in that Ottavino covered the windows with black paper.

The space was a creative solution to a problem. Ottavino, a Brooklyn native, lived in the city with his wife and two-year-old daughter. In previous off-seasons, he had traveled to Long Island to throw, but with a young daughter, the commute was becoming a burden. To compound the problem, his throwing partner of previous winters, the Mets' Steven Matz, had moved to Nashville. Ottavino knew that another Met, Matt Harvey, was one of the few professional pitchers who also lived in Manhattan. Ottavino asked Harvey if he was interested in looking for a place to throw with him. Harvey declined.

"At that point, I was kind of screwed," Ottavino said the following May. "I didn't know what to do."

This wasn't just any off-season. Ottavino's career was in jeopardy: he had been left off of the Rockies' Wild Card roster that October and was coming off the worst year of his career. He had walked 6.5 batters per nine innings, second worst in the majors among pitchers who had thrown at least fifty frames. He was thirty-two years old, and he was entering the final year of his contract. He needed a place to throw. He needed a place to improve. He needed a place to *experiment*.

Ottavino's father-in-law, who's involved in real estate, offered a suggestion. He had an unoccupied property in Harlem a block from a subway stop. Ottavino could use the space that winter to create his own indoor bullpen. There would be a price: a signed bat from his All-Star teammate Nolan Arenado. That was quite a discount; the last tenant, a Nine West shoe store, had paid $22,000 per month.

"Not very many people knew what was going on," Ottavino said. "Just the security guy, Thomas, and my father-in-law, and the people in his office."

Unlike other Manhattan training facilities, Ottavino's new workshop featured a Rapsodo unit and an Edgertronic camera. One of the lessons of talent development is that it doesn't take much space, or an ostentatious facility, to get better. The storefront was about eighty feet deep, just enough to accommodate a pitch. It wasn't glamorous, but it was all he needed to turn his career around.

Rockies coach Jerry Weinstein, the winner of *Baseball America*'s 2018 Tony Gwynn Lifetime Achievement Award and a proponent of player adaptability long before it came to be called "growth mindset," says, "There isn't anything that we can't develop."

Weinstein has been in the business since the 1960s and was among the first to try radar guns, weighted balls, and overload/underload bat training. The seventy-five-year-old, whom Kyle Boddy has dubbed "the godfather of baseball," regards fear of the unknown as an opening to exploit. "The man with the information wins," he says. "The information is king."

When development began to be overhauled, the people with the information were independent instructors and front-office analysts. But as the movement blossoms, those people are players. "The best lessons are self-taught," Weinstein says. "I tell [players] my job is to eliminate my job. My job is to teach them how to develop themselves." That's among the most exciting facets of modern development: Rather than allow themselves to be sorted and weeded out, players are empowering *themselves* by seizing the means of production.

In the midst of his struggles in 2017, Ottavino had begun looking for answers. After reading about Trevor Bauer's work at Driveline and seeing Boddy proselytize on Twitter, he wanted to learn more about pitch design. Most professional pitchers had at least heard of Driveline by then, but Ottavino says there was still considerable suspicion about what was going on there. In October, he traveled to Seattle to investigate for himself.

"The rap on Driveline was kind of negative around the game . . . and that kind of attracted me more," Ottavino says. "They don't really care what other people are thinking. They're doing something that they think is working. . . . And, honestly, seeing a guy like Trevor commit to going there year-round is such a stamp of approval, even without knowing him, just because of the type of pitcher he is."

The team at Driveline decided not to alter Ottavino's delivery. He was throwing in the mid-90s, and he had already addressed alignment issues in his crossfire motion on his own. What they did discuss were ways to improve his command. Like Josh Tomlin, Ottavino had gotten "internal." He needed to be "external."

Matt Daniels explained the merits of differential training with weighted balls. Ottavino would bring that command program back to his mini Driveline in Harlem. He also bought a pitching pad, a rubberized strike-zone-like target to throw toward. It included colored and numbered regions. As he went into his delivery, a training partner—when he had one—would call out a number or colored zone to target.

Ottavino also brought back something else: pitch-design science. Although Bauer had embraced that effort early, few other established major leaguers had followed his lead by late 2017, so it remained to be seen whether Bauer's process was replicable. "Ottavino is really the first significant test of that," Daniels said.

Ottavino arrived in Seattle with one of the best breaking balls in the game. It's classified as a slider, but Daniels said it's really a sideways curveball due to Ottavino's low arm slot. The sweeping, Wiffle-like breaker boasts remarkable horizontal movement. But in 2017, oppo-nents had stopped swinging at the pitch, partly because only 43 percent of his pitches were thrown within the confines of the strike zone and partly because it was so hard to hit that opponents learned to lay off.

Opponents swung at his slider at a 38.1 percent rate in 2016, but that rate fell to 28.2 percent in 2017. Only Dellin Betances induced a lower overall swing rate (34.6 percent) than Ottavino's 35 percent, which had fallen from a 42.2 percent mark in 2016.

The idea at Driveline was to create another pitch to complement his slider in a similar tunnel but stay more often in the strike zone, falling between his fastball and slider in movement and velocity. Dan-iels was a point man on the project.

When Ottavino first arrived, he was shown video of cutter-slider hybrids, breaking pitches that would have similar vertical movement to his slider (very little) but less horizontal movement. Emulating one would give him a third, distinct movement profile. Ottavino went to the mound of the R&D building and began to throw.

"We looked at [Luis] Severino and [Rockies teammate] Jon Gray, and initially that's what we tried to do," Ottavino said. "But I had a really hard time throwing that pitch as hard as I wanted to. Basically, you try to impart true bullet [or gyro] spin on the pitch, but still throw it in the upper 80s, low 90s."

Using Edgertronic and Rapsodo, Ottavino and Daniels tinkered with different grips and settled on something of a hybrid gyro-cutter-slider. Daniels said they were looking for "15 percent spin efficiency" on the Rapsodo, or 15 percent transverse spin/85 percent gyro spin.

"We marked down when the spin efficiency was in the range we wanted, and when it wasn't," Ottavino said. "Then we would go to the video. I could see what the difference was in my finger pressure when the spin was right. We kept adjusting the grip. And pretty much in one day we were like, OK, we think this is it."

One day: the magic of deliberate practice coupled with the Edger-tronic and Rapsodo.

The hybrid cutter had another key characteristic: it tunneled well with his two-seamer. He dropped his four-seam usage from 30 per-cent in 2017 to 5 percent in 2018. "I started alternating between my two-seam and [the cutter] to try to see if I could throw them comfortably out of the same slot and how they would look next to each other, and that was pretty much it. We just practiced it for a few days, and then I went home."

Ottavino hadn't just learned how to create a new pitch. He had learned how to optimize practice.

For several days a week over a four-month period in Harlem, Ottavino threw his new cutter and his two-seamer and slider, monitoring all of them with his own Rapsodo and Edgertronic. He threw weighted balls and aimed at the pitching pad. Sometimes he found a catcher to meet him at his tiny lab. Sometimes he just threw a five-gallon bucket of balls into a net by himself. The cutter, which he would throw 10.1 percent of the time in 2018, was an important addition, but more than that, he welcomed the improved feel and command. He reported to spring training in Arizona with his weighted balls and Edgertronic camera. He was the only Rockies pitcher using either. The righty felt more prepared than ever. Still, seeing was believing, and the Rockies' staff hadn't seen the new Ottavino yet.

"I did get called into the office to basically tell them what I've learned and why I think it's gonna make me better," Ottavino says. "As long as you have a good reason, they can't really argue with it."

Even so, the Rockies were skeptical about the camera. "Is this gonna put more things in your head?" asked Rockies manager Bud Black and his staff.

The self-effacing Ottavino had a reputation as an intelligent player but also as a "thinker," which can be a dangerous label in a major-league clubhouse.

"When a person who's perceived as intelligent or a thinker struggles, they think you're overthinking," said Ottavino, describing an issue also plaguing Bauer. "That was part of what I was hearing [in 2017] is, 'Oh, you're just overthinking things.'"

Ottavino countered that the Edgertronic would make him think *less*, narrowing his focus. "I'm gonna think either way," Ottavino told the coaches, "but this makes me know what to think *about*."

The Rockies staff had fewer doubts when he began to throw. On the backfield bullpens at the Salt River complex in Arizona, a handful of pitching mounds run parallel to each other. On a quiet February morning, Ottavino climbed one of them and demonstrated his new pitch with several coaches behind him, observing with arms folded. The last time they'd seen Ottavino throw, he had been a mess. Then he showed them his cutter. It tracked on a straight line for most of its journey before breaking subtly near the plate. Soon he took his remade self into simulated games.

"I pretty much dominated everybody in my live BPs, and coaches were excited about it. All of a sudden I was making a lot of pitches that I wanted to make," Ottavino said.

This was a different-looking guy. The new Ottavino was a *dude*. After getting hit in his first Cactus League outing, he threw six perfect innings in a row. The last thing he needed to prove was that it could carry over to regular-season action.

The Rockies and Ottavino opened the season on March 29 at Arizona. His first batter of 2018 was Diamondbacks star Paul Goldschmidt. He started Goldschmidt with a sweeping slider. It buckled Goldschmidt's knees and broke back over the plate for a strike. Everyone had seen that pitch before. They hadn't seen what followed. Ottavino next threw his very first gyro-spin-cutter-slider hybrid. Goldschmidt watched the tight-breaking, 88 mph pitch cut through the zone for strike two. Ottavino took a deep breath, returned to the rubber, and threw a 94 mph two-seamer that started outside. Laminar flow propelled it back over the plate for a called third strike. Goldschmidt walked back to the dugout without protest. Jake Lamb followed by waving at a darting two-seamer for a strikeout. After walking Daniel Descalso, Ottavino quickly regained his command and struck out Alex Avila swinging on another sharp-breaking two-seamer.

"I was like, I had it," Ottavino said on a June afternoon. "And then I did it again the next night, and right away I was just very locked in."

Ottavino faced fifty-five batters in April. He struck out *thirty* of them. He allowed four hits, four walks, and one run in sixteen innings. No reliever was more dominant. It wasn't a fluke: in May, he faced forty-four batters and allowed just four hits and two runs.

Ottavino posted a 1.62 ERA in the first half, and he finished the season tied for the sixth-highest WAR by a reliever. His K-BB rate improved from 9.9 percent in 2017 to 24.6 in 2018, the third-biggest increase in the game, and he lowered his walk rate by 4.4 percentage points, the ninth-greatest decrease.

In 2018, Ottavino's cutter had 3.8 inches of horizontal movement, which ranked fourth among relievers. It also had 3.9 inches of vertical movement. It was a weird pitch; few moved like it, but it worked. Ottavino threw the newly created pitch 129 times in 2018, and it generated whiffs on 50 percent of swings, a staggering mark that was tops among all pitches labeled as cutters. The pitch had the horizontal movement of a lesser-breaking slider, but it moved in the opposite direction and had the same sink as his two-seamer. Ottavino's slider moved like it always had, averaging 9.5 inches of horizontal movement, which ranked fifth among all pitchers. But because it was paired with a new pitch and improved command, batters were back to swinging at a 41.1 percent rate and whiffing on 36.8 percent of those swings.

In the Rockies clubhouse in June, Ottavino showed teammate Chad Bettis the Edgertronic. Bettis handled the cube-shaped device with curiosity.

"Bettis is using my camera tomorrow in his bullpen," Ottavino said. "[Tyler] Anderson and Gray want to go [to Driveline] this coming off-season. Things are just heading in that direction. I think the biggest thing is, it's not going to be—it shouldn't be—taboo."

On the strength of his 2018 campaign, Ottavino signed a three-year $27 million contract with the Yankees in January 2019. If his father-in-law's lot isn't available in future years, perhaps he can use Yankee Stadium.

On the night of September 2, 2018, at Citizens Bank Park in Philadelphia, Cubs shortstop Addison Russell pinch hit for Kyle Schwarber with two outs in the top of the eighth. Phillies pitcher Austin Davis, a rookie left-hander who'd entered the game at the start of that inning, reached into his back pocket and pulled out a lineup card, on which he had written information about how to handle each hitter.

Third-base umpire and crew chief "Cowboy" Joe West, a sixty-five-year-old in his record forty-first year of MLB service, saw Davis do it. He ambled over to the mound and held out his hand as if he'd caught the pitcher passing notes in study hall. Davis surrendered the card, and West stuck it into his own back pocket and waddled away despite Davis's objections. Gabe Kapler came out to argue as well, but West stuck to his interpretation: Davis, he said, had violated rule 6.02(c)(7), which states that "the pitcher shall not have on his person, or in his possession, any foreign substance." West could confiscate the card, but he couldn't make Davis forget what he'd already read. Russell struck out swinging.

It was, in a sense, a clash between baseball's old ways of thinking—or *not* thinking—and its new ways. West broke into the big leagues in 1976, a time when the only advantages at pitchers' disposal were ways to doctor the ball. Although some pitchers still seek that same edge, the new breed of ballplayer benefits more from information than sticky substances. West was labeling *information* "foreign"—which, in fairness to him, it *was* for most players until very recently.

Davis, who made his MLB debut in late June, says he first consulted a card on July 14 in Miami. It's become common for outfielders to carry positioning cards and even for catchers—who have to work with more pitchers per game and per season than ever before—to wear wristbands that remind them about the proper approach for each pitcher and opponent. But Davis is believed to be the first pitcher ever to consult a card on the mound, and the idea was his own.

The twenty-five-year-old former twelfth-rounder is a typically open-minded modern player. Over the winter, he works with former first-rounder Luke Hagerty—a Driveline adherent who launched a tech-propelled comeback attempt in 2019, at age thirty-seven, after a battle with the yips and a thirteen-year absence from affiliated ball—at a facility in Scottsdale, where he uses Rapsodo to fine-tune his grips. Carrying cards into games is an extension of the same desire to perfect his pitches. With the card, he says, "I can throw with full conviction, no second-guessing in the back of my mind. . . . And then from the coaching-staff side, they know that I'm throwing what

I know to be true based off what the analytics are. There's so much information now, why would you not take advantage of it?"

Before every game in which he's available to pitch, Davis grabs a spare lineup card and jots down notes about strengths and weaknesses from the Phillies' advance scouting reports, which he says are "super digestible" by the time they're presented to the players. For him, having a few words for each hitter to remind him between batters of how he wants to pitch—particularly when he's in the midst of a multi-inning outing or facing an unscheduled hitter—functions as a psychological "security blanket."

In the thick of the action, some kinds of thinking can be counterproductive, but like Ottavino with the Edgertronic, Davis regards his cards as a means of cutting down on distractions. In 2016, Red Sox pitcher Rick Porcello started writing down scouting reports on lineup cards because it helped him retain the information; previously, he told the *Boston Herald*, he "would kind of get mixed up when I was out there." But Porcello still left his cards in the dugout when he was on the mound. Davis went one step further. "Why waste the mental energy to try and memorize all this stuff and understand every single hitter that you could possibly face . . . when you could just have it on a card in your back pocket?" he asks. Some pitchers would worry about being perceived as "bush league" by not being off-book in games, but as Davis says Kapler told him, "To do something or not to do something based off what the optics would be is not a good reason to do it."

In early August, Davis disregarded what his card told him to do against the Diamondbacks' A.J. Pollock, and Pollock crushed a ball that would have been over the fence had Phillies right fielder Nick Williams not leaped and brought it back. That close call, Davis says, was a reminder that if you're not using all of the information available, "you're putting yourself at risk to get hit hard." Later that month, Brian Bannister's former clubhouse co-conspirator Zack Greinke followed in Davis's footsteps and peeked at a card of his own, which Davis—who finished the season with a 3.68 FIP and more than a strikeout per inning—saw as a sign that his own reasoning was sound.

After West's encounter with Davis in September, MLB spoke to its senior umpire and told him the rookie was right. Davis's cards were officially legal. Cowboy Joe called the Phillies' clubhouse to apologize. Information wasn't foreign after all.

Via traveling analysts, conduits, and inquisitive coaches, forward-thinking teams have focused on, as Astros outfielder Tony Kemp says, "taking the information and really utilizing it on the field." But that effort is relatively recent, and some teams are still lagging behind. In at least one case, a star player on a late-adopting team went outside the organization in search of statistical support.

In early 2011, a writer for a statistically oriented website got an e-mail through the site's contact form. The message came from one of the best hitters in baseball, who suggested an article on a topic of interest to him. The writer also found the topic intriguing, so he produced a post. The player liked it, and the two stayed in touch.

Eventually, the player asked the writer to help him come up with contract comparables for an upcoming negotiation; although he had an agent, he wanted to consult with someone who wouldn't stand to benefit from his signing a deal. "I helped him with his contract, and after that, he was like, 'Why don't you actually do some regular stuff for me?'" the writer recalls. In 2013, the writer became a part-time, secret, statistical consultant to the analytically inclined star. "From what I understand, like 90 percent of his teammates would go out on a Friday night, go to the clubs, and he'd be texting me about his chase rate," the writer says. "This was an obsession for him."

The player asked the writer to sign an NDA, not wanting it to be known to his team that he was seeking this sort of assistance. "He was very concerned up front [that] they would not be happy that he was getting outside advice that might conflict with what they were going to tell him, and he didn't want to come off as uncoachable," the writer says. Although plenty of hitters see personal swing coaches, a personal stathead was something new. The player didn't want to ruffle any feathers in the front office or clubhouse, but he wanted to be better, and he didn't trust his team to deliver the data he craved.

"Most of it was based around game prep," the writer says. "Eighty percent of what we did was figuring out what the context of that specific day's opponents was going to be for him." The team's scouting reports were standard fare: what the pitcher threw and how hard and how often he threw it. The player wanted to know more: how often hitters swung against certain pitches, what happened when they did, and what the umpire's and catcher's strike zones looked like. Prior to his work with the player, the writer had viewed slumps as largely random. But helping the hitter analyze how pitchers were attacking him and how he could counter gave him a glimpse at a cat-and-mouse contest most outsiders don't see. "There's definitely some element of, 'OK, pitchers have figured out how to do this one thing to me, I have got to figure out how to respond to that thing to make them pitch me differently,'" he says.

In addition to sending scouting reports, the writer provided analysis of the player's performance via a set of statistical markers that captured his process rather than his results: chase rate, ground-ball rate, pull rate, hard-hit rate. "All he really cared about was, am I squaring up the ball, am I not swinging and missing, and am I swinging at strikes," the writer says. The writer sent the hitter a weekly report on his performance in those metrics over the previous week, along with his rolling and seasonal averages. "He thought that helped because it basically allowed him to get away from, 'I went 3-for-19 this week, I need to make some adjustments,'" the writer says. "That was probably the most impactful thing for him, just getting him to stop tinkering."

Studying the combination of catcher and umpire was a big advantage, too. In given games, the hitter could disregard certain spots, confident that pitches up and in or low and away wouldn't be called strikes. "I would watch him take a pitch we had talked about pregame, like, 'This pitch is just an auto-take today,' no chance of this getting called even though it was in the zone," the writer says. "And he would take a 3–1 fastball on the inner half and just drop his bat and start walking up to first, and the pitcher's having a meltdown on the mound, and he would just smirk because he was like, 'Yeah, you didn't know that pitch wasn't going to be a strike today, but I knew.' . . . He knew the day's strike zone better than any pitcher in the world."

When a call did go against him, the hitter would want to check the umpire's work. "Pretty regularly he would come in the dugout between at-bats, like, 'Hey, I want to see the [strike-zone] map,'" the writer says. So the writer arranged for him to be able to access a live site where he could check pitch locations during games, as well as pitch types and other information.

After Statcast came out, the player and his stathead assistant found a use for that data too. In one post-Statcast season, the player rated poorly as a fielder according to most defensive metrics, which displeased him. "He was like, I get that I'm getting older, but I do not want to be an embarrassing defensive player," the writer says. The writer called in a few favors and obtained Statcast information that allowed him to recommend changes to the player's positioning that would help him hack his stats. "We basically fixed his defense in an off-season," the writer says.

Aside from that defensive overhaul, the writer says he was never sure how much his work was helping the hitter, who had been successful before their first interaction. A few years into their professional relationship, though, the writer changed jobs and had to stop helping the hitter. And although it may have been a coincidence, the hitter had a down year without him. "He felt like it was a real loss for him to not have this [information]," the writer says. The writer suspects that the *thought* of not being prepared may have hurt the hitter as much as the absence of information itself. When he walked to the plate, the writer says, the perfectionist player wanted to be thinking, "I did literally absolutely everything I could have done to try and make myself as good as possible today." And if his team wasn't helping him think that, he'd find someone who would.

Every year, more players are eager to learn, and fewer teams are unequipped to give them the tools they need. But players may have reasons to mistrust teams: maybe they don't want wearable data in the hands of their employers, or maybe they think teams that aren't currently contending will be more interested in suppressing their salaries in arbitration than enhancing their stats. That creates an opening for a new vector for development: the agency.

Traditionally, agents have tried to make players the most money they can given their past performance, but they haven't done much to improve that performance. Caleb Cotham is the model for a new type of player agent, one who can, as he told us in May 2018, "help you with your curveball but also help you with arbitration."

Cotham was a fifth-round Yankees draft pick in 2009 who climbed to Triple-A by 2013 but seemed stalled at that level, recording a 5.46 ERA in twenty-six games from 2013 to 2014. "I couldn't have felt farther away from the big leagues," he said, adding, "My window was closing very fast, and I think I knew I needed to take a little more risk in my training." After the 2014 season, he spent a month and a half at Driveline. He went through the velocity-training program, raised his average fastball speed from 89 to 93, and used Rapsodo and Edgertronic to sharpen his slider. In 2015, he started the season with a 2.17 ERA in twenty-seven games between Double-A and Triple-A, striking out more than a batter per inning, and in late July, the Yankees called him up, which he attributes entirely to his winter's work. "If I would have kept doing what I was doing, no chance," he said.

Cotham's time in the big leagues was brief, but at least he'd made it. Late in his career, Cotham switched his representation to The Bledsoe Agency, a boutique outfit just south of Nashville that was founded in 2009 by brothers Hunter Bledsoe (a former pro player) and Dustin Bledsoe (who went to law school while his younger brother was pursuing his playing career). "They went about the representation model a little differently, just in the sense that they [believe] being a really good player should be the primary goal," Cotham said. "If you're not good, nothing else matters . . . so we start with the idea that we should do everything in our power to get the player as good as possible."

Cotham retired as a player after spring training 2017 and began working for the Bledsoe brothers. He became a certified agent and helped the agency construct an in-house, Driveline-style training area with a weight room and a technology-equipped hitting and pitching facility. Many of the agency's twenty-some clients—a few big leaguers and 2018 first-overall draft pick Casey Mize among them—worked with Cotham in person over the off-season, and others he advised via video.

Cotham viewed his value partly as preparing players to utilize the training they could expect to receive in pro ball, and partly as preemptively inoculating them against misinformation. "If you understand the principle behind all these cues and drills, then you're going to have a better chance of not going down a weird alley that might derail your career," he said. But he was also a resource for players who might have fallen through the cracks in organizations that didn't make their improvement a priority. In most cases, the interests of teams, players, and agencies should align—in theory, they all want the player to be better—but an agency may be able to offer more personalized service. "There are a lot of guys that [teams] have on their plate," he said. "They want to get everyone better, but I think sometimes you might not get the information you need in the time you need it. The Double-A pitching coach might have the one cue you really need, but you're stuck in High-A." That's where Cotham came in.

In 2016, when he was still pitching for the Reds, Cotham, future Bledsoe Agency client Tony Cingrani, and a couple of other Reds pitchers used to meet before and after batting practice to play Blokus, an abstract strategy board game. While they competed to place Tetris-shaped pieces on the board in a particular pattern, they talked about how to make the missing components of their pitching plan fall into place. Like Cotham, Cingrani visited and swears by Driveline, but his fortunes changed most dramatically after he was traded from the Reds to the Dodgers in July 2017, the same month he hired The Bledsoe Agency. In Cincinnati, Cingrani says, the support staff "was a lot of old-school baseball guys, as opposed to [LA], it's trying to embrace that analytics side." Although the Reds shared some information with players, it was barebones and not tailored to individual skill sets. "We were kind of on our own," he says, adding, "It was just like, 'Hopefully you have success. Good luck.'"

The Reds have addressed that deficiency: in January 2019, they hired Cotham as their assistant pitching coach, bringing him back to a modernized version of the organization where he ended his own athletic career. "I'm really excited to explore what this side looks like now and help players that are at the tip of the spear," he says. Although he won't be helping players on the agency side, he believes others will be, saying, "I think the rabbit's out of the hat on that. . . . If you're paying attention, it's tough to miss that that's an opportunity in the offseason to provide guys with that type of resource."

The next generation may not even need Cotham's help. Nate Freiman, a six-foot-eight former major-league first baseman who's tied for the title of tallest-ever nonpitcher, played for the A's in 2013–2014. Almost immediately after retiring at thirty-one in March 2018, he dedicated himself to learning more about the sport he'd stopped playing. Freiman knew the game was "accelerating toward the data now that teams are catching onto ways to use it in player development," and he wanted to keep pace.

Freiman, who minored in math at Duke, started taking online courses in machine learning and the programming languages SQL and R. He voraciously read analytical writing about the game, and soon he started producing his own, becoming the first former big leaguer to write for FanGraphs, where he posted repeatedly as part of a residency program in August 2018.

With nine big-league homers, six FanGraphs posts, and multiple programming languages on his résumé, Freiman was a unicorn candidate for a conduit job, and in December, the Indians hired him to take on a far-ranging role in baseball operations. "If a current or former player were to ask, I would say don't be afraid of being wrong and don't be afraid to say you don't know," he says. He'd also advise picking up programming. "At the very least," he concludes, "it shows a willingness to learn." For the modern major leaguer, that's the best quality to have.

17

NO CEILING

The game's gotten harder. . . . The next generation's here,
and they're really good.
— **THIRTY-TWO-YEAR-OLD MLB OUTFIELDER ADAM JONES**

On October 26, 2018, a few hours before the first pitch of World Series
Game 3, legendary home-run hitter Hank Aaron sat at a dais alongside
MLB commissioner Rob Manfred, Christian Yelich, and J.D. Martinez.
The latter two were there to receive the Hank Aaron Award, an annual honor bestowed by broadcasters and fans on the best hitter in
each league during the regular season. Aaron, one of the leading con-
tenders for the title of "best living player," name-dropped one of his
primary competitors for that post. "I told Willie Mays that if he and
I were playing [today], they'd probably be sending us to Class D ball
because we wouldn't know how to hit these [pitchers]," Aaron said.
He gestured to Yelich and added, "I watched him play and walk up to
the plate and hit somebody that was throwing 100 miles an hour, and
I said, 'Oh my God, I couldn't do it.'" Not long after Aaron's comments,
Adam Ottavino—who hasn't thrown 100, but has thrown 99.8—told
MLB.com's *Statcast Podcast*, "I would strike Babe Ruth out every time."

Because baseball players' performance is always relative to their
contemporary opponents, it's difficult for fans to assess skill across
eras. But in April 2007, Hardball Times writer David Gassko performed
a study on the quality of competition in baseball. He examined all
players ages twenty-six to twenty-nine in each year dating back to
the beginning of the big leagues and compared their performance in
season x to their performance in season x+1. Hitters in that cohort
should be largely resistant to age-related decline, so a change in their

collective results from one year to the next should reflect a change in the rest of the league's talent.

Gassko discovered something surprising: players, it seemed, had stopped getting better. "Over the past 15 years, the quality of competition has been essentially flat," he wrote. "I think it's pretty clear that we are hitting some kind of wall of physical ability."[1]

That seemed true at the time, but it's usually a losing proposition to bet against human beings getting better. With help from sabermetrician Mitchel Lichtman, we've updated Gassko's study. Here's what MLB's quality of competition has looked like postplateau:

MLB Quality of Competition, 1992–2018

Not only have MLB players not *stopped* improving, but they're improving at one of the most rapid rates in history. If there is a ceiling, we haven't come close to it yet.

The heightened competition of recent seasons has coincided with a historically significant youth movement. Weighted by WAR (so that more productive players have a higher impact), the average hitter age in 2018 was the league's lowest since the advent of the designated hitter in 1973, and for the first time since 1977, every team had an average hitter age below 30. Hitters twenty-five and under accounted for their largest share of MLB plate appearances since 1978, when free agency was just getting going. Relative to the league, they collectively had their highest walk rate and second-highest isolated power in history, with a better strikeout rate than normal. If we lump together all players (both pitchers and position players) twenty-five and younger and thirty-five and older, we find that the "old" group accounted for the lowest percentage of league-wide WAR since the nineteenth century in 2017 and barely rebounded in 2018. The "young" group's share, meanwhile, was close to a thirty-five-year high. The difference between the two proportions was at its widest since 1974.

A multitude of factors can affect the league's quality of play, including the size of the pool of potential players (which has increased as a result of the breaking of the color line, the growth of the domestic population, and the internationalization of the sport); competition from rival baseball leagues; competition from other sports and forms of entertainment; increasing salaries and incentives to pursue playing baseball; expansion in the number of teams; and improvements in player evaluation. But improvements in player development should ensure that the caliber of play keeps climbing. "The difference between the best player and the worst player is really, really small in the big leagues," Dave Bush says. "This type of information, if it makes you 1 percent better, that may be enough to keep you up there."

Because today's technology allows for more rapid evaluation, one might surmise that players are debuting younger than ever. Not so: the average debut ages for batters (24.8) and pitchers (25.1) in 2018 were the same as the averages over the previous twenty seasons. Nor are hitters or pitchers receiving less minor-league seasoning, on average, before making the majors.

Some clubs keep blue-chip prospects in the minors longer than necessary to delay starting their service clocks. Others, out of old habit, may be behaving too cautiously in abandoning veterans and promoting prospects. Because players who've benefited from new developmental measures are competing against similarly enhanced competition, MLB's bar is higher and may take just as long to clear. It's also possible that there's a hardwired amount of experience players must accrue to be big-league quality. "We could move pitchers more quickly, but it seemed like there was something with hitters where they needed to see a lot of game pitches at new levels to adapt to better pitching," Mike Fast says. That may be because prospects' brains are still growing; the prefrontal cortex, the last brain region to complete its development, plays a part in pattern recognition, and perhaps in adapting to pitching.

Lastly, promotion patterns may only seem static because recent technological advances aren't just boosting prospects, they're also helping players who weren't considered major-league material until new technology and techniques intervened. Left-handed pitcher Brandon Mann made his MLB debut for the Rangers in July 2018, a few days before his thirty-fourth birthday, making him the oldest American-born player to break into the bigs since 2002. Texas had signed him in January after watching him throw at Driveline, whose weighted-ball program he credits for propelling his fastball from the mid-to-high 80s to the low-to-mid 90s. Mann spent almost half his life pitching professionally—in four teams' farm systems, Japan, and indy ball—before his opportunity in Texas arrived. "Where baseball is now, I don't feel older," he told *Hill Country News*. "I work with all the spin rates and (data) and try to use all of that to my advantage. That's where baseball has gone. I just wish I did this when I was twenty-five, not thirty-four."[2]

Although an increasing capacity for player improvement sounds like an unalloyed positive, the spread of the movement presents multiple problems for the sport that could come to a head within the next few years. "I think that any of this innovation and advancement hopefully leads to better players, who make more money, who create a better game," says A's GM David Forst. In practice, though, that may not be true beyond the "better players" part.

The first red flag is financial: the massive strides teams are making in player development are destabilizing the compensation structure that has reigned supreme in the sport since the 1970s, when the reserve clause binding players to teams was abolished and replaced by a service-time-based system that pays players via arbitration and free agency. Prearbitration players make close to the league minimum regardless of how good they are, but in theory, those who maintain their performance for several seasons can count on cashing in via free agency. Starting with the winter of 2017–2018, though, that model seemed to stop working, as free agents who once would have been in line for big paydays went without offers or settled for seemingly below-market contracts. The average MLB salary fell for the first time since 2004 and only the second time in the past fifty years in a season without a strike or collusion.

Although there was more than one cause of the market crash, one culprit appeared to be the increasing efficiency with which front offices obtain talent. On a dollars-per-win basis, free agents have never been the best investments. By the time players qualify for free agency, they're typically past their peaks and headed for decline, yet they expect salaries commensurate with their past production. As the last of the late-adopting teams belatedly embraced data-driven analysis, awareness of aging patterns and projected performance began to govern every transaction, and the supply of overexuberant bidders dried up. Suddenly, no one was willing to pay top dollar on the free-agent market for depreciating players, and increasingly, teams even opted not to tender contracts to players approaching the end of their arbitration eligibility.

Increasingly, potent player development exacerbated the problem. Dating back to Branch Rickey, excelling at development has provided teams with an excuse not to spend on external solutions. Today's teams try to create talent rather than importing proven veterans. Why pay a premium for a name-brand free agent when one could extract the same stats from a generic equivalent? With the right swing alteration or tweak to a pitch, today's bench player or bullpen arm could be tomorrow's successful starter, for a far lower salary than the better-known veteran on the verge of decline.

Although MLB still doesn't have a salary cap, the luxury tax (essentially a soft cap on player payroll) exerts downward pressure on salaries, and bonuses on the domestic and international markets are now tightly controlled. With fewer places to direct their dollars without paying penalties, teams are funneling funds into R&D. Analysts and executives with the know-how to improve players more than pay for themselves, so when teams get a chance to pluck a key staffer from a franchise that's further ahead, a front-office feeding frenzy results. "It's not really publicized," Brian Bannister says, "but the free-agent market in front-office hirings, to me, is hotter than on the players side."

Owners often come from financial sectors, and they know a wise investment when they see one. "What is a $6,000 high-speed camera if you hit on two out of five international pitchers instead of one out of five?" Bannister says. "If you produce another major-league player because you spent $6,000 on a camera, it's a no-brainer." Despite the obvious advantages, there remains a vast asymmetry between teams in resources devoted to development, partly because more miserly owners are consistent in their unwillingness to spend. "The teams with more resources for their major-league payroll are going to have more resources in this area as well," Forst says. "It's not the difference between $200 million and $80 million, as it is in payrolls, but there's still a gap there."

Amid all of those investments in off-the-field infrastructure, star players are still getting paid, and some of those stars are reclamation projects, such as Hill, Turner, and Martinez, who have made more money than they could have imagined midway through their careers. While the recent revolution in player development has helped individual players perform better and make more, though, it may be costing players collectively. The player-compensation system—and by extension, baseball's labor peace—rests on a foundation of free agency, and that foundation is fragile.

Moneyball was a movement led by low-payroll teams that were searching for ways to keep pace with big spenders. Eventually, the big spenders got smart and erased that small-market edge. As a consequence, some of the early practitioners of progressive development were also the teams with the greatest resources, including MLB's bicoastal behemoths, the Yankees and Dodgers. For now, the concentration of talent in the cheap, prearbitration ranks favors teams that wouldn't win bidding wars for free agents, but as Forst asks, "How long do you think that's going to last?"

Players hope they'll have to wait only until the current CBA expires on December 1, 2021. If front offices are going to keep bypassing the big-ticket items and converting raw talent into productive, pre-free-agency players with relatively little earning power, it's imperative for the Players Association to adjust its own strategy. As the CBA's expiration approaches, the MLBPA will work to get players paid earlier in their careers, but the league won't make that concession lightly.

Posturing and rhetoric between the league and the union are already growing more heated as owners rack up value that the players don't share via franchise appreciation, giant TV deals, and income from MLB's digital arm, which have collectively decoupled profits from onfield results, suppressing the incentive to spend. Even if they're earning a lower piece of the overall revenue pie, major leaguers may be reluctant to rock an MLB boat that still pays them handsomely by normal-citizen standards. But the ingredients are in place for a more contentious round of bargaining than the past few CBA cycles have seen, and it's partly player development's fault.

The other existential problem that the one-two tandem of Moneyball and the post-Moneyball focus on player enhancement poses for the sport is stylistic and aesthetic. Sabermetrics cemented the importance of pitchers preventing balls in play, as well as a few facts about offense: walks are valuable, strikeouts aren't worse (on average) than any other out, and high-strikeout hitters tend to draw walks and hit homers, which makes them more productive than high-contact types. As high-strikeout pitchers became increasingly prized and the stigma surrounding high-strikeout hitters dissipated, competitive pressures pushed strikeout rates ever upward. Strikeouts pay, particularly for pitchers; as the Astros' Cy Sneed says, "There's never a situation where you strike a guy out and you're like, aw, man."

In the stands, though, that's a common reaction. And here, too, the movement has helped baseball double down on a concerning trend. Teams are no longer limited to the existing supply of high-strikeout players; through pitch design, pitch-mix changes, velocity gains, and batters trading contact for power, they can *create* more Ks. MLB's strikeout rate has climbed for thirteen consecutive seasons. In 2018, strikeouts outnumbered hits for the first time in history, and the rate of "three true outcomes"—strikeouts, walks, and homers—reached a record 33.8 percent of plate appearances. Throw in hit-by-pitches, which are also at an all-time high in the sport's modern era (thanks to faster fastballs, more breaking balls, and evidently not enough sticky stuff), and nearly 35 percent of plate appearances don't require the batter to run or a batted ball to be fielded.

"Baseball traditionalists hate that we're trying to take balls out of play, [but] when your goal is to win, you're trying to control the outcome as much as possible," Bannister says. The better batters get at driving the ball, he adds, the more crucial it is for pitchers to steer clear of contact. And advanced development has barely started scratching the surface of fielding. "Eventually, the world of technology is going to get into fielding too," says Mike Fast, who notes that fielding is difficult to train because it involves so many movements that are challenging to track. "You can get the Statcast data or FIELDf/x or whatever, and that's great," he says. "But when you try to show your players to train them, well, they don't want to see a dot moving on a screen. They want to know how they were moving." Some teams have started capturing high-speed video of defenders with an eye toward enhancing fielding technique.

Defense has already improved behind the plate, where a new emphasis on framing rather than blocking and throwing has rapidly remade the catching landscape. In the decade during which tracking technology has been available, the difference in framing performance between the best and worst teams—as measured by Baseball Prospectus's framing runs—has been cut in half, while the variation among all teams has also reached a record low. "The average framer is now better than he was five years ago because clubs are able to coach him to get better," an NL GM says. And that means more strikeouts even when hitters don't swing.

The ongoing campaign against contact is a case of misaligned incentives. Players and teams are trying to do what's best for them, but in baseball—as opposed to football or basketball, where deep passes and three-pointers, respectively, are both smart *and* entertaining— the optimal plays from a competitive perspective may not be optimal from a fan standpoint. "On the club level, we're trying to create better players and a better formula for winning," Forst says. "[On] the industry-wide question of whether it's a better game, I will let Mr. Manfred handle that one."

Aside from speechifying, Manfred hasn't handled it decisively so far, although in fairness to the commissioner, the power of the Players Association makes it more difficult for the league to impose sweeping changes. There's plenty that baseball could do to promote balls in play: deadening the ball, shrinking the strike zone, lowering the mound, or moving the mound back. Pitchers are taller than they used to be, and they're releasing their pitches closer to the plate.

Baseball could learn from golf, which entered its talent-transformation era earlier and has already wrestled with the ramifications. As pro players used data to hit the ball farther and more efficiently, they began to break golf, getting too good for old courses. "The traditionalists really dislike that, and some of the players say it's part of the evolution—'We're better, and that's just one of the by-products,'" says Columbia Business School professor Mark Broadie, the Bill James of golf. "The improvements in players, both in their skill and perhaps in technology . . . have been intentionally offset by increases in course difficulty so that scores remain the same. . . . On the PGA Tour, you'll almost never see a pin in the middle of the green anymore."

In contrast to sports that tinker constantly with their products, MLB hasn't made a meaningful move to curtail strikeouts since lowering the top of the strike zone in 1988, although in 2019 it announced plans to implement a three-batter minimum per pitcher appearance in 2020. They also set up a partnership with the independent Atlantic League to test a new mound distance, a TrackMan-assisted strike zone, and other experimental measures. MLB's official historian, John Thorn, wrote in late 2018, "The dilemma for owners and players and fans may be understood as The Paradox of Progress: we know the game is better, so why, for so many, does it feel worse? I submit that while *Science* may win on the field, as clubs employ strategies that give them a better chance of victory, *Aesthetics* wins hearts and minds." It won't matter how good players get if fewer people want to watch them.[3]

Without MLB's intervention, the strikeout-rate rise probably can't be stopped. But for those who fear a boring brand of baseball, there is hope that the increase could be slowed or temporarily paused. Although strikeout rates have generally risen over time, they haven't done so during every era. The strikeout rate in 1911 was higher than in 1951. The strikeout rate in 1963 was higher than in 1993. More recently, the strikeout rate in 1997 was the same as in 2007. As the Astros' aforementioned recommitment to contact suggests, Ks can move in more than one direction. But to make more contact, hitters will have to solve spin.

When pitcher Jim Creighton began to spin balls by batters in the early 1860s, he changed baseball from a game whose core was contact, fielding, and running to one in which the pitcher-batter battle took precedence. That conflict is still the centerpiece of the sport, and with blazing fastballs becoming commodity goods, teams have taken their cue from Creighton. "Spin is really the driving factor for everything now, because you can find velocity anywhere," Bannister says, adding, "Pitch design is going to be the next five years of baseball. I think that's where everybody's going."

The latest skirmishes in this centuries-spanning war, Bannister explains, are being waged by "hitters getting on the perfect swing plane, [and] pitchers trying their best to get off of that swing plane with every pitch they throw." Hitters craft their swings to take advantage of the fat part of the pitch-trajectory bell curve: most pitches come in on a roughly 6 degree downward plane, so most hitters swing up at the same angle to maximize their margin of error and exit velocity. Pitchers on enlightened teams, in turn, are trying to work away from that hitting sweet spot, throwing 8 degree breaking balls down and 4 degree fastballs up—ideally disguised so that hitters can't tell the difference. "The good teams are just expanding more than ever, more pitches outside the zone," Bannister says. "It's just that dance."

A lot of hitters haven't learned the steps. "Most hitters, even if you throw a high pitch, they still try to hit it with their 6 degree swing," Bannister says. That's changing. Baseball's prevailing strategies are cyclical: When pitchers were still throwing low in the zone, hitters started swinging up to punish those pitches. When hitters went low, pitchers went high. Now some teams are trying to teach their hitters to go high also.

Astros outfielder Tony Kemp says the biggest benefit of TrackMan for him has been recognizing which pitchers do and don't have hop on their heaters. Before every series, Astros coaches brief the hitters on which pitchers have high spin, and the hitters adjust accordingly. "You've been trained to hit the ball obviously where it's pitched," Kemp says. "But now that you have spin rate, and you have guys who can understand how to spin the baseball with four-seam hop, you can see that the baseball's actually going to end up above your barrel. So now we're talking about swinging above the baseball."

That isn't any easier than it sounds—imagine trying to hit a high-90s fastball that isn't where it appears to be—but it's the future of hitting. "It's all about fine-tuning your skills to match the pitcher," says Kemp, who adds, "I definitely can say that I've altered my swing in a way to adjust my barrel through the zone to hit pitches." So have his teammates. In 2018, Astros hitters produced a .359 wOBA on four-seam fastballs in the upper third of the zone and above, easily topping the Red Sox and Indians for the major-league lead.

One factor holding back hitters is an inability to train against the same stuff they're seeing in games. Pitching machines can't currently match the spin rates of MLB's outlier arms. "It doesn't matter if you turn up the velocity, the spin rate is still the same," Bannister says. "So you never actually, as a hitter, have any way to practice against really, really elite-spin-rate pitchers."

Virtual reality may offer a solution long-term, but its visual fidelity isn't yet up to snuff. Still, teams are testing it; Forst, a former independent-league player, recently donned a headset to face off against (and have trouble catching up to) a virtual Trevor Bauer. "It still remains to be seen how much can we use a tool like virtual reality to teach a guy what's a strike and what's not and see how it improves their performance," he says. Whenever the next tech breakthrough comes, hitters will have one factor in their favor: they can take many more max-effort practice swings without hurting themselves than pitchers can throw practice pitches. If hitters keep hacking, maybe they can catch up.

Or maybe they don't have to hack. Maybe hitting is all in their heads.

With each advance in technology, the cutting edge takes another step back from basic, box-score outcomes. For more than a century, all we knew about batters was their results: strikeout, single, home run. Later, with tools like TrackMan, we learned how well each ball was hit, which allowed us to estimate how a hitter was performing independent of results. But even a snapshot of the ball in the instant after contact is measuring a result: the outcome of a swing and the body movements that produced that swing. Lately, we've gained insight into those parts of the process. Now teams are trying to study what's happening in the brain even before the body and bat start moving. With each step along this ontological quest to understand athletes, new paths to improvement appear, enabling earlier interventions.

Jason Sherwin and Jordan Muraskin are the founders of deCervo, one of the companies trying to bring neuroimaging and brain training to baseball. They met during their doctorate studies at Columbia University, where Sherwin was analyzing how expert musicians process music and Muraskin was using imaging to measure the ways in which expertise shapes the brain. They joined forces to study baseball players, designing custom software that tested users' speed and accuracy in recognizing simulations of certain pitch types, in conjunction with a wireless EEG cap whose electrodes could detect the neural predecessors of their responses—the signals in their brains that were saying "slider" or "curve." Testing on Division I college players revealed "an enhanced perception-action coupling" and "enhanced inhibitory control" compared to nonplayers—neural markers of athletic aptitude.

Sherwin and Muraskin initially envisioned their product as a scouting tool, capable of identifying players with preternatural pitch recognition—like Mookie Betts, who reportedly impressed the Red Sox with his predraft scores on a test administered by a Cambridge-based deCervo predecessor called NeuroScouting—or screening out those who were slow to pick up pitches. When they started working with teams, though, their clients viewed those initial measurements as a starting point, not the last word. "The next question was always, 'How do we do it better?'" Sherwin says. "So we very quickly learned that the interest was more on development."

In 2018, four MLB organizations used deCervo's software in the minors, with one of them employing it at five affiliates. The company has introduced a mobile app that can be used without a headset, reducing expenses and the need for experts to be present to conduct the tests. Although it's difficult to prove causation, deCervo claims to have established strong correlations between performance improvements in the app and performance improvements on the field. Its next step may be partnering with companies that make swing sensors or wearables, which could yield a grand unified tracking system capable of assessing a player's performance from first thought to last action and from Little League to the big leagues. "I personally think it could have the most impact for kids that are younger," Sherwin says, citing an age range of "seven to twelve, because those are extremely formative years when it comes to the nervous system."

Sherwin says one of the first teams to experiment with deCervo concluded after one season, "the more the players used it, the better they did." That answers one question, but it raises another: why some players practiced regularly while others, Sherwin says, would "play around with [it] for a few minutes and then go onto Instagram." That dilemma may lead back to the unknown that drew Sherwin and Muraskin to the field in the first place: how experts get so good and whether their proficiency stems from something innate. "I think what's really hardwired is the foundations to allow them to train more efficiently and train smarter and train harder," Muraskin says. What teams would really like is a way to identify other players who share that part of Bauer's brain. "We're close to being able to spot some of this information," Muraskin says.

Until *all* **players** get the benefits of transformative techniques from an early age, player performance will be subject to sudden spikes, all of which will surprise projection systems that aren't privy to proprietary info. "The predictive nature of advanced analytics today is going to be thrown a curveball," says Andy McKay. "This player-development technology is going to provide enough information that the players that are willing to go for it can make quantum leaps in their careers."

One way for teams to minimize that uncertainty is to take an even more proactive role in player development, turning what began as a bottom-up movement into a top-down one.

In the off-season, Alex Hassan notes, players have historically had little contact with their teams. "A lot of the off-season is like, 'Hey, go get 'em, we'll see you next year.'" That's about to change. Teams are hiring many of the former independent instructors at the leading edge of development. New ideas and new voices are invading dugouts; as Eno Sarris, a writer at The Athletic, observed, the average tenure of a major-league hitting coach in December 2018 was only 1.4 years, the lowest figure in at least a decade. Only five hitting coaches at the start of 2019 had been with their respective teams for more than three years.

"I definitely don't fault guys for going and seeking outside help wherever they can get it," Dave Bush says, adding, "I look at it like if you're sick and you're going to see a specialist, you're not always going to go to your regular doctor because you know there's someone else out there that may know a little bit more about a particular topic." If that specialist could be *inside*, though, that would be even better from the team's perspective, leading to lower risk of a player seeing someone who isn't qualified, less potential for conflict between internal and external coaches, and tighter integration with the team's analytical resources.

In the past, teams were often so hesitant to tamper with players that they would wait until they failed, reducing the perceived risk of screwing them up. By not helping them, though, they were already hurting them—and indirectly driving them to people like Latta and Boddy. Now, Bannister says, "We're trying to give them the personalized, Driveline-type experience. . . . They don't have to go see a guru in the off-season in order to get that type of exposure to better player-development information." Teams that develop a reputation for providing players with the proper support may make themselves more appealing landing spots for free agents in need of career rejuvenations. Over the 2018–2019 offseason, MLB teams hired eight former Driveline employees, including Ochart and Daniels.

Bannister expects more players to take a cue from PGA pros (and Bauer) and purchase their own sensors, trackers, and cameras to continue their training year-round. Although that could lead to more mastery and greater technological literacy, it may also exacerbate another growing problem with the sport. At the lower levels, baseball is becoming a more expensive undertaking and potentially a more discriminatory one.

According to a 2018 report by the Aspen Institute, only 34 percent of children from families earning less than $25,000 played a team sport in 2017, compared to 69 percent from homes earning more than $100,000. Between 2011 and 2017, the participation rates in households earning at least $75,000 increased, while the participation rates in lower-earning households decreased. Organized sports are often an unsupportable expense.

Baseball, wrote star outfielder Andrew McCutchen in a 2015 piece for the Players' Tribune, "used to be a way out for poor kids. Now it's a sport that increasingly freezes out kids whose parents don't have the income to finance the travel baseball circuit." Deliberate practice is powerful regardless of one's economic origins, but it requires time, technology, and instruction, all of which may be in short supply for children from lower-income families. Similarly, tools like TrackMan help amateur talents get spotted and drafted, but only if they can afford to play on teams and in tournaments where those systems are installed. In the post-Moneyball era, the have-nots are only falling further behind the curve.

In late 2016, MLB and USA Baseball began to combat the pay-to-play structure of youth baseball by forming the Prospect Development Pipeline, a series of free, team-attended, invitation-only events for high-school players. In late 2018, MLB expanded the program by forming the PDP League, a Royals Academy-esque "development and showcase" experience scheduled for mid-June through early July 2019. The announcement on MLB.com promised that the eighty participants would receive "evaluation using modern technologies to tailor an individualized development curriculum for each player."

MLB and USA Baseball also teamed up in 2018 to launch the Trainer Partnership Program, which in part will bring "all of the state-of-the-art evaluation tools that have become so common at the major-league level to the international market." In November, the program held a three-day showcase in Boca Chica that featured 120 Dominican players who'll be eligible to sign in 2019 and 2020. Every pitch, batted ball, and run time was meticulously tracked.

These initiatives are addressing real problems for young players, but MLB isn't funding them out of purely altruistic motives. Both programs are rectifying a problem for teams by feeding decision-makers' insatiable desire for data. On the international market, teams can verbally commit to players up to three years before they're eligible to sign, but they can't bring those players to their academies until one year before. That leaves a window during which teams are dependent on trainers for data, and the trainers have taken advantage. "It's getting wild out there," Bannister says. "The earlier you can get data on [a player, the better], but you can't bring him into your academy. So now it's all about setting stuff up in a portable format, or now buying it from the [trainers]." Or luring players to a free showcase and letting the cameras roll.

For good or ill, the youth baseball experience worldwide is about to be more information-rich than ever. If anything, though, objective measurements provide fuel for competitiveness and a new way to hook kids on an old game. The same people who say stats suck the joy out of following baseball may also say that launch angles and spin rates suck the joy out of playing it, but just as there's nothing joyless about understanding the sport in a different and deeper way, there's nothing joyless about being better at it.

Eventually, early exposure to data may help restore a species that Moneyball made almost extinct: the MLB player turned general manager.

According to data provided by Baseball Prospectus writer Dustin Palmateer, 44.1 percent of GMs hired in the 1980s were former MLB players. Among GMs hired in the 2010s, only two, Dave Stewart and Jerry Dipoto, have been big leaguers. The percentage of new GMs who were once minor leaguers has fallen from 67.6 percent in the '80s to 20.6 percent in the 2010s. Almost 40 percent of GMs hired in the 2010s have been Ivy Leaguers; from the '70s to the '90s, that rate never rose above 3 percent. Although it's a sign of progress that nonplayers are no longer excluded from the team-running ranks, front offices have swung so far in the other direction that they've merely traded one type of homogeneity for another, morphing into a slightly younger and far nerdier brand of old boys' club. GMs are exclusively male, overwhelmingly white, and increasingly Ivy League educated. That lack of demographic diversity is likely leading to a lack of diversity of thought.

Dipoto says that in contrast to a previous generation of players that was left behind by baseball's statistical revolution, today's players are "learning as they go, and as a result, I think you're going to see some players start to matriculate back toward front-office or player-acquisition-type roles like they did twenty-five, thirty-five years ago." Rays conduit Cole Figueroa adds, "I truly believe there is a harmonious middle ground where one day we will see players running teams again, and even more progressive-thinking people who didn't play at all [sitting] in the dugout." In December 2018, Figueroa's team took a step along the latter path by installing its director of analytics, Jonathan Erlichman, as the majors' first "analytics coach." Erlichman, who never played the game beyond T-ball and majored in math at Princeton (where he wrote his senior thesis on "Gravitational Redshifts in Galaxy Clusters"), will be in uniform as a member of manager Kevin Cash's staff in 2019, a stathead in coach's clothing. "People are just excited for what we're potentially going to learn from this," Erlichman told the *Tampa Bay Times*.

In 2015, Bill James said, "My view on the world is we have an ocean of ignorance and a small island of knowledge." He wasn't speaking specifically about baseball, but the observation applies, even to one of the most obsessively chronicled and comprehensively quantified human hobbies. "I feel like, yeah, our island is one hundred times bigger than it used to be," Fast says. "But does that make the ocean that much smaller?"

It's scary not to know things. But it's also exciting, because it means there's more to learn.

Inside the self-contained bubble of baseball, being better can accomplish only so much. Expansion aside, there's a finite number of roster spots in the majors and a finite number of wins to be distributed among the thirty (or, in the future, thirty-two or thirty-four) franchises. No matter how good teams get at developing players, the average team will finish at .500, the average player will be worth no more than before, and the team that wins the World Series will still start out 0–0 the next spring.

Outside of sports, though, there are no such constraints. We can be better without making something else in the world worse. Each of us individually, and all of us collectively, could be Justin Turner before changing his swing, Rich Hill before fully embracing his curveball, Trevor Bauer before redesigning his slider. Maybe humanity is about to break out. As James said, "We haven't done anything yet to compare with potentially what we could do."

EPILOGUE

THE RESIDUE OF DESIGN

Success breeds complacency. Complacency breeds failure.
Only the paranoid survive.

   —ANDY GROVE, former Intel CEO and semiconductor pioneer

Brian Bannister's father spent fifteen years in the majors and pitched in one playoff game. That was one more than Bannister himself experienced. Neither of them ever went to the World Series. So when the 2018 Red Sox made the ALCS against the Astros and then the World Series against the Dodgers, following back-to-back division series losses in the two preceding seasons and a playoff no-show the year before that, Bannister thought the same thing as the rest of the Red Sox: we can't waste this opportunity.

More so than any other major sport, modern baseball becomes a different beast in the playoffs, morphing from an everyday activity in which teams and players pace themselves to one in which they ratchet up their intensity in response to extra off days and higher stakes. Managers pull their starters early, furiously cycle through a parade of relievers (some of them regular-season starters), and ask closers to go longer and dig deeper than they do during most of the year. And as teams deploy their best pitchers, pitchers deploy their best *pitches*, throwing close to their maximum speeds at all times. The October mantra, Bannister says, is: "Best pitch quality, best pitch execution, best pitch mix."

All of the above is particularly true in the World Series, a best-of-seven sprint in which there's no need to hold anything in reserve. "That's when all the seeds that have been planted, in that year, in previous years on the development side, [come] together," Bannister says. "This is no longer a development scenario. This is pure execution."

In a sense, though, the ongoing revolution is blurring the line between development and execution. Although big projects such as swing overhauls and new pitches are typically reserved for the off-season or spring training, today's cutting-edge coaches and players are constantly tweaking and tuning in a more focused way than their predecessors. Bannister's portable pitching lab and Fenway's suite of sensors allowed the Red Sox to scout themselves, scouring their staff for any noncompliant pitches that could give a game away. "Maintaining breaking balls is a full-time job now," Bannister says. "[A breaking ball] will waver between a 60 and a 70 pitch, just based on 15 degrees of spin axis. And that can be grip, that can be fatigue as the year goes on, it can just be getting out of whack slightly."

Entering the playoffs, the Red Sox faced this problem with right-handed relievers Joe Kelly, thirty, and Heath Hembree, twenty-nine, two key cogs in a bullpen that projected to be Boston's biggest vulnerability. Both Kelly and Hembree have sliders that rate as their best secondary pitches when they're working well. In the 2016 playoffs, Bannister says, Kelly's slider had been "as close to throwing an 80 as you could throw," coming in at up to 93.5 mph with a wicked shape. In his three postseason outings that year, Kelly threw the slider 41 percent of the time, more often than any other pitch. At the start of 2018, Kelly's slider was still formidable, as was Hembree's, whose movement Bannister describes as "perfect."

Over the course of the regular season, though, both Kelly and Hembree had slowly lost their nasty sliders. Relievers who throw a lot of sliders, Bannister says, tend to release them with their hands slightly turned to the side, as if they're throwing a football. That hand position imparts extra spin to the slider compared to holding the hand more square to home plate, which adds extra hop to the fastball. When the season started, Kelly and Hembree had their hands at an angle and threw spin-efficient sliders with less hop on their heaters, but they both began to suffer from the same affliction. "As the year went on, for whatever reason, their hand[s] [were] getting more and more square on their fastball[s], and they were getting more and more carry on

their four-seamer[s], and we started to see them lose their sliders,"
Bannister says. The wipeout pitches they'd been throwing in April had
devolved into "baby cutters" that weren't missing many bats.

There was one happy by-product of this unintended alteration:
pitchers who throw with their hands square to home also tend to
have better curveballs. And so, Bannister says, "We actually saw Joe
and Heath's curveballs getting better while their sliders were getting
worse."

Thanks to sensitive tools like Edgertronic and KinaTrax, the Red
Sox learned in 2018 that there's value to placing pitchers into buckets
based on their arm actions. Two pitchers with identical release points,
as measured by TrackMan, can reach those release points via very different mechanisms, and that sequencing of actions—the relationship
between shoulder, elbow, and hand—can be used to group pitchers
together. "You can only throw a ball so many ways," says Bannister,
who uses golf analogies to describe the angle at which pitchers' hands
come through the ball: hook, draw, square, fade, and slice. Classifying
pitchers, he says, "allows us to be better coaches because we can address their needs very specifically based on those specific angles and
ratios."

The Red Sox discovered that once a pitcher's arm action starts
drifting in a certain direction, it's difficult to reverse the trend, just as
it is to change a golf swing overnight. Kelly and Hembree had morphed
from "draw" pitchers to "square" pitchers. At first, the team had tried
to fight it, but accepting it soon seemed the smarter course. "Once we
identified, 'Hey, they're switching what bucket they're in' . . . we knew
we needed to address their needs differently and come up with a different game plan," Bannister says.

With the playoffs approaching and both pitchers unable to trust
their sliders, Red Sox pitching coach Dana LeVangie, Bannister says,
made a bold decision: "Let's just completely eliminate the slider, and
let's go to [the] curveball." Although both pitchers' ideal sliders were
better than their ideal curves, they couldn't execute the sliders, and
they *could* execute the curves.

Kelly threw his last slider of the season on September 19. Hembree
threw his on September 29. The chart shows how Kelly (solid lines)

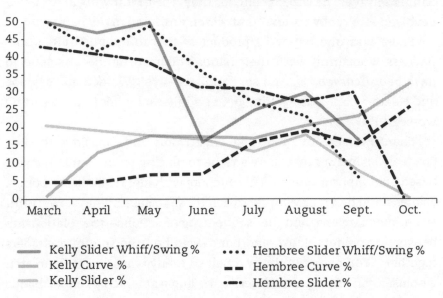

Joe Kelly and Heath Hembree
Slider and Curve Usage and Slider Whiff/Swing Percent by Month, 2018

Kelly Slider Whiff/Swing %   •••• Hembree Slider Whiff/Swing %
Kelly Curve %   ▬ ▬ Hembree Curve %
Kelly Slider %   ▬•▬• Hembree Slider %

and Hembree (dotted lines) saw their slider whiff rates sink month by month through September. It also reveals how their usage of sliders gradually gave way to curves, culminating in a slider-less October.

The strategy worked wonders. Hembree allowed zero runs in his four playoff appearances, including a routine 11th inning in an epic World Series Game 3. The Red Sox reliever with the next-lowest ERA was Kelly, who led the bullpen with 11 1/3 innings pitched over nine games and allowed only one earned run, striking out 13 without issuing a single free pass—an extraordinary feat for a pitcher who's normally not stingy with walks. Despite his pedestrian regular-season stats, he signed a three-year, $25-million deal with the Dodgers in December.

Boston's technology had failed to prevent Kelly and Hembree's sliders from degrading. But by helping the Sox understand what went wrong—and, in the case of their curveballs, what went right—the data suggested a solution. "If we didn't have the tools, and we didn't have the knowledge of the biomechanics and the physics of what was actually happening, there was no way we would have ever come to that conclusion," Bannister says.

Bannister reached back to his 2015 playbook to boost Boston's postseason staff in other ways. Another right-handed reliever, Matt Barnes, was already reliant on curves, throwing them 39.1 percent of the time during the regular season, which ranked eighth among pitchers with at least forty innings—one spot behind Rich Hill. But on one crucial occasion, Bannister convinced him to drastically ramp up that rate.

"Every once in a while [Barnes] goes, 'What do you got for me?'" Bannister says. One of those times came on October 14, in the pitching lab in right field before ALCS Game 2 against Houston, with the Sox trailing the Astros 1–0 in the series. "I just said, '[Lance] McCullers and [Ryan] Pressly are going out there and, for lack of a better term, McCullers-ing us to death with breaking balls,'" Bannister recalls. He suggested to Barnes, "Why don't you just go out there and just mirror them and do it right back?"

That night, Barnes relieved David Price with two outs in the fifth inning, runners on first and second, and Boston up by one run. Facing Marwin González, he threw four consecutive curves to end the threat: called strike, swinging strike, foul, swinging strike three. The next inning, he threw ten curves in eleven pitches, going groundout, pop fly, groundout. He'd thrown 93 percent curves, easily exceeding his career high in an outing of more than two pitches. "That just said [to the Astros], 'Hey, if you're going to do that, we have guys that can do that too,'" Bannister says.

Not only was that appearance pivotal—Barnes got the win in Boston's series-tying 7–5 victory—but it may have had a psychological impact on the rest of the ALCS. In an era of rigorous, data-driven scouting, one outlier outing in which a player strays from his history sows doubt. "Once you've established that you'll do something that's so many standard deviations away from what you'd normally do, I think it actually makes you better for the rest of that series and the rest of the playoff run," Bannister says, adding, "All the advance reports go out the window."

Speaking of pitch selection and psychological impact: two innings after Barnes left the game, Rick Porcello entered it. Porcello, who was pitching out of the pen between starts, threw his sinker more often than any other pitch during the regular season. Statistically speaking, it wasn't one of his better pitches—his four-seamer and slider were better—but it helped him induce contact and create quicker at-bats, allowing him to stay in games longer. In a playoff relief role, though, he wouldn't need to be economical; he'd only need to miss bats. "Three best pitches, three best locations, and just live or die by that," Bannister says. "You're not a sinkerballer anymore, you're Rick Porcello, the eighth-inning setup guy."

His first playoff appearance of 2018, a short but sweet hold in the eighth inning of ALDS Game 1, marked the first time in his ten-year career that he'd ever appeared in an MLB game without throwing a sinker. ALCS Game 2 was the second. Porcello got Tony Kemp to ground out with a curve, struck out González with a four-seamer, and then ended the inning by convincing Carlos Correa to chase and swing through a slider down and away. As he walked off the mound, he screamed and pumped his arms.

"I thought that was a defining moment of the whole run," Bannister says. Before then, "the narrative had always been we were one reliever short, or the bullpen was the vulnerability of our team, and seeing Rick step up and be that stopgap . . . was just such a boost for the entire team. At that moment, we were like, 'We're going to do this.'"

When they did do it, in Game 5, it was behind three homers off of Clayton Kershaw (including bombs by J.D. Martinez and impending MVP Mookie Betts) and a third consecutive strong start by David Price, who had entered the month with an ugly October track record. Price had only added to his choker reputation in his shaky first two postseason starts of 2018, allowing two homers on his cutter without recording any Ks, which prompted a recommendation.

"I always prefer, especially in the postseason, if you can take away a pitch that is a weak-contact, weak-exit-velo pitch and replace it with a higher-swing-and-miss pitch," Bannister says. Years after he helped Hill, Bannister still sometimes sounds like a broken record when he gives feedback after games, frequently repeating, "He didn't throw his best pitch enough." This time, an important pitcher took the tip to heart.

In Price's ALCS-sealing, six-inning gem at Minute Maid Park, he subtracted from the weak-contact column, using his low-whiff cutter—which he had thrown almost 30 percent of the time during the regular season—a little more than 10 *percent* of the time. Price threw the changeup (by far his highest-whiff offering) on 43 percent of his pitches in Game 5, a career record, and in each of his two World Series starts—both of which were dominant—the lefty threw the cutter less than 7 percent of the time, his lowest usage rates in any game since the first half of 2015. That tweak made him a hero.

According to the historical stats and analysis site The Baseball Gauge, the playoff pitching performances of Kelly, Hembree, Barnes, bullpen Porcello, and postcutter Price collectively increased Boston's probability of winning the World Series by 37.1 percent. The Red Sox won 108 games during the regular season, but they won the World Series in part by being willing to deviate from full-season patterns when the data told them to. It takes a little luck to win in October, but luck, according to Branch Rickey, is the residue of design. For the Red Sox, luck was the residue of *pitch* design. Bannister still hasn't thrown a pitch in the playoffs, but he has helped determine the playoff pitches that other pitchers threw. Fittingly, he abandoned his usual midgame station in the clubhouse to join the rest of the team for the final few minutes of the clincher, MLB bylaws about coach counts in the dugout be damned.

"I've never been in the dugout [as a coach] except for the ninth inning of Game 5," Bannister says. "[I] wasn't going to miss that moment." Nor should he have. He helped make it happen.

Weeks before the Red Sox dogpiled at Dodger Stadium, the Indians returned home for Game 3 of the best-of-five ALDS, playing to save their season. Kluber had been rocked in Game 1. In Game 2, the bullpen, including Bauer, had allowed an early lead to slip away. On October 8, Mike Clevinger took the mound in Game 3 with the season on the line and shut the Astros down, striking out nine and allowing one run over five innings. In the bottom of the fifth, Francisco Lindor slammed a Dallas Keuchel pitch over the left-field wall and off a digital clock on the facade of the elevated walkway to a parking garage. The crowd was euphoric. The Indians led 2–1, clinging to a shred of hope against a formidable Astros team. Francona gave the ball to Bauer, his third relief appearance in the series.

Bauer's fastball was back, averaging 95 mph in the series, but he still hadn't really rounded into form following his long layoff. He allowed a leadoff single to Tony Kemp, who advanced to third on an errant Bauer pickoff throw. George Springer reached on an infield single. Alex Bregman bounced a weak grounder back to Bauer, who tried to start a double play but threw the ball into center field. González followed with a double to score two and gave the Astros a 4–2 lead. Although Houston hadn't hit him hard, it was an ugly inning. The afternoon shadows grew long as the minutes remaining in Cleveland's playoff life grew short. The game, and the Indians' season, ended in an 11–3 rout.

The Astros celebrated on the Progressive Field grass. The Indians retreated to a somber postgame clubhouse. Bauer answered a pack of reporters' questions promptly and departed. The rest of the team would soon disperse, and many would take a break from the game, resting their bodies and minds. Not Bauer. The next night, he had dinner with Boddy in Cleveland. Then he went back to work.

Days after the season ended, Bauer began his off-season routine of having his elbow and shoulder imaged at Stanford and his delivery mapped. Bauer's archive of images of his delivery and his arm's interior is likely unrivaled by any other pitcher in professional baseball.

"He goes and gets his biomechanics captured every year from the same exact person even though there are better methods, including ours. It's not a point of precision, it's a point of his *history*," Boddy says.

Bauer assembles all the information, and he and outside experts evaluate what adjustments he might need to make to his training regimen or delivery. After his imaging and mapping in November 2018, he made another trip, to Nashville, where he met with Caleb Cotham at The Bledsoe Agency and helped design an off-season development plan for Neil Ramírez.

Bauer remains a complicated teammate. After helping Ramírez— good teammate!—he sent a tweet on November 29 that gave the opposite impression to some who saw it, writing, "Plot twist, I was better than Kluber this year." He added in a separate, clarifying tweet that "Klubes was outstanding but so was I." He said he wasn't trashing a teammate. A number of statistics said Bauer was correct about being better than Kluber in 2018. Yet Kluber was a finalist for the Cy Young Award, and Bauer was not. (Tampa Bay's Blake Snell won the award, while Bauer finished sixth.) Few players would wade into the waters of social media to rank performances within a clubhouse. As he saw it, he was just setting the record straight for posterity.

MLB Network invited Bauer on air to talk about his social-media missives and another big story line: reports that the Indians were shopping him. Bauer obliged. During the live remote interview, he said that if the Indians were to trade him, they ought to do so after the 2019 season. He'd have more "surplus value" in 2019, he reasoned. Bauer was unwilling to discuss an extension. He wants to be the first player to go through the arbitration process for a fourth time in the winter of 2019–2020, and it's unlikely the Indians would want to pay the salary he'd command, which could exceed $20 million.

Bauer won his second consecutive arbitration case against the club in February 2019 and was awarded a $13 million salary for the forthcoming season. Arbitration hearings typically feature arguments based solely upon on-field performance, but Bauer accused the lawyers arguing the case for the club of "character assassination" in the final ten minutes of their presentation before the arbitrator, which included mentioning Bauer's "69 Days of Giving" charity effort from 2018, in which he gave away $420.69 a day to sixty-eight different charities over the course of sixty-nine days. "They didn't mention it was a charitable campaign, just mentioned the name," Bauer told USA Today. What else did they say? "Basically, that I'm a terrible human being."[1]

Bauer had created more controversy on social media in January when he engaged in a two-day-long, back-and-forth Twitter skirmish with a college student. Bauer responded to the young woman after she levied a pair of insults. She soon faced an avalanche of responses from Bauer and some of his 134,000 followers. The woman said she felt harassed. After facing criticism for recklessness and insensitivity,

Bauer tweeted, "I often defend myself against internet trolling" but resolved to "wield the responsibility of my public platform more responsibly in the future."

Most pitchers start ramping up their velocity in February, the month they report to spring training, but Bauer had begun crow-hopping and max-efforting 105-plus mph throws into netting in the main Driveline facility in November. He was testing everything he had, including his latest project: building a better changeup.

The one area Bauer struggled to attack in 2018 was low and away to left-handed hitters. Although Bauer's changeup missed bats at an above-average rate, yielding one of the ten lowest batting averages and slugging percentages of any starter who threw the pitch at least one hundred times in 2018, it lacked the horizontal or vertical movement he wanted, and he had trouble locating it consistently. On the same mound in the Driveline R&D building where he commenced his slider project, he began again, with the Edgertronic and Rapsodo watching and measuring. Bauer wanted a pitch shape that would move in the same tunnel as his slider but break in the opposite direction. He and Driveline pitch-design guru Eric Jagers (who'd be hired by the Phillies in March) used a black marker to draw a stripe on the balls Bauer was throwing, making the spin axis easier to track. On some throws, the black stripe looked like a tilted equator. Progress.

Bauer and the Driveline staff made video overlays to compare his pitches' movement. A green loop overlaid on the video represented the tunnel that he wanted the pitches to travel within for as long as possible. Bauer's slider, four-seam fastball, and changeup all inhabited the loop for about half the journey to the plate. Then the slider broke off to the left and the changeup faded down and away.

Bauer began throwing live at-bats earlier than he had the previous off-season. A player peanut gallery gathered around the cage as he threw to a motley crew of hitters and HitTrax quantified the results. Bauer grunted as he threw his entire arsenal of pitches, which often resulted in whiffs from overmatched hitters, drawing laughs from the audience.

Bauer believes he will be even better in 2019, but he has fears. He'll be twenty-eight in 2019, statistically already at or even past the typical player's physical peak, though he'd like to challenge that notion. (His velocity increased in 2018, when the standard aging trajectory would say it should have declined.) He hasn't yet won the first of the three Cy Youngs he covets. He worries about what will happen when more talented pitchers, like the Dodgers' Walker Buehler or even Adam Ottavino, start to adopt his practices. "[Bauer] thinks there's a road-map issue," Boddy says. "I have done this additional work to prove I can do this. . . . And everyone will start doing it." Other pitchers' ceilings will be higher than Bauer's.

"His fears are not stupid," Boddy says. But Boddy comforts him with this: few, if any, pitchers are willing to work as hard, to put in the necessary deliberate practice. "I was like, 'Can you name a single major or minor leaguer that works as many hours as you in the off-season?'" Boddy says.

Bauer couldn't.

"Well, it doesn't matter then, does it?" Boddy told him. "You haven't fixed the problem that us humans have, which is that we don't like to work very hard. If you fix that problem, you're in line to make billions of dollars doing something else."

Just as most players are behind Bauer, most (likely all) teams are trailing the Astros, even though Sanstreak sold out three months' stock of Edgertronic cameras in one day in January as other clubs belatedly got on board. As Boddy tweeted in February 2019, "Most teams are still in denial and use technology because they feel they have to. They're still way behind actual integration." We're still in the early stages of this movement, perhaps just the end of its beginning.

This era of development depends on adopting and integrating technology and data to spur players to new heights. But each transformation starts with something innately human: a desire to be better. Only the curious and the driven will excel in the future of enlightened athletics. Only the paranoid will survive.

Boddy is built for that world, but he says he doesn't want to work in a major-league front office. He seemingly doesn't need to. His company, which employs more than thirty people, has become a brand:

the third building of the Driveline campus is a warehouse whose slow-to-illuminate fluorescent lights reveal wooden crates stacked to the ceiling. The crates contain weighted balls, wrist weights, and other Driveline products, all manufactured in China and shipped over by boat. At the 2018 Winter Meetings, Boddy offered MLB teams ninety-minute meetings to explain the latest innovations at Driveline, and he filled all of the available slots. He also hosted curious media members for an event in Driveline's Mandalay Bay hotel suite, which was soon so packed that the crowd spilled into the bedrooms.

In the fall of 2018, the *Puget Sound Business Journal* recognized Driveline as Seattle's second-fastest-growing minority-owned business. The magazine pegged Driveline's revenue in 2017 at $3.12 million, an increase of 374 percent from 2015. But there is one job Boddy would leave for, a position in which he would morph from the ultimate outsider to the ultimate insider: MLB pitching coach.

On October 30, the Angels anointed ex-Astros bullpen coach Doug White as their new pitching coach. White, who never played professionally, got into the game by opening his own facility in Southern California. The news touched off a Twitter exchange between Boddy and Bauer.

BODDY: Christ sakes they let anyone become a big league pitching coach these days. (Congrats, Doug!)

BAUER: I guess there's hope for you after all Kyle. Big if true.

BODDY: Pitching coach of the Phillies, 2023, here we come.

BAUER: C'mon man don't be pulling an Elon Musk and delaying the timeline ok? I want my model three and that looks like you in Oakley's in a Phillies uniform in 2021 ok?

Maybe one day the game's two ultimate outsiders would *both* be in uniform. Until then, though, they had a changeup to perfect. In early January 2019, Bauer stepped back onto the mound in the R&D building at Driveline and threw another five-gallon bucket's worth of balls. Opening Day was approaching, and Bauer had to be better.

ACKNOWLEDGMENTS

BEN LINDBERGH: Many industry insiders have little incentive to speak frankly about baseball's final frontier. We're grateful to those who talked to us anyway, in some cases because they cared deeply about sharing knowledge that might help players improve. Without them this book would've been a lot shorter.

Thanks to Sam Miller, Steve Goldman, Zach Kram, and Rob Neyer for early reads and recommendations; to Craig and Cathy Wright for research help and hospitality; to Richard Puerzer for graciously sharing his archive of clippings; to Paul Kuo for wrangling clients; to Rob Arthur, Mitchel Lichtman, Rob McQuown, and Daren Willman for statistical assistance; to the writers whose work informed ours, including R.J. Anderson, Mark Armour, Russell Carleton, J.J. Cooper, David Laurila, Joe Lemire, Dan Levitt, Lee Lowenfish, Eno Sarris, Jeff Sullivan, and Tom Verducci; and to Bill Simmons, Sean Fennessey, Mallory Rubin, and Justin Sayles at The Ringer for letting me moonlight again. On the home front, love and gratitude to my wife, Jessie Barbour, and to my tiny writing companion, Grumkin, for their patience and support.

Our reporting was the product of a great many recorded conversations conducted in a terrifyingly short time. Those interviews would've been worthless without the army of helpers who pitched in to transcribe them: Gavin Whitehead, David Seeger, Jared Beaumont, Chris Baber, Lee Sigman, Kenny Kelly, Michael Carver, Alex Bazeley, Bobby Wagner, Scott Holcombe, Keith Petit, Luke Lillard, Mitch McConeghey, Roland Smith, Troy Carter, Mohamed Hammad, Andrew Calagna, Aria Gerson, Hector Lozada, Jason Marbach, Joe Corkery, John Stookey, Jordan Epstein, Mark Neuenschwander, Matthew Fong, Ricky Gaona, Zach Brady, Aaron Wolfe, Bern Samko, Bradley Beale, Colby Wilson, Eric Oliver, Eric Peters, Greg Vince, Jeremiah Nelson, John Gilbert, Jorma Vaughn, Joseph Bunyan, Kazuto Yamazaki, Michael

Hattery, Michelle Lenhart, Mitchell Krall, Molly McCullough, Robert Frey, Samuel Ujdak, Tim Moore, and Andrew Berkheimer.

One of the hardest things about this project was keeping track of the whereabouts of everyone we interviewed, seemingly half of whom changed jobs while we were writing, as teams doubled down on data-driven development. Another challenge was knowing when it would be overkill to include yet another example of a player transforming himself. Thanks to all of the self-improving players we talked to but couldn't do justice to in the text, among them Jarod Bayless, Sean Boyle, Tony Cingrani, Tyler Flowers, Bryce Montes De Oca, Michael Plassmeyer, David Speer, Kohl Stewart, Ross Stripling, and Matt Tracy. The ranks of progressive players like them are swelling by the season.

Thanks to our agent, Sydelle Kramer, for enduring our (OK, mostly *my*) many e-mails, and to our editor, Jeff Alexander, for helping us make the book both briefer and better. And thanks, of course, to Travis, for being a patient, dependable, and cooperative coauthor. The best thing about cowriting a book is not needing to write a whole book. The next-best thing is having a partner with whom to split the stress.

TRAVIS SAWCHIK: To report this story, we conducted scores of interviews and traveled all over the country to get behind the curtain: from spring training camps in Arizona, to business parks in LA and Seattle, to a sleepy town in Montana, in addition to plenty of trips to Crocker Park in Westlake, Ohio. This book was only made possible because there were enough key figures involved in this revolution willing to explain their talent-creating, ceiling-raising magic. As a reporter, you hope to learn as much as you can about a subject and share it with an audience. I learned so much about a game I thought I knew well. We will always be indebted to the people you have read about in the preceding pages. It is my hope they feel we did justice to their stories and to the idea that we can all be better.

I owe a debt of thanks to our wonderful agent Sydelle Kramer, who brought Ben and me together to work on this book. Sydelle was incredibly patient in helping us from the book's proposal stage to our manuscript deadline. Our editor Jeff Alexander was something of a miracle-working personal trainer in getting the text in shape. I am grateful that Basic Books believed, as we did, that this is an important story. And I am also grateful that Nate Silver and David Appelman allowed me to hold day jobs while writing this book over the course of 2018–2019.

I couldn't ask for a better partner on this project than Ben. What I believe you most want in a coauthor is someone who cares deeply about the project. Ben's tireless work on this book in addition to his day job and podcast was something to behold. I believe because we reported and wrote this together, the end result is better than it would have been had we worked alone.

My wife, Rebecca, was a patient sounding board throughout the writing process. Without her support, this task would have been exponentially more difficult. I'm indebted to my mom and dad for developing me into, hopefully, at least a fringe-average author. And I will always be grateful that Duke Maas gave me a chance to write about baseball as a newspaperman. Duke passed away early in 2019. Thank you, Duke. What I know to be true is that reporting and writing a book are anything but solitary endeavors.

GLOSSARY

Abbreviations

ABCA: American Baseball Coaches Association

AL: American League

ALCS: American League Championship Series

ALDS: American League Division Series

BABIP: batting average on balls in play

BP: batting practice

CBA: collective bargaining agreement

DSL: Dominican Summer League

ERA: earned run average

FIP: fielding independent pitching

GM: general manager

IL: injured list

ISO: isolated power (slugging percentage minus batting average)

MLB: Major League Baseball

MLBAM: MLB Advanced Media

MLBPA: MLB Players Association

MVP: most valuable player

NCAA: National Collegiate Athletic Association

NL: National League

OBP: on-base percentage

OPS: on-base plus slugging

PD: player development

PDP: Prospect Development Pipeline

PECOTA: player empirical comparison and optimization test algorithm

PGA: Professional Golfers Association

SABR: Society for American Baseball Research

SEC: Southeastern Conference

TPI: Titleist Performance Institute

WAR: Wins Above Replacement

WARP: Wins Above Replacement Player

WHIP: Walks plus Hits per Inning Pitched

wOBA: weighted On-Base Average

wRC+: weighted Runs Created Plus

Terms

A-ball: A lower level of the affiliated minor leagues.

Bauer Unit: The mph/rpm reading of a pitch; used to quantify spin.

Big 12: An NCAA Division I athletic conference.

changeup: A pitch type thrown slower than a fastball and designed to fade away from a batter.

Class D: How the lowest level of the minor leagues was defined prior to 1962.

College World Series: The NCAA Division I championship tournament.

curveball: A breaking pitch that departs from a straight trajectory due to its spin axis and spin rate.

Cy Young Award: The annual award bestowed by the Baseball Writers Association of America on the best pitcher in each major league.

Division I, II, III: The levels of intercollegiate athletics, from highest (Division I) to lowest (Division III).

Double-A: The second-highest level of the minor leagues after Triple-A.

draft pick: A player selected in baseball's first-year player draft, which is held each June.

Edgertronic: A type of high-speed, high-definition camera manufactured by Sanstreak and applied to pitch design.

fastball: A pitch type that generally features the greatest velocity and the least movement.

fly ball: A label for an elevated batted ball.

40-man roster: The group of players eligible to be added to the 25-man active roster, including players on the 25-man, some minor leaguers, and players on the injured, bereavement, or paternity leave lists.

four-seam fastball: The fastest and straightest pitch, thrown with the fingers perpendicular to the seams.

Golden Spikes Award: The award given to the best player in Division I baseball each year.

Gold Glove Award: Honor bestowed upon the best fielder at every position in each major league.

Great Wall of Groundball Prevention: A ring of screens stationed around the infield to encourage hitters to aim up, designed by Indians coach Pete Lauritson while at the University of Iowa.

gyroball: Theoretical pitch thrown with a spin axis in line with its movement, making it immune to the Magnus effect.

High-A: Between Low-A and Double-A in the minor-league hierarchy.

hit-by-pitch: Term for when a batter is hit by a thrown pitch.

indy ball: Independent baseball; collective term for all professional leagues unaffiliated with MLB teams.

K rate: Percentage of plate appearances that result in a strikeout.

Laminar Express: Nickname given to Trevor Bauer's two-seam fastball.

laminar flow: A principle of fluid dynamics that can make a sphere (such as a baseball) curve away from its initial course.

leverage index: A measure of a plate appearance's importance in determining each team's win probability within a game.

L-screen: An L-shaped protective net designed to shield batting practice pitchers.

Magnus effect: The force exerted on a spinning sphere or cylinder that creates a pressure differential on opposite sides, leading to movement.

newton metre: A unit of torque.

Opening Day: The first day of the MLB season.

PITCHf/x: A camera-based pitch-tracking system that debuted in MLB ballparks in 2007.

Players Association: The union representing MLB players.

pop fly or pop-up: A mishit batted ball that is hit high but not far and is typically easily caught.

pulldown: A max-effort practice throw.

pull side: The left side of the field for a right-handed batter, or the right side of the field for a left-handed batter.

Rapsodo: A portable tracking unit capable of measuring pitch speed, movement, spin, and spin efficiency.

Rookie ball: The lowest level of the domestic minor leagues.

Rookie of the Year: Award given to the best new player in each of the major leagues.

Rule 5 draft: An annual player selection process designed to prevent teams from hoarding too many young players in their minor-league systems; players selected must be added to the new team's MLB roster or returned to their old team.

sabermetrician: An analyst devoted to obtaining objective knowledge about baseball, often employing statistical or mathematical methods.

Saber Seminar: Annual Boston-based sabermetric conference for charity.

sidespin: The type of spin that makes a breaking ball or changeup move horizontally.

sinker: A fastball gripped parallel with the seams that travels slower and moves more than a four-seamer, generally thrown to induce ground balls; also known as a two-seam fastball.

slider: A breaking pitch with more velocity and horizontal break than a curveball; has the highest average whiff rate of any pitch.

spike (half, full): Grip classifications pertaining to the placement of a pitcher's index finger on a ball; with a full spike, a pitcher jabs the tip of his index finger into the ball.

spin axis: The axis around which a ball or sphere spins, which determines the direction of its movement or break.

spin rate: Frequency with which a pitch rotates around its spin axis; plays a role in determining how much a pitch will break.

Statcast: A comprehensive player-tracking system that debuted in all MLB ballparks in 2015, combining optical cameras and TrackMan radar.

super-utility player: A versatile player capable of playing a number of defensive positions.

TrackMan: A Doppler radar-based tracking system that began in golf and measures the speed, movement, and spin of pitched and batted balls in almost all high-level ballparks.

Triple-A: The highest level of the minor leagues.

tunnel: A pitch's path to the plate: by throwing different types of pitches within the same tunnel, a pitcher can camouflage his pitches' true natures until it's too late for hitters to react to their movement.

Voros's law: "Any major league hitter can hit just about anything in 60 at-bats": a cautionary maxim about the perils of small-sample performance, coined by baseball analyst Voros McCracken.

Winter Meetings: Annual baseball industry convention, often accompanied by a flurry of player transactions.

0-for-4: The stat line of a batter who had no hits in four at-bats.

NOTES

Chapter 1: Saviormetrics

1. Michael Lewis, *Moneyball: The Art of Winning an Unfair Game* (New York: Norton, 2003).

2. Bill James, "An Interview with Billy Martin," *Esquire*, May 1984, 71–72.

3. Mark L. Armour and Daniel R. Levitt, *Paths to Glory: How Great Baseball Teams Got That Way* (College Park, MD: Potomac, 2004), 312.

4. John Harper, "A's GM Still Putting 'Money' Where His Mouth Is," *New York Daily News*, August 3, 2003.

5. Phil Birnbaum, "Eliminating Stupidity Is Easier Than Creating Brilliance," Sabermetric Research, June 13, 2013, http://blog.phil birnbaum.com/2013/06/eliminating-stupidity-is-easier-than.html (blog).

Chapter 2: A Natural Maniac, an Unnatural Athlete

1. Harry Hillaker, "Tribute to John R. Boyd," *Code One Magazine,* January 28, 2015, www.codeonemagazine.com/f16_article.html?item_id=156.

2. Angela Lee Duckworth, "Grit: The Power of Passion and Perseverance," TED Talk, published May 9, 2013, www.youtube.com/watch?v=H14bBuluwB8.

3. Ben Brewster, "Four Ways to Improve Your External Rotation to Throw Harder," *TreadAthletics*, August 5, 2016, https://treadathletics.com/external-rotation-throw-harder/.

4. Tianyi D. Luo, Gregory Lane Naugher, Austin Stone, Sandeep Mannava, Jeff Strahm, and Michael T. Freehill. "Ultra-long-toss vs. Straight-line Throwing for Glenohumeral Range of Motion Recovery in Collegiate Baseball Pitchers," *Orthopaedic Journal of Sports Medicine*, July 31, 2017, https://www.ncbi.nlm.nih.gov/pmc/articles/PMC5542142/.

5. Kevin E. Wilk, "Insufficient Shoulder External Rotation Increases Shoulder Injury, Surgery in Pitchers," *Healio: Orthopedics Today,* December 2015, www.healio.com/orthopedics/sports-medicine/news/print/orthopedics-today/%7Bb565af15-810c-4ec0-8b50-8acedc98391a%7D/

insufficient-shoulder-external-rotation-increases-shoulder-injury-surgery-in-pitchers.

6. Lee Jenkins, "Trevor Bauer Will Not Be Babied," *Sports Illustrated*, August 15, 2011.

Chapter 3: Making Mules into Racehorses

1. Mark L. Armour and Daniel R. Levitt, *In Pursuit of Pennants: Baseball Operations from Deadball to Moneyball* (Lincoln: University of Nebraska Press, 2015), 70.

2. Ibid., 75.

3. Ibid., 78.

4. Ibid., 74.

5. Ibid., 78.

6. Lee Lowenfish, *Branch Rickey: Baseball's Ferocious Gentleman* (Lincoln: University of Nebraska Press, 2007), 113.

7. Fresco Thompson, *Every Diamond Doesn't Sparkle* (Philadelphia: David McKay, 1964), 71.

8. Lowenfish, *Branch Rickey*, 122.

9. Thompson, *Every Diamond Doesn't Sparkle*, 125.

10. Richard J. Puerzer, "The Chicago Cubs' College of Coaches: A Management Innovation That Failed," *The National Pastime: A Review of Baseball History*, no. 26, Society for American Baseball Research (2006): 3–17, http://research.sabr.org/journals/files/SABR-National_Pastime-26 .pdf.

11. Christopher D. Green, "Psychology Strikes Out: Coleman R. Griffith and the Chicago Cubs," *History of Psychology* 6, no. 3 (2003): 267–283.

12. Charlie Grimm with Ed Prell, *Jolly Cholly's Story: Baseball, I Love You!* (Washington, DC: Regnery, 1968), 240.

13. Al Wolf, "Cub Pilot Plan Poses Problem," *Los Angeles Times*, February 15, 1961, C2.

14. Edward Prell, "Col. Whitlow Takes Over—Cubs Appoint Athletic Director," *Chicago Daily Tribune*, January 11, 1963, C1.

15. Kevin Kerrane, *Dollar Sign on the Muscle* (New York: Beaufort, 1984), 128.

16. Ibid., 128.

17. Richard J. Puerzer, "The Kansas City Royals' Baseball Academy," *The National Pastime: A Review of Baseball History*, no. 24, Society for American Baseball Research (2006): 3–13, http://research.sabr.org/journals/files/SABR-National_Pastime-24.pdf.

18. Spike Claassen, "42 Survive Cuts for Royals' Academy," *The Sporting News*, September 5, 1970.

19. Spike Claassen, "Kauffman Dedicates 'Dream' Academy," *The Sporting News*, April 3, 1971.

20. Ibid.

21. Ted Williams and John Underwood, *The Science of Hitting* (New York: Simon & Schuster, 1970), 14.

22. Leigh Montville, "A Gripping Tale: The Accidental Discovery of a Two-Seam Changeup Has Made Atlanta's Tom Glavine Baseball's Best Pitcher," *Sports Illustrated*, July 13, 1992, www.si.com/vault/1992/07/13/126807/a-gripping-tale-the-accidental-discovery-of-a-two-seam-changeup-has-made-atlantas-tom-glavine-baseballs-best-pitcher.

23. *Peter King's Football Morning in America*, "Week 2," aired September 17, 2018, NBC Sports, https://profootballtalk.nbcsports.com/2018/09/17/patrick-mahomes-chiefs-nfl-week-2-fmia-peter-king/?cid=nbcsports#the-lead-mahomes.

24. Craig R. Wright, *The Diamond Appraised* (New York: Simon & Schuster, 1989), 24.

25. Ibid., 12.

Chapter 4: First Principles

1. Elon Musk, "The Mind Behind Tesla, SpaceX, SolarCity," TED Talk, February 2013, www.ted.com/talks/elon_musk_the_mind_behind_tesla_spacex_solarcity#t-232078.

2. Chris Anderson, "Elon Musk's Mission to Mars," *Wired*, October 21, 2012.

3. Barry Bearak, "Harvey's Injury Shows Pitchers Have a Speed Limit," *New York Times*, September 16, 2013, www.nytimes.com/2013/09/17/sports/baseball/harveys-injury-shows-pitchers-have-a-speed-limit.html.

4. Michael G. Marshall, *Coaching Pitchers*, section 9, chapter 36, www.drmikemarshall.com/ChapterThirty-Six.html.

5. Kyle Boddy, "Reviewing ASMI's Biomechanical analysis of Dr. Marshall's Pitchers," Driveline Baseball, October 10, 2011, www.drivelinebaseball.com/2011/10/reviewing-asmis-biomechanical-analysis-of-dr-marshalls-pitchers-focus-performancevelocity/ (blog).

6. David McCullough, *The Wright Brothers* (New York: Simon & Schuster, 2015), 63.

7. Ibid.

8. Kyle Boddy, "Weighted Balls, Safety, and Consequences," Driveline Baseball, March 3, 2016, www.drivelinebaseball.com/2016/03/weighted-baseballs-safety-and-consequences/ (blog).

9. Frans Bosch, *Strength Training and Coordination: An Integrative Approach* (Rotterdam, Netherlands: Uitgevers, 2010), 227.

10. Eric Cressey, "Weighted Baseballs: Safe and Effective, or Stupid and Dangerous?," Eric Cressey, December 15, 2009, https://ericcressey .com/weighted-baseballs-safe-and-effective-or-stupid-and-dangerous.

11. G. S. Fleisig, A. Z. Diffendaffer, K. T. Aune, B. Ivey, and W. A. Laughlin, "Biomechanical Analysis of Weighted-Ball Exercises for Baseball Pitchers," *Sports Health* 9, no. 3 (May/June 2017): 210–215, www.ncbi.nlm.nih.gov/pubmed/27872403.

12. Brendan Gawlowski, "Soft Toss: Behind Driveline Baseball," Baseball Prospectus, December 23, 2015, www.baseballprospectus.com/ prospects/article/28102/soft-toss-behind-driveline-baseball/.

Chapter 6: The 10,000-Pitch Rule

1. K. Anders Ericsson, *Peak* (New York: Houghton Mifflin Harcourt, 2016), 31.

2. K. Anders Ericsson, Ralf Th. Krampe, and Clemens Tesch-Römer, "The Role of Deliberate Practice in the Acquisition of Expert Performance," *Psychological Review* 100, no. 3 (1993): 363–406.

3. Rod Cross, "How to Curve a Baseball or Swing a Cricket Ball," January 24, 2012, www.youtube.com/watch?v=t-3jnOIJg4k.

Chapter 7: The Conduit

1. D.K. Willardson, *Quantitative Hitting: Surprising Discoveries of the Game's Best Hitters* (Hitting Tech, 2018).

2. Seymour B. Sarason, *The Culture of the School and the Problem of Change* (Boston: Allyn and Bacon, 1971), chapter 2, https://archive.org/ details/cultureofschool00sara.

3. https://groups.google.com/d/msg/rec.sport.baseball/0RK6WRWEQks /R80tkdYC5bQJ.

4. Nick Piecoro, "Dan Haren, Burke Badenhop Among New Wave in Front Office," Azcentral Sports, USA Today Network, March 26, 2017, https://www.azcentral.com/story/sports/mlb/diamondbacks/2017/03/26/ dan-haren-burke-badenhop-among-new-wave-front-offices/99521052/.

5. Larry Stone, "Bannister Digs into Stats to Pile Up Pitching Feats," *Seattle Times*, April 20, 2008.

6. Tyler Kepner, "Use of Statistics Helps Greinke to A.L. Cy Young, *New York Times*, November 17, 2009, www.nytimes.com/2009/11/18/sports/baseball/18pitcher.html.

Chapter 8: Perfect Pitch

1. Adam Kilgore, "'Granny' Shot Master Rick Barry Is Glad Someone Had the Guts to Bring It Back to the NBA," *Washington Post*, December 27, 2016.
2. Kellie Green Hall, Derek A. Domingues, and Richard Cavazos, "Contextual Interference Effects with Skilled Baseball Players," *Perceptual and Motor Skills* 78 (1994): 835–841, www.gwern.net/docs/spacedrepetition/1994-hall.pdf.

Chapter 9: We're All Astronauts

1. Carol Dweck, "What Having a 'Growth Mindset' Actually Means," *Harvard Business Review*, January 13, 2016, https://hbr.org/2016/01/what-having-a-growth-mindset-actually-means.

Chapter 12: The All-Star Player-Coach

1. Travis Sawchik, "For Pirates' Alvarez, the Struggle with the 'Yips' Is Real," *Trib Live*, August 9, 2014, https://triblive.com/sports/pirates/6571471-74/alvarez-sax-blass.

Chapter 14: Just Be Better

1. David Laurila, "Prospectus Q&A: Craig Breslow," *Baseball Prospectus*, December 18, 2006, www.baseballprospectus.com/news/article/5769/prospectus-qa-craig-breslow/.

Chapter 15: Soft Factors

1. Alan S. Kornspan and Mary J. MacCracken, "Professional Baseball: The Pioneering Work of David F. Tracy," *NINE: A Journal of Baseball History and Culture*, University of Nebraska Press 11, no. 2 (Spring 2003).
2. Dan Kopf, "The 2008 Financial Crisis Completely Changed What Majors Students Choose," *Quartz*, August 29, 2018, https://qz.com/1370922/the-2008-financial-crisis-completely-changed-what-majors-students-choose/.

Chapter 17: No Ceiling

1. David Gassko, "League Difficulty (Part 4)," Hardball Times, April 16, 2007, https://tht.fangraphs.com/tht-live/league-difficulty-part-4/.

2. Zach Smith, "Never Say Die: Brandon Mann Makes MLB Debut After More Than 16 Seasons," *Hill Country News* (Cedar Park, TX), July 11, 2018, http://hillcountrynews.com/stories/never-say-die-brandon-mann-makes-mlb-debut-after-more-than-16-seasons,77745.

3. John Thorn, "The Sky Is Falling, Baseball Is Dying, and the Roof May Leak: The Consolations of History in Calamitous Times," Our Game (blog), November 19, 2018, https://ourgame.mlblogs.com/the-sky-is-falling-baseball-is-dying-and-the-roof-may-leak-e3f7e0b0e48d.

Epilogue: The Residue of Design

1. Bob Nightengale, "Trevor Bauer Says He Suffered 'Character Assassination' but Insists There's No Ill Will with Indians," *USA Today*, February 14, 2019, www.usatoday.com/story/sports/mlb/columnist/bob-nightengale/2019/02/14/trevor-bauer-cleveland-indians-arbitration/2869671002/.

INDEX

ABOUT THE AUTHORS

Jason Hall

BEN LINDBERGH is a staff writer for The Ringer and hosts the *Effectively Wild* podcast for FanGraphs. The coauthor of *New York Times* bestseller *The Only Rule Is It Has to Work*, he lives in New York, NY.

Stephanie Strasburg

TRAVIS SAWCHIK is a staff writer for FiveThirtyEight. The author of *New York Times* bestseller *Big Data Baseball*, he lives in Bay Village, OH.